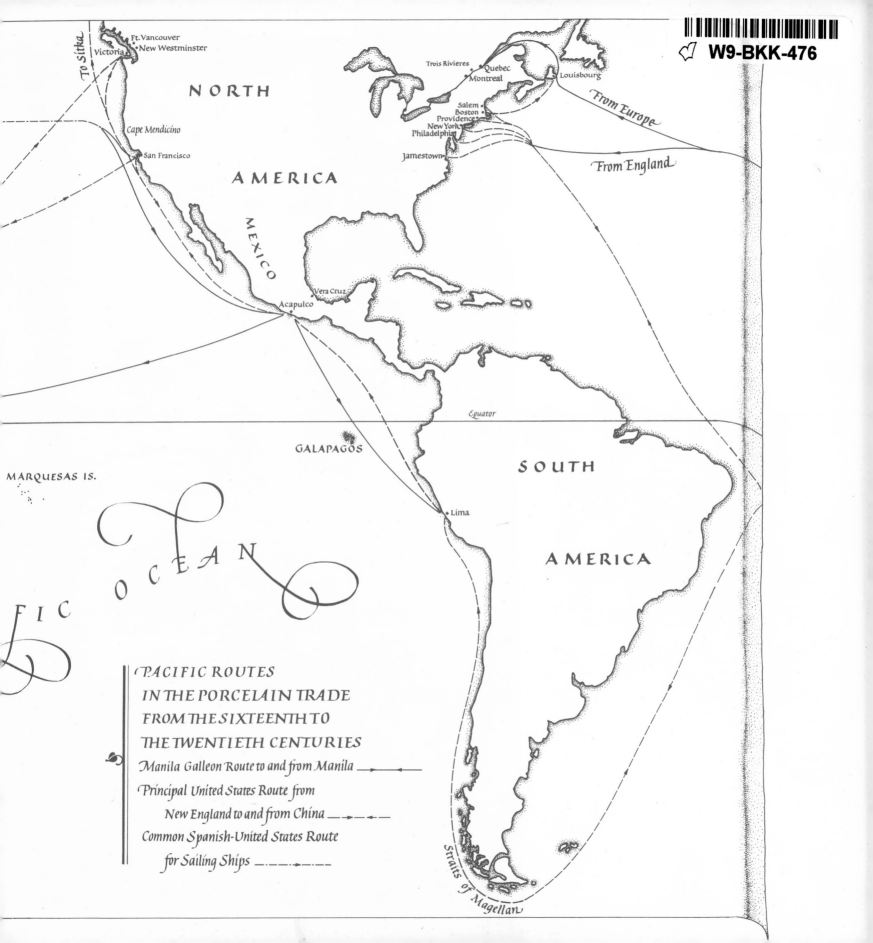

W9-BKK-476

NORTH

AMERICA

To Sitka

Ft. Vancouver
New Westminster
Victoria

Cape Mendicino

San Francisco

MEXICO

Vera Cruz
Acapulco

Trois Rivieres
Quebec
Montreal
Louisbourg

Salem
Boston
Providence
New York
Philadelphia

Jamestown

From Europe

From England

Equator

GALAPAGOS

MARQUESAS IS.

SOUTH

AMERICA

Lima

FIC OCEAN

Straits of Magellan

PACIFIC ROUTES
IN THE PORCELAIN TRADE
FROM THE SIXTEENTH TO
THE TWENTIETH CENTURIES

Manila Galleon Route to and from Manila ——————

Principal United States Route from
    New England to and from China ——————

Common Spanish-United States Route
    for Sailing Ships ————————

0057083

COLLIN COUNTY COMMUNITY

3 1702 00088 6675

CHINESE
EXPORT PORCELAIN
IN NORTH AMERICA

DATE DUE	
FEB 17 1992	
DEC 0 4 1992	
FEB 2 7 1993	
FEB. 2 4 1994	
MAR. 1 7 1994	
MAY 6 1994	
APR AY 30 1995 96	
MAY 08 1996	
ILL 5·8·99	
BRODART, INC.	Cat. No. 23-221

Learning Resources Center
Collin County Community College District
SPRING CREEK CAMPUS
Plano, Texas 75074

WITHDRAWN

JEAN McCLURE MUDGE

CHINESE EXPORT PORCELAIN
IN NORTH AMERICA

DESIGNED BY HERMANN STROHBACH

Clarkson N. Potter, Inc./Publishers

DISTRIBUTED BY CROWN PUBLISHERS, INC.

NEW YORK

Copyright © 1986 by Jean McClure Mudge

All rights reserved. No part of this book may be reproduced or transmitted in any form or by any means, electronic or mechanical, including photocopying, recording, or by any information storage and retrieval system, without permission in writing from the publisher.

Published by Clarkson N. Potter, Inc., 225 Park Avenue South, New York, New York 10003 and represented in Canada by the Canadian MANDA Group.

CLARKSON N. POTTER, POTTER, and colophon are trademarks of Clarkson N. Potter, Inc. Manufactured in Japan

Library of Congress Cataloging-in-Publication Data

Mudge, Jean McClure.
     Chinese export porcelain in North America.

     1.   China trade porcelain—North America.
2.   Porcelain, Chinese—Ming-Ch'ing dynasties,
1368-1912.   I.   Title.
NK4565.5.M83   1986   738.2'0951   86-18744
ISBN 0-517-54470-9
10 9 8 7 6 5 4 3 2 1

First Edition

Photo opposite title page: Detail of Fig. 91

FRONT ENDPAPER. Pacific routes in the porcelain trade
BACK ENDPAPER. Atlantic routes in the porcelain trade
All maps are by Robert Williams

Contents

for William McClure Mudge

ACKNOWLEDGMENTS

Over the six years of making this book, the combination of research, analysis, informed conjecture, photographic art, and editorial and design skill represented here is due to the interest and help of many people. I am delighted to acknowledge their assistance. First, however, I wish to give tribute to Francis Ross Carpenter, a China scholar and former associate director of the China Trade Museum in Milton, Massachusetts, now incorporated with the Peabody Museum, Salem. Frank suggested I use the museum's collection as the basis for expanding my first book, a task so vast that encouragement was essential. More than the suggestion, however, Frank successfully applied for funds from the National Endowment for the Arts as the first financial support for my study. I had previously benefited by an exploratory grant from the American Philosophical Society. Private individuals were also supporters; I am most grateful to Pamela Lammont du Pont Copeland and to Stevens T. M. Wright for their gifts toward the expenses of this project. I am also indebted to Joan Evans, formerly of the China Trade Museum.

Willing researchers had specific areas requested of them. Without the aid of Beth Bailey, Robert Decker, Eve Gribi, the late Patricia Fleming, Susan Floyd, Marie Kalat, Linda Johnson, Jean Krase, Claire Lincoln, and Lewis, Robert, and Anne Mudge, certain crucial corners in this study would have remained unseen. Three translators—Mary Ho, Kathlyn Liscomb, and Amy McNair—provided me with English equivalents of the latest Chinese scholarship. Ms. McNair also tracked down certain obscure details and provided one of the drawings. Robert Williams expertly drafted the maps and line drawings for this book. The accomplished work of several photographers enhance the text; their names appear in the photo credit list on page 300.

Many curators supplied information about objects in their collections or references to articles and books, as did dealers and collectors; thus they are listed together. Four people lead this group for the extraordinary time and attention they paid to endless requests for information: Lucy J. Butler and William Sargent of the Peabody Museum; Carol A. Kim, formerly of the China Trade Museum; and Charlotte Wilcoxen of the Albany Institute of History and Art.

Other curators, keepers, dealers, archaeologists, and collectors whose assistance I gratefully acknowledge are Virginia Armella de Aspe, John Austin, John Ayers, Ralph C. Bloom, Elaine Bonney, Hector Rivero Borrell, C. Boschma, Marley R. Brown III, Susan J. Brown, Robert F. Burgess, Joseph T. Butler, William Butler, Manuel Carballo, Cary Carson, Alice Caulkins, Alfonso Cervantes, María Teresa Cervantes de Conde, Paul Chase, Mark A. Clark, J. D. Cleaver, Craig Clunas, Elizabeth Collard, José Ignacio Conde y Diaz-Rubin, Edward F. Conley, Edward S. Cooke, Jr., Suzanne Corlette, Andrée Crépeau, Julia B. Curtis, Phillip H. Curtis, Ellen P. Denker, Diana De Santis, Ulysses G. Dietz, Marie-France Dupoizat, Robert Egleston, Marie Elwood, Alan D. Frazer, Laura G. Fecych, David L. Felton, H. A. Crosby Forbes, Jaime Rincón Gallardo, Monica C. de Rincón Gallardo, Felipe García-Beraza, Alexandra R. Garfield, James L. Garvin, Derek Gillman, Robert L. Giannini III, Nancy Gleason, Geoffrey Godden, Jonathan Goldstein, Emmet Gribbin, Edward T. Hall, Lewis Hanke, Peter Hardie, Barbara Harrisson, Ingmar Hasselgreen, Sandra Helmer, Norman Herreshoff, Janet Holmes, David S. Howard, Kee Il, Helmuth W. Joel, Frances F. Jones, C. J. A. Jörg, Peter Kaellgren, Patricia E. Kane, Kazushiga Kaneko, David Kingery, Cynthia Koch, Rodrigo R. Rivero Lake, Peter Lam, Barbara Langworthy, Thomas Layton, Jean Gordon Lee, Ann LeVeque, Howard A. Link, Florence C. Lister, D. L. Lunsingh Scheurleer, Pauline Lunsingh Scheurleer, Kathryn A. McCutchen, Carol Macht, Consuelo Maquívar, Mrs. Duncan Mauran, Richard J. Menn, Lord Methuen, Tsugio Mikami, George L. Miller, John C. Milley, Mrs. Peter Milliken II, Eleanor B. Monahon, Patricia Moore, Mrs. Rafi Y. Mottahedeh, M. B. Munford, Milo M. Naeve, Christina H. Nelson, Timothy C. Neumann, Josephine G. Northrup, Richard C. and Jane C. Nylander, Kerry A. O'Brien, Thomas W. Parker, Walter W. Patten, Jr., Charlotte Patten, Donald C. Peirce, Karin E. Peterson, Carmen Peréz de Salazar de Ovando, Carlos de Ovando, Beatriz Sanchez-Navarro de Pintado, José de Pintado, Leonor Cortina de Pintado, Robert A. Porter, Jean Bruce Poole, Marita Martinez del Rio de Redo, Leonor Riba, Nancy E. Richards, Deborah M. Roebuck, Christian Rohlfing, Norman S. Rice, Nan A. Rothschild, Diana E. Roussel, Lewis Rumford II and Rose C. Rumford, Teresa Sanchez-Navarro, Sondy Sanford, Penny J. Sander, P. Hairston Seawell, Elizabeth Sharpe, Emily Scolov, Clarence Shangraw, Kevin Stayton, Margaret Stearns, Garry W. Stone, Beatrice K. Taylor, Hilary Toren, Mary Tregear, Henry Trubner, William Tuttle, Aline Ussel, Earle D. Vandekar, Eugenio Sisto Velasco, Kazuo Yamasaki, Suzanne C. Valenstein, Pamela Vandiver, Edward Von der Porten, Page Warden, James C. Y. Watt, Michael F. Weber, Ronald E. Whate, James W. Whitehead, Roderick Whitfield, Cara L. Wise, Henry T. Wright, Zhang Fukang.

Other collectors and collections are acknowledged in captions. And still others, with numerous archaeologists, are listed under "Manuscripts" in the Bibliography for the original documents in their possession.

Clare Le Corbeiller, associate curator of European Decorative Art at the Metropolitan Museum of Art, kindly shared her expertise on export wares made for the West in a critical reading of this book in manuscript. Her questions have saved me from error; she has suggested clarifications and elaborations. I am indebted to her for providing, in effect, a safety-net review of these pages.

Institutions in this country and abroad whose collections have served this study, either as background information or with objects, include the Adams National Historic Site, Quincy, Mass.; the Albany Institute of History and Art; the Art Institute, Chicago; the Ashmolean Museum, Oxford; Asian Art Museum, San Francisco; the Association for the Preservation of Virginia Antiquities; Baltimore Museum of Art; Baur Collection, Geneva; the Bostonian Society; City of Bristol Museum and Art Gallery; the British Museum; the Brooklyn Museum; the Charleston Museum; Chaupultepec Castle, Mexico City; the Chrysler Museum, Norfolk, Va.; Cincinnati Art Museum; Colonial Williamsburg Foundation; Concord

Antiquarian Society; the Cooper-Hewitt Museum, New York City; Daughters of the American Revolution Museum; Percival David Foundation, London; the Dietrich Brothers Americana Corporation; the Edison Institute; Henry Ford Museum and Greenfield Village, Dearborn, Mich.; the Essex Institute, Salem, Mass.; Fondation Custodia, Institut Néerlandai, Paris; the Fortress of Louisbourg, Louisbourg, Canada; the Fries Museum, Leeuwarden, the Netherlands; the Gemeentelijk Museum Het Princessehof, Leeuwarden, the Netherlands; the Groninger Museum, Groningen, Holland; Gunston Hall, Lorton Va.; Historic Annapolis, Inc.; Historic Cherry Hill, Albany; Historical Society of Pennsylvania; Idemitzu Art Museum, Tokyo; Thomas Jefferson Memorial Foundation, Charlottesville, Va.; the Kurita Art Museum, Tokyo; the Metropolitan Museum of Art, New York; Minnesota Historical Society; Museo Isidro Fabela, Mexico City; Museo Franz Mayer, Mexico City; Museum of the City of New York; the Museum of Early Southern Decorative Art, Winston-Salem, N.C.; the Museum of Fine Arts, Boston; the Museum of Fine Arts, Houston: the Bayou Bend Collection; the Museum of London; Museum of New Mexico; Nacional Museo del Virreinato, Tepotzotlán, Mexico; the U.S. National Park Service: Colonial National Historical Park in Yorktown, Hyde Park in New York, and the Independence National Historical Park in Philadelphia; the Newark Museum; the New Hampshire Historical Society; the New Haven Colony Historical Society, New Haven, Conn.; the New Jersey State Museum; New Jersey Historical Society; the New Jersey State Museum; Newark Museum; New York Historic Sites Bureau; New-York Historical Society; Norwalk Historical Commission; Nova Scotia Department of Education; Old Barrack Association, Trenton, N.J.; Parks Canada, Archaeological Research Division, Ottawa; Peabody Museum, Salem, Mass.; Philadelphia Museum of Art; Phoenix Art Museum; the Preservation Society of Newport County, Rhode Island; Rijksmuseum, Amsterdam; Princeton University Art Museum; Rhode Island Historical Society; Rhode Island School of Design; Royal Ontario Museum, Canadiana and New World Archaeology Departments, Toronto; Shelburne Museum, Vermont; Sleepy Hollow Restorations; Smithsonian Institution, Washington, D.C.; Society for the Preservation of New England Antiquities; Tokyo National Museum; University of King's College, Halifax: the Weldon Collection; U.S. Department of State, Diplomatic Reception Rooms; Van Cortlandt Museum Mansion; Victoria and Albert Museum; Virginia Research Center for Archaeology; Washington and Lee University, the Reeves Collection, Lexington, Va.; the Henry Francis du Pont Winterthur Museum; Yale University Art Gallery.

As with the gathering of information for this book, so with its presentation: collaboration of the most pleasant sort has made it possible. I should like to thank my agent, Carol Mann, for interesting Nancy Novogrod and others at Clarkson N. Potter in publishing this work. The staff at Potter has been so patient in waiting for my delivery of manuscript that in the process two editors have come and gone. Now Pam Krauss has ably supervised the final stages of editing after a major editorial review by Martina D'Alton. Without the intelligence and probing interest of Ms. D'Alton, a sprawling text would still be struggling for order and succinctness. Bogged down by detail, I was reinvigorated to bring new ideas and structure to the book and saved from many errors. For Ms. D'Alton's contribution, I cannot be more grateful. For saving me from further errors, I should also like to thank Kate Davis, the careful copyeditor of the Harkavy Publishing Service. In Potter's design department, Gael Towey has been a helpful consultant as well. The designer, Hermann Strohbach, has presented beautiful photographs with an expertise immeasurably enhancing both objects and text. Finally, I should like to thank my son, Bill Mudge, for his patient help with two word-processor programs, which I mastered imperfectly, but enough to save considerable time in producing readable copy. For his tireless technical help, photography in these pages, and interest in art history, I dedicate this book to him.

Jean McClure Mudge
Hyde Park, Chicago, 1985

Preface

I must study politics and war that my sons may have liberty
to study mathematics and philosophy. My sons ought to
study mathematics and philosophy, geography, natural history, naval architecture, navigation, commerce, and agricul-
ture, in order to give their children a right to study painting,
poetry, music, architecture, statuary, tapestry, and porcelains.

—John Adams to Abigail Adams, May 12, 1780

Chinese porcelains came to North America from the late-sixteenth to the early-twentieth centuries, precisely when the historic trade of China's ware to the West reached its climax. First Spanish galleons, then Dutch, British, and French East Indiamen, and, finally, U.S. ships brought chinaware to ever-increasing buyers on this continent. The influx of Westerners in the Far East—following Portugal's sixteenth-century lead—coincided with the Golden Age of porcelain under the first three emperors of the Qing dynasty: Kangxi, Yongzheng, and Qianlong, successively in power from 1662 to 1795. This unprecedented imperial support to the porcelain industry led to increasing supplies of excellent export as, simultaneously, European demand for Chinese porcelain swelled. Even in the nineteenth century, when that demand declined (fulfilled in part by Western porcelains), the aura of prestige accorded Chinese ware by nearly a millennium of trade only slowly faded. Today, as this venerable industry experiences a revival, the term *Chinese porce-*

lain continues to evoke a sense of respect and value.

In that heyday of trade, China's supply of porcelains was hitherto unparalled in variety of type—particularly in a swift adaptability to Western models—style, size, color, number, and quality. Quality should be emphasized. Export ware has been wrongly dismissed as always inferior to porcelain kept in China for court use. Imperial ware—by definition, destined for the emperor—*was* indeed specially made to be finer than any intended for export. Nonetheless, wares going overseas might still have been of high merit, even up to official standards, and occasionally with the imperial *nianhao*, or reign mark. Furthermore, export pieces are valuable now as material evidence of a past era, special symbols of the East-West interchange.

From Yuan times (late-thirteenth century) and through the Ming dynasty (1368-1644) green wares (celadons) and blue-and-white china, on display in Turkey and Iran today, testify to the value of medieval trade pieces to the Middle East, reflecting the desires of the sultans and caliphs who purchased them. Among foreign buyers an expectation of worthy porcelains suited to their tastes continued well into the nineteenth century. But especially in the Qing dynasty, the West ordered some of the most exquisite work Chinese expertise could produce. (It also requested, and received, some of the most bizarre!)

This book probes the nature of the West's purchase of Chinese porcelain—for North America via European colonial powers—in its intricate history, considerable artistic range, and symbolic richness. To do so requires touching base with many disciplines. Serious students of porcelains are no longer exclusively collectors, museum curators, or dealers. For some time, anthropologists and archaeologists have exhumed shards and occasionally whole pieces, cherishing even the smallest sliver, whose identification number is sometimes longer than the shard itself. Joining the ranks of porcelain scholars are ceramic scientists. They have devised inventive ways to test body or glaze compositions and firing temperature by chemical analysis, optical microscopy, and scanning electron microscopy (SEM) with energy-dispersive X-ray (EDXR). Equally ingenious are the tests for probable date by the use of thermoluminescence and magnetic analysis.

Clearly, art historians and other humanist students of porcelain now must correlate their facts and assumptions with the laboratory results of these relative newcomers to the subject. Fortunately, papers and conversations presented to assemblies in the several disciplines allow for a cross-fertilization of findings. Such an opportunity was available in Shanghai in November 1982, at the first International Congress on Ancient Chinese Pottery and Porcelain. At this writing, its proceedings have not yet been published, precluding the mining of all that might have been presented there. Yet my notes from several papers and conversations with specialists have found places in this book.

Along with this recent, multidisciplined interest in porcelain has been an extension of the subject of inquiry: from first-class, imperial wares to those of various qualities made for foreigners. Chinese export porcelain has come into its own for a variety of good reasons. It is found literally worldwide, by initial or secondary trade, by loss at sea, or by discard or burial on site. An apparently surprising example, a bowl recovered off the coast of Ireland from the wreck of the *Trinidad Valencera*, one of the ships in the Spanish Armada (1588) returning home via a northern route around the British Isles, becomes less startling when seen as an early, far-flung survivor of the Manila Galleon trade across the Pacific (discussed in chapter 2). Export ware adds historical, social, and economic dimensions with multinational implications to the study of Chinese porcelains. It has been recognized as having a value all its own, not only as an amusing memento of a historic East-West trade.

The attention paid export ware dates from the 1950s for the most part, so the field is still young, especially from the archaeological side, despite an impressive spread of discoveries (see appendixes C and D). Such shard study along with laboratory test results will amend and add to the data, especially to the overview, formerly the province of art historians. Despite its youthfulness, the subject of porcelain study has an impressive list of scholars by reputation and geographic spread. Their works, listed in the Bibliography, are indispensable sources for this book.

My own approach was formulated in an earlier book, *Chinese Export Porcelain for the American Trade, 1785–1835* (see Bibliography), in which I pursued two tracks—history and art history. When interwoven together and strands of economic history added, the three fields illuminated each other. In addition, I was intrigued by the possibility of decoding the "language" of the objects as symbols of the interaction of China and the United States, their mute but concrete vocabulary of signs. I wished to explore what has now become basic in the study of American material culture in a package of considerations: the physical nature of a piece, its form and decoration; its probable use; the communication of values it embodies; the acceptance, rejection, or ignorance of those values; and, to some degree, an evaluation of the object in light of the present. The seed for this sort of analysis lay in Susan Langer's *Philosophy in a New Key* (1941) and *Feeling and Form* (1953), twin volumes on the theory of art. Anthony Garvan, professor of American Studies at the University of Pennsylvania and adjunct professor at the Winterthur Museum, was testing Langer's views on specific American decorative arts, such as Puritan ecclesiastical silver. Through Langer and Garvan, I came to see a symbolic valence inherent in the physical object waiting to be translated into words.

The same encompassing perspective has directed this book. In the pages that follow—from captions as well as text—facts of nation, place, and time, of body and glaze paint, of importations and owners will occasionally be accompanied by commentary that probes the aura surrounding a piece. I say "occasionally" because doing so for each object would double the length of the text. It is enough to provide a model of my technique at the end of chapter 1, using figure 38 as an example; I invite the reader to make the same extended analysis to any piece illustrated here or elsewhere. Privately then, one may understand the "message of the pot," a special combination of mutual attitudes of China and the West, varying according to period and object. In short, scrutiny and informed conjecture reveal international attitudes and assumptions captured in time and timelessly available on the hardy porcelains.

Historic cultures—in this case China, Spain and New Spain (Mexico), Holland, England, France, and the United States—interpreted from the present but from knowledge of the past, are represented by the porcelains. They are historical envoys rather than merely attractive trade pieces sent out in a wide diaspora from the China coast. Export porcelain becomes a mirror of the mutual reactions of East and West, adding a major dimension to its already accepted uniqueness in world ceramics.

Some knowledgeable students of export have seriously questioned whether or not American buyers really distinguished levels of china that were not special orders. Did they rely almost solely on the ceramics supplied by their local china merchant? The question implies doubt about taste in North America. A response has at least two parts. One is the definition of "American." In this study, as in others, it encompasses our Latin and Canadian neighbors. From the beginning and in successive generations, they and their Dutch and English counterparts often selected porcelain based on the best Western culture of the time. In fact, they came to determine the dominant forms and decorations and to play a role in determining the nature of the market. As chapters 2 and 3 will show, the Spanish and Dutch helped to stimulate, even revolutionize, the export scene with demands for higher quality wares fitted to their specifications. The English followed them, joined by the French, preeminent among tastemakers. All foreigners knew the difference between "fine" and "coarse" wares, a distinction long held by the Chinese themselves. (It is repeated endlessly by the Dutch, who sold to many foreign markets other than their own.)

Prices were based on these distinctions, of course. By cost alone anyone could tell that one porcelain was better than another. China of different qualities in a single household did not indicate utter dependence on only the merchant's open stock supply. Rather, a single family might function as today with two or more types, loosely divided between "everyday" and "company" ware. Documentation for these statements lies in the repeated concern of the directors of the supercargoes who bought in China for the home market, whether in Mexico City in the early-seventeenth century, in London a hundred years later, or in Boston and New York a century after that. From the start, they instructed their agents to buy what would sell well to the largest market. A prime example is an order placed by the British East India Company in 1740 for four hundred chests of china, samples included, as for a square-form "Pattern Saucer." All of the samples sent were known to suit popular taste, for at the end of this long, specific list of open-stock ware is the note: "Observe that the Colour of the Blue in No. 3 (Chest) will do for the blue and White China throughout, for most people like a Pale Blue, and the China thin. . . ."[1]

Time and again the rule was to buy good ware—not necessarily fine, but well made, pleasing in design, and, until the nineteenth century, not too heavy (then, heavy porcelain was sometimes requested!). The orders from the directors were not without a link to the buyer: the pressure of consumer taste ultimately authorized them. The answer to the query posed above, then, is finally found in this grass-roots marketplace, an exchange seen in detail in the pages to follow.

Normally, scholars in this field have wisely limited their studies to particular collections, for example, Phillips and Le Corbeiller examined objects left to the Metropolitan Museum of Art by Helena Woolworth McCann, with a few later purchases; Howard and Ayers examined those assembled by Rafi and Mildred Mottahedeh. In my first book, however, I found it essential to move beyond the porcelains at the Winterthur Museum, and not only because blue-and-white was then greatly underrepresented in that collection. There were too many important pieces elsewhere. In this book, I have cast my net even farther, pulling in objects from this country, Mexico, Canada, England, and Holland, in private homes, historical societies, and museums. Selecting from such a large compass was difficult. Pieces constantly competed for inclusion. If someone's favorites have been left out, their

disappointment is my own. But my philosophy of choice lay in the approach given above and the geographical focus of my study—North America—even though some of the pieces illustrated had to come from collections in England and Europe.

Another stylistic consideration in writing this book was the type of Romanization of Chinese characters to use. I have selected pinyin and not included either the Wade-Giles nor Chinese character equivalents. Pinyin has become standard in the Western press and its atlases. In another generation, Wade-Giles will be known only to a few scholars in China and the West. The single exceptions to this rule are my use of Wade-Giles in parentheses after the pinyin form of certain cities, and the imperial *nianhao*, because at present, these terms are more familiar in this form. Also, Chinese characters for these and other words have been omitted, assuming that those Asians who may read this book will know English.

In these pages a quantity of information and analysis awaits the reader. Yet much work remains to be done in the field, especially in area studies. Some have been published, but many wait for the patient sifting of more documents and the gathering of the objects themselves. If well chosen, such studies will add to the number of illustrated pieces for the pleasure of a worldwide readership.

The growing pantheon of export porcelains shines in its jewellike brilliance. In a fractious world, these productions of the East for a demanding Western market are a triumph of collaborative inventiveness, taste, and trade. For some viewers, they stimulate a sense of profound pride in being part of the human family. In the epigraph to this book, John Adams, writing over two hundred years ago, looked forward to the day when his progeny would be studying art, including porcelain. We are his spiritual kin, inheritors of his legacy, and warm assenters to his insight that the study of porcelain is a significant part of the vast scape of knowledge we call the humanities.

The Nature and Variety of Chinese Porcelain

It may seem curious at first that the word *porcellana* (pig) was the term medieval Italians gave the pure white Chinese ceramic which had no duplicate in the West. Yet they had already used *porcellana* or *porcelletta* (piglet) to dub the cowrie shell, because its body, back, and snout resembled a pig's (fig. 1). Now the cowry's thin, hard body and stainless, glossy finish were identified with the body and glaze of Chinese porcelain. The association was further suggested when the cowry, used first in ancient China as currency and eventually in international exchange, was applied as decoration to pottery in the Middle Ages.[1] Linked by their surface similarity, combination on pots, and value, the shell and the ceramic readily became identified by the same word. By the time an account of Marco Polo's travels was translated into French (1298), cowries and chinaware were both labeled *porselaine*,[2] indicating that the rest of Europe would follow Italy's coinage.

In the West since the eighteenth century, porcelain has been defined as ware whose body is made of china stone (*petuntse*) and china clay (*kaolin*) of a particular gray-to-pure-white color, which vitrifies and becomes translucent as well as sonorous when fired at a high temperature. From this definition (open to revision if new data confirms that kaolin was not used until much later), Western scholars have dated porcelain to the middle of the Tang dynasty (A.D. 618–907).

In China, stoneware, the varicolored clay that becomes hard and glasslike when fired and rings when struck, is also considered porcelain; their term *ci* signifies both. Because stoneware evolved from coarser ware during the Eastern Han dynasty (A.D. 25–220), porcelain is, to Chinese scholars, eighteen hundred to two thousand years old.[3] However, stoneware (*ci*) is not to be confused with earthenware of coarse clay (*tao*), fired at a lower temperature, and requiring a glaze to be water impermeable. In both East and West, earthenware is of another class. Both cultures also agree on the generic term for earthenware, stoneware, and porcelain—namely, "pottery."

1. *Cowrie shells*, two egg-shaped, one plain.

Four general categories may be used to distinguish porcelains according to quality and to the intended owner: imperial, domestic, export, and special or private order (*chine de commande*). The classifications should not be considered hard and fast; they may overlap.

Imperial Porcelain

Imperial or "official" ware was primarily destined for the emperor and his court, but some pieces found their way to rich merchants and through them to overseas buyers. Official ware had to be state-of-the-art perfect. In the Tang dynasty, one or two mandarins appointed by the emperor supervised the making of the court's stonewares and porcelains. By the Northern Song dynasty (A.D. 960–1127), white porcelaneous wares from Jizhou and Ding and greenware

(formerly celadons) from centers such as Longquan came together at the emperor's court. Later, in the Southern Song dynasty (1127–1279), blue-gray crackle-glaze stoneware from Hangzhou and white porcelain with a thin bluish or greenish glaze (*qingbai* or *yingqing*) from Jingdezhen were favored. Though even the best ceramics for some centuries were thought to be inferior to gold, silver, and other metalwork,[4] the worthiest ceramics were still admired and included in the eighth-century Chinese law that forbade exportation of "precious and rare articles" on pain of imprisonment.[5] Roughly seven centuries lapsed from the discovery of porcelain until the Ming rulers began marking wares made exclusively for them with reign marks (*nianhao*) in a double circle in blue under the glaze. But this practice was not standard until the first high point in Ming porcelain production during the reign of the Xuande emperor

2. *Saucer*, marked Xuande (1426–35), probably Yongzheng period (1723–35), D 14.8 cm. *Doucai*, imperial quality.

3. Reverse of fig. 2, showing Xuande period mark.

(1425–36) (figs. 2 and 3). His standards apparently excelled those of his successors; there are later Ming emperors whose marked ware is not first class.[6]

Domestic Ware

Domestic or "people's" ware could also be nearly "perfect." Of some pieces made in the Qing dynasty (1644–1911), only a trained eye can detect body differences or the slightly off-center painting of a mark in relation to the obverse design.[7] Widely ranging in quality from the earliest period, domestic ware might be quite commonplace, though still good, and reasonably priced, even cheap. Marco Polo, who must have been familiar with imperial porcelains at the court of Kublai Khan and elsewhere during his travels in China (1275–92), only wrote about the domestic/export wares of the Yuan dynasty (1280–1368):

> The most beautiful vessels and plates of porcelain, large and small, that one can describe are made in great quantity . . . more beautiful than can be found in any other city. And on all sides they are much valued, for none of them are made in another place but in this city [Tingiu (Tong'an), south of Quanzhou, Fukien Province], and from there they are carried to many places throughout the world. And there is plenty there and a great sale, so great that for one Venetian groat you would actually have three bowls so beautiful that none would know how to devise them better.[8]

Export Porcelain

Polo was writing for fellow Westerners, telling them that they, too, could have what he had seen, for these nonimperial, less-than-perfect domestic porcelains were exportable (see map 1). In short, domestic ware might also be export ware, especially that which was produced in large quantity. This virtual identity had been true since the Tang dynasty, when the empire stretched from Persia to Korea. Under the Tang,

Guangzhou (Canton) first became an important seaport, and by the eighth century, it boasted a thriving resident community of Arab merchants with mosques and business houses.[9] During the Southern Song dynasty, the government greatly encouraged maritime trade abroad. Through the joint efforts of Chinese, Persian, and Arab shippers, porcelains were exported from three major ports on the southern coast—Wenzhou, Quanzhou, and Guangzhou[10]—each with its own superintendent of trade. Traders not only went south to the Philippines, Borneo, and the Moluccas, but west to Vietnam, Thailand, Java, Sumatra, and even farther to Zanzibar on the African coast and to Fostat near Cairo. Porcelain, largely white and green wares, was the main cargo.[11]

During this time, the port of Quanzhou (Ch'uanchou, or, for Polo, Zayton) in Fujian Province rose to first prominence, a role it maintained for roughly two hundred years (1250–1450). As Polo noted, it was "one of the two ports in the world where most merchandise comes, *for its greatness and convenience.*"[12] Kilns in the three southern provinces of Zhejiang, Fujian, and Guangdong, as well as the nascent future capital of porcelain making, Jingdezhen in Jiangxi Province, supplied the pots streaming out of this port (figs. 4–6).[13] Marco Polo's seventeen-year stay bridged the end of the Song dynasty and the beginning of the Yuan dynasty under Kublai Khan. On Polo's return to Europe in 1292, he reputedly brought back porcelains with him, including a small white jar, quite stained, now in the Treasury of St. Mark's, Venice.[14] Into the fourteenth century, the Yuan dynasty continued the favorable overseas trade policies of its predecessors for good reason: 5 percent of the Song's total revenue had come from international trade.[15] This centuries-old exchange and the welcome given foreigners under the Yuan[16] help to explain one of the most important Western contributions to, even an indirect collaboration with, the Chinese potter: the introduction of cobalt blue painted under the glaze, the

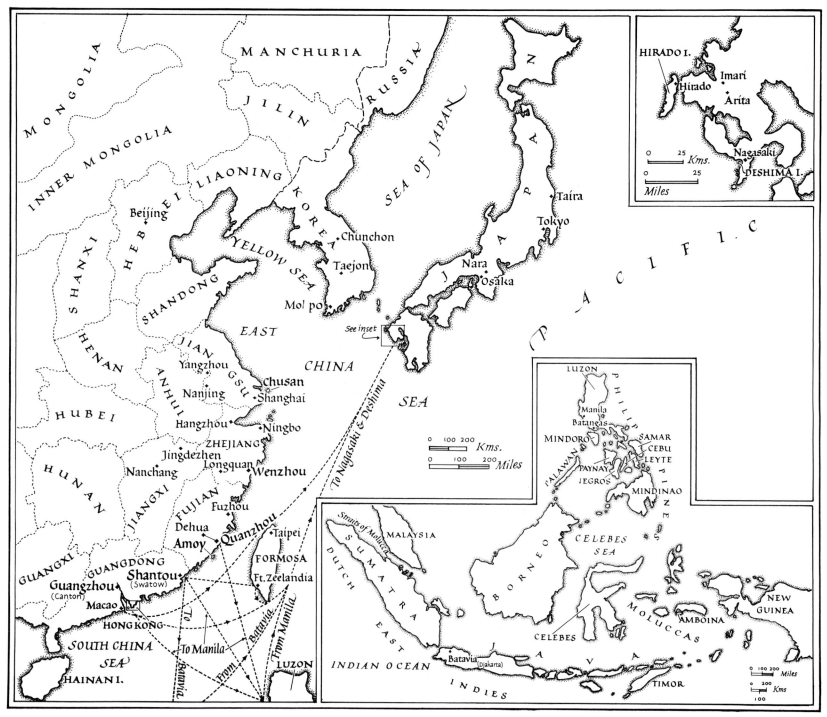

MAP 1. Trade routes between China, Japan and the Philippines.

blue-and-white (*qinghua*).[17] Such porcelain has been ardently admired in the West and eventually came to be highly valued by the court as well.

Cobalt, a mineral ore, had been known in the Tang dynasty. A well-stratified Tang shard of blue-and-white, part of a pillow with a Near Eastern–style design, was found in Yangzhou in 1975, but it is too slight an example to argue for the widespread practice of blue brushwork on the unfired body.[18] The Tang cobalt may have been imported from the Near East in the form of glass bricks. It was fritted, or fused, with a lead glaze, but, on the usual examples, the cobalt was only used to color the glaze (as did red and yellow pigments). During the Tang, it was not painted onto the body before glazing.[19] Some Song blue-and-white is also known.[20] But the indisputable development of underglaze cobalt was in the Yuan.

The Persians not only may have created the demand for underglaze blue wares, but also have provided the Chinese with quality cobalt—*sulimānī*, as Near Eastern merchants called it—containing arsenic, with which to do the job. The Persian painter on earthenware had difficulty preventing the blue from running. Even the Chinese, working on finer, less permeable porcelain, had trouble when the blue ran in the glazing, but less often than his Middle Eastern counterpart and with more tolerable effects. In the early Ming dynasty (late-fourteenth century), the temporary closure of China's ports to foreign trade made cobalt scarce. When it was available again, it was mixed with native Chinese ore, in use, by best evidence, after 1426,[21] the beginning of the Xuande reign. Simultaneously, *sulimānī* became known as "Mohammedan blue," no doubt to distinguish it from Chinese cobalt.

Visually, one cannot tell the two cobalts apart. The difference is chemical and can only be made in the laboratory, where in tested Chinese ores, more manganese has been found. Other untested ore samples, however, may yield less manganese.[22] Consequently,

4. An artisan throws a pot, 1982, Jian Guo Porcelain Factory, Jingdezhen, where traditional hand methods of porcelain production are standard.

opinion in China is divided about whether the cobalt used in early wares was imported or not. Of those in the West who believe it was, the fact that more manganese appears in wares after the mid-fifteenth century suggests that a new source of ore had been found, namely in China.[23] Whatever the nationality of the cobalt, in response to the new demand for blue-and-white, the native potter made a tremendous advance in his craft: he could now high-fire cobalt as well as iron and copper under the glaze.[24]

Learning Resources Center
Collin County Community College District
SPRING CREEK CAMPUS
Plano, Texas 75074

5. A painter applies a circular line on a vase neck with the help of a wheel, 1982, Jian Guo Porcelain Factory, Jingdezhen.

kilnsite about three miles from Jingdezhen.[26] Apparently, blue-and-white was not immediately favored by the Chinese court. Along with the five-color wares, the Chinese, accustomed to the thick, varied glazes of Song monochromes, labeled blue-and-white "vulgar."[27] For a time, then, export blue-and-white differed from both domestic and imperial porcelains in suiting overseas buyers of a special sort, most notably sultans and caliphs of taste and wealth.

Today these collections exceed in number any like them in China. Two are unique in the number of objects of known date and in quantity of porcelains. The Archaeological Museum, Teheran, has over a thousand pieces, all originally at the shrine to Shah Abbis at Ardebil and dating no later than 1612. The other collection, at the Topkapi Saray Museum in Istanbul, has over ten thousand porcelains, of which eight thousand are Chinese, dating from the sixteenth through eighteenth centuries. Not surprisingly, the earliest blue-and-whites in each of these two groups depart from Chinese tradition, not in form nor even decorative motifs but rather in the overall composition of the decoration. The Arabic preference for even-numbered divisions of the whole plate or of borders often prevails. In short, reflecting the demanding tastes of wealthy Middle Easterners, among the best survivors in these collections are those of a hybrid Islamic and Chinese design.

Recent discoveries, however, show that imperial-quality blue-and-white developed earlier than previously thought. One pagoda-topped vase from a 1319 tomb[28] now replaces the 1351 twin temple vases, known as the "David" pair, as the earliest dated example of native blue-and-white.[29] The elephant-head handles and dragon-painted bodies of the "David" pair and the pagoda feature of the earlier vase give strong middle and late Yuan evidence that the foreign-inspired style was on its way to being translated into court taste well before the Ming dynasty (1368–1644). Of course, overglaze enamels remained and were

While this technical achievement may be credited to the Chinese alone, it was first stimulated by the export trade; without foreign interest, blue-and-white might never have been perfected. In the early Yuan, overseas orders evidently exceeded the supply of domestic ware, and Chinese potters created a whole new line—the blue-and-white—to join white and green wares for shipment abroad. Chinese literature about the period, which usually deals only with imperial ware, does not mention blue-and-white.[25] Yet shards of this type of export have been found at the Hutien

combined with the underglaze blue-and-white in the *doucai* (dovetailed colors) and *wucai* (five-color or polychrome) wares,[30] although they took second place to the pristine blue by itself. Eventually, the blue-and-white won favor at court, where it gradually replaced the rich Song monochromes, the delicate pure whites, and the luminous greens of Longquan ware.[31] Imperial taste thus adapted to a foreign mode, eventually transforming China's potting industry.

That change was accelerated in the early Ming period by the concentration of China's ceramic industry at Jingdezhan, east of Poyang Lake in Jiangxi Province. There, on Jewel Hill, an imperial factory was established in 1369. Almost immediately a growing number of private factories joined this one in making not only domestic ware but also assigned orders for the court.[32] In any of the private kilns, then, both domestic and imperial wares could be produced, facilitating the cross-fertilization of form, decoration, and even quality between the two, though artisans producing official wares no doubt worked separately from those making domestic and export pieces. The proximity and sharing of production between imperial and private factories may explain the occasional appearance of reign marks upon export pieces other than the rare official wares that were inevitably spirited out of the country for a price (see appendix A).

Under the second Ming emperor, Yongle (1403–24), the Chinese admiral Zheng He led seven large expeditions west as far as the Somali coast and the Persian Gulf, but restrictions concerning foreign contacts soon followed. Officially, subjects were forbidden on pain of death to emigrate or trade.[33] Unofficially, however, the lucrative trade, which had become standard during the Song and Yuan, continued apace, and apparently more porcelain was sent abroad than ever before.[34] Instead of encouraging its own shipping, the Ming brought other nations' merchants to China's ports to participate in a scheme of "tributes," known since Song times. Goods were given as the tribute

owed to an emperor—chief of the Celestial Kingdom at the center of the world—by a foreign "vassal" state. They in turn received merchandise more valuable than those they brought, and were thus forever kept in debt.[35]

The tribute system was an early, subtle form of an unfavorable balance of trade, for trade, in fact, is what it was. Under this scheme, though the total amount of export porcelain rose, individual purchases of the best available blue-and-white were rationed. Tribute missions to Beijing were limited to fifty sets of it,[36] and prices for this sort of ware were high, according to Chinese records. The price list of export goods during the reign of the Hongzhi emperor (1488–1505) shows plates and vases at 500 guan, bowls at 300, and wine jars at 1500 guan. A tael of gold was worth 50 guan, thus the wine jar cost 30 gold taels, or more than $45

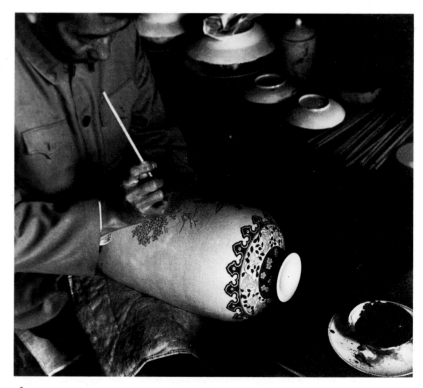

6. A master painter retraces cobalt blue on a previously sketched design, 1982, Jian Guo Porcelain Factory, Jingdezhen.

8. *Ewer*, c. 1575–1600, H 19.5 cm. Dark underglaze blue, above-average export. Courtesy of the Ashmolean Museum.

7. *Jar*, c. 1573–1620, H 34 cm. Underglaze blue, fine domestic/export.

then, since a tael (a silver ounce) was worth $1.50 until the late-nineteenth century (fig. 7).[37]

The overwhelming popularity of blue-and-white in the West for four centuries and through three dynasties—the Yuan, Ming, and the first decades of the Qing (1644–1911)—allowed ample time for the appearance of many sorts of forms and decorative motifs (figs. 8–14). The early Near Eastern blend of Islamic taste with the Chinese gave way to a hybridization of the ware with European preferences after Western traders advanced upon China beginning in the early-sixteenth century. In 1514, the Portuguese arrived, followed by Spanish, Dutch, English, and French agents. Their lust for the riches of the East exceeded civilized behavior, especially in the case of the Portuguese who allied themselves with Chinese or Japanese coastal pirates, thus earning a reputation among the Chinese as the

9. *Kendi*, c. 1600–20, H 19.4 cm. Underglaze blue, average domestic/export. Private collection.

10. *Bottle*, c. 1628–44, H 39.2 cm. Blue mark on base (lotus?), fine export. Courtesy of the Weldon Collection, University of King's College, Halifax, Nova Scotia.

12. *Jar*, c. 1680, H 45 cm. Underglaze blue, fine domestic/export. Private collection.

11. *Plate*, c. 1680–1710, D 20.3 cm. Underglaze blue, average domestic/export. Private collection.

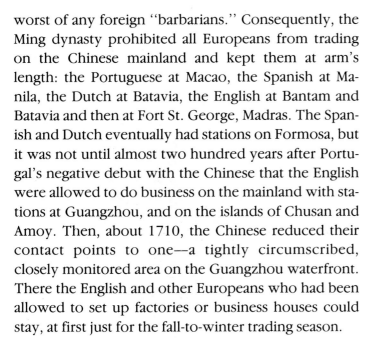

13. *Cup and saucer*, c. 1715–30, cup: D 7.6 cm, saucer: D 14.6 cm. Chinese ''Imari'' with iron-brown edge, average ware. Courtesy of the Peabody Museum.

14. *Saucer*, c. 1725, D 11.9 cm. Blue interior, brown exterior. Courtesy of the Society for the Preservation of New England Antiquities.

worst of any foreign ''barbarians.'' Consequently, the Ming dynasty prohibited all Europeans from trading on the Chinese mainland and kept them at arm's length: the Portuguese at Macao, the Spanish at Manila, the Dutch at Batavia, the English at Bantam and Batavia and then at Fort St. George, Madras. The Spanish and Dutch eventually had stations on Formosa, but it was not until almost two hundred years after Portugal's negative debut with the Chinese that the English were allowed to do business on the mainland with stations at Guangzhou, and on the islands of Chusan and Amoy. Then, about 1710, the Chinese reduced their contact points to one—a tightly circumscribed, closely monitored area on the Guangzhou waterfront. There the English and other Europeans who had been allowed to set up factories or business houses could stay, at first just for the fall-to-winter trading season.

Special-Order Porcelain

Porcelains now purchased by these Westerners were not only what was available but what they had specifically requested. This latter sort of ware was called *chine de commande*, special-order porcelain (figs. 15–

27). Beginning with the blue-and-white in the sixteenth and seventeenth centuries and also including some polychromes, special-order wares were carried home by the ships of Europe's East India companies. The desire for these wares, which was immediately responsive to each wave of fashion, eventually led to three other Western contributions to the Chinese potter–painter in the eighteenth century: black-gray line painting (also called *grisaille, encre de chine,* or penciled ware); an overglaze rose enamel made from a chloride of gold; and the use of isometric perspective and shading to simulate three-dimensionality. The first two techniques were probably introduced to the imperial court by Jesuit missionaries; the third definitely was. Both black line painting and the gold-red, which underwent experiment during the 1720s, were on the market for overseas purchase by the 1730s.[38]

While black line painting was based upon a technique that merely needed improvement so that the black did not fade in firing, the introduction of the rose palette was more than the addition of one color and its hues. It added a new range in the Chinese painter's palette. Technically, the gold-red, as the Chinese translate it today to distinguish it from copper-

15. *Dish*, c. 1700, H 24.1 cm, D 27.3 cm. *Doucai*, perhaps unique; fine export. Courtesy of the Victoria and Albert Museum.

17. *Jar*, c. 1723–35, H 84 cm. Chinese ''Imari'' with overglaze blue and gold-red, fine, special-order export, possibly unique. Courtesy of the Museo Nacional del Virreinato, Mexico.

16. *Vase*, part of a garniture set, c. 1710–22, H 38.1 cm. Overglaze enamels: iron-red, black, gilt, fine domestic/export. Private collection.

19. Detail of fig. 18, Fo-lion finial, pawing gold brocade ball.

18. *Jar*, c. 1735–40, H 50.8 cm. Overglaze enamels, fine domestic/ export. Private collection.

20. *Tureen*, c. 1750–75, H 22.2 cm, L 26.6 cm. Overglaze enamels, fine export. Private collection.

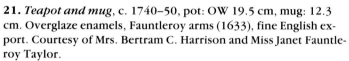

21. *Teapot and mug*, c. 1740–50, pot: OW 19.5 cm, mug: 12.3 cm. Overglaze enamels, Fauntleroy arms (1633), fine English export. Courtesy of Mrs. Bertram C. Harrison and Miss Janet Fauntleroy Taylor.

22. *Soup bowl*, c. 1810–20, D 20.5 cm, H 4.7 cm. Overglaze pastel enamels, unidentified arms, initials, and insignia of an archbishop, fine Spanish export. Courtesy of the Peabody Museum.

23. Detail of fig. 22, insignia of Spanish archbishop.

24. *Soup bowl*, c. 1800, D 24.7 cm, H 3.81 cm. Sepia vignette, "MONTICELLO" and "THOMAS JEFFERSON" in script, fine American export. Courtesy of Dr. Wesley Gallup.

25. Detail of fig. 24.

26. (far left) *Figurine*, woman playing a *pipa*, c. 1750–75, H 22.4 cm. Overglaze enamels, fine domestic/export. Courtesy of the British Museum.

27. (left) *Twin boy figurines*, the Merry Spirits of Union and Harmony (*he he er xian*), c. 1700–20, H 27.6 cm. Overglaze enamels, average domestic/export. Courtesy of the Franz Mayer Collection, Mexico City.

red, was combined with a white oxide of arsenic and fired in a low-temperature kiln. The white not only gave a spectrum of rose hues from deep ruby to the palest pink but could be combined with enamels of any color, thus making "soft" or "pale" colors—pastels. Foreign colors (*yangcai*) refers, then, not only to the rose range but also to the pastel enamels (*yuancai*). *Famille rose,* the nineteenth-century French term for the new rose hues, is also translated *yangcai,* but *famille rose,* or rose palette, ought to be replaced with gold-red, which specifies the chemistry of the color rather than the color alone, and places it with copper-red and iron-red, long accepted terms among art historians.

In contrast to the delayed acceptance of blue-and-white in the Ming, the gold-red was immediately adopted by the Qing court. In the early part of the Qianlong era (1736–95), the rose and soft colors came to surpass in popularity the long-preferred blue-and-white (figs. 28 and 29). This shift occurred even though the blue reached new aesthetic heights during the reign of Kangxi, and has in fact, always remained the favorite of many collectors.

Excellent evidence supports the theory that the Jesuits transmitted the Renaissance techniques of achieving three-dimensionality through the use of perspective and chiaroscuro to the Chinese court artists, and through them, to painters in Jingdezhen. Like their predecessors in Beijing a hundred years before, the eighteenth-century Jesuits were knowledgeable in the latest Western sciences and arts. By their era, these included astronomy, physics, mathematics, medicine, geography, history, music, ceramics, and perspective. Father Giuseppe Castiglione (1688–1768), the highly favored painter to the emperor Kangxi and his two successors, was one of the most instrumental. He was also a friend and teacher of painting to Nian Siyao, director of the imperial factory at Jingdezhen under the

28. *Plate*, c. 1740–60, D 23.1 cm. *Doucai*, above-average export, now rare. Courtesy of Norman Herreshoff.

29. *Dish*, c. 1820, D 27.5 cm. Overglaze gold-red and gilt FitzHugh design, superior export. Courtesy of the Peabody Museum.

emperor Yongzheng (1726–35). With Castiglione's help, Nian translated Andrea Pozzo's *Perspective Pictorum et Architectorum* (1729; 2d ed., 1735), writing in his preface, ''I am now, thanks to Lang Shining [Castiglione], capable of drawing a Chinese subject in a Western style.''[39] Castiglione probably taught other Chinese at court to paint on a few selected porcelains. Such wares came undecorated from Jingdezhen to the emperor's summer palace, where a number of artisans, including enamelers and ivory workers, gathered.[40] In his turn, Nian must have influenced painters at Jingdezhen and possibly Guangzhou as well. As imperfectly as the foreign notion of perspective was rendered by the Chinese, some objects received remarkably realistic spatial treatment. This feat was all the more an achievement when the object to be painted was curved (fig. 30).

Figure 31 shows one of four similar but not identical plates of eggshell thinness. Western influences immediately arrest the viewer: the composition itself,

the use of gold-red, and the treatment of light and dark to achieve modeling. A European couple and their child appear in three plates (two are the exact reverse of each other); the couple alone is depicted in one. Yet in all but one plate, the subjects' features are oriental, as were those of all foreigners painted by the Chinese, a natural and sure signature of the artist's nationality.[41] Two of the plates are marked Yongzheng, another is unmarked, and the fourth is marked Qianlong. This last alone depicts the Europeans much more as a Western painter might, with rounder eyes and fuller, wider lips, possibly painted by Nian Siyao or another Chinese painter closely supervised by Castiglione.[42] The Yongzheng plates are pastel polychrome, including gold-red; the Qianlong is much more vividly painted in rose hues. All attempt to render the three-dimensionality of the figures with shading. Given these examples, it is highly probable that Castiglione was a major link between Western knowledge of the rose color and perspective techniques and

30. *Saucers*, c. 1790, each D 13.0 cm. Overglaze enamels, fine export. Courtesy of Dr. Wesley Gallup.

the experimentation with them by Chinese painters.

Other Jesuits also played an artistic intermediary role. In 1712, just three years before Castiglione arrived in Beijing, Father Francois Xavier d'Entrecolles (1664–1741), missionary in Jiangxi from 1698 and pastor to a congregation of Jingdezhen potters, complained of a request made to him by certain merchants there. Stating a belief in the singular genius of Western invention, they urged him to find something novel from Europe to be made up for the emperor. Whether or not d'Entrecolles complied in this instance he does not say, but he noted that the poor potters could be put to predictable failures by impossible demands from both European buyers and the emperor. D'Entrecolles indicated he would rather not add to their burden; after all, many were members of his congregation.[43] But his evidence, as well as Castiglione's, shows that in these last years of Kangxi, during Yongzheng and into the first years of Qianlong, that is, c. 1690–1740, the Jesuits transmitted Western taste to the Chinese who decorated porcelain for the emperor, and in turn, for export.

Among all Catholic orders, the Jesuits' longstanding, exclusive connections with the Chinese court naturally led to the habit of calling porcelains with Christian subjects ''Jesuit ware,'' even if ordered by other Catholic brothers or converts. From a certain view, the Jesuits deserve having china bear their name, since not only did their eighteenth-century introduction of highly popular Western techniques increase the export market, but two centuries before, they were among the first after Marco Polo to republicize the virtues of porcelain to the West. Father Matteo Ricci, writing about China in the period of his residency there (1582–1610), observed:

> The finest specimens of porcelain are made from clay found in the province of Kiam (Jiangxi), and these are shipped not only to every part of China but even to the remotest corners of Europe where they are highly prized by those who appreciate elegance at their ban-

31. *Saucer*, c. 1736–50, mark and reign of Qianlong, D 17.4 cm. Overglaze enamels on thin body; ruby-red on reverse, imperial ware. Courtesy of the Baur Collection, Geneva.

quets rather than pompous display. This porcelain, too, will bear the heat of hot foods without cracking and, what is more to be wondered at, if it is broken and sewed with a brass wire it will hold liquids without any leakage.[44]

These comments from Ricci's diary, first published in 1615, could have been read in Latin (four editions), French (three editions), German, Spanish, Italian (one edition each), and excerpts in English, all within the first half of the seventeenth century.[45] His report would have impressed all intelligent, tasteful, and practical readers. (A hundred years later, d'Entrecolles noted that porcelain repairs at Jingdezhen were done almost invisibly by specialized workers who drilled small holes in the broken pieces, and, like repairers in

Ricci's day, made them water-tight "with a very delicate brass thread."[46]

The appeal of Chinese porcelain, with its adaptability to the latest styles, unique gray-to-white clay, bluish-white glaze, and novel scenes of a land still exotic to most Westerners, remained steady and strong into the nineteenth century. The nature of that fascination changed considerably over the three hundred years of this present study. Beliefs such as the sixteenth-century claim that porcelain detected poison by instantly breaking on contact with it,[47] or the long-standing superstition in primitive societies that porcelain contained mystic charms in this life and should be the container to hold food and other items for the deceased in the next,[48] gradually faded. A more basic admiration of its usefulness or the beauty of its decorative forms and designs in new hues or color ensembles came to dominate. A practical feature

32. *Sugar bowl*, c. 1790, H 13.7 cm. Overglaze enamels on typical Western form, a composite armorial: elements of the English, Prussian, and (below) Dutch royal arms, fine export. Private collection.

33. *Gouache*, from a series on porcelain production by a Guangzhou artist, c. 1825, c. 38.5 × 53 cm. Potters at work. Courtesy of the Peabody Museum.

played no small part as well: because of its quartz content and molecular structure, porcelain broke cleanly and was, therefore, much easier to mend than the jagged edges of broken earthenware.

Mixed with these sure assets was a desire to see a national or personal identity reproduced in the ware ordered after the Europeans arrived in the sixteenth century (fig. 32). The export porcelain produced over the centuries, then, becomes a symbol of intercultural values, a mirror of the best and sometimes the worst of the basic concerns of East and West. By their materials of body and glaze, a rich story of achievement in ceramic science may be read (figs. 33–37). But even more fascinating, the attitudes of widely separate strangers are frozen in time, in a variety of forms and designs. In fact, export embodies so many interna-

34. *Gouache*, c. 1825, c. 38.5 × 53 cm. Potters and molds. Courtesy of the Peabody Museum.

35. *Gouache*, c. 1825, detail of a view of painters and inspector. Courtesy of the Peabody Museum.

36. *Gouache*, c. 1825, c. 38.5 × 53 cm. Glaziers with ware drying. Courtesy of the Peabody Museum.

37. *Gouache*, c. 1825, c. 38.5 × 53 cm. Chinese and European traders in Guangzhou factory. Courtesy of the Peabody Museum.

38. *Goglet*, c. 1845, H 31.1 cm. Overglaze enamels, unique American export. Courtesy of the Winterthur Museum.

which to analyze any export object. By separating the elements of date, quality, form, decoration, and use, a piece may be understood in context, its "language" may be read, and the message of Chinese export enjoyed beyond its physical appeal alone. The goglet is a significant form in the most basic sense; it defines space absolutely, standing alone as a created object. By carving out intentional room, it commands attention, fulfilling its function as a made object (the question of quality is put aside for the moment). Its simple shape—a long neck and round body—is historic Chinese, a heavier, nineteenth-century version of Yongzheng prototypes. The elephant-head handles, much better molded and sculpted than any predecessors, would be too heavy on a thinner piece. As bearers of the Buddha's jewels, the elephants—introduced with Buddhism from India—had by now, in their appearance on porcelain and other ceramics, become wholly Chinese in artistic origin.

If the form is oriental, then the decoration is almost purely Western, specifically American, with minor exceptions. The bold eagle, taken from the 1782 seal of the United States, holds not only the U.S. but the Chinese imperial flag in its talons. Floral sprays, whose origin was probably French, fill the background and the opposite side. The decoration is well painted on a smooth body, and the whole is a pleasing novelty with familiar elements uniquely joined. No other porcelain objects known to this author bear Chinese and Western flags in a focused pairing.

The piece combines Eastern and Western elements in a harmonic whole as simple and straightforward as its lines. It implies the special relationship Americans enjoyed with Chinese merchants and with their government in the nineteenth century. That era of good feeling was to last longer for the United States than for any other Western power. Probably an American buyer ordered the goglet, which may account not only for the eagle but for the form (in this period, Americans often wanted to have native forms and dec-

tional sources of ideas and tastes that it is unique in world ceramics. This contribution alone rescues it from past disdain based solely on judgments of body or glaze. Now this ware speaks with another voice to those interested in a history, anthropology, and sociology of ceramics.

As we trace the coming of porcelain to North America in the pages to follow, the intricate fusing of its physical and emblematic meanings are there for the curious reader, building from the example of the goglet in figure 38. This goglet establishes the criteria with orations). Less likely, the piece might have been a gift from a Chinese merchant to an American, but the featured eagle hints of a predominant Western choice, using Chinese elements to symbolize a new, extensive period of East-West unity and cooperation. Thus the goglet, which was probably intended largely for display, is a quintessential example of special-order export porcelain: the coalescence of traditional Chinese art with the demands of occidental taste in a specific statement of either national or individual identity. No other ceramics from any country had this extensive significance.

JAPANESE PORCELAIN

Along with Chinese export in imitation of Japanese wares—the familiar Chinese ''Imari''—porcelains from Japan were imported into North America. They are easily confused with Chinese specimens, especially as shards. But they are later and less numerous, because the Japanese porcelain industry, born at Arita Hizan about 1605, was not well developed until the mid-seventeenth century.[49] That was a decade after the Japanese, fearing Western penetration, in 1639 expelled all foreigners but the Dutch and Chinese.[50] Afterward, Chinese junks probably supplied the Manila market, and through it, Mexico, with incidental Japanese ware, largely blue-and-white ''Old Imari'' porcelain.

In the late Transitional period, 1658–82, however, when Jingdezhen's fine wares for export diminished, Manilians and Mexicans looked to Japan as a substitute source: its industry was ready to meet a new demand. On both sides, however, China's role as an intermediary was still necessary; foreigners were excluded from mainland Japan, and neither Manilian nor Mexican merchants wished a direct Japan-Mexico connection, a clear threat to their own lucrative China trade. Such had long been the case in Mexico. When a Japanese diplomatic and trade delegation had arrived in Mexico in 1614, the viceroy expelled them ''on payne of death.''[51] Japanese export porcelain thus made a circuitous and circumscribed route on its way to the New World.

Some historical documents specify Japanese porcelain was in the Dutch and English colonies on this continent, but similar manuscripts in Mexico and Peru have not yet come to light. However, remaining objects are vivid evidence. They may or may not be representative, but at least they are diverse. The bottle in figure 39 is shorter than its Chinese prototype (see fig.

39. *Bottle,* Japanese Arita, c. 1690, H 12.0 cm. Underglaze blue and overglaze enamels. Marked bottom: overglaze stylized flower, above-average domestic/export. Private collection.

40. *Pair, "Korean Fo Dogs,"* Japanese Imari, c. 1661–72, H 19.36 cm. Overglaze polychrome, above-average domestic/export. Private collection.

Elsewhere in North America, typical scalloped, multipaneled, wide-bordered bowls in the Japanese Imari style of the late-seventeenth century and plates of the eighteenth century are not uncommon, brought by the Dutch and English to our East Coast as well as by the Spanish to Mexico (fig. 41). But the Japanese wares suffered telling handicaps. They might be average in quality, yet more expensive than the Chinese competition. Despite protests by the Dutch and others, the Japanese kept their prices high with an additional increase by middlemen. Also, unlike Chinese export, porcelains from Japan were usually for a general market, not on order for the West. In chapters to come, a few examples of Japanese wares will be included with the Chinese for comparison, some in the same illustration. Chinese export, however, will remain the focus, beginning with its first arrival in North America via the long-lived Manila galleons.

141), like other Japanese rectilinear bottles,[52] and its careful painting is distinctive in its borderless simplicity. In figure 40, the pair of "Korean Fo dogs" (so-called by the Japanese) are wildly colorful adaptations of the Chinese guardian lions; the color imparts power. A larger, white-and-gilt pair is also in Mexico today.[53] In addition, in Lima, large Japanese jars are still displayed in churches with others from China; they are also both part of private collections (see appendix E). The superb craftsmanship of Japanese porcelain at its best indicates why the West sometimes preferred porcelains from Japan over China, and why the former became models for the Chinese potter, either in entire styles, such as Chinese "Imari," or in particular motifs, after the early 1680s, when the kilns at Jingdezhen were restored.[54]

41. *Sugar bowl*, Japanese Imari, c. 1690, H 9.5 cm. Overglaze polychrome, average export. Private collection.

CHAPTER 2

Manila Galleons to Mexico

The Spanish in Mexico were the first to import porcelains to this continent. As early as the sixteenth century, galleons from Manila brought Chinese goods to Mexico, but internationally, collectors, connoisseurs, dealers, and even curators (if they acknowledge this fact) are vague about details of the exchange, especially its long history. In addition, it has been falsely assumed that most of these goods were carried overland through Mexico en route to Spain, even though historians have known that much of the galleons' cargoes remained in New Spain. The West's ignorance, even indifference, is due in part to an exclusive focus on northern European countries—Holland, England, and France—and their colonies. In English-speaking countries, Spain and New Spain have been eclipsed, while Mexican authors, writing in their own periodicals, have told the story, but only in the most general way.

The oversight is understandable. Serious study of export wares dates only from World War II, an offshoot of Western scholarship about classical Chinese porcelains, which was itself a relatively new field, only a century old in the West. That interest in export was dependent upon historic collections of porcelain on the Continent or in England, which, if private, were exhibited, or if in museums, were readily accessible. In contrast, porcelains in Mexico are not found in quantity in any major museums. The best Chinese export wares are mainly in private homes and are rarely, if ever, on public view.

In addition, the fortunes of Spain and New Spain have been thought to be essentially the same: if Spain's power declined, as it did in the early-seventeenth century (simultaneously with the arrival of the Dutch and English in the Far East), then so too must Mexico's. Such, however, was apparently not the case. A century-old Mexico exhibited economic and even political muscles that would lead to her independence in the nineteenth century.

R. L. Hobson, a Venerable Bede of Chinese porcelain scholarship, has remarked that history as well as technique is fundamental to the understanding of ceramics. Since Mexico has suffered from ignorance of her China trade, a brief background to her porcelain imports is basic to making known her early preeminence and continuing role. That role allows us to define most of the range of export pieces to North America—except for special-order wares—from the earliest period on. But their first association with

Spain emphasizes Mexico's place as first importer and significant tastemaker in this hemisphere.

OPENING THE PACIFIC OCEAN

From the broadest perspective, New Spain's China trade was based upon Spain's competition with Portugal for the commerce, Christianization, and political control of the Far East, first in Japan, and then in China. Pope Alexander VI had tried to forestall rivalry between the two Catholic monarchies by proclaiming separate spheres of activity for each when both countries launched their overseas empires from the Iberian Peninsula in the late-fifteenth century.[1] By the Treaty of Tordesillas in 1494, the dividing line was the meridian 370 leagues west of the Cape Verde Islands. Spain, eager to compete for Portugal's profit in pepper from the Moluccas, argued about the position of that line on the opposite side of the world.[2] The geographical focus of that confrontation, in which Spain eventually triumphed, was the Philippine Islands. There, Manila

42. *Box*, c. 1803, D 6.1 cm, and its model, a 1785 Carolus dollar (8-real piece), Mexico City; above-average export. Courtesy of Dr. Wesley Gallup.

became the center of Spain's power and trade, a way-station of such superb location that every Western nation coveted its control.[3]

Although Manila eventually funneled goods to Mexico from all over the world, not just the Orient, the bulk still came from ports in the ancient arc of Southeast Asia, from India in the west to Siam, Cambodia, Borneo, Thailand, Malaysia, Japan, and especially China.

Two nearly simultaneous events set the stage for the Manila–Mexico axis. In the period 1519–21, while Hernán Cortés conquered the Aztec capital of Tenochtitlán—now Mexico City—Ferdinand Magellan entered the Pacific Ocean from Cape Horn on the first circumnavigation of the world. His party also explored in the Philippines, sending back much valuable information to the Spanish crown. With land and sea claims uncontested for a time, Spain could implement a grand plan of mercantilism in her Pacific lake. She could send New World silver and gold to the Far East and in return import treasures made famous by Marco Polo three centuries before. The Chinese wanted specie above all else, and Spanish-Mexican silver dollars—eventually called the Carolus dollar for Charles III (first minted in 1772)—became the standard coin for the trade and remained so until the mid-nineteenth century (fig. 42).

A little over four decades after Magellan, in 1565, Miguel Lopez de Legaspi arrived in Cebú to establish the first Spanish station in the Philippines. But it was his pilot, Andres de Urdaneta, who made the most crucial discovery for the future of the Pacific trade—a feasible return route. Instead of fruitlessly heading due east into the trade winds, as had his predecessors, Urdaneta directed his ship northeast past Taiwan, the Ryukyus, and Japan to about 40° north latitude, picking up both the Japanese current and northwest winds. He then proceeded to the California coast. Subsequent voyages refined this *tornavuelta* so that at Cape Mendocino the ships turned south to follow the coast and eventually arrive at Acapulco.[4]

The return trip was fraught with problems: storms from Southeast Asia, if the ships did not leave early enough in the fall; a radical change in temperature from the tropics to the North Pacific; and most dire, a vast landless stretch of sea, north of the Hawaiian Is-

lands, where, for five or more months, no port would be touched, no fresh supplies of food or water would be available. When it rained during the passage, any container, especially jars, would be used to collect the water.[5] Ornamental jars and vases may even have been brought from below, the bigger the better. The Spanish preferred jars to casks for their storage of grains, oil, wine, and other liquors.[6] Coupled with their life-saving function on the homeward route, and their decorative value, no wonder a great quantity of jars appear to remain in Mexico in comparison to survivors in other countries in the China trade (figs. 43–47).

When Manila became the capital of the Philippines

43. *Jar*, stoneware, "Martaban," c. 1773–1810, H 41.2 cm. Six molded panels, brown glaze, common utilitarian export. Courtesy of the Field Museum of Natural History.

44. (below left) Detail of a panel on jar in fig. 43, bust of Charles III, from a coin in circulation well after its first minting in 1772.

45. (below right) Detail of a panel on jar in fig. 43, Arabic "Fatimah's Hand" with European ruff. Open right hand thought to be protection from the "evil eye," an Arab superstition, also common among Christians and Moslems.

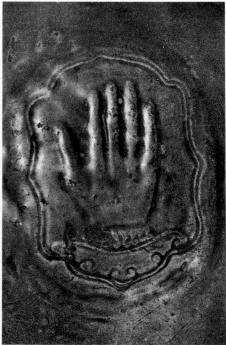

46. *Vase* (one of a pair), c. 1730–50, H 132.5 cm. Size "no. 1" vase in Spanish market, first-class export. Courtesy of Mr. Arthur A. Houghton, Jr.

47. Detail of phoenix in fig. 46.

in 1571, chosen to supercede Cebú because of its proximity to China, the route between New Spain and the islands had been tested for six years. Ships on this line, the *naos de la China*—better known as the Manila Galleon—became legends in their own time for the real and supposed value of their cargoes. The actual annual figure varied from 1.5 to 2 or sometimes 3 million pesos. Exaggerated estimates of three or four times these amounts were rumored, the larger by those furthest removed from the trade.[7] During its unparalleled 250-year history, the Manila Galleon carried the booty every foreign privateer or pirate understandably craved. After 1815, ships of independent Mexican or foreign merchants replaced these government galleons in their Pacific ellipsis, but the trade by then was much diminished.[8]

PORCELAIN IN THE PHILIPPINES

Once firmly in the islands, the Spanish tapped into, radically changed, and increased a centuries-old trade in Chinese, Siamese, and Annamese pots. From mid-Tang times, earthenware vases (*Yue*) from China, notable for their hardness, found their way to the Philippines, as did the first porcelains of the eighth and ninth centuries.[9] It was not until the Song and Yuan dynasties that considerable numbers of mass-produced pottery and porcelain, some of excellent quality, arrived. Their importation continued into the Ming.[10]

Chinese records of the thirteenth century are the earliest documentation of this trade. In 1225, Zhao Zhuguo (Chao Chukuo), superintendent of foreign trade at the port of Quanzhou (Ch'uan-chou), wrote his handbook on foreign commerce, *Records of Various Barbarous Nations* (*Zhu Fan Zhi*), mentioning the Philippines three times. He described Chinese junks anchoring in island harbors, near established marketplaces or in more primitive areas, announcing their presence by the beating of a drum. The natives then boarded the vessels to barter their own goods for porcelains, metals, lead, tin, variegated glass beads, pearls, iron needles, and black satin and other colored fabrics. Zhao Zhuguo recounted certain perils, especially with one isolated tribe, the Hay-tan, whose members lived in treetops, from which they might shoot arrows at strangers. Quite readily, however, they could be distracted by tossing "a porcelain bowl, [which] they would joyfully pick up and hop away shouting."[11]

Most of the porcelains came from kiln sites in Chinese provinces on the southern coast—Zhejiang, Fujian, and Guangdong—within a two-to-three-week sailing distance of the Philippines. No doubt Jingdezhen was another source in this early period. A variety of china came, but especially the blue to greenish white wares (*qingbai*) and the celadon, or greenware. Less common were pieces with underglaze floral designs or verses in brown beneath a yellowish green glaze; lead glaze pieces; underglaze brown objects with *qingbai* glaze and carved border designs; carved phoenix-head jars; large carved plates; a type of molded white ware (*shufu*); blue-and-white; and underglaze red wares.[12]

Whether from burial sites or by the passing of porcelains from one generation to the next, the evidence of wares in the islands before the Spanish is considerable, varied, and can be of high quality. Magellan and his men had seen such wares when they ate with native chiefs: large porcelain platters for rice and meat and so-called porcelain—but probably stoneware—jars for rice and wine.[13]

In the 1560s, Miguel de Legaspi was, in essence,

conducting market research in porcelain and other Chinese goods. On his pioneer trip in 1565, he encountered a junk owned by Borneo Moors trading in the Philippines and took samples of its cargo, including some gold and porcelains. Twice more, in 1569 and 1570, Legaspi reported on the islands' exchange, again mentioning porcelains.[14]

Also in 1570, a junior officer, Captain Juan de Salcedo, encountered two Chinese junks and for the first time noted wares of high quality. Besides earthenware jars and dishes, on the decks of both ships were porcelain vases, plates, bowls, and "fine porcelain jars, which they call *sinoratas.*" In the cabins were more valuable cargoes, among them, "gilded porcelain bowls" and "gilded waterjugs," Salcedo reported, "although not in a large quantity, considering the size of the ships."[15] The waterjug was doubtless a "kendi," with a mammalian spout of which few gilded ones exist.[16] Similar luxury wares were no doubt among the possessions of Raxa Soliman, the wealthy Muslim king of Manila prior to the coming of the Spanish. Before his sumptuous house was destroyed by fire, it had been filled with supplies of money, copper, iron, wax, cotton, blankets, vats of brandy, and porcelain.[17]

With this sort of data, Legaspi's successor, Guido de Lavezaris, could make informed recommendations about the trade. In 1573, he wrote his superiors: "The Chinese have come here on trading expeditions since our arrival, for we have always tried to treat them well. Therefore during the two years we have spent on this island, they have come in greater numbers each year, and with more ships; and they come earlier than they used to, so that their trade is assured us." Further, he continued, they were bringing "better and much richer wares." Then he proposed a plan, prophetic in its implications: "If merchants would come from Nueva España, they might enrich themselves, and enrich the royal customs in these parts—both through trade and through the mines, the richness and number of which are well-known to us."[18] It was just this scheme that the Spanish crown implemented.

Lavezaris's report succinctly tells what happened to the Philippine trade in porcelains after the establishment of Spanish rule. Despite taking second place to silks, more and better wares rapidly arrived. Instantly, Spain controlled and regularized her dealings with the Chinese merchants. By making transactions only to fit her larger mercantilistic policies, she caused the near demise of the native market, and for another noncommercial reason: natives of the seacoast communities became Christians under Spanish rule and gave up their "pagan" burial practices and other ceremonies. In other communities where Christianity was not adopted, the old traditions continued; today, natives may still be found fermenting wine in Chinese jars and using porcelains in their ceremonies.[19]

Archaeological evidence pinpoints the types of wares that were part of the bonanza in porcelains after the Spanish came. The early-twentieth-century archaeological pioneer, H. Otley Beyer, found "a great flood" of blue-and-white whole pieces and shards dating from the reign of Wanli on. Among the sites he excavated were the best stratified deposits of late-sixteenth-century wares in Manila, in the old China-town called the "Parian" (marketplace) and in the Escolta.[20] Beyer's discoveries also included overglaze polychrome wares, "frequently with decoration in silver," he reported. The others were early-sixteenth-century pieces of yellow, turquoise, and purple, or later-sixteenth-century wares decorated in red, green, and black.[21] In short, the Spanish initiated a brilliant new period in the porcelain trade, stimulating the Chinese kilns that produced export, and eventually ordering a few forms especially for Hispanic taste.[22]

In 1570, three galleons arrived in Manila from Acapulco, but their return cargoes are unknown[23] (see map 2, New Spain). In early 1574, by chance during the first year of the reign of Wanli, two galleons, the *Santiago* and the *San Juan*, had their goods noted in a joint cargo list.[24] It shows both the general types of porcelain brought and its order of importance among other imports in the early years of the trade:

448	marcos of gold, of different degrees of purity
712	pieces of all kinds of silks
312	quintals of cinnamon
22,300	pieces of fine gilt china, and of other kinds of porcelain ware
11,300	pieces of cotton cloth, each worth 2 pesos or more of common gold
930	arrobas of wax, each arroba worth 15 pesos of common gold
334	arrobas of cotton thread, each arroba worth 17 to 20 pesos of said gold.

King Philip II (1527–98) and Queen Anne of Austria (d. 1580), both avid ceramic collectors,[25] received this report via Mexico. In its pages, their majesties no doubt enthusiastically read that in addition to these items were gifts for them from native chiefs: "many jewels and crowns of gold, with silks, porcelains, earthen jars, and other very excellent things."[26]

Over the next twenty years, sometimes four similarly laden galleons annually made the round trip from Manila to Acapulco. By 1593, fearing the loss of too much silver to China, afraid of Chinese competition with Spain's silk industry, and apprehensive that excessive profits might accrue to Mexican merchants, Spain cut the number of official galleons to two ships of 300 tons each per year. However, with profits running 100 to 300 percent annually, government regulations became a game to break rather than to obey; an unknown amount of smuggling ensued, in ships ranging from the prescribed size to 2,000 tons. Still from 1593, one or two galleons was the recorded average until 1720, when official policy dictated that there should definitely be only two galleons of 560 tons each. Any increase, legal or illegal, was somewhat offset by an occasional shortage of ships or interference in the trade by the Dutch or Portuguese.[27] Despite these setbacks, Mexico's first half-century of trade with China, until about 1620—the end of the Wanli period—was unprecedented in value and numbers of items, setting a standard that perhaps even the Dutch never matched.[28]

Acapulco, normally a nondescript little fishing village, nonetheless readily replaced La Navidad as the galleons' home port; its harbor was unparalleled for its deep waters and sheltering mountains. Once unloaded and inspected, the Manila goods were quickly sold at an annual fair in January, a few weeks after the arrival of the galleon. Buyers came from all over Mexico—Puebla, Guadalajara, Jalapa, Saltillo, Mexico City—and from as far away as Peru. Traders, merchants, government officials, seamen of many nationalities, vagabonds, and fair followers eagerly attended, making a scene that was medieval in color, celebration, and compressed humanity.[29]

The Peruvians, who brought their own good supply of silver and raised prices, were especially popular. After 1582, they came regularly to Acapulco, when a royal edict aborted plans to establish direct trade between their country and the Philippines. The government feared too much competition with its own galleons, which sailed from Portobelo and supplied this area with Spanish goods. Five years later, another ban prohibited trade in Chinese goods by the "Lima ships" between New Spain and Peru and was repeatedly issued throughout the seventeenth century, but to little avail. According to reports of the

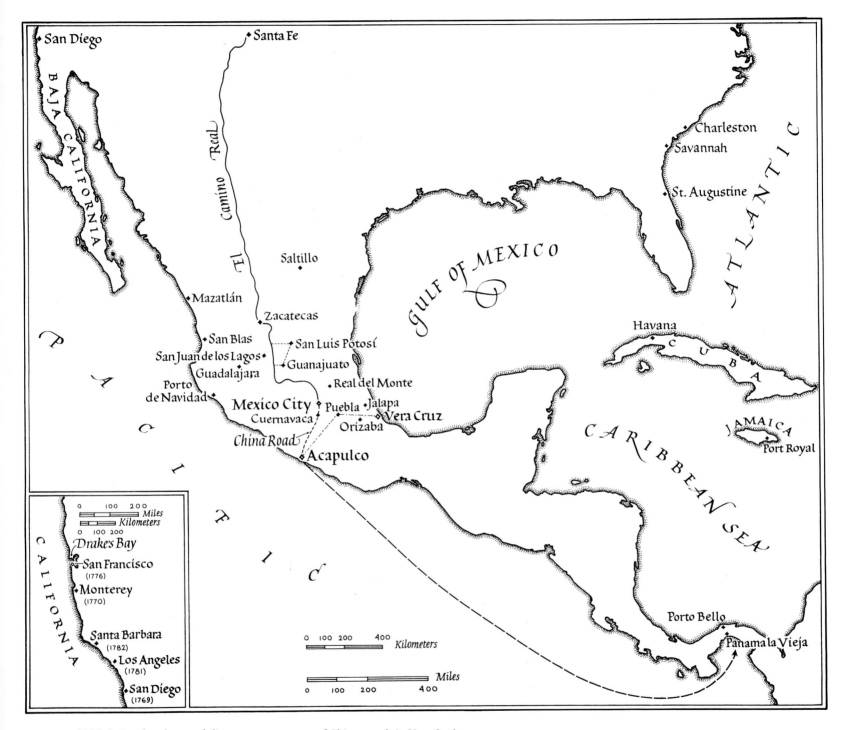

MAP 2. Land and coastal dispersement routes of China goods in New Spain.

day, Lima equalled Mexico City in the taste, wealth, and ostentation of its Asian objects. And the twentieth-century evidence of handsome porcelains in Lima's churches, museums, and private collections still tells of continuous, considerable smuggling, carried on at the highest levels, even in the church.[30]

The extent of Chinese porcelain's influence in Peru is still to be explored fully. In Chucuito, Puno, in the south Peruvian highland, 15,000 feet above sea level, on the northwest short of Lake Titicaca, where pottery making has been a major activity since ancient times, a large deposit of Chinese shards was found in a centuries-old rubbish heap within part of a temple compound. Such evidence suggests that porcelain was of great interest to the local potters.[31]

Once unloaded in Acapulco, the porcelains continued their odyssey in Mexico via two routes: either to Vera Cruz (as it was then spelled) through Puebla and Orizaba for transshipment to Spain, or to Mexico City by the "China Road." This last threaded up and down through every possible terrain from sea level to the capital at 7,000 feet, a journey of 110 leagues (depending on the period, 2.4 to 4.6 mi.).[32] According to Gemelli Careri in Mexico in 1693, the bulk of the porcelains traveled the China Road north to Mexico City, "being too burdensome to transport to Europe."[33] The relative paucity of porcelains in Spain today supports his statement. Many more are in Mexico. And the rough ride by mule train to Mexico City must have multiplied the colony's supply of *chiñitas* (porcelain shards used as small change) even as it added to its total of whole pieces.

Most of the porcelains and other China goods were on consignment to the *almaceñeros* (merchants) of Mexico City. These spiritual heirs of Cortés and the conquistadores shared a similar passion—gold. Their treasure was more diverse, however, and, through an intricate network of domestic and international trade, their profits, which came to exceed those of Cadiz,

vaster. On the east coast of Mexico they were connected with the mother country by the yearly fleets that arrived at Veracruz from Seville, having stopped in various Spanish possessions in the Caribbean. North of Veracruz, at Jalapa, at an annual fair like Acapulco's, the merchants exchanged silver for most of the ships' cargoes, reselling items to provincial traders or later at northern fairs at San Juan de los Lagos and Saltillo.[34] They stored the rest of the Spanish shipments with the greater part of the Manila galleons' cargoes in warehouses in the capital. From here, they continued to control the finer disbursement of foreign wares throughout the colony, transporting goods to the silver-mining districts northwest of Mexico City— Zacatecas, Guanajuato, Real del Monte, San Luis Potosí, and other towns—via the Camino Real, a highway ready for service by the early 1550s.[35] They also distributed goods to the south and invested capital there. When, in 1592, they established a Consulado (a merchant guild and court), the *almaceñeros* were, in effect, announcing their oligarchy. Even socially, they were Mexico's true aristocracy and foreshadowed what was to happen elsewhere in the New World: colonists in English and European territories who engaged in international trade also became the ruling elite.

The octopus connections of the Consulado were indispensable for the continuation of the Manila Galleon. Spain suffered a general decline in the seventeenth century, but New Spain experienced only a temporary decrease of silver production in the Zacatecas area from the 1630s to 1660s. New capital from Mexico City led to a gradual renaissance in the mining areas, and by 1690, Zacatecas had reached a new peak of output, exceeding a high point reached between 1620 and 1625.[36] By 1720, it emerged as the undisputed leader of mining in Mexico. This development and other factors assured that Mexico would be able to assert a certain economic, if not a political, independence from Spain. As early as 1620, one historian argues, Mexico had successfully established a diversified capitalistic economy and did not need to trade with Spain as much as before. She "became the financier of her own defense, the supplier of her own needs, and the home of her own distinctive society."[37]

EARLY COLLECTORS AND COLLECTIONS

In 1625, Thomas Gage, an English Dominican, noted the extraordinary wealth of Mexico City, then one of the largest, richest cities of the world, attributable in part to her Asian trade. In the Alameda, a promenade area not far from the city's center, a parade of social classes gathered regularly to stroll and exhibit their finery. Commenting upon their pageantry, Gage enumerated articles that were all imports from the Orient:

> Both men and women are excessive in their apparel, using more silks than stuffs and cloth. Precious stones and pearls further much this vain ostentation. A hat-band and rose made of diamonds in a gentleman's hat is common, and a hat-band of pearls is ordinary in a tradesman. Nay, a blackamoor or tawny young maid and slave will make hard shift, but will be in fashion with her neck-chain and bracelets of pearl and her ear-bobs of some considerable jewels.[38]

In Veracruz on the east coast, Gage also reported the mixture of East and West in the apartments of a clergyman whom he visited the same year. Prior of the Dominican monastery, he was a "young spark," in love with high living, intoned Gage disapprovingly. In a softer vein, for Gage enjoyed good food, he described the dinner served him. A first course, "the Indian drink called chocolate," was followed by a sumptuous meal of native delights. Afterward, the friar invited his guests to see his luxurious rooms, where Gage noted pictures and hangings of cotton-wool and colored feathers from Michoacán, tables covered with silk, and "cupboards adorned with several sorts of China cups and dishes, stored within with several dainties of sweetmeats and conserves."[39]

Clergy, then, like the merchants and populace at large, enjoyed the luxuries of the East. A 1695 painting of the Plaza Mayor (now the Zócalo) of Mexico City depicts the colorful crowds and rows of canopied stalls where riches and foods were sold (fig. 48).[40] In the plaza, too, was the "Parian," a miniature of its namesake in Manila; within its walls goods from both Europe and the East were available.[41] Porcelains fit well into this conspicuously consuming society. The merchant with his pearled hatband could supply silk-clad, bejeweled clients with anything that Chinese and sometimes Japanese markets could produce.

The chinaware—both practical and decorative—seemed almost designed by Renaissance or baroque architects to enhance the capital's elegant townhouses and stately churches. In the large inner patios and corridors of two-story *casas* facing the city's wide streets, enormous jars displayed bold curves and gorgeous colors. Some of them bore the arms of their owners, repeating in polychrome precision the massive *escudos* above the large entrance doors. Others similarly enlivened public lecture halls. Tableware, vases, and jars also decorated living and dining rooms.[42]

References to porcelains from scattered sources over a hundred-year period provide glimpses of the wares in individual homes, government buildings, or churches. In the 1645 inventory of Don Juan de Cervantes Casaus is listed "*un tibor de loza de China alto*" (a tall jar of Chinese porcelain).[43] Three years later, Father Fernandez de Navarrete, Dominican missionary with service in China, noted a disastrous fire in the Royal Pharmacy in Acapulco, where "flasks and other vessels, all of fine Chinese porcelain" were destroyed.[44] And in inventories of 1645 and 1650 were

Chinese imports of chests, lacquer trunks, worked velvet pillows, and an orange Chinese canopy. One of 1688 listed a cupboard with three shelves each laden with fine Chinese blue-and-white in "a variety of bric-a-brac." On top, with a large glass jar, were smaller jars of porcelain.[45]

Other forms, usually large, of tankards, ewers, cylinders, beakers, and jars—rarely dishes or bowls—were also known, but few have survived in Mexico. And in the churches, tall vases fit well with the gilded, ultra-baroque style of the central altars. Humbler church jars, fitted with an iron lid and key, stored precious oil for altar lamps (fig. 99), and similar ones, often blue-and-white, were also used in private homes. Still others held flowers to honor a grave, a custom still practiced today.[46] In issues of the *Gazeta de Mex-*

48. Oil on canvas, Spanish, *La Plaza Mayor de México* (1695) by Cristobal de Villalpando, 2.12 × 2.66 m. Courtesy of Colonel Paul Methuen, Bath, England.

ico of 1730, and again in 1737, references to 120 and 108 barrels of porcelain, respectively, indicate the quantity of wares rivaling the massive importation of the years 1573–1620.[47] Certainly, the Chinese production for the foreign market was at a new high, while in New Spain, by 1720, the silver mines were exceeding their previous output.

Dispersement of these wares followed Mexico's hierarchical society, rigidly divided into sixteen classes. Those receiving the best, of course, were the *peninsulares*, or derogatively *gapuchines* (from *gapuchine* or spur)—Spanish-born whites. Immediately below them were native-American Spanish [Creoles] or *criollos*. These two upper classes, the *gente de razón*, were ranked considerably above those below them, members of *la plebe*, who were, in descending order of legal and social power, the mestizos of Spanish and Indian heritage; the mulattoes of African, Spanish, and Indian blood; the chinos, largely of Chinese and Filipino origin; and, at the very bottom, the Indians.[48] Despite their humble position, if Christianized and skilled, like an unknown number of goldsmiths, some Chinese achieved a certain status. Gage reported that such chinos along with the Indians had "perfected the Spaniards in that trade."[49] Thus, Chinese as well as indigenous artisans may be credited either with the silver mounts on porcelain or its gold and silver repairs. Possibly, they were the major artisans in this craft, considering the aversion of the upper classes to manual labor.

Despite these distinct levels, no true middle class existed. One Mexican clergyman put it succinctly: "In America there are no graduations or middle ranges: everyone is either rich or miserable, noble or contemned [*sic*]."[50] Still, in a society permeated by the promise of wealth, rank by race and birth could give way to rank by worth, though without the most desired civic privileges. One could become a mestizo merchant of some standing, or slip and find oneself a white Spaniard employed as a simple laborer. It was even possible for creoles and wealthy mestizos to purchase a coat of arms from the Spanish crown.[51] Given this mobility among classes and the range in quality of export china, everyone was familiar with it. The *gente de razón* may have claimed the best, but even broken porcelains had their place. *Chiñitas* passed as small change, always at a premium in Mexico,[52] and were probably almost as plentiful as the cacao beans used by the Indians since pre-colonial times. From intact fine ware to humble coin, then, the porcelains coming to Mexico played significant aesthetic, domestic, and economic roles for the whole society.

SURVIVING PORCELAIN IN MEXICO

Today Mexico retains only a fraction of the treasures from her once-vast exchange with China. Ordinary usage, revolutions, church and state confiscation, neglect, and sale abroad have all gradually eroded her accumulation of splendor since the late-sixteenth century. Spices and silks naturally had a limited life, but furniture, ivories, carved woods, lacquerware, metal objects, and porcelains might have passed intact to the present. Fortunately, porcelains are not the rarest of the lot: they are survivors by nature. From the commonest blue-and-white to the most exuberant of the polychromes, the export china of Mexico is a cool, brilliant symbol of this continent's first trade with the Far East.

As early as 1574, about two hundred settlements existed in New Spain. From a growing number of these, porcelain shards recently recovered are like a breadcrumb trail of the types of chinaware imported (see appendix D). They include pieces washed ashore from shipwrecks of the Spanish fleet returning to Ca-

49. *Jar*, Wanli, c. 1575–1600, H 38.1 cm. Underglaze blue, emblems of Spanish monarchy under Philip II (1556–98), with Chinese designs, possibly unique export. Private collection, Mexico City.

50. Reverse of fig. 49.

diz via the Bahama Channel near the Florida coast. The shards, whole objects, and the written record give us the following picture, beginning with the most costly pieces.

Mexican Forms

Among Spanish-Mexican porcelains, jars for every purpose in each period are the primary shape. One of the earliest known to be made for this market is a late-sixteenth-century blue-and-white hexagonal piece (figs. 49 and 50) similar to one in a Portuguese collection.[53] Without ears (loops for rattan rope), probably this one was intended for decorative rather than useful storage, if for storage at all. The dominant bicefal eagle with crown, adopted during the reign of Philip II (1556–98), perches upon a heart-shaped object. Another such eagle above and right appears to be sitting

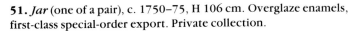

51. *Jar* (one of a pair), c. 1750–75, H 106 cm. Overglaze enamels, first-class special-order export. Private collection.

52. Detail of fig. 51, arms of Fernando de Valdés y Tamón.

on a garlic bud. Two arrows pierce each base. These Western emblems catch the eye before the Chinese motifs on other panels—phoenixes and elephants, saddled horses, lions, and birds—symmetrically laid out between trees or flowers beneath unidentified friezes of bottle-shaped clusters. The white-on-blue stylized lotus border is a longstanding Ming device, but the overall design is possibly from a Portuguese or Spanish textile source.

Today in Mexico, *tibors* (large Chinese jars), are ranked according to size from no. 1, the largest (up to 1.7 m tall), to no. 4, the smallest (35–40 cm). Size no. 2 is 70–80 cm, and size no. 3, 50–55 cm. The magnificent jar in figure 51, one of a pair, is a size-one piece, tapering in profile to minimize its height, a feature that makes such jars impractical for anything but sentinels of power and authority. Captain Fernando de Valdés y Tamón, governor of the Philippines, was the original owner of this pair; his arms are carefully painted on the neck (fig. 52). Valdés, summoned to Madrid, died en route in Cuernavaca, leaving many of his belongings in New Spain. A Mexican artisan replaced the Fo lion finial on one of the lids with a lacquer one, dating it 26 August 1846, almost a century after the jars were first made.[54] Larger and more expensive than any other porcelains, such jars were eschewed by the Chinese themselves as unwieldy and expensive, according to d'Entrecolles.[55] At the other end of the scale, common blue-and-white, unusually wide size-two jars may still be seen in Mexico. Their sketchily painted landscapes are similar to the smaller ginger jars known farther north.

Large jars of a range of quality appear to have influenced Mexican potters, especially those working in Puebla de los Angeles. From their products, the Chinese models inspiring them may be deduced, perhaps indicating preferred types. Wide-mouthed jars—variants on the *guan*—rather than elegant, narrow-lipped *meiping* shapes, were the preferred form. The one in figure 53 has a Sino-Italian form and features a husky spotted deer, typical of the Mexican chinoiserie style.

As an aside, it is unlikely that Chinese potters or painters worked in Puebla, or if they did, only in the humblest positions. The Potter's Guild regulations of 1653 strictly forbade all but Spanish of "unmixed blood," the *gente de razón*, to become master potters. Furthermore, none of the Puebla faience in the Chinese style shows anything but a Mexican hand. Finally, the Chinese, accustomed to finer clay and well employed at home, would have had little incentive to leave China to work elsewhere.[56]

Figures 54 and 55 show a size-three jar, also one of a pair. Distinctively Mexican with the Hapsburg eagle, it bears the crown of the Conde de Santiago de Cali-

53. *Vase*, earthenware, c. 1625–50, Puebla, Mexico, H 16.6 cm. Ex. coll. Francisco Pérez de Salazar. Private collection.

maya, a little town near Talucca. The design on this piece is bolder than most, but the possibility is remote that a Mexican artisan painted it; the firing process would have been risky on such an expensive object. During the turbulent nineteenth century, the lid to this jar was lost. Other jars of the period were less damaged, losing only their finials, which had been mistaken by revolutionaries for the Spanish lion. (Such dismembered lids are either still used with their jars, or have been converted into the tops and bottoms of hanging lamps.)

The square bottle in figure 56 was known in Europe as a Geneva or gin bottle, named after its glass proto-

54. *Jar*, c. 1760–80, H 66.0 cm. Overglaze enamels, first-class special-order export. Private collection.

55. Detail of arms of the Conde de Santiago de Calimaya (Ignacio Gómez de Cervantes).

type. Such bottles held liquor and were popular beginning in the seventeenth and continuing through the eighteenth century. An intact bottle and the shards of other similar ones were found off the Florida Keys in the 1733 wreck of the merchant ship *San José y las Animas*.[57]

A humbler drinking vessel imported into Mexico from the earliest period, though of purely Asian ori-

gin, was the kendi. One example (fig. 57) once had a longer neck, and its lipped mouth was thus formed by smoothing the remaining base, probably by a Mexican artisan. Even in Asia, its decoration is rare.[58] The latticework around the top and as a ground for the reserved phoenix on the body have been overpainted in red enamels to match the spout's reserve. In typical "Swatow" style, touches of turquoise and yellow

56. (far left) *Bottle*, c. 1715–40, H 22.5 cm. Underglaze blue, overglaze red, green, and gilt; above-average export. Private collection.

57. (below) *Kendi*, c. 1680–1700, H 12.1 cm. "Swatow"-type, overglaze red, green, turquoise, yellow, white; above-average export, rare. Private collection.

58. (left) *Albarello*, c. 1725–35, H 22.2 cm. Heart-shaped reserve, blank for label, pierced by two arrows (cf. fig. 49); overglaze enamels, above-average export. Courtesy of the Victoria and Albert Museum.

combine with the dominant reds and greens. Over the years, Westerners adapted the kendi for use as a waterpipe, or narghile (onomatopoetically, a "hubblebubble"). To accommodate this purpose, their necks lengthened as their spouts shrank by the mid-eighteenth century.[59]

From twelfth-century Persia came another form, the albarello, a drug jar used for balsams, powders, or other concoctions, introduced to Europe through the spice trade. Rare in Mexico in export porcelain, a few examples from the seventeenth and eighteenth centuries have survived. On the body of this example in figure 58, is a heart twice pierced by diagonal arrows, above which a black hat with looped and knotted tassels signifies a lesser prelate of an urban church or ca-

59. *Mancerina*, c. 1750, D 23 cm. Overglaze enamels and gilt panels, fine export. Courtesy of the Museo Nacional del Virreinato, Mexico.

60. *Mancerina*, majolica, c.1730–49, Alcora, Spain, D 17.8 cm. Underglaze blue, yellow, and red. In orange, signed Ferrer (Vicente Ferrer). Courtesy of the Victoria and Albert Museum.

thedral. The blank space defined by the heart is for a label to the solid or liquid within.[60]

Another object given a Hispanic flavor was the *mancerina* (fig. 59) or *trembleuse*, a cup-holder attached to its own often shell-shaped saucer. Apparently, as the story goes, the twenty-third viceroy of Mexico, the Marqués de Mancera (in office 1664–73) had the palsy and popularized the all-in-one shape. If so, no examples of his era survive. In fact, the earliest prototypes in Spain, made in Alcora faience, are from the second quarter of the eighteenth century (fig. 60), the same period as the Chinese export piece in figure 59. The majolica models are normally smaller in diameter (about 18–20 cm) than their porcelain copies, and their cup-holders are a bit higher.[61]

Recalling the dominant Catholicism of New Spain, the eighteenth-century baptismal basins, such as the one in figure 61, replaced the export bowls of the two preceding centuries in Mexico. Hard evidence that such export bowls were imported in the seventeenth century is suggested by the appearance of the form in Pueblaware blue-and-white faience of that period.[62] One dated circa 1680 in the Art Institute, Chicago, shows unmistakable links to Kangxi paneled designs. Figure 61, in its heavy potting and detailed painting, is an especially fine basin. Family practice reserved it for the baptism of male babies, and when the male line ran out, this one became merely a decorative object.

The goose tureen, another uncommon eighteenth-century form, is known internationally. The example

61. *Basin*, c. 1740–60, D 63.5 cm. Overglaze iron-red and gilt, fine export, rare. Private collection.

62. *Tureen*, c. 1760–80, H 41.3 cm. Overglaze enamels and gilt, arms of Cervantes on center back, first-class export. Private collection.

63. Detail of head in fig. 62.

64. Detail of feathers in fig. 62.

in figures 62, 63, and 64, bearing the arms of the Cervantes family identical to those on the tureen in figure 61, was probably based on faience prototypes from a Strasbourg factory, possibly designed by Adam von Lowenfinck. Two other identically shaped but differently decorated examples also have Spanish associations with the Asteguieta and the Gálvez families.[63] This linkage of Spanish taste with northern European design in a Chinese object is no surprise, considering the Hapsburg ties of the Spanish royal family in the seventeenth century and the introduction of a Bourbon line on the ascension of Philip V, born at Versailles in 1700. The tureen shown is an exceptionally vivid, well-painted example.

Other tureens were shaped like fish, specifically the carp. Though Sweden has similar examples, in Mexico, when the ceramic lid on the underbelly of the fish was broken, it might be replaced with a silver one, carefully wrought with scales to blend with the body painting. In some cases, heraldic arms were painted on the tail or head (figs. 65 and 66). Both tureens illustrated probably once had stands painted

65. (below) *Tureen*, c. 1775–1800, L 48.3 cm. Overglaze enamels, arms of Gálvez near mouth, fine export. Private collection.

66. (above right) Detail of arms of Don Matias de Gálvez y Gallardo, viceroy of New Spain, 1783–84, on a plate (identical to arms in fig. 65). Courtesy of the Franz Mayer Collection.

71. (above left) *Dish liner*, c. 1720–40, L 23.2 cm. Overglaze iron-red and green, above-average export. Private collection.

72. (above right) *Figurine*, Westerner with dog, c. 1715–30, H 15.2 cm. Overglaze green-grey and orange-brown, above-average export, now rare. Private collection.

not common forms in Mexico today. Apart from an unknown number of Guanyin goddesses, which may have been imported from the early-seventeenth century, there are the roughly executed Kangxi twin figures of harmony (*Hehe er xian*, the deities of Chinese merchants in general and potters in particular), and occasional images of Chinese men. Quite unusual is the figure of a Westerner with his dog (fig. 72). The roosters in figure 73, however, were probably popular; cockfighting, a national sport in Mexico, had its aficionados then as today. These pieces were not ex-

73. *Pair of cocks*, c. 1740–60, H 39.7 cm. Overglaze iron-red combs on brown base, fine export. Courtesy of the Franz Mayer Collection.

74. *Shaving bowl*, c. 1740–50, L 33.6 cm. Overglaze gold-red and enamels, above-average export, unusual painting. Private collection.

75. *Flowerpot* (one of a pair), c. 1740–50, H 17.1 cm. Overglaze iron-red and gilt, fine export. Private collection.

clusive to New Spain nor were the shaving bowl (fig. 74) and the flowerpot (fig. 75), but they do have Mexican pedigrees.

Several representative pieces from an extraordinary service of the turn of the nineteenth century are seen in figures 76–79. The set may be unparalleled in its grand but chaste design; its elegant classical lines are simultaneously fluid but contained and well balanced. Quite unusual are four different finial styles shared within the set and represented by the pieces illustrated. These objects summarize the exquisite taste achieved earlier and maintained for the entire history of the Manila Galleon, a permanent tribute to both the Hispanic buyer and the Chinese potter.

76. *Pieces from a tea/coffee/dinner service*, c. 1790–1800, chocolate pot: H 20.3 cm.
Overglaze enamels, fine export. Private collection.

78. *Tureen*, c. 1790–1800, H 35.5 cm.
Same service as fig. 76. Private collection.

77. *Sauceboat on stand*, c. 1790–1800, L 36.8 cm. Same service as fig. 76. Private collection.

79. *Dish cover*, c. 1790–1800, H 18.4 cm. Same service as fig. 76. Courtesy of the Franz Mayer Collection.

MEXICAN DECORATIONS

Gilded Porcelains

The Spanish, discovering gilded and silvered wares among the Filipinos, found a combination they could not resist: precious metals wedded to a precious object. Since the Northern Song (A.D. 960–1127), the Chinese had been decorating Ding porcelains with gold and silver.[64] Records of the Yuan (1280–1367) also indicate that along with painting and enameling, gilding and silvering—however primitive the results—were known.[65] Apparently, a new height in this technique was reached in the reign of Jiajing (1522–66)[66] from the evidence of a number of masterfully gilded whole pieces. A pair of white bowls with a meander lotus pattern in gold represents the simplest form of gilt ware of this period (fig. 80). Although reminiscent of Spanish-Moorish copper lusterware,[67] these bowls and others like them are a finer product. A few more bowls of about the same size, identical in decoration but on enameled monochrome surfaces or with blue-and-white underglaze painting inside and on the base, are in London, Hong Kong, and Tokyo.[68]

Most of these rare pieces are now owned by the Japanese, who have labeled them *kinran-de* (gold brocade style). Brocades from Turkey, at their peak in the early sixteenth century, or Chinese lacquerware patterns may have inspired the designs on these gilded porcelains.[69] Other known forms include tall, footed bowls and tall vases, teabowls, incense burners, faceted and double-gourd-shaped bottles, covered jars, and ewers.[70] In figure 81 is a solid, rounded ewer in red and gold, based upon a ceramic model. Other gilded ones may derive from metalwork forms and are more attentuated, as is one in the Baur Collection, Geneva.[71] Ewers similar to this one are also known in Indonesia, which indicates they may also have been exported from China to Mexico. Many of the export wares from Southeast Asia have twins in New Spain.[72]

No whole gilded pieces from the first years of trade have survived, although archaeologists such as Gon-

80. *Pair of bowls*, c. 1550–1600, D 10.2 cm. White porcelain with gilt, fine domestic/export. Courtesy of the Percival David Foundation, University of London.

81. *Ewer*, c. 1522–66, H 21.1 cm. Overglaze enamels red, green, and gilt (*Kinran-de* ware), superior export. Courtesy of the Idemitsu Museum of Arts, Tokyo.

zalo Lopez Cervantes have turned up Ming shards with gold. They confirm the 1574 cargoes' list of 22,300 pieces of "fine gilt china." The gold, combined with the most common enamel colors, red and green, had a universal aesthetic appeal but especially for the Spanish. Of course, such objects were of the finest quality, surpassing most export ware, and perhaps inspiring one English observer in Mexico City in 1582 when he noted, "Earthenware plates of such fine quality are brought from the newly discovered islands of China that he who can obtain one of them will give its weight in silver. . . ."[73]

Possibly a cheaper imitation of the gilded china from Jingdezhen, was a type of red, green, gilt, and underglaze blue "Swatow" ware.[74] A variety of "Swatow" ware, including this sort, was widely distributed throughout Southeast Asia and, in quantity, to Japan in the early-seventeenth century.[75] Doubtless, it too found its way to Mexico, and shards yet to be recovered would not be surprising finds.

A single shard from the Mexico City subway excavations represents another sort of gilded ware (fig 82). However, this piece is late-seventeenth or early-eighteenth century, produced during the Kangxi restoration of quality porcelain production; thus it is finer and younger by a hundred years than gilded shards, or whole objects, which may surface in the fu-

82. *Shard*, c. 1700–25, Mexico City, 6.66 × 9.20 cm. Private collection.

83. *Shards*, clockwise from left: carrack with deer, carrack with figure, "Chinese aster" or palmette design; first two, c. 1600; last, c. 1700–20. Mexico City. Largest shard, 9.52 × 9.52 cm.

ture with an authentic Mexican pedigree of the late-sixteenth century (see appendix B).

Blue-and-White Porcelains

To move from gilt wares to blue-and-white is to shift from the highest style to the most common, although the best of the blue-and-white—once thought foreign and vulgar—came to be the most prized by the Chinese themselves. Like its gilded shipmates, the underglaze blue wares coming to Mexico also predate the sailing of the Manila Galleon. They, too, go back to Jiajing and Longqing, because the latter period, 1567–72, was so short that the former's decorative style carried through to Wanli.[76]

Unlike the earliest gilt wares, blue-and-white whole pieces of the late-sixteenth, early-seventeenth centuries may still be seen in Mexico. The many shards of these porcelains indicate how plentiful they once were (fig. 83). Unearthed in the excavations for the Mexico City subway and under the Templo Mayor, shards have also been found in the states of Puebla and Michoacán. The bowl in figure 84 indicates a typi-

84. *Bowl*, c. 1590–1610, D 12.5 cm. Underglaze blue (compare fig. 83, third shard), common export. Courtesy of the Rijksmuseum.

cal whole piece, similar to one of the shards in figure 83.[77] Other evidence of blue-and-white has come to light in the former northern territories of Mexico. For example, in northeastern Arizona at the Franciscan mission of Awatovi, occupied 1603–1701, such shards have been found. And at the Palace of Governors in Santa Fe, the northernmost point of the famed

El Camino Real, seventeenth-century blue-and-white shards were recovered. One of them had been fashioned into a scraping tool.[78] Still another shard of blue-and-white with a scroll design has been unearthed with other objects at a site fifteen miles north of Albuquerque where there had been an Indian-Spanish settlement in the early 1600s.[79]

Two general types—*kraakporselein* (mid-sixteenth century to about 1650) and Transitional ware (1620–80)—overlap each other. The first is a Dutch term given porcelains found in Portuguese carracks (galleons), which they captured in 1602 and 1604.[80] *Kraakware*, or carrack in English, is usually light and brittle, tending to chip at the edges. Its range of blues, though considerable, is often in the silvery, gray-blue area, going from dark to light and watery. Carrack may occasionally be heavy, but rarely is it as solid as Transitional ware, soon to be discussed, which also has many more shapes. The latter is thicker and brighter, and its decorations more distinct than car-

rackware. Both apparently were made in the Jingdezhen area in private kilns.

Carrackwares came to Mexico before any other colony in North America and in greater quantity. They appear to have outnumbered Transitional pieces, in part due to a decline in the China trade during the silver industry's temporary depression in the early-seventeenth century and in part for carrack's more pronounced Arabic flavor. Its echoes of Moorish taste—paneled composition, ogival reserves, palmette leaves—must have appealed to Spanish buyers familiar with blue-and-white and with these design elements after centuries of Muslim domination and influence, even if, by this period, these devices had long been incorporated into Chinese decorative art.[81]

Faience dishes and bowls dating from as early as the ninth century hint of their influences on the carrackware of five centuries later (figs. 85–87). Moorish features also appear on higher style blue-and-white made for the Arab market in the thirteenth and fourteenth

85. *Dish*, 9th century, Nishapur, Iran, D 19.7 cm. Underglaze black-brown, green, and yellow (compare fig. 94). Museum für Kunst und Gewerbe, Hamburg; after Jakobsen, pl. 2, p. 37 (see Bibliography, "Books")

86. *Bowl*, 13th century, Kasan, Iran, D 21 cm. Underglaze blue and black (compare figs. 11 and 13). Kunstgewerbemuseum, Köln; after Klein, p. 169 (see Bibliography).

87. *Dish*, c. 1530–40, Isnik, Turkey, D 26.7 cm. Underglaze blue (compare figs. 157, 206 and 207). Victoria and Albert Museum; after Lane, pl. 30, pp. 51–52 (see Bibliography).

[Drawings: Robert Williams]

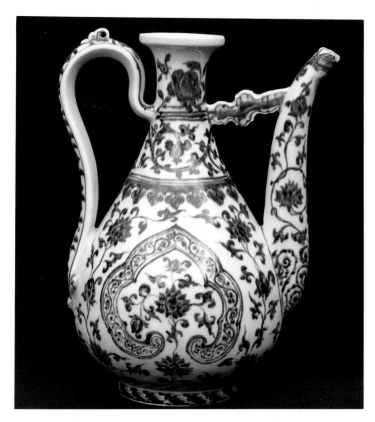

88. *Ewer*, c. 1685–1700, H 28.6 cm. Deep underglaze blue, fine domestic/export. Private collection.

Eastern sources as to seem native. Certainly the painting draws upon well-known Chinese mofits, for example, a woman on a porch, a grasshopper on a rock amid flowers, or a duck or fish swimming through water weeds, combined with panels of symbols, sprigs, flowers, and fruit. By this time, too, certain Western bottle shapes, considered "barbarian" by the Chinese in the late-fourteenth century,[84] had, in large part, become assimilated.

Stylistic dating of carrackwares into seven overlapping periods from 1550 to 1640 has been outlined by Brian McElney.[85] Later ones may now be extended to the 1650s. The recent recovery of a large load of carrack and Transitional wares—called the Hatcher Collection, for its salvager—from a Chinese junk of about 1645 indicates carrack's continuing popularity to the mid-seventeenth century.[86]

While McElney's findings are a welcome guide, he

89. *Dish*, c. 1550–70, D 21.2 cm. Underglaze blue *shufu*, common domestic/export. Private collection.

centuries.[82] In Mexico, porcelains of this quality, though uncommon, are known, such as the ewer in figure 88.[83] Carrackware, less precise in form and painting than more costly blue-and-white, has the high merit of folk art. Its molds and edges, patterned after metalwork models, are extraordinary on such thin bodies, and its painting flows freely. In the best pieces, that boldness of stroke is combined with great precision and detail. Painters and potters of carrack could be inspired artists.

Hybrid to some extent in form and decoration, carrack leans more toward the East than the West. Historic Chinese cup, bowl, plate, and dish shapes predominate. Pointed, lobed, and S-shaped lines—separately or combined—in reserves are subordinate additions, so well-integrated from Indian and Near

90. *Dish*, c. 1560–80, D 19.7 cm. Underglaze blue, fine domestic/export. Private collection.

91. Detail of fig. 90.

92. *Cup*, c. 1585–1620, D 15 cm. Underglaze blue, common domestic/export. Private collection.

93. *Shard*, dish, Mexico City, c. 1590–1620, D 19.05 cm. Underglaze blue "Swatow" ware, common domestic/export. Private collection.

omits one type of carrack found in Mexico and elsewhere (fig. 89) that combines molded white ware, a latter-day type of *shufu*, with blue-and-white. Similar design elements derived from *shufu*, known since the Yuan dynasty,[87] appear to have continued into the sixteenth century. Cups in this style parallel in size and form paneled carrack cups, which McElney dates 1585–1600, and which might be called *shufu*-carrack.[88] But the direct tie of this ware to past prototypes should make them part of McElney's first group, c. 1550–70. Also, though these prototypes were made in the official kilns, more were produced in the private ones and exported, as was true as well of their carrack descendants.[89] This example also indicates that tight dating can be useful only as a guide; a particular style might continue to be popular past its introduction or peak period. Yet—as is true of all ceramics—one combination of form with decoration has a specific life-span; if it dies out and then is reproduced, the latter-day copies are notably different.

Other Mexican carrackwares illustrate some of McElney's groups. Typical motifs, idiosyncratically rendered, are usually well done even though the body may be poor or the firing uneven. The dish with two deer beneath a pine tree in the moonlight (figs. 90 and 91) is a superior example of its type, with a unity in the delicate body and brushwork; a balance in composition between the waterweed-lotus outer border, the plain cavetto, and the well-spaced central design; and a light but sure energy in its seemingly off-hand lines. (Plates with reverse blue-and-white, yet with similar composition and of the same date also exist in Mexico.)

Of the same period and often found as a shard, is a paneled cup or bowl; the two terms are often used interchangeably, East and West[90] (fig. 92). Its bird, at least on the inside, is singing in the moonlight. The cup's paneling and painting is often repeated in other designs: floral sprays may replace the bird, bordered by narrow panels of bowed, streaming ribbons. A

third sample, a shard of a dish (fig. 93) with a phoenix, is large enough to show its identity with four others of the late-sixteenth century recovered from Drake's

94. *Dish*, c. 1605–25, D 47.6 cm. Blue-and-white, common domestic/export. Private collection.

95. Detail center of fig. 94.

96. *Bottles*, c. 1610–20, left: H 27.9 cm, right: H 26.7 cm. Underglaze blue, above-average domestic/export. Courtesy of the Franz Mayer Collection.

Bay.[91] An established pattern among "Swatow" wares, "Phoenix standing in a garden," the shard indicates that coarse wares were produced at each period of trade, thus quality is not a sure guide to dating.[92] Finally, the largest piece of this group, a low bowl with flared, cusped edge—the only one without a moon—covers a rather crude body with a vigorous but uneven composition (figs. 94 and 95).[93]

Carrack bottles bear the same details as the objects just seen. In addition, the two in figure 96 illustrate another common mythical animal, the *qilin* (ch'i-lin). One gallops horizontally, the other vertically, to fit the panel style. To repair chipped lips or cracked necks of such bottles, the Mexican silversmith sometimes made a protective sheath, an appropriate combination of riches from West and East. The carrack ele-

phant kendi in figure 97, an example of which was in the collection of Philip II (d. 1598),[94] was recovered from a Dutch East Indiaman, the *Witte Leeuw*, sunk off St. Helena in 1613.[95] A less frequently seen carrack design is the pattern of leaved gourds with vines, as on the lobed jar in figure 98.[96]

The jar in figure 99 is an adaptation of an otherwise conventional carrack piece. Fitted with a lockable iron lid, it became a "money jar," used for storing valuables.[97] Money jars, often protected by rattan guards, were known among the Filipinos and other Malays before being imported to New Spain.[98] Mexicans called them *chocolateros*, since they stored cacao beans and other choice items like spices and oil. The ironwork is often well executed and sometimes identifies its owners; for example, the lid of one *chocolatero* has incised in capitals, "Convento de Nuestro Padre Sn Francisco"[*sic*].[99]

97. *Kendi*, c. 1612, H 17.0 cm. Underglaze blue, recovered with the *Witte Leeuw* (1613). Courtesy of the Rijksmuseum and the National Geographic Society.

An exceptional piece in size and type of decoration, the lattice or fretwork (*linglang*) bowl, remains intact in Mexico (fig. 100), an enlarged version of the common rice or soup bowl in China, known there as "wine seas."[100] The Spanish probably used it for food and drink as well, or for handwashing and baptism, before they ordered bowls specifically for that ceremony (fig. 61). The popular Mexican drink, *pulque* (a fermented juice of the maguey plant), or wine from Spain, may once have filled this wine sea, but it is notable that not many punchbowls remain in Mexico as compared to other Western countries. A warped circumference assured that this piece would remain unmarked, but its latticework links it to known Wanli bowls, and its decoration to late-sixteenth-century styles.[101]

98. *Jar*, c. 1600–20, H 15.5 cm. Underglaze blue, average domestic/export. Private collection.

99. *Jar* (*chocolatero*), c. 1590–1620, H (with lid, without key) 27 cm. Underglaze blue, common domestic/export, now rare. Private collection.

100. *Bowl*, c. 1600–20, D 35.5 cm. Underglaze blue, above-average domestic/export. Private collection.

101. *Pot*, c. 1612, H 19.0 cm. Underglaze blue, recovered from the *Witte Leeuw* (1613), common domestic/export (compare fig. 103). Courtesy of the Rijksmuseum and the National Geographic Society.

102. *Plate*, c. 1560–80, D 26 cm. Underglaze blue, fine domestic/export. Private collection.

The pot in figure 101 could also have been used for *pulque*, or chocolate, the drink that the Aztecs introduced to the Spanish[102] (predating tea's popularity in the West by nearly a century), or *atole*, also an Indian drink or rather thick pap, served hot in pots.[103] For Mexico, these pots are not associated with any one drink.

Blue-and-white carrackware appears in reverse emphasis in the plate in figure 102. Though not a design of New Spain, it is a reminder of both the quantity of fine late-Ming ware pouring into Acapulco and the hybrid Chinese-Arabic roots of some of the dominant patterns of the period. In this case, the swiftly drawn but striking cranes are framed in the hexagonal ogival reserve, known on Persian wares as early as the fourteenth century, an adaptation of ancient Chinese designs.[104] Though of eighteenth-century origin, a Persian plate with seven partridges bears a compositional resemblance to this piece, perhaps indicating a reverse borrowing.[105]

A carrackware pot, three cups, and a bowl in a Spanish painting of about the 1630s (fig. 103) represent late carrackware, contemporary for about twenty more years with another, heavier blue-and-white, called Transitional ware in the West. The transition was between the Ming and Qing dynasties, from 1620, the end of the Wanli period, until 1683, the year Cang Yingxuan (Ts'ang Ying-Hsuan) was appointed director of the imperial factory at Jingdezhen. The last three Ming emperors, successively ruling from 1620 to 1644, oversaw a period of dynastic disintegration. The imperial kiln nearly ceased operations, forcing private ones to assume more and more official work,[106] while also producing more wares for foreign demand. With less control by the government, their production of export pieces freely incorporated new shapes and decorations. Some Transitional pieces may show their hybrid nature; others remain almost purely oriental.

Compared to carrack, fewer examples of Transitional ware remain in Mexico. The first half century of the Manila Galleon, 1573–1620, was a peak period of import not duplicated again until the late-seventeenth century.[107] During the lull in trade, while China underwent a turbulent change of dynasties, Mexico's silver industry entered a thirty-year slump (although incomes among a few reached new highs; fortunes of

four, eight, and in one case nine hundred thousand pesos were reported in the 1650s).[108] In addition, from the early 1600s, Dutch ships waylaid Chinese junks or Portuguese carracks bound for Manila loaded with yearly supplies, and despite the sixty-year union of Spain and Portugal (1580–1640), the Portuguese often acted quite independently of Madrid, managing to monopolize the import of silks to Manila from 1619 to 1631, and possibly porcelains as well.[109] Transitional wares of fine quality may have been increasingly scarce at the end of the 1660s and beginning of the 1670s, but the coarser ones were still in some supply. Fortunes in Jiangxi Province went from bad to worse in 1673, when the Ming insurgent, Wu Sangui, staged a rebellion, burning and razing the imperial work-

103. *Still Life of Fruit and Porcelain*, oil on canvas, Spanish, by Juan Zurbarán (1620–d. before 1664), 36.3 × 62.8 cm. Underglaze blue cups, a pot, and dish, c. 1620–50. Courtesy of the Cincinnati Art Museum.

104. *Beakers*, c. 1650–80, H 5.5 cm. Underglaze blue, common export. Private collection.

shops. They were rebuilt four years later, and at least a handful of private potters kept alive some semblance of the industry. Meanwhile, export wares of a more humble nature, many direct from Canton, continued to reach the West throughout the 1670s to 1682, when a new era of porcelain production began.[110]

That renaissance under the Kangxi emperor (1662–1722), produced objects, made early in his reign, that reflect the end of one era and the beginning of an-

other. The trio of three miniature beakers in figure 104, indicate the continuing popularity of paneled decoration combined with a form that dates from the mid-1600s. A pair of urinals in figure 105, deftly designed for each sex, show landscapes typical of Transitional pieces with the sacred fungus, *ling-chih*, emblem of longevity. This style of the motif is associated with the underside of Kangxi pieces, as on the plate in figures 106 and 107. The fungus is most fertile, thus prized, when grass is sprouting from it, as in these pieces, which are quite typical renderings.[111] The plate, of fine white clay, is carefully painted, although there is a common perspective problem in rendering the riverside wall. And its composition skillfully balances a broad patchwork border (a design borrowed from Japanese porcelains) with the uncluttered, peaceful central scene.

The precarious reception Christianity received in the Far East is well represented by the cup and dish in figure 108. It is typical of the quality of early export ware illustrating religious subject matter, often called

105. *Urinals* (pair), c. 1680s, left: L 24.13 cm, right: L 20.3 cm. Underglaze blue, common export, now rare. Private collection.

106. *Plate*, c. 1685–1710, D 28.8 cm. Underglaze blue, mark on base—fungus, above-average domestic/export. Private collection.

107. Detail of fig. 106, spotted deer.

108. *Cup and dish* (not a pair), c. 1685–1710, cup: D 8.6 cm, saucer: D. 12.7 cm. Underglaze blue, the Crucifixion, common Christian domestic/export. Courtesy of Dr. Wesley Gallup.

"Jesuit" ware. No doubt the fame of the first Jesuits in sixteenth-century Beijing—especially Father Matthew Ricci—has made their order preeminent in China in the popular mind. But other Catholic orders—Augustinians, Franciscans, and Dominicans—long resident in Macao, Canton, and Manila, may have been equally responsible for ordering such ware.[112] Still other customers might have been pious merchants and Chinese or Japanese converts. More accurately, the ware might be called simply "Christian" ware. The design source for the Crucifixion scene in figure 108 may be a cartoon, part of a European engraving, which in its boldness suggests a woodblock original.[113] Seventeenth century blue-and-white Christian wares were distinctively simpler and less detailed than their penciled and polychrome successors in the eighteenth century.

Mexicans will tell you today that Christian ware is not known in their country. However, in its day it was no doubt imported and later was largely destroyed (the Jesuits were expelled from Mexico in 1767, and the church in general suffered confiscations by the state during the nineteenth century). Probably, it was no great loss; aesthetically, it cannot compete with the Chinese ivories and wood carvings representing Christ that are still in Mexico.

In the Kangxi reign, a multipaneled blue-and-white export ware with a repeated, bold "China aster" motif, actually a palmette variation, appeared. A bowl in this design was recovered from the 1715 shipwreck of the *San José* off the coast of Florida (fig. 109).[114] As noted before, the foliate edge, paneled border, and broad leaf shape link this pattern with Middle Eastern taste. The leaf, in whole or in part, appears five times in the center and structures the palmettes as well. It is one of the motifs, possibly the commonest, frequently found on earthenwares from the Arab world[115] and on sixteenth-century textiles from the Ottoman Empire.[116] The whorls about the leaves are also an Arabic device used as a solid background or as clusters with other figures in a border design (fig. 11).[117]

Returning to more ordinary wares, a blue-and-white platter of the eighteenth century shows that Mexicans

109. *Bowl*, c. 1714, D 12.1 cm. Underglaze blue, recovered from the *San José* (1715), average export. Courtesy of Dr. Charles Fairbank, University of Florida.

110. *Platter*, c. 1750–70, L 41.9 cm. Underglaze blue, above-average export. Courtesy of the Franz Mayer Collection.

shared with Europeans stock patterns made in large quantity (fig. 110). The piece, though nicely painted, is heavy and rough, the glaze curdling in the familiar "potato soup" or "orange peel" manner. A quantity of such ware, internationally imported, was also familiar throughout Mexico in the eighteenth century. A rare Mexican still life, *The Cupboard* (1769), by Antonio Pérez de Aguilar, shows a common blue-and-white plate of about 1725–50, that resembles those salvaged from a 1745 shipwreck near Gothenburg, Sweden.[118] On the shelf above it, the underside of a carrack dish is visible.[119]

Monochromes and Polychromes

White wares had been popular in the Philippines before the coming of the Spanish. White was a premium color for the Spanish as well, parallel to their desire for Chinese silk of similar purity.[120] The gilt-and-white bowls in figure 80 represent the combination, then, of two highly prized possibilities in porcelain. But the *qingbai* (pale blue or greenish, thin-glazed white) or true white wares and the gilded pieces differ from the so-called *blanc de Chine* of the last half of the seventeenth century, many of which were made at Dehua, Fujian Province. It could vary from a lardlike, greasy-to-the-touch porcelain (prized by the Chinese) to a nearly blemishless, smooth ware. The cup in figure 111, with its applied prunus branch, crackle, and silver embellishment, is an example of the attention given such wares in Mexico. Similar shards have been found in Mexico City excavations.

Normally the extremely popular goddess of mercy, Guanyin (Kuan-yin)—in *blanc de Chine* represented more often than the Buddha himself—sits or stands, dressed in flowing gown and wearing precious jewels.[121] At times, however, she holds a child (fig. 112) and may be found with a cross as pendant, both suggesting Christian images to a Westerner; but the cross may actually have been a Chinese addition his-

111. *Cup* with silver cover, c. 1690–1710, H 12 cm. Dehua white, above-average, now rare; Mexican silverwork, superior. Ex. coll., Francisco Pérez de Salazar. Private collection.

112. *Guanyin with child* (headless), c. 1690. Jingdezhen or Dehua white, recovered off Port Royal, Jamaica, on letter reporting two-thirds of city submerged by 1692 earthquake; above-average domestic/export. Courtesy of the National Geographic Society.

torically unrelated to Buddhism.[122] The child was probably borrowed from Hariti, another Chinese deity, and represented the baby hoped for by the infertile woman who prayed to the goddess.[123] These elements confused some Christians about her true nature, and as early as 1556, the Dominican friar Gaspar da Cruz, visiting a monastery temple on a small island off Canton, wondered if the goddess he saw with babe in arms was the Christian madonna. Cruz also mistakenly thought St. Thomas had once been in China.[124] Although these figures may have been called "*Sancta Marias*" in English shipping records,[125] that term probably originated in Portuguese or Spanish as a casual reference. In English, they are usually not called "madonnas" but loosely "Mary," or "woman with child."[126] In short, most Guanyin statuettes were not imported by Westerners for religious purposes but as art objects or souvenirs. An exception may be the rare figurine in figure 113, clearly an attempt to imitate Mary and infant Jesus.

Celadons, or greenwares, and other mono-

113. *Westernized Guanyin with child*, late 1700s/early 1800s, H 48.9 cm. Jingdezhen or Dehua white, rare. Courtesy of the Victoria and Albert Museum.

chromes—coral red, turquoise, pale blue, and black, for example—are part of Mexican collections today.[127] The greenwares, a subject in themselves, do not exhibit features of East and West; they remain purely oriental. And the monochromes, among the most difficult of porcelains to date, are outside of this study, because they were not originally made for export and rarely found their way to the West before the late-nineteenth or early-twentieth centuries.

Polychrome pieces, however, bring us into a world of new splendor in the Manila Galleon story. In the first decades, the shard finds show that such wares were plentiful and varied: the overglaze enameled fragments excavated in Manila were yellow, turquoise, and purple wares of the early-sixteenth century; red, green, and black of the late-sixteenth century. Frequently, shards included silver decoration.[128] Not surprisingly, shards similar to those found in Manila have been unearthed in Mexico, and others, equally rich, may be expected to be found as archaeology continues.

The shards in figure 114 represent some of the earliest polychromes in New Spain recovered from Mexico City excavations. The bottom of a small bowl (left) of fine clay and painting shows a border of small triangles and part of a panel in slightly worn overglaze enamels of red, green, and yellow. (To compare with a whole piece, see figs. 115 and 116.) The underglaze blue mark appears to be Jiajing. On the inside center is part of an underglaze blue, well-painted lion or dog. Similar in style but not of such quality, is the round shard, the bottom inside of a larger bowl, painted with similar red, green, and yellow triangles on the reverse. A standard, swiftly drawn late-seventeenth-century red and green flower pattern (right) was a popular color combination. It appears in the vase in figure 117, a form common to the Transitional period.

On the iron-red, white, and gilt dish (fig. 118) the peony and willow tree pattern was as popular in Mexico as elsewhere. However, it is uncommon today; the

114. *Shards*, c. 1573–1600, Mexico City. Private collection.

115. Base of fig. 116.

116. *Bowl*, c. 1580–1600, D 9.18 cm. Exterior: overglaze enamels in red and green; interior: central convex medallion in underglaze blue; average export, now rare. Courtesy of the Princessehof Museum.

117. *Vase*, c. 1600–20, H 22.8 cm. Underglaze blue, overglaze red and green, average domestic/export. Private collection.

118. *Dish*, c. 1715–30, D 16.5 cm. Overglaze iron-red and gilt, above-average domestic/export. Private collection.

willow usually appears in underglaze blue. The same palette, with the addition of "*capuchino*" brown and green, was used for the much finer painted tureen in figure 119. This type is not usually found in other national Western collections, but the phoenix in this pose is a familiar bird in both high-style porcelains

119. *Tureen*, pumpkin-shaped, c. 1715–30, H 17.1 cm. Overglaze enamels, fine export. Private collection.

120. *Beakers* (pair), c. 1730–40, H 11.1 cm. Overglaze enamels, fine export. Private collection.

(figs. 46 and 47) and in "*Nonya*" ware, so called by overseas Chinese living in the Malacca Strait for "*Nonya*" or female (the ware was inherited matrilineally).[129] The phoenix is known thus in Mexico as well. The combination of form, colors, design, and the quality probably mark this piece especially for the Hispanic market.

The use of gold-red on Mexican export produced a number of notable examples. Among general patterns was gold-red with black enamel, a stunning combination. It makes its appearance in the 1740–60 period as on the beakers in figure 120. This arresting contrast, set off by touches of turquoise, yellow, and green appears on other contemporary forms in Mexico; large jars, covered cups, and kendis, apparently more in demand here than elsewhere.[130] Much more delicate is the gold-red decoration of the charger in figure 121. Its bold, subtly shaded peonies are complemented by the outer border with its alternating gold-red and aqua sections surrounding white-on-white floral reserves. The cock and hen, symbolic of the emperor and empress, emphasize the East in this "foreign color" style; the plates in figure 122 are clearly Western in subject matter. The life of Christ series were special-order wares and may be found in several countries. The precise renderings indicate fine engravings rather than woodblock prints as sources, but the Chinese painter's unfamiliarity with human anatomy evidently made even copying from detailed sources a problem.

Gold-red with gilt dominates the extraordinary stand in figures 123 and 124. The acrobatic rooster, balancing a basket on its back, may be a playful celebration of the cock, on order for a Mexican client, or the bird from the Chinese painter's repertoire for imperial porcelains, as in figure 122. Compare the basket on the boar's head in figure 67. The basket probably derives from an emblem associated with one of the Eight Immortals, Lan Caihe, the patron of gardening, who is often depicted carrying a spade and basket of flowers.

121. *Charger*, c. 1750, D 38.1 cm. Overglaze gold-red and enamels, first-class export. Private collection.

122. *Plates*, c. 1730–40, left and right: D 22.9 cm, center: D 20.9 cm. Left to right: the Adoration of the Shepherds, the Crucifixion, the Resurrection; fine export. Courtesy of Dr. Wesley Gallup.

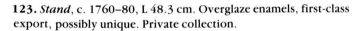

123. *Stand*, c. 1760–80, L 48.3 cm. Overglaze enamels, first-class export, possibly unique. Private collection.

124. Detail of center of fig. 123.

Penciled ware, black painted with a fine hairbrush in imitation of engravings, was on the general export market by the 1730s.[131] An excellent example of such work in Mexico is a plate bearing the arms of the Ovando family (fig. 125). The single Chinese motif, a latticework background, doubtless was not part of the original coat of arms. An unusual feature is the addition of the family's name spelled out in capitals clockwise around the outer edges of the central decoration (fig. 126). Other New Spain coats of arms make generous use of gilt and gold-red for a very rich effect (fig. 127). Among those known, Mexican armorials were once probably plentiful, but today only eighteen or twenty survive. Many of them may be seen at the Mayer Collection in Mexico City.

Public arms complemented private ones. On the ascension of Charles IV to the Spanish throne in 1788,

both Mexico City and its Consulado of merchants, in celebration of the event, had services of porcelain made with their arms (figs. 128 and 129). The design of the Consulado's arms is taken from a medal by the Spanish engraver Jéronimo Antonio Gil (1732–98), who had been sent to Mexico in 1778 to supervise the Royal Mint. He designed a similar medal for the city of Puebla on Charles IV's enthronement as well as the seal of the Royal Academy of Fine Arts of San Carlos in New Spain, founded in 1785 (fig. 130). (Gil was the quasi director.)[132] An unusual melding of public and private interests occurs in the seal of Valladolid; its chief officer's likeness is featured in the center (figure 131). Such works are reminders of the role these cities played in the success of the China trade, which was in its last phase as they were produced.

What happened to Mexico and her import of porce-

125. *Plate*, c. 1740, D 26.3 cm. Penciled and gilt, arms of the Ovando family (1734), first-class export. Private collection.

126. Detail of Ovando arms, fig. 125.

127. *Plates*, c. 1730–50, left: D 23.2 cm, right: D 24.4 cm. Overglaze enamels. Left: unidentified arms, right: arms of Ahedo family; first-class export. Private collection.

128. (below) *Pitcher*, c. 1790, H 13.3 cm. Overglaze enamels, arms of Mexico City, first-class export. Courtesy of Dr. Wesley Gallup.

129. (right) Detail of saucer, c. 1790. Overglaze enamels, arms of the Consulado of Mexico City, first-class export. Private collection.

131. *Cup*, seal identical to plate on right in fig. 130, c. 1790; first-class export. Courtesy of Franz Mayer Collection.

130. *Plates*, c. 1790, left to right: D 26.4 cm, D 30.5 cm, D 20.6 cm. Arms of the city of Puebla, seal of the Royal Academy of San Carlos, seal of Valladolid; first-class export. Private collection, U.S.A.

lains in the nineteenth century? Today one can find a range of objects in "Rose Mandarin," "Rose Medallion," and other designs found elsewhere in the West and in North America, but they did not come under the aegis of the Manila Galleon alone. It had suffered from competition with the Royal Philippine Company, loosely operating from 1766 (but only officially founded in 1785) to trade directly between the Philippines and Spain. Galleon power also gave way to English, French, and American traders, who began to call at the West Coast ports of Spanish America. In 1811, Mexican rebels seized the silver about to be sent to China from Acapulco and two years later burned the town. When the monarchy was restored under Ferdinand VII, a decree decisively terminated the Manila ships.[133] With their demise, international traders continued the supplies of porcelain, and evidence of it may be found in surprising places.

Colonial monuments, called *riscos* (rocky cliffs or crags) were decorated with a potpourri of porcelains, native earthenware plates and tiles, whole or as shards, in unique baroque structures. Today only one remains—the wall of a fountain in the former home of the late Don Isidro Fabela in the Plaza de San Jacinto in San Angel (figs. 132 and 133).[134] For the student of the trade in Chinese porcelains to Mexico, this *risco* is a good place to begin and end. Items from the Ming dynasty are edge-to-edge with objects made over two and three hundred years later, and their display is bordered by Mexican pottery. The proximity of these two sorts of ceramics symbolizes the close connection between native wares and their Chinese models over the years—another enduring tribute in Mexico to the inventiveness, artistry, and steady labor of the Chinese potter.

132. *Risco fountain*, begun c. 1739–40. Casa de Don Isidro Fabela, Plaza de San Jacinto, San Angel, Mexico City.

133. Detail of fig. 132.

CHAPTER 3

Trade Triangles in the Atlantic

The Dutch and English inextricably shared the history of export porcelain in North America. From shard evidence, the earliest known ware on the East Coast of America north of Mexico belonged to English colonists in Virginia, but Dutch ships were chiefly responsible for its arrival here. True, the English East India Company re-exported from England three-quarters of its imports in the early-seventeenth century;[1] also true, England was responsible for most of the goods entering Virginia from 1630 to 1700;[2] however, random remaining cargo lists do not include ceramics, and enumerate only the principal items—mainly necessary staples. Even if ship manifests were more complete, china-ware in commercial loads would not have been included, and personal orders, if any, were few and small.

England was not yet a major nation in the trade with China. Beyond all other Westerners, the Dutch and Spanish dominated the seventeeth-century exchange, and even Dutch East Indiamen, like the *White Lion* (1613), which carried a quantity of porcelain, did not always note it in their cargoes. Porcelain was pop-ular, but not the major money item in the trade. Of East India wares in demand, spices and textiles far exceeded china.

A century before, politics and commerce linked Holland to the Hispanic world, a tie naturally promoting the Dutch to succeed Portugal, then Spain, as the first European nation trading with China. In 1506, Spain assumed control of the Netherlands. At the same time, Antwerp became the chief entrepôt to pass goods—largely spices imported by the Portuguese—to the rest of Europe. Antwerp maintained this position until 1560, when Dutch ships replaced the Portuguese in the carrying trade from Lisbon, and Amsterdam gradually became the primary northern funnel of Eastern goods.[3]

Soon afterward began the long war for Dutch independence from Spain (1568–1648). The Protestant northern Netherlands, with Amsterdam as its major center of trade, had a geographically superior position from which to win that struggle against its Catholic foes. She also had a better navy than both the Spanish and the Portuguese, who, under Spanish control from 1580 to 1640, were a second enemy. When the Dutch took two Portuguese carracks loaded with porcelain in 1602 and 1604, Amsterdam was the natural place for it to be auctioned. This china, among the first ware to enter the country in quantity, drew notable foreigners to its sales. Among the avid royal buyers were Henry IV of France (1533–1610) and James I of England (1566–1610).[4] Holland's scope of trade with China included carrying goods from the mainland to numerous ports within Southeast Asia and to others on the return route to Europe. For a time she far outdid any competitors, Eastern or Western—the Indians, Arabs, Siamese, Malays, and Japanese as well as the Iberians and the English.[5]

With this sort of activity, and largely in ships from the Netherlands, the Dutch uncontestably provided the English market with the better part of their East India goods, including porcelains. Based upon figures given by Sir Walter Raleigh in the late-sixteenth century, ten Dutch ships to every English vessel engaged in trade between the two countries,[6] a ratio that meant only a trickle of porcelain might reach America via London in the early-seventeenth century. The meager beginning of the English East India Company reinforces this assumption.[7]

Despite England's successful pirating of Spanish galleon treasure in the late-sixteenth century under Gil-bert, Hawkins, Raleigh, and Drake, Queen Elizabeth's efforts to establish England in the East fell well behind the Dutch. She founded an East India Company in 1600, two years before Holland had its own, but it was small and private while the Dutch was large and national. In addition, the English company had trouble establishing a firm base in the East, shifting in the 1620s between Bantam and Batavia. Not until 1643 was England regularly operating out of Fort St. George, Madras, but still distant from the Chinese mainland. Her purchase of porcelain could not compete with the quantities carefully ordered by the Dutch, who for nearly forty years, 1624–62, were well positioned on Formosa at Fort Zeelandia to buy the bulk of their wares from Chinese suppliers. A smaller share of Dutch export wares came from a second major trading headquarters in Batavia.[8] Their most-favored-nation status with the Japanese after 1639, when all others except the Chinese were expelled from that island, gave her, and her alone among European nations, access to both China and Japan. These advantages, coupled with Holland's success in frustrating several major English efforts to trade with the Chinese, kept England at a distance for the better part of the century.[9]

VIRGINIA

In North America, independent Hollanders and the Dutch West India Company (1624) were as sure and successful as her East India Company on the other side of the world. Holland regularly sent ships, sometimes even armed naval vessels, up Virginia's James and Potomac rivers with their many convenient inlets. Dutch merchantmen bartered manufactured goods for a coveted product: the colony's tobacco, which filled other European pipes besides their own.[10]

Well before that, however, independent Dutch ships arrived in Virginia; the first, in 1619, brought West Indian slaves.[11] Others, like the *White Dove* (1621) and *Flying Hart* (1629) also came. In the period 1624–46, however, the West India Company's monopoly among Dutch ships was probably fairly tight with only occasional exceptions. After 1646, private merchants in Holland, including English traders resident there, were allowed to traffic throughout her possessions, and the thirty-year-old trade increased accordingly. Not only would goods enter in new quantities, but the Netherland merchants thereafter appointed Virginians as their agents or factors, cementing a long-standing friendship between the colony and Holland. The English Civil Wars (1642–49) had encouraged such a bond when the Dutch provided scarce manufactured goods, which had fallen off from the mother country. Also, the Dutch further gained in popularity by keeping the price of tobacco high and bringing items the English could not supply.[12]

The Dutch West India Company's open-door policy to independent traders occurred just after the peak of Chinese porcelain buying by the Dutch in Asia. Although in the following decade, 1646–57, fine chinas became rare,[13] coarser china continued to be available and was bought by the Dutch in great quantity until 1662. That year they lost their post on Formosa to the Chinese pirate, Koxinga, who thereby broke Holland's best contact with the Chinese mainland.[14] The export ware that reached Virginia in Dutch ships reflected these changes: fine chinas were available to the early 1650s, rougher ware until about 1662. (A few years before, 1658–59, the Dutch East India Company bought the first quantity of Japanese export porcelains—whose production had been gearing up to a mass market since about 1650—to fill the gap left by the Chinese.)[15] Some Transitional wares, which could be of high artistic merit, did find their way to North America after 1657, and they will be discussed in pages to follow.

Meanwhile, the English, anxious about Dutch maritime superiority since the late-sixteenth century and increasingly jealous of her profitable trade in Virginia's tobacco, began to pass a series of stringent acts preventing ships other than her own from carrying goods into or out of her ports. Her chief aim was to cripple the Dutch. In 1651, the first Navigation Act took effect, at a moment when there was a large surplus of Dutch merchandise in Virginia,[16] thanks in part to the arrival of twelve ships from Holland two years

before.[17] In 1660, a stronger act cut down the total tonnage brought in Dutch holds, but exemptions included East India goods, at least those loaded south and east of the Cape of Good Hope.[18] Legally, a Dutch ship bringing items directly from the Far East could unload them in Virginia. In fact, it is probable that considerable illegal trade from Holland to Virginia continued in these articles.

In brief, the Dutch involvement in the coming of porcelain to Virginia is inseparable from the English side of the story. England's primacy in the China trade did not occur until the eighteenth century. For the first three-quarters of the seventeenth century, she depended not only upon Dutch supply but also, in part, upon Dutch taste.

Shards and Inventories

One early reference to what may be Chinese porcelain in Virginia was made in about 1622, just after the famous Indian massacre in Jamestown. To quiet fears about immigrating, Edward Waterhouse wrote a tract for English readers, advertising the colony's assets. The following experience he related, however, referred to the Potomac, not the James River area. In an Indian chief's "house," Waterhouse reported, a "*China-Boxe*" was found. The chief said that he had received it from another chief who lived "*West* over the great Hils, some tenne dayes journey, whose Countrey is neare a great Sea." In his turn, the second chief had gotten the box from "a people . . . that came thither in ships, that weare cloaths, crooked swords, and somewhat like our men [Englishmen] dwelt in houses, and were called *Acanack-China*." Waterhouse hoped that this information would lead to the long-sought Northwest Passage to the riches of the Far East.[19] The "great sea" may have been the Gulf of Mexico, the "people," Spaniards or Dutch (often roaming the West Indies), and "*Acanack-China*," yet to be determined. Whatever the source, this "China-

134. *Box*, c. 1522–66, H 7.6 cm. Mark: ***chuan xia bian yong*** ("seal box for use as required"). Overglaze enamels; inside, a *qilin*; fine domestic/export. Courtesy of the trustees of the British Museum.

Boxe," if porcelain, could have been a square, rectangular, circular, or oblong box (fig. 134).

In contrast to the scarcity of early written references, physical evidence—in the form of shards—is becoming plentiful. Archaeologists have only been at work in Virginia since about 1955, with most digs done since the 1970s. Still, the first signs are sufficient to make a few working generalizations. The average porcelains brought to Virginia between 1607 and 1698 were probably similar to those known by the middle classes in Holland; others, yet to be found, could have been of the best quality. Quantity was relative to the total population, which in 1616 was 351 people.[20]

Among the earliest evidence are the shards of six small wine cups from a frontier settlement, known as the "Maine," near Jamestown, occupied from about 1618 to 1635 (fig. 135).[21] They are almost identical to one type of cup found in the 1613 wreck of the *White Lion*, at St. Helena in the South Atlantic.[22] A rare casualty to Portuguese seamanship, the *White Lion* carried a varied load of porcelain along with jewels and

spices, whose recovery in 1976 provides a rich touchstone for dating several kinds of carrackware. The "Maine" cups are fine in body, though some are more casually painted than their *White Lion* counterparts. Because they would have cost even more after crossing the Atlantic, their humble ownership is, then, something of a surprise.[23] No less surprising are the porcelain shards found in eighteenth-century slave quarters, although they were probably damaged castoffs, still useful or perhaps valued as decorative miscellany.[24] Contemporary with these pieces and a little later are shards from a tenement on Kingsmill Properties (north side of the James River between Wareham's River and Harrup House), occupied about 1620–50; they are parts of a cup identical to the "Maine" fragment, and of a bowl with a bottom-hole exterior base.[25]

Some sister shards of the Ming and, later, more sizable numbers of Qing porcelains have been excavated in Tidewater, Virginia (fig. 136). Unless otherwise noted, most are underglaze blue-and-white. At another site, "Flowerdew Hundred Plantation," near

135. *Cup* (60 percent reconstructed), c. 1610, D 4.5 cm. Underglaze blue, above-average domestic/export. Courtesy of Colonial National Historic Park, Yorktown, Virginia.

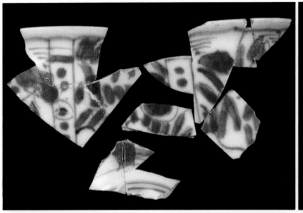

136. *Cup shards*, left: carrack, c.1615; right: c.1685–1700. Shards from the Drummond/Harris Plantation, the Governor's Land near Jamestown. Average to above-average domestic/export. Courtesy of the Virginia Research Center, Yorktown, Virginia.

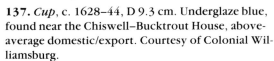

137. *Cup*, c. 1628–44, D 9.3 cm. Underglaze blue, found near the Chiswell–Bucktrout House, above-average domestic/export. Courtesy of Colonial Williamsburg.

138. Detail of base mark on fig. 137. *Jigutang* ("Hall of Investigating Antiquity"), hallmark of Gao Chengyan (1603–48), a famous bibliophile and poet.

Richmond, more shards, largely eighteenth and nineteenth century, may rival in quantity the previously known porcelains concentrated in the Jamestown area.[26]

The Jamestown evidence is of teacups, rice and soup bowls, plates, and small vases.[27] These, like the "Maine" pieces, were apparently owned by culturally middle-to-lower-class colonists whose money had come quickly in the early years of tobacco farming.[28] Their possession of porcelain is a symbol not of taste and refinement, as was common in Europe or England, but of a boomtown economy with a precarious future. (The "Maine" houses, for example, were impermanent structures, and the community's burial practices primitive at best: sometimes bodies were buried without their limbs arranged or benefit of coffins or, apparently, clergy.[29])

Along with the Wanli pieces is an intact Transitional cup (fig. 137), which may be dated at 1628–43 (fig. 138),[30] the same period as shards recovered from the

139. *Cup shard* (left), c. 1640–60. Underglaze blue, associated with Col. Thomas Pettus (d. by 1669) and his son, Capt. Thomas Pettus (d. 1691). *Bowl shard* (right), c. 1690–1720, associated with Capt. Pettus and James Bray II. Courtesy of the Virginia Research Center, Yorktown, Virginia.

140. *Plate*, c. 1740–60. Underglaze blue and eroded overglaze enamels; associated with Thomas Bray's son, James Bray III, and his sister, Elizabeth Bray Johnson; above-average domestic/export. Courtesy of the Virginia Research Center, Yorktown, Virginia.

site of Colonel Thomas Pettus's substantial frame house. Occupied about 1640–92 by Pettus and his son, Captain Thomas Pettus, the house was abandoned and destroyed.[31] The Pettus shards overlap with pieces dating from the period of the Pettus family's successor, James Bray II (fig. 139). Separating the possessions of the two men, even at the time, was dif-

ficult; Nathaniel Bacon, appraiser of the Pettus estate in 1692 noted, "as for the household goods when we went to inventory them, the time agreed on Mr. James Bray told us that we came too late for he had carried them away."[32] Bray also "carried away" Mrs. Pettus, who shortly became his wife. Bray, like Pettus, a reasonably well-to-do English colonist, built a brick house and within it enjoyed blue-and-white and Chinese "Imari" porcelains (fig. 140).[33] Here were settlers whom one might expect to have such chinaware, in contrast to the "Maine" tobacco farmers.

For the collections already gathered and for future discoveries, facts of population and trade illuminate the quantity and the social context of the ware. Despite severe setbacks from the first years of settlement, a slow steady growth occurred. By 1625 there were 1,478 colonists, including 269 women and 23 blacks.[34] Up to this time and through the 1620s, Virginia's leaders were from the aristocracy. In the next period, beginning with a doubling of the population during 1630–35, early successful planters came into power, replacing the educated élite who left or died.[35] Representatives of the English upper classes again asserted their political and social dominance, arriving during the English Civil War and continuing to emigrate through Oliver Cromwell's Commonwealth, altogether spanning the years 1642 to 1660. Along with other, humbler sympathizers with the monarchy, they found a haven in royalist Virginia. Among the newcomers were the families of Richard Lee, Edward Digges, William Randolph, George Mason, and John Page, who with others founded distinguished dynasties for the eighteenth century. By 1660, then, men of culture again controlled Virginia, and the colony now numbered 30,000.[36]

Both these groups could afford to own similar porcelains, although the élite probably had more of better quality. Figure 141 illustrates what a prominent Virginian, of noble or native birth, might have owned at this time. In York County, Virginia, a 1671–72 inventory included "one dutch case & bottles."[37] Porcelains made in the 1660–80 period would have been Transitional Chinese (fig. 142) or fine and coarse Japanese. At present, the assumption of such ownership is based upon shard finds and Virginia's contact with Dutch sources for the porcelain before 1660, as well as Japanese wares. Samples of seventeenth-century estate inventories of Accomack, Northampton, and York counties even among the very wealthy do not name china per se.[38]

However, such inventories may reflect appraisers' ignorance or may lump together precious and inconsequential objects, especially when concentrating on form, or if on material, then focusing on metalwork pieces of silver (plate) or pewter. Listings of specific

141. *Bottle*, c. 1665, H 31.4 cm. Underglaze blue, silver screw top, above-average export. Courtesy of the Ashmolean Museum.

142. *Tankard*, c. 1645–65, H 22.6 cm. Underglaze blue, above-average export. Courtesy of the Ashmolean Museum.

objects—plates, dishes, jugs, porringers, salts, cups, and saucers—may have included china. Often appraisers could not distinguish it from other ceramics, especially delft; even today the two are sometimes confused. Later appraisers may have purposely omitted references to East India goods because if their source was Dutch, they were contraband. (In 1670/71, the appearance of one East India tablecloth and five East India napkins is an exception.[39]) Spanish tables, guns, money, shoes, and leather in York County estates clearly indicate Virginia's trade with a culture apart from the English. The hints of porcelain beyond the often lean facts given in appraisals make these inventories only one part of the complex data needed to reveal Virginia's actual ownership of china in the seventeenth century. More archaeological evidence compared with more period documents, including inventories, will give a surer view.

NEW NETHERLAND

Ironically, while in North America (1609–64), Holland probably found more porcelain buyers in the English colonies than in her own. New Netherland[40] included New Amsterdam, Fort Orange (Albany), and two forts on the Connecticut and Delaware rivers. Hollanders and other European arrivals to this area found a much different situation than the English in Virginia. Both groups had their severe hardships: dissension in the ranks; lack of food; disease; and Indian troubles. However, while Virginia's population inched upward then increased rapidly in about 1630, the population in New Netherland rose only to about 300 colonists by 1630, and by 1643 had actually dipped slightly. In contrast, Virginia by 1638 had reached 30,000 colonists. The Dutch even offered patroonships—land grants for the wealthy with West India Company support—beginning in 1629, but to no avail. Only Rensselaerwyck in present-day Albany was successful.[41] For the rank-and-file of first English settlers in Virginia, the primary attractions were economic opportunity and the promise of social mobility. Hollanders at home were too content with their solid burgher lives. To emigrate would be to work only for the company and risk losing a relative prosperity. Peter Stuyvesant, on becoming governor in 1647, found only 250, or at most 300 men who could bear arms.[42]

A shift upward began slowly in 1650, when passengers were induced to come from Holland, often at their own expense, buy the promise of furs, fruits, and the climate in the new colonies. Even so, by 1660, a rough estimate indicates at most 10,000 inhabitants, one-third of Virginia's population,[43] and of these, about 6,000 were Dutch.[44] By the end of the seventeenth century, twenty-six years after New Netherland had become New York, the total population was just over 18,000, or a little more than half of Virginia's in 1660. Of that number only 5,066 were white males.[45] Statistics such as these suggest a bleak prospect for the porcelain trade in New Netherland, but other sources tell a slightly different story.

Shards and Inventories

Recent excavations on the southern tip of Manhattan have produced a quantity of porcelains, although only two of them—both blue-and-white—may date from the seventeenth century. On one site stood the Dutch Stadt Huys, first a tavern in the 1640s, then the city hall in 1654. It served this function until about 1697, and was the hub of the colony's business and drinking—a common pairing in the colony. On the other site, adjacent to the Stadt Huys, Lovelace Tavern was built in the 1670s, after the English had taken control from the Dutch. From the Lovelace area, a lone blue-

and-white shard of the seventeenth century has been recovered. In contrast, about 374 porcelain shards of the eighteenth century were found on both sites.[46] The fragmentary nature of the shards prevents describing the porcelains as vessels typical of a tavern.[47]

Nearby, in a landfill made from 1680 to 1700 and afterward built upon (7 Hanover Square and 64 Pearl Street), a second shard has been found amidst much more evidence of eighteenth-century porcelain, along with Dutch blue tiles and everyday earthenwares.[48] So new and singular are these pioneering projects that they may be atypical of forthcoming finds. However, combined with population figures and the immigration history of New Netherland, they support a working thesis that porcelains were not commercially imported in quantity but were more commonly brought by other means.

Any china before the 1640s was probably carried, in large part, by the immigrants themselves. A good early example is the ware belonging to a wealthy Danish sea captain and landed farmer Jonas Bronck, who arrived in 1639 on the ship *De Brant van Trogen* (*The Conflagration of Troy*). He bought 500 acres from the Indians, north of the Harlem River at the outpost of civilization of New Amsterdam,[49] and though not the only wealthy landowner in this area, Bronck nonetheless gave it his name—the Bronx. From Bronck's inventories, the contrast between his wilderness farm, Emaus, and his sophisticated possessions is striking. Taken a year after his death in 1642, one inventory indicates he had "6 little alabaster plates," which were doubtless porcelain with a minimum of blue-and-white decoration. The other inventory also lists these plates, and in addition "1 chest containing various pieces of porcelain."[50]

Bronck (1600–42), a Dane employed by the West India Company, had lived in Amsterdam. With his maritime connections, he would have found ready purchase there of Far Eastern goods, Japanese or Chinese.[51] He owned a Japanese cutlass and two mirrors, one of ebony and the other of gilt, both typical of the oriental trade. If his plates were Japanese, they would have been rare, early examples of "Old Imari" (*Ko-Imari*) ware; if Chinese, they might have been similar to the plate in figure 143.[52] The now-lost porcelains referred to in Bronck's trunk are tantalizingly undescribed, but clearly, they were pre-1640, and thus would have been late Ming, early Transitional.

Richer inventories will be discussed, but an early archaeological find fits chronologically here. In 1970–71, through persistent efforts by archaeologist Paul Huey, the area of Fort Orange in Albany was excavated. Inside the fort, from a deposit dating about 1650–60, in a house belonging to the prosperous trader Hendrick Andriessen van Doesburgh, were found three shards, reconstructed and illustrated in

143. *Dish*, c. 1630–40, D 20.9 cm. Underglaze blue; on reverse: four crude whorls; average export piece, now rare. Courtesy of the Ashmolean Museum.

figure 144.[53] From a survey of illustrated Transitional export ware, this type of symmetrical, scroll-leaved decoration on the rim of an object limits the piece to a mustard pot, can, tankard, or chamberpot (fig. 145, and see fig. 142). These are slight clues but concrete proof of the presence of porcelain when the colony's population was at last growing. Also, supplies to Albany regularly arrived from New Amsterdam when,

as early as 1633, a packet service was established.[54] Other digs, then, might reveal everyday porcelains similar to and even earlier than van Doesburgh's.

The listed chinaware of Pieter Claerbout, a contemporary of van Doesburgh and also a successful trader, complements the shard data. In 1659, he left an inventory showing he owned the following porcelains, valued in guilders (florin) and stivers:

144. *Shards* (reconstructed), edge of vessel, c. 1650–60. Underglaze blue, border in open-scroll leaf motif, above-average export. Courtesy of Paul Huey, senior archaeologist, New York State Parks and Recreation, Waterford, New York.

145. *Mustard pot* and *salt*, Japanese; *mustard pot*, Chinese. left: *ko-Imari* (Old Imari), c. 1690, overglaze enamels; pot, H 11.4 cm; right: Chinese pot, c. 1645–65. Japanese objects: fine; Chinese pot: average. Courtesy of the Ashmolean Museum.

3 porcelain cups	f5.05
3 porcelain cups	4.04
2 porcelain dishes	6.16
6 porcelain plates	5.05
7 porcelain plates	6.13
3 porcelain platters	5.10
3 porcelain platters	5.00
3 porcelain platters	9.00[55]

The average value of these thirty pieces was 1.52 florin, or six times the cost of fine porcelain shipped out of Batavia for the Netherlands in 1647. This is the last recorded year of a bulk load of quality porcelain carried home by the Dutch before the near-closure of trade in chinaware ten years later.[56] Were Claerbout's pieces of such quality? Only more contemporary inventories showing the difference in price between fine and coarse porcelain would tell for certain. A man of Claerbout's means would have been able to own good pieces. Also, if they were coarse, their increase in value would not have been as great as 600 percent. This figure is explained by middlemen surcharges between China and Albany, and also by the scarcity of quality pieces after the late 1640s and early 1650s. Claerbout's, then, were probably fine porcelains, according to export standards set by the Dutch at the point of origin. The dish in figure 146, a period example, indicates the type.

In mid-century, the declining supply of chinaware in the Far East was felt in New Netherland. Either some wealthy folk did not care to own it, or in the decade or so before their deaths it had become scarce.[57] In April 1662, Susanna Van Rensselaer in Holland wrote her brother, Jeremias, administer of Rensselaerwyck in Albany: "I had much trouble in procuring the small table plates, as not many are being made, for the people now all use pewter, so that I could not get any better ones."[58] Because delft and other tablewares were produced in abundance at the time, porcelain is the likeliest ceramic referred to.[59] The brother of Susanna and Jeremias, the Reverend

146. *Dish*, c. 1640–60, D 37.5 cm. Overglaze enamels, carrack underglaze blue pattern, fine export. Courtesy of the Ottema-Kingma Foundation, the Princessehof Museum.

Nicholaus Van Rensselaer, who came to New Amsterdam in 1674 from an Episcopal congregation in England, left five "chany" plates in his 1679 estate, along with other earthenwares.[60] The Van Rensselaer sister and brothers thus illustrate two sorts of private importation: by purchase abroad and by new immigration.

Private enterprise of a more dramatic sort, confiscation and piracy, probably brought more seventeenth-century porcelains to New Netherland than any other means. In 1655, for example, goods from a Spanish ship, commandeered by the Dutch in Jamaica, were sold in New Amsterdam.[61] In addition, beginning under Dutch rule, smuggling and piracy were everyday occurrences in and near New Amsterdam and continued well after the English came in 1664. Pirates out of

Madagascar, their headquarters, sold their booty with impunity in the colonial capital, and East India goods were the chief items bought.[62] In fact, ships carrying such pirated goods were often owned by merchants of the city who commissioned the pirates to obtain the wares.[63] The colonists thus circumvented not only the Dutch East and West India Companies, but also private merchants in Amersterdam. Even though most of the pirates were English, after English rule began piracy increased by leaps and bounds, at least until the example of Captain William Kidd (c. 1645–1701), a once-respected privateer turned pirate, who was captured and hung. (Kidd's treasure, which included East India goods, was seized by the British government, but rumors that part of it remained inspired Poe's "The Gold Bug" and Stevenson's *Treasure Island*.[64]) There is no easy way to estimate the amount of china entering by illicit trade, but the Madagascar–New Amsterdam connection no doubt accounts for a large portion of it.

Increasingly, general trade was another source; in the 1630s, private traders did only a limited business in the colony. After 1638, they were allowed by the West India Company to buy furs, the area's first and most attractive product. With such inducement, they brought a variety of manufactured goods to exchange for this coveted item.[65] No doubt East India wares were part of their trade.

The implication of a healthy start in such goods is clear in a 1657 petition from Amsterdam merchants to the West India Company. It shows that before this time their ships brought East India goods to New Amsterdam, where the English were in the habit of buying them (and from there, presumably supplied such goods to New England). The merchants protested that the 4 percent duty charged by the colony's director general, Peter Stuyvesant, had led the English to turn to Amsterdam to buy East India wares, which were shipped to England or directly to Virginia and New England, thereby depriving the petitioners "of a con-

siderable share of their trade."[66] Furthermore, the complaint read, if the duty was not payable in beavers or silver coin, Stuyvesant took "the value of it arbitrarily out of the cargo, advancing the prices fifty per cent against those, declared here at the Company's office."[67] Besides requesting that the duty be reduced and be payable in wampum instead of furs or coin, the petitioners wished to be refunded or credited for the overcharges they had paid "during the last year."[68] This phrase suggests that Stuyvesant's measures had not been in effect too long. Two facts should be noted: the goods in question were East Indian, and the year was 1657, the last season of direct trade in fine Chinese porcelains for about twenty years. These cargoes had undoubtedly included some chinaware.

Exchange in East India items was proportionate to the three-way trade between Holland, New Amsterdam, and Virginia. Known to exist in the 1630s,[69] this trade was voluminous by the 1650s,[70] and, in fact, was only part of a vast network of goods carried by the West India Company and independent shippers involving the Chesapeake Bay, the New England colonies, and the Dutch Caribbean (e.g., Surinam and Curaçao)—in short, the whole of North and South America.[71] Holland's complex of connections meant that some of their cargoes unloaded in New Amsterdam undoubtedly included porcelains.

So great was the threat of the Dutch to the success of England's own mercantile scheme for her colonies that in 1664 England invaded and conquered the New Netherlands. But afterward, resident Dutch merchants greatly outnumbered the English, and the new government had to compromise. The resulting Dutch-English New World nexus continued to depend upon Amsterdam's role as entrepôt of porcelains and other Eastern wares well into the last quarter of the seventeenth century. After the surrender, trade between the colony and Holland was allowed to continue for six months; restrictions then grew, but largely upon the West India Company, to the benefit of independent

New Amsterdam merchants. These merchants had retained their political power by supporting the English victors in business. In short, English governors and the Dutch merchants composed a new oligarchy.

This alliance continued through the brief recapture of New Amsterdam by the Dutch and the resumption of control by the English under Sir Edmund Andros. Like his predecessors, Andros became deeply allied with the Dutch mercantile community, effectively maintaining the trade in East India and other goods for the decade 1664–74 to the great benefit of the Dutch on both sides of the Atlantic. Beginning in 1674, two to four Dutch ships left Amsterdam annually for New York with stops in England to pay duties. Even though that same year saw the first serious threat of competition from English merchants, Andros was nonetheless charged with favoring Dutch interests in New York to the detriment of his countrymen. He was finally recalled to England in 1680. By 1682, five English ships were en route to New York from London, and from that time onward, English business interests would grow. Even so, they could not eclipse the Dutch. In part, this was because the interconnections between merchants in Holland, England, and New York were sometimes familial as well as mercantile.[72] Dutch families in New York thus continued to dominate the economic and social scene well into the nineteenth century.

Early Collectors and Collections

This view of New Amsterdam–New York in the late-seventeenth century illuminates the position of porcelain in quantity and quality among contemporary Dutch families. The collection of Peter Stuyvesant (1592–1672), the director general for seventeen years, is not surprising. Before coming to New Netherland in 1647, Stuyvesant—who grew up in the era of Dutch hegemony in the China trade—had served the West India Company in Curaçao, where no doubt he devel-

oped a taste for porcelain. Curaçao and other ports often launched Dutch marauders to intercept Spanish galleons supplying forts in the West Indies or en route to Seville.[73] Stuyvesant's predilection for such cargoes is clearly seen in his later confiscation of Amsterdam East India goods whose duties could not be paid in New Amsterdam. Perhaps among them were the "three great China pots," which his widow, Judith, left to her cousin Nicholas Bayard in 1674, possibly similar to the beaker in figure 147. To her son, Nicholas William Stuyvesant, she gave the rest of her porcelains.[74]

147. *Beaker*, c. 1660–75, H 51 cm. Underglaze blue with overglaze enamels, superior domestic/export. Courtesy of the Ashmolean Museum.

148. *Teapots*, right: both porcelain, c. 1685–1700; left: Ixing redware, c. 1736–1820. Dehua white pot, D 18.6 cm. Courtesy of the trustees of the British Museum.

The vast "purcelaine" collection of the barber–surgeon Dr. Jacob De Lange was inventoried in 1685; its range and volume, accumulated over the years, show what a true collector could amass. It also testifies to the well-known reputation of the Dutch for luxurious furnishings in North America as elsewhere. With other East Indian items—an expected part of any valuable New Amsterdam inventory—they fit well in De Lange's spacious interiors. In an Old World fashion common to the wealthy, the doctor's porcelains were displayed in at least three ways: in a cupboard, on the chimney piece, and on the walls, where they were hung separately or rested on cornices and brackets in the style made popular on the Continent by Daniel Marot. Most of the collection was arranged in De Lange's "Side Chamber," which was also an office and painting gallery. His "East India Cupboard" may well have been like others of the period, carved and inlaid with porcelain, mother-of-pearl, or ivory.[75]

Besides the cupboard, the mantel and chimney wall held the following pieces: 127 teapots—including two white teapots and seven small red teapots (Ixhing); sixty-seven saucers with five others; thirty-three butterdishes and six double butter dishes; seven half basins, two great and five small basins and one barber's basin; six small flasks, two presumably larger flasks, and two flaskets; five oil pots; four small cans and three small oil cans; five dishes; four drinking glasses; four saltcellars; three small mustard pots; two small cups; two fruit dishes; two tobacco boxes; two belly flagons. Also included were single examples of a can with a joint, another with a silver joint, a sugar pot, a small and a great goblet, a small chalice, a small spice pot, and a small spoon. Except for three "white men," the figurines were almost all small: six men, two swans, one duck, and one dog.[76] The variety of form among this useful and decorative collection indicates that every sort of porcelain enjoyed in Holland would have been available to the rich in New Netherland as well (fig. 148).

Ten years later, another notable collection was inventoried. The Reverend Rudolphus Van Varick of Long Island was a domine who had served three parishes (Flatbush, Utrecht, and Brookland). He had been naturalized in 1686 and lived eight years longer.[77] His wife, Margrita, died a year later, and the inventory of their shop (Van Varick appears to have been a merchant as well as a minister) and joint possessions was made in 1695. East India cabinets, trunks, and boxes richly embellished with silver or brass were given to their children with the following china: a cup set in silver, eleven "Indian babyes" (toys or dolls), six large dishes, six small dishes, two white cups with covers, and two groups of "pieces"—thirty-nine small porcelains and twenty-three porcelains of unspecified size. Because bequeathed by Margrita directly to her children, these were among the most prized china and were listed without a price. The remaining household ware (none is specified as shop merchandise), included at least some fine cups. In the appraisal by her executors, one of whom was Nicholas Bayard, they were valued as follows:

3	Large China Disshes (crakt & broke at 20s)	£3:00:—
10	China Disshes at 12s	6:00:—
4	ditto Crakt	1:00:—
2	China bassens at 10s	1:00:—
1	ditto crakt	0:05:—
1	China smaller bason at 6s	0:06:—
2	ditto crakt at 3s	0:06:—
3	fine China Cupps at 9s	1:07:—
1	China Jug at 10s	0:10:—
4	China Sawcers at 3s	0:12:—
6	ditto smaller tea disshes at 3s	0:18:—
1	ditto crakt at 2s	0:02:—
6	painted tea disshes at 4:6s	1:02:—
4	tea dishes at 2:6s	0:10:—
5	tea Cups at 3s	0:15:—
3	ditto: one at 2:6s and two at 1:6s	0:05:06
4	ditto painted browne at 2:6s	0:10:—
6	small ditto at 1:6ns (pence)	0:09:—
3	ditto painted read and blew at 3s	0:09:—
2	East India flowr potts white at 6s	0:12:—
1	ditto crakt at 3s	0:03:—
3	ditto smaller at 4s	0:12:—
2	ditto round at 4:6s	0:09:—
1	China Inck box & 2 Sand boxes at 12s	0:12:—
1	Lyon 9s 1 China Image 9s	0:18:—[78]

Some of these objects may once have been displayed in a "painted wooden rack to set china ware in" valued at £1.7. Figures 149–153 illustrate pieces

149. *Bowl*, c. 1630, W 19.2 cm. Silver mount marked A 1632 MS, for Leeuwarder Minne Sickes. Courtesy of the Fries Museum.

150. *Bowls*, right: c. 1690, D 6.6 cm; left: 1740, D 6.9 cm. Right with cover: underglaze blue, overglaze brown; left: overglaze enamels, common export. Courtesy of Mr. and Mrs. Lewis Rumford II.

151. *Cups*, c. 1685–1710, left to right: H 6.4 cm, 6.7 cm, 6.4 cm. Can and octagonal cup in overglaze enamels; Dehua white cup, above-average export. Courtesy of the trustees of the British Museum.

contemporary with and probably similar to the Van Varick collection.

In both the De Lange and Van Varick collections, each comprising well over a hundred pieces, no sets of china appear, not even for tea, which had become a Dutch staple by the late 1630s. (The East India Company had shipped tea to Holland from Japan in 1610, but it became popular only twenty years later. Teacups, originally an Asian trade name, were first ordered in quantity—twenty-five thousand—by the East India Company in 1643.[79]) Nor do other period inventories list any china sets. For example, the goods of

the Reverend Mr. Patrick Gordon, valued at £375 in 1702, included "1 Small Tin Box wth Tea, 2 Tea Pots with some China & Delph Cups & Dishes," all worth £.04.[80]

Far from having a set, Mr. Gordon evidently mixed at least two types of ceramics when serving tea. The red teapot, known in China to preserve nuances of taste, had a particular use: for specially flavored teas such as saffron, or, for a variation in summer, peach leaves.[81] In an oil painting of 1720, *The English Family at Tea*, such a red pot (either Ixhing or Staffordshire stoneware) sits in the middle of the tea table, perhaps not only for saffron and other teas but also for hot water.[82]

The style of varied lushness in interior design evident in these inventory lists was paralleled by the range of taste in Chinese pots and porcelains within a single collection. As a touch of the exotic and even of the bizarre, porcelain was valued for its deliberate variety and piquancy.

Another wealthy merchant and the last Dutch mayor of New Amsterdam, Cornelis van Steenwyck (d. 1684), had in his "Great Chamber," along with a valuable collection of silver worth over two hundred

pounds, "nineteen china, or porcelain, dishes." Placed prominently in the house along with a French nutwood cupboard, twelve Russian leather chairs, two velvet chairs with fine silver lace, and probably decorating the chimney on top of "a flowered tabby cloth," these porcelains could only have been first-class.[83] The plate in figure 154 is of such a quality. Another object, a "children's ship," was in Steenwyck's foreroom or general sitting room. It could have been of wood, but perhaps it was porcelain, resembling a junk of later date (fig. 227).

The chocolate pot is not known to be distinguished

152. *Lion whistle*, c. 1690–1720, H 12.3 cm. Dehua white, common domestic/export. Courtesy of the Groninger Museum.

153. *Figurines*, Chinese scholars, c. 1690–1710, both H 14.0 cm. Three-color ware, common domestic/export. Courtesy of the trustees of the British Museum.

154. *Plate*, 1672, D 27.3 cm. Underglaze blue and copper-red. Mark on base in blue: *Kangxi renzi Zhonghe tang zhi.* ''The renzi year of the Kangxi reign [1672], made in the Zhonghe Hall'' (Hall of Central Harmony, Forbidden City, Beijing); imperial quality. Collection of F. Lugt. Courtesy of the Fondation Custodia, Paris.

155. *Coffee/chocolate pot*, c. 1690–1710, H 28.0 cm. Underglaze blue, one of five known examples, above-average export. Courtesy of the Victoria and Albert Museum.

from pots used for coffee or tea until the late-seventeenth century. Outside of New Spain, chocolate drinking was expensive and not well known until a hundred years later, and then largely in court circles. However, William Pleay's New York inventory of 1690 lists a silver ''jocolato pot.''[84] Perhaps he had a ''Spanish connection'' (either by business or piracy), as obviously did Capt. Nicholas Dumaresq (d. 1701) of New York. Among Dumaresq's effects were many exotic items of international trade, including forty pieces of Spanish and French gold (£12), twenty yards of ''Spanish Druggett'' (pure wool or wool woven with

either silk or linen), a Spanish cup (valued at 11s, possibly silver because listed with his plate), and ''one Chocollatto pott,'' not appraised, thus no doubt ceramic, and if so, possibly porcelain (fig. 155).[85] Japanese porcelain coffee/chocolate pots date from about 1680 (fig. 218), and because the first such pots in metalwork appear about the same time, Chinese porcelain models would postdate them and possibly their Delft contemporaries. But by the 1690s, they could have been among those objects ordered by fashion-conscious buyers from the newly revived kilns at Jingdezhen.[86]

Without a direct source of East India goods in quantity in the seventeenth century, early English immigrants to the Massachusetts Bay Colony and nearby probably saw less china than their counterparts in Virginia. The Bay Colony was smaller and grew more slowly than Virginia;[87] fewer people meant fewer porcelains, as did the difference in the class of people emigrating from England. Though led by the squirearchy, those who settled in Massachusetts were largely from the middle and lower classes, at least during the first century, while Virginia and the South came to attract more of England's gentry along with humbler folk.

Although immigrants were not prevented from bringing favorite pieces, in the North or South ceramics were not included on the lists of recommended equipment printed on broadsides for prospective colonists.[88] In addition, at this early date, few Englishmen were investing in the Far East. A relevant exception was Matthew Cradock, who increased to two thousand pounds sterling his stake in the East India trade in 1628, the year before the forming of the Massachusetts Bay Company. Cradock was also the East India Company's first governor, but his role in the possible transfer of East India goods from England to America is unknown. At best, he would probably have been instrumental in obtaining a few pieces of porcelain for relatives or for gentlemen friends from East Anglia, like John Winthrop, Thomas Dudley, and Emmanuel Downing, who did emigrate. Cradock himself remained in England.[89]

During the English civil wars (1642–60), while royalists and others came to Virginia in even greater numbers than before, both immigration and shipment of manufactured goods to New England actually shrank.[90] New Englanders, who had principally been farmers in their first decade as colonists, were now forced to take to the sea in search of trade for needed merchandise. Soon, ships built in Massachusetts were

in great demand, and merchants who organized this great exchange were dealing with the whole Atlantic basin. A complex web of shipping lanes connected New England with coastal ports in Pennsylvania, Maryland, Virginia and the Carolinas, in Newfoundland, Nova Scotia, and the Bermudas. From the coast, New England ships sailed first to the West Indies then to Portuguese possessions, Europe, and, of course, England.

Boston, Salem, and Cambridge, with constant contacts overseas, took the lead in commercial and thus economic affairs. With a massive shipbuilding industry underway, Boston was not only chief carrier to the other East Coast colonies, but by 1676 was considered "the mart town of the West Indies."[91]

West Indian imports—cotton, dyewoods, ginger, indigo, molasses, and, for a short time, tobacco— were key to the growth of commerce in New England. She could only pay for cloth, ironwares, and luxury items from England by bills of exchange, gold, silver, and tropical wares coming from the Caribbean. Not until 1700 was the codfish industry so well established as to be the backbone of Boston's prosperity.[92]

If Boston was chiefly responsible for the coastwise carrying trade, if her captains put into New Amsterdam to buy Dutch goods, and if she regularly sent ships overseas to other ports where East India goods were exchanged, she should have had a reasonable importation of such goods, including porcelains; but apparently she did not. Although in 1640 the city had three times as many inhabitants as New Amsterdam— about twelve hundred versus four hundred—and kept this lead to the end of the century and later, she could not boast of the same sizable porcelain collections as those of New Amsterdam.[93]

Like the Holland-Virginia nexus, there was also a close commercial bond between Virginia and New England. The partnership of Edmund Scarburgh of Virginià and Edward Gibbons of Massachusetts was formed before mid-century. The brothers Bowdoin, John and James, both captains from Boston, traded with Virginia's Eastern Shore and even owned land there.[94] In the 1690s, William Pepperell traded New England goods in Virginia, then carried barrels of pork and beef to Barbados before returning home with West Indian products[95] in a triangular trade familiar to other New Englanders. The close connection between merchant, mariner, and landowner could, as in the case of the Bowdoins, become an identity.

Inventories

Despite these and other contacts abroad, New England inventories are at present the best evidence of a decided difference in the ownership of porcelain between the English colonies North and South, and New

Netherland: no verifiable seventeenth-century shards have been found. Ironically, in New England, which probably had less china than Virginia, references to chinaware *do* appear, although they are rarer, limited in quantity, and less precise than the Dutch lists. Of course, some appraisers were less careful than others in distinguishing ceramic types.

As in Virginia, porcelains may have been buried in listings of basins, bottles, bowls, cans, cups, dishes, flasks, flagons, inkstands, plates, platters, tobacco boxes, and other objects. This was especially true when such pieces were grouped together as a unit. As a result, coarser types of ware may have been lumped with earthenware, or porcelain may not have been recognized for itself. Another possibility is that it may have been given away, for example as a wedding gift, thus omitted from estate lists. On the question of mislistings, possibly the thin, handleless cups of the sort found in Virginia (fig. 135) were included in the terms *dram* and *wine* cups. As in New Amsterdam, tea, coffee, and chocolate cups were not distinguished until the end of the century, although as early as 1670 Dorothy Jones of Boston was licensed to sell "coffe and chuchaletto."[96]

Of the china listed (often spelled as pronounced: "cheyney," "cheenie," "chaeny," etc.), porcelain flatware—dishes, plates, and saucers—emerges as the chief form owned by the first seventeenth-century New Englanders. These comparatively easy-to-pack pieces would have been carrack and Transitional wares comparable to those imported into Mexico. The 1641 listing of "1 Chaynie Dish" for Thomas Knocker of Boston is a prototype for the rest of the century. The plate in figure 156 is a period carrack plate.[97] At such an early date, before New England went to sea, it is reasonable to assume that Knocker brought this piece with him when he immigrated. In

156. *Plate*, c. 1585–1600, D 38.1 cm. Underglaze blue, above-average export. Private collection.

fact, probably most of the first generation brought items purchased in London, originating with the Dutch, or less often by importers like Cradock.

A 1647 list of the possessions of the wealthy widow Martha Coteymore (a cousin of Cradock's, soon to marry John Winthrop), included "one parcel of cheyney plates and saucers" worth one pound. (On Winthrop's death in 1649, his estate did not include these or any china. Tin, pewter, and an unidentified ceramic ewer and flagon were his tablewares.)[98] A John Davenport, however, left four pounds worth of "Cheyney" in 1648.[99] Because there probably were not many pieces, the price indicates the best late-Ming export. Another rare, early piece was a "cheney basen" in the estate of Governor Theophilus Eaton of New Haven on his death in 1658; the type is represented in figure 157.[100] (Eaton's basin may have come with him to the New World twenty years before when he left a prosperous mercantile business in London with connections in Denmark and Holland.)

Of the five notices of china in the Essex County court records for the period 1636–83, only "dishes" are surely identified as porcelain. They date respectively from 1647, 1661, 1662, 1666, and 1672, though probably they were owned for a period from five to fifteen years before (similar to fig. 158). A possible exception is "One siluer tipt Jugg," noted in the 1650 estate of Elizabeth Lowle, which may be porcelain or another ceramic, but one worthy of the metal used to repair it. Otherwise, dishes dominate.[101] According to room-by-room descriptions, they were displayed in a hall or parlor. Given Salem's prominence in trade abroad, this scanty appearance of porcelain suggests an incomplete record rather than reality (fig. 159).

The same slight references, again often to dishes, are true of similar records in Boston and Watertown.

157. *Basin*, c. 1635–60, D 35 cm. Dark underglaze blue, above-average Dutch export. Courtesy of the Ottema–Kingman Foundation, the Princessehof Museum.

158. *Bowl*, c. 1612, D c. 21 cm. Underglaze blue, recovered from the *White Lion* (1613); average export. Courtesy of the Rijksmuseum and the National Geographic Society.

In fact, in the latter town in 1669, wealthy Deacon Samuel Thatcher owned "eleaven cheany dishes," an unusual number for the time. Six years later, at the other end of the economic scale, the appraisers of Jonathan Shattuck, who was apparently a tailor, recorded five pieces of chinaware worth two shillings, six pence.[102] More typical were the "6 cheny Dishes 3s" of Peng Heath of Roxbury listed in 1671, and the "china Bason" of Joseph Rock of Boston, 1683.[103] These pieces may have been ten to twenty years old, thus Chinese, but after 1660, an occasional Japanese

159. Shelves of carrack, c. 1573–1620. Cups, dishes, plates, and bowls. Courtesy of the Princessehof Museum.

piece could have come to New England via the Dutch (fig. 160).

However rarely it appears, "china" is at least an item in New England estates, whereas it was seldom listed in Virginia inventories of the same time period. (Even in the Connecticut River Valley, more sparsely settled than the coast, "cheney-ware" was listed in estates above 200 pounds sterling in the 1660–80 period. In the years 1685–1705 china remained rare but appeared in roughly nine percent of a sample of inventories recently studied.)[104] But in New England, unlike Virginia, there are no known whole pieces or even shards of seventeenth-century porcelain, in spite of their presence in inventories.[105]

Scarcity may have sharpened the New World distinction between those who owned porcelain and those who did not. (Gluts on the Amsterdam market in the early-seventeenth century made some coarser porcelains well within the purse of the average Dutch householder.) Most colonial owners were middle-to-upper-middle class, and owned it in order of occupation: merchant, mariner, or minister.[106] Ministers may have been given china in return for services, but most clergy were cultivated and often linked to the merchant class by marriage,[107] and thus had a taste for porcelain.

The known range of quality between inventoried china is difficult to specify. For example, in 1662, John Andrews's Ipswich estate, valued at £1083.19.06, included "5 chanye dishes," while ten years later, Samuell Jacob, also of Ipswich, left an estate worth £356.10.06, which included an unspecified number of "cheny dishes," probably of lesser quality than his wealthier neighbor's. Some pieces of known value are a rough guide to quality. In Roxbury, Peng Heath's six dishes were worth three shillings. This was the same value of a Spanish table in Virginia at the time, an item often owned by middle-to-upper-middle-class southern householders. Heath's pieces

160. *Dishes*, Japanese porcelain, mid-to-late 1600s, enameled wares, left: c. 1670–80, D 32.8 cm; center: mid-to-late 1600s, *ko-Imari*; right: c. 1660–70, Chinese carrack-inspired. Above-average export. Courtesy of the Ashmolean Museum.

were probably of average-to-good quality. The very wealthy could have even better wares and more variety of form.[108] In addition, the lower-middle class could have owned coarse or cast-off china, either ignored or lumped together with the ubiquitous phrase, "a parcell of earthenware."

In this state of rarity, large porcelain collections would have been the exception (figs. 161 and 162). Quite unlike the Dutch in New Amsterdam, New Englanders did not have the conditioned taste for porcelain nor the relatively easy chance to buy it. Almost without exception, merchants were tied to England by political loyalty, commercial bond, and family connections as well. In foreign ports, they preferred to deal with resident Englishmen.[109] And when trading

with non-English ports, as in New Amsterdam, such necessities as iron and cloth would be the first purchases. Also, it was illegal to buy from the Dutch after 1660. Furthermore, any china coming to New England by commercial carrier would have been classified as luxurious "sundries," for the most part, and probably obtained in miscellaneous, individual orders until the 1690s, rarely, if ever, in bulk loads. In 1699, John Higginson in Boston informed his brother in London, who had written to inquire about the market in East India goods, "China and lacker-ware will sell if in small quantity. . . ."[110]

Another deterrent to high living, including collecting, was the strength of the Puritan plain style. The pious Congregational eye was no less appreciative of va-

162. Detail, vase on lower left shelf in fig. 161.

161. Shelves of Transitional ware, c. 1620–80. Courtesy of the Princessehof Museum.

riety and richness than the average; although devout, the colony's leaders were upper-middle-class gentlemen or merchant gentlemen of substance and taste. Both clergy and laity enjoyed their "cheyney" (silk) drapes, Turkey carpets, silver, brightly polished pewter, the many delights of a wide variety of fermented liquors, and spices like pepper, cinnamon, ginger, and nutmeg. Still, the New England worship of God usually preceded a devotion to domestic decor. Unlike the Dutch, Bay colonists did not turn their interiors into minor art galleries. While the Dutch had paintings *and* porcelains, the few china dishes of New England homes were often their only "paintings." The furnishings of even the wealthy remained relatively chaste.

Like their counterparts in Virginia, they were for the most part land rich and object poor.

After 1660, a new breed of merchant entered the Boston scene, and piety among commercial types gradually took second place to profit, comfort, and finery, much to the consternation of the Reformed clergy.[111] After the early 1680s, Chinese export ware came to Boston as well as New York, legally or clandestinely, in the holds of merchant or private ships. The plate in figure 163 from Mexico could easily have had a twin in the North. Pirate loot was traded to welcome buyers in Massachusetts, Rhode Island, New York, and the Carolinas (fig. 164).[112] Even then, however, from the evidence now available, pepper and other spices took precedence over porcelain in seventeenth-century Massachusetts Bay and colonies nearby.

Midway between South and North, of course, was the great experiment of William Penn on the Susquehanna. Philadelphia's birth in the 1680s coincided with England's growing role in the Far East, thus quite early it felt the effects of her presence there. Philadelphia, in fact, was to become one of the major centers of the China trade in both colonial and republican days.[113]

Besides the porcelains enjoyed by the Penn family itself (fig. 165), other well-to-do immigrants also had a number of pieces. One Philadelphian, Henry Waddy, owned on his death in 1694 "1 Japan dish crackt, 3 china plates, 1 Japan bowl, 1 china cup and 1 china dram cup," all valued above average.[114] This amount of precious ware was unusual for the period, even among ceramic fanciers, such as the weaver John Busby (d. 1699). Among over thirty ceramic pieces in Busby's estate was a lone "Cheiney cup."[115] Another

group of porcelains, slightly later in date but unusual as documented heirlooms, was collected between 1832 and 1875 by the Philadelphia Quakers Elizabeth Clifford Morris Canby (1813–92) and her daughter, Elizabeth Canby Rumford (1848–1933). Their objects represent a number of early-eighteenth to mid-nineteenth-century wares from the Philadelphia and Wilmington areas, and many of them are illustrated in these pages (see figure 150, for example).[116]

Like Virginia, and in sharp contrast to New Amsterdam/New York, New England had a wider access to East India goods only after the turn of the eighteenth century. The dramatic advent of new goods to suit new tastes—a cornucopia of chinaware comparable to Mexico's at the turn of the seventeenth century—would affect the whole East Coast of America, even though its start was more gradual, as the next chapter describes.

163. *Plate*, c. 1685–1700, D 38.1 cm. Underglaze blue, fine domestic/export. Private collection.

164. *"Puzzle" jugs* (pair), c. 1690–1710, H 23.4 cm. Overglaze enamels, reed-painted; hollow handles and rim for liquid to pass when jug turned sideways; fine export, curiosities in their day. Courtesy of the Newark Museum.

CHAPTER 4

English Hegemony in the Eighteenth Century

From the first decades of the eighteenth century, porcelains exported to the West came principally in ships of the English East India Company. England's lead among all other Westerners in China was achieved in part by her success in becoming the first foreign power in modern history allowed to trade on the Chinese mainland. Still, the exchange took place either on islands—Chusan and Amoy—or, by 1710, only at a limited area fronting the river at Guangzhou (Canton). There, by 1730, the English had been joined by the Dutch along with the French, Danes, Swedes, and Germans (the Ostend Company). To serve foreigners' special orders in overglaze decoration, Chinese painters established themselves on Henan Island just south of Guangzhou. Overland in the north, especially at Kiakta, the Russians intermittently traded, too. At Macao, the Portuguese played a much diminished role, while the Spanish continued a vigorous trade from Manila.

European commerce in porcelain, though independent, was actually interconnected, sometimes intimately, nation to nation (fig. 165), with a definite effect upon the export ware reaching the American continent. Although the Spanish controlled Mexico's and California's supply of porcelain, the cargoes captured from her ships in the Caribbean or Atlantic were as salable in Boston and New York as anywhere in the Spanish realm.[1] Apart from a number of special-order Mexican forms or the adaptation of forms to local use, and apart from a few particular decorations, the common wares bound for New Spain were similar to other countries' imports. The French, as shards reveal, brought their own porcelains to a number of settlements in North America, and the English were the principal shippers of chinaware to their East Coast colonies. However, their preferences were hardly exclusive. In China, the English might buy porcelains ordered according to Dutch and French taste,[2] and in England, the Dutch might readily sell wares made for them.[3] Along with a closeup view of china entering the North American colonies, the national and international aspects of the trade in china are an integral part of this chapter, beginning first with the English, then moving to the Dutch and French, and finally, to the Spanish in California (fig. 166).

In the same way that China distinguished coarse

and fine porcelain in any era, the English generally separated their imports into the commoner pieces sold in large lots through the English East India Company and better objects bought in small quantity for private trade.[4] Also, private trade both preceded and succeeded the East India Company's porcelain buying. From the suppliers of the first London porcelain shop, opened in 1609,[5] to the china importers of the nineteenth century,[6] all were private traders. Later, officers of the East India Company were allowed to engage in their own limited thus "private" trade. Not until the nineteenth century did they sail in ships other than the company's Indiamen. (Warehouse auctions of large lots of everyday ware might include privately traded pieces, but most of the latter were ordered in advance for known individuals as commissioned purchases or as gifts.) Most of the best English colonial china surviving today was private-trade not company-bought porcelains, according to types listed in extant company records. This natural treasuring of choicer pieces explains why some of the more ordinary objects, such as mustard pots and porringers, listed in gross amounts in late-seventeenth and early-eighteenth-century shipping records (and appearing in colonial inventories) are now so rare. (To balance this view, archaeology is recovering shards of everyday wares with each excavation; see appendix D.)

Though the East India Company had been chartered in 1600 and had established posts in India and the Indonesian archipelago, its activities had been small compared to the Dutch. Also, the English Civil War and interregnum froze funds and trade, but by the late-seventeenth century, the company again attracted capital, and London slowly began to rival Amsterdam as an entry point of Eastern goods. By 1709, this strength was confirmed in the merging of two competitors in the trade, the Old and New East India companies, as the United Company.[7]

Well before that, however, the importation of china by private or company means had had a variable but important history in the late-seventeenth century. According to remaining records, the porcelains entering England in 1669 were worth a mere £10, but rose to a value of £2,746 in 1685, then to another high of £6,275 in 1693, to reach £13,067 in 1697, and £15,282 two years later. For three years—1694, 1696, and 1700—no china was recorded, no doubt reflecting market gluts brought about by the years of large purchase. The peak year, 1704, indicated a value of £20,815, the highest for the whole first half of the century.[8] This uneven supply occurred during an initial trial period when the percentage of porcelain to total

165. *Dish*, c. 1710–20, D 38.7 cm. Arms of Magellan, now Mechlin. *Figurine*, probably a French courtier, c. 1700–15, H 22.2 cm. *Mug*, c. 1720, H 12.6 cm. Arms of Penn. *Teapot*, c. 1735, H 11.4 cm. Arms of Hanbury with Comyn in pretence. Fine export. Courtesy of Dr. Wesley Gallup.

166. *Cup and saucer* (left), c. 1730–40, cup: D 6.3 cm, saucer: D 10.5 cm. Mark on base: VOC. *Dish* (center), c. 1740, D 22.9 cm. Dutch ships at Capetown, Table Bay, South Africa. *Cups* (right), c. 1750–70, D 5.4 cm. British ships. Dish: superior; cups and saucer: above-average export. Private collection.

imports might reach as high as 20 percent. After 1712, when demand determined purchase, its proportion did not exceed 2 percent.[9] A minor place in cargoes from the East, however, belies the great influence export porcelain had upon European taste and the ceramic industries of Portugal, Spain, Mexico, England, Holland, France, and Germany. The growth of their production was one of the key reasons for the eventual decline in demand for Chinese wares in the nineteenth century.

COLLECTORS ON THE EAST COAST

In this era of experiment before regular shipments began, some reexport of china to America took place, and scattered references indicate that a few more porcelains reached North American households than before. The Dutch-English connection between Amsterdam, London, and New York, piracy, smuggling, the taking of prizes, and the sophisticated demand of New Yorkers all continued to play a part in the first two decades of the eighteenth century in keeping New York ahead of all others. Though no porcelains are listed among items passing customs from 1701 to 1709,[10] the inventories of leading citizens during this period show that they had access to china by private purchase or irregular means. In 1700, Cornelius Jacobs's estate listed a china lacquered bowl and twelve new plates in a parcel of china and earthenware of the same period as the plate in figure 167. Two years later, Abraham DeLanoy's goods included 120 dishes, cups

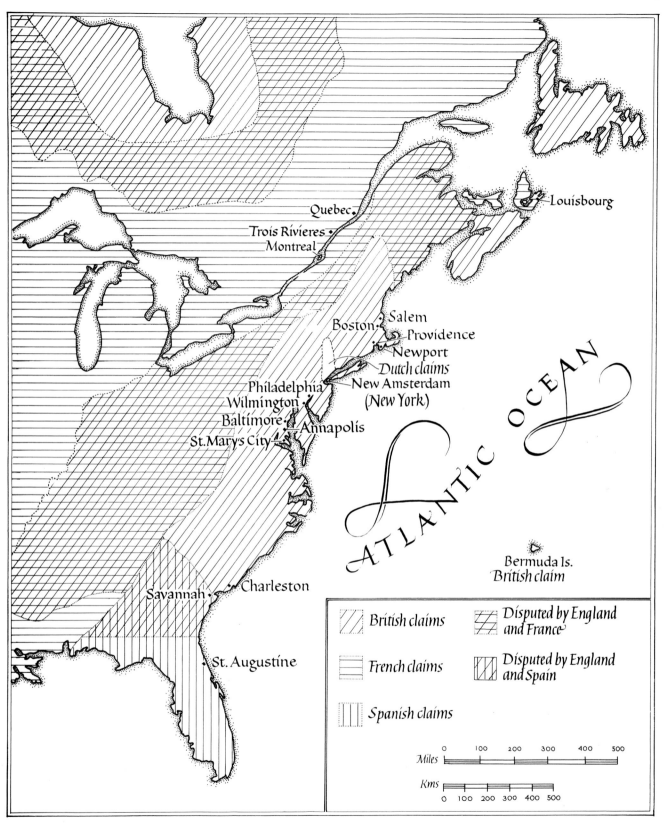

MAP 3. English and European colonial claims on the east coast.

Quebec.
Trois Rivières .
Montreal

Louisbourg

Salem
Boston .
Providence
Newport
Dutch claims
New Amsterdam
(*New York*)

Philadelphia .
Wilmington .
Baltimore .
St.Mary's City .
Annapolis

ATLANTIC OCEAN

Bermuda Is.
British claim

Savannah .
Charleston

St. Augustine

British claims

French claims

Spanish claims

Disputed by England
and France

Disputed by England
and Spain

Miles
0   100   200   300   400   500

Kms
0   100   200   300   400   500

167. *Plate*, c. 1690–1710, D 35.3 cm. Mark: underglaze blue Kangxi *nianbao*. Underglaze blue and copper-red, fine domestic/export. Private collection.

168. *Coffee/chocolate pot*, c. 1690–1720, H 29.2 cm. Underglaze blue, nineteenth-century Dutch silver mounts, fine export, now rare. Courtesy of the Newark Museum.

and saucers, making him a collector comparable to Jacob De Lange in 1685. In 1705, Col. William Smith's china was valued at £5; and four years later, Joseph Bueno was reported to own seven china cups, twelve cups and saucers, and five ''images in glasses.'' In the next decade, in 1718, Capt. Giles Shelly's china included twelve images, six lions, three basins, a sugar box and a red teapot (either of Ixhing ware, known to have been owned in Salem in the early-eighteenth century, or Staffordshire red stoneware, in imitation of Ixhing ware, first made in the late-seventeenth century then again in the 1740s). In 1729, William Burnet (1688–1729), governor of New York until 1728, then for a year governor of Massachusetts, left an estate with over three hundred pieces of china worth over

£130. The coffee/chocolate pot in figure 168 might well have been the sort Burnet owned. His successor as governor of New York, John Montgomerie (d. 1731), owned a set of china appraised at £75.[11] Contemporaries had porcelains equaling his (see fig. 169). Figure 170 is of a soup dish once associated with Jacob Leisler, in New Amsterdam from 1660 until his death in 1691, but the form and decoration postdate Leisler.

These generous listings contrast, sometimes sharply, with other colonists' chinaware in the North or South. In Boston, in 1718, Isaac Caillowell's pieces, unlike Shelley's, were all utilitarian: five dishes, a dozen plates, two mugs, two slop bowls, a teapot, four cups, six saucers, and a spoon dish. In this

169. *Tea service* (partial), c. 1730–35. Teapot: H 11.1 cm. Overglaze penciled and gilt, owned by Hendrik and Catharine de Peyster Rutgers (m. 1732); superior export. Ex. coll., Waldron Phoenix Belknap, Jr. Courtesy of the Museum of the City of New York.

early period, Elizur Holyoke also had an unitemized amount of porcelain.[12] In Annapolis, of fourteen inventories of 1665–1700, only one, for Henry Constable, a planter, shows "two china board bowls," indicating where they were displayed or most commonly used. In the first decades of the eighteenth century, as elsewhere in the English colonies, more Annapolis families enjoyed china. The owners were predictable: marine or military captains, tobacco planters, or professionals, including ministers. However, humbler colonists, such as the tailor Matthew Beard, with an estate worth £47, might have a piece or two of china along with earthenware, and that quite early, about 1700–1709. The cup and saucer in figure 171 would have been the sort Beard might have owned.[13] By the 1720s, imports from the previous ten years meant that many more citizens of Annapolis recorded china in

170. *Plate*, c. 1710–25, D 22.2 cm. Underglaze blue with gilt, fine export. Courtesy of the Museum of the City of New York.

171. *Cup and saucer*, c. 1730–35, cup: D 6.4 cm, saucer: D 10.5 cm. Underglaze blue; in 1740, owned by David and Mary Lefevre Deshler (m. 1739); average domestic/export. Courtesy of Mr. and Mrs. Lewis Rumford II.

172. *Cups and saucers* (pair), c. 1740–45, cup: D 8.3 cm, saucer: D 12.7 cm. Chinese "Imari," called "caudle cups." Above-average export. Courtesy of Mr. and Mrs. Lewis Rumford II.

their estates, and the number increased in the next few decades (fig. 172).[14] After New York, Annapolis may have been in a class of its own: a rich tobacco economy with direct sailings to and from London supported a sophisticated city quickly adapting to the latest fashions from England (figs. 173 and 174).

St. Mary's City, the colonial capital of Maryland until 1694, where archaeologists have extensively probed key sites, contrasts with Annapolis. Digs of the first house of John Hicks, a sea captain, sheriff, and judge, have uncovered twenty-one shards of tea porcelains and a large number of other ceramics, dating from about 1741. However, these fragments are atypical. Another citizen of St. Mary's, William Deacon, was the only other person in the 1740s known to have owned a quantity of ceramics, including a dinner service for twenty, according to his inventory.[15] Not surprisingly, in the early-eighteenth century, porcelain ownership was more common nearer the coast, in commercial ports such as Annapolis.

The hard data on Annapolis in the late-seventeenth and early-eighteenth centuries indicates that more porcelain was in Virginia than is presently known from available inventories. Though East India goods are mentioned occasionally in estate lists (silk dresses and sashes, ivory combs, callicoes, spices, and so on), no references to china per se occur in the seventeenth century (see chapter 3). Appraisers may commonly have lumped all ceramics under the term *earthenware*. Thus in James Whaley's York County house in 1701, his "parcel of earthenware" that decorated the mantelpieces in his hall and chamber may have included porcelains.[16] In the next year the York County records clearly distinguish such ware, listing a single "Jappan Mugg" (which may signify either Japanese or Chinese) belonging to Capt. Charles Hansford.[17] Of course, popular porcelain forms such as flowerpots (of which one was recorded in 1703/04) were possibly china, as may have been coffee cups (1709); butter basins, butter plates, and porringers (1711); tea cups and fruit dishes (1712); mugs and cans (1713); cruets (1714); punch bowls and an oil jug (1716).

Only after the early-eighteenth century would porcelain be properly denoted, and even then, only occasionally. The first such reference in the York County records appears in 1717–18.

Along with a japanned chest of drawers and a tea table with furniture, John Marrott had glasses and china cups worth £0.07.06. This seems a pittance compared with his fellow colonists to the north, especially for a wealthy man whose estate was valued at £904.11.1 (fig. 175).[18]

173. *Spittoon*, c. 1720–25, H 7.0 cm. Underglaze blue, tobacco harvest and consumption; based on dated Delft model, 1721; above-average export, now rare. Courtesy Ottema-Kingma Foundation, Princessehof Museum.

174. Bird's-eye view of rim in fig. 173.

183. *Plate*, c. 1725–40, D 23.4 cm. Underglaze blue, overglaze red and gilt touches, fine export. Ex. coll. G. R. Curwen. Courtesy of the Essex Institute.

first small Alley on the Long Wharf, Boston."[27] And the next year, William Welsteed, a Boston merchant, offered a large number of plates and "pickle caucers [*sic*]"[28] (fig. 183).

An ever-growing commercial supply of porcelain supplemented the private orders now that the East India Company was past its experimental stage. Even though Mrs. Hannah Wilson and John Buining advertised supplies of china in 1730, it is likely that the wares in John Jekyll's Boston estate, inventoried in 1732, represent a private purchase. They are too fine for the normally commonplace shop or warehouse china. Jekyll owned "2 Burnt China Bowls worth £2, 6 Chocolate Bowls £2, 1 Pr China Candlesticks Tipt with Silver £4, 12 Coffe cups with handles £1 7s." "Burnt china" probably refers to gilded ware and was the top of the line. Jekyll's candlesticks are especially noteworthy, being even more valuable than his burnt bowls. He also had a set of burnt china (fig. 184) at a time when sets of china were unusual. Jekyll's ownership of one suggests that they began to be available sometime in the 1720s.[29] Jekyll's uncle, Sir Joseph Jekyll, had his arms painted on a porcelain service made about 1720.[30]

Evidence from larger consignments of porcelain, available from the late 1730s, further suggests that the first sets were for tea, though at this time, dinner services were also available. In September 1737, on Scarlett's Wharf, the following were on sale: "A Parcel of fine large Enamel'd Dishes. Ditto of divers Sizes of Bowles burnt & Enamel'd. Ditto of all sorts of Plates. Sundry Complete Setts of Furniture for the Tea Table. Blue & White Bowles; Blue & White Cups & Sawcers. Several sorts of small Baskets, etc."[31] (fig. 185).

By 1732, Charleston, South Carolina, was the

184. *Coffee and tea cups, saucer*, c. 1720–40, coffee cup with handle: D 6.0 cm, saucer: D 12 cm, cup: D 7.5 cm. Incised underglaze "artichoke" or "lotus" leaf pattern, part of a full tea service, fine domestic/export. Courtesy of Norman Herreshoff.

fourth largest town on the Atlantic seaboard.[32] From the earliest Board of Trade quarterly reports in 1716, ships carrying "European goods," including china, are recorded entering Charleston. In the first six months of 1717, twenty-four ships with such cargoes arrived[33] from London, Plymouth, Liverpool, Bristol, Philadelphia, and Boston. Charleston therefore had the same sorts of wares as did Boston, but in smaller quantities. (Boston's population in 1720 was twelve thousand to Charleston's thirty-five hundred.)[34]

By the 1730s, newspapers refer to the china as a familiar staple. In fact, in 1735, there were twelve notices in *The South Carolina Gazette* similar to one that appeared in 1732: "To be sold by Yeomans and Company" along with ironware, guns, powder, "indian trading glasses," haberdashery, tea, textiles, and groceries—"setts of china ware."[35] Throughout the 1730s, such phrases as "a choice parcel of china ware," "china ware of all sorts," "a great choice of China-Ware cheaper than usual," and even "fine China Wares, viz. Plates, Bowls, and Tea cups and

185. *Platter*, c. 1725–40, D 31.1 cm. Overglaze enamels, above-average export. Private collection.

186. *Cups and saucers*, c. 1730–40, left: cup: D 6.6 cm; center: cup: D 6.4 cm; right: cup: D 6.3 cm. Center set: older Chinese "Imari," other two: newer gold-red; fine stock-pattern export. Courtesy of Mr. and Mrs. Lewis Rumford II.

187. *Shards* (reconstructed): slop bowl, two coffee cups, one teacup, one plate, c. 1720–40. Overglaze enamels and gilt, from the Heyward–Washington House, Charleston, S.C., fine export. Courtesy of the Charleston Museum.

188. *Bowl* (reconstructed), c. 1740–60. Underglaze blue, from the Heyward–Washington House, Charleston, S.C., above-average export. Courtesy of the Charleston Museum.

sawcers, and nice Pint Basons'' tempted buyers (fig. 186). Many notices refer to the wares as recently imported from London, but others not so advertised may have come from other colonial ports. Trade statistics for Charleston in 1735 showed the following ten towns in order of frequency as points of origin for entering ships: New Providence (twenty-eight ships),

Philadelphia (twenty-two), Boston (nineteen), Barbados (seventeen), London (fifteen), Jamaica (fourteen), Cadiz (fourteen), St. Augustine (twelve), Africa (eleven), and Bristol (ten).[36] Though one-third the size of Boston, Charleston seems to have had the same sort of cosmopolitan contact by sea as her larger northern sister, and doubtless identical porcelains.

A major setback to Charleston's shops and private collections occurred on 18 November 1740 when an extensive fire burned down three hundred houses in addition to wharves, stables, and storehouses in the oldest part of town, costing in merchandise alone over £200,000.[37] Spunky citizens immediately recovered, as a note in the *Gazette* one month later indicates: "James Reid being burnt out of his House in Elliot-street keeps now his store at Mrs. Le Brasseu's large House opposite to the French Church and has the following goods just imported by the Concord, James Young Master from London, landed since the fire, viz. silver coffee pots . . . " and an extensive list of English and Far Eastern wares including china.[38] By

1749, more fulsome lists lured readers: "to be sold by David Crawford in Broad-street, a large assortment of China Ware, as breakfast cups and saucers, dishes, plates and bowls of all sorts, tea and coffee cups and saucers, also 3 compleat sets of colour'd china for a tea-table" (fig. 187).[39] And in another notice of John McCall's, those who had been waiting for punch bowls and white or brown teapots as well as the usual porcelain dishes, plates, cups and saucers could get down to Tradd Street and enjoy the cargo of the ship *Appollo* recently in from London (fig. 188).[40] Proportionately, Charleston was keeping up with any city north of her.

Because Providence sent the most ships of any entering at Charleston in 1735, that northern port's ownership of porcelain provides a rough guide to its buyers in the southern city. A study of Providence inventories of 1750–1800 by Barbara Gorely Teller covers a later period, but it gives a gauge for comparison. Teller found that Providence porcelain owners spanned the low-to-high income groups. "Complete tea sets" were owned by members of both groups, while "large parcels" of porcelain were found only among the wealthiest. Predictably, as in Mexico, merchants led all others in quantity and worth; sea captains, gentlemen, mariners, and widows following them in order. Teller also describes the room-by-room appearances of porcelain in Providence. Her samplings doubtless reflect practices up and down the coast among English colonists, with slight variations. In Providence halls or parlors, "closets" or "beaufatts" might display china. (In the south, the hunt or sideboard in such rooms would be a commoner place for this use, as in Henry Constable's Annapolis inventory, noted earlier.) In Rhode Island, porcelains might also be exhibited in first-floor bedrooms, used for entertaining in the eighteenth century. Even in upstairs bedrooms friends as well as family gathered for tea, where tables were set with services for both decoration and easy use. (The inventory studies of Abbott

Lowell Cummings in rural Massachusetts (1675–1775) and Alice Hanson Jones in Philadelphia (1774) support Teller's room-use findings.)[41]

There is one important exception to taking Teller's data as normative in Providence or elsewhere for the early-eighteenth century: lower-income people in the 1700–1750 period rarely owned porcelains, according to inventories. With this one proviso, her profile for Providence probably applies safely to all the English colonies on the East Coast from the first days of bulk importation on. As mid-century arrived, all income groups owned the ware—the merchants having the most and the best, though of every quality.

Inventories and newspapers together show that the entire range of china that the English were importing was being reexported to her colonies in the first half of the eighteenth century, some of the highest quality (fig. 189). How much was sent? Only a rough estimate is possible. Demand as well as size and number of ships per year determined supply. Demand depended upon population. By 1755, Pennsylvania led the other colonies with 250,000 inhabitants, followed by Massachusetts Bay with 220,000; New York and Connecticut each with 100,000; Maryland and Virginia, each 85,000; North Carolina, 45,000; Rhode Island, 35,000; New Hampshire and South Carolina, each 30,000; Georgia, 6,000; and Nova Scotia, 5,000.[42] Probably 10 percent, or 105,100 people could buy fine china; added to the additional 20 percent who could afford coarser ware, 210,220, the total made about 315,320 buyers of fine and coarse china—a considerable number for the day (fig. 190).

The second factor, size and number of ships per year, can be answered only in part, excluding smuggled goods. While most of the East Indiamen of the British Company in the heyday of their trade averaged 400–450 tons, the American-built ships, normally the carriers of East India goods to the colonies, weighed only about 70–100 tons. Later and until the American Revolution, larger brigantines and snows (like brigs

189. *Plates*, c. 1725–35, left: D 31.8 cm, right: D 22.0 cm. Overglaze enamels, owned by Miss Susan Ingersoll of Salem, superior domestic/export. Ex. coll. George R. Curwen. Courtesy of the Essex Institute.

190. *Sauceboat with stand*, c.1745–65, boat: L 21.6 cm, stand: L 18.4 cm. Underglaze blue, from a dinner service owned by the Ropes family of Salem, common pattern, above-average export. Courtesy of the Essex Institute.

but with supplementary "snow" rigging on a trysail mast close behind the mainmast) of 100–300 tons imported the wares.[43] Perhaps twenty sailings per year with such goods were made to each of the major ports, according to the Board of Trade quarterly records. Given the weight of the china and the size of the average ship, it would seem that over 300,000 buyers were in short supply, if not at one port then at another, a factor that each city counted upon. That may

have been one reason that English and European ceramics, especially Delft, found ready sales here; their cheaper price may have been another. It certainly meant that the choicer pieces of porcelain would be coveted by the colonists, even more so than they were in England.

Porcelains' appeal, for its fineness and novelty, held firm despite the duties gradually placed by the British—to protect their nascent home ceramics industry—upon china entering English ports. In 1704, the duty (which was then solely for revenue) was 12.5 percent, imposed on Japanese and Chinese porcelains alike. By the early 1790s, when large-scale English commercial production was well underway, it had reached almost 50 percent, and in 1799, a new act increased the rate to over 100 percent.[44] But when the East India Company reexported the porcelains, they received a "drawback," the return of duties paid. It is possible, then, that for importers, reexport of surplus supplies was an increasingly attractive alternative.

In America in the early 1750s, taxes on tea, coffee, and East India ware began.[45] Despite this onerous excise, which led to the Boston Tea Party in 1773 and finally to the Revolution two years later, chinaware continued to be imported, though in lesser quantities until the break with England. For example, in Boston in 1772, despite the recent opening of a Staffordshire and Liverpool Warehouse in King Street, so named for the ceramics in which it dealt, Samuel Gray "At the Three Sugar Loaves in Cornhill," offered "A neat Assortment of India China Ware of many forms and sizes *much cheaper than they are usually sold*," except for cups and saucers, no doubt to compete with the English wares.[46]

In the years just before the Boston Tea Party, two opposite trends affected porcelain supplies and distribution in Massachusetts Bay. One was the expectation of conflict by Loyalists to the crown, who, preparing to leave the colony, sold their estates. Those goods often included china.[47] Related to this gradual exodus was the increase, by 1773, of appeals from Boston merchants to "Country Traders" and "Town Shopkeepers." The latter might be more willing to "entertain" the factors of the East India Company and buy their goods, being less fired with patriotic zeal than were the Bostonians.

Independence-minded colonists were beginning to advocate a "buy American" plan.[48] In 1771, there had been thirty-three advertisements for East India china; there were only twenty-eight the next year, and by 1773, nineteen. In 1772, American-made fabrics were featured by one merchant, who nonetheless was hedging his bets; his goods also included imported English wares.[49] Thus estate sales and loyalty to British interests outside of Boston meant a dispersal of porcelain to both those who were planning to remain in the colonies and those in provincial areas, even though the total amount of imported china was declining in this half decade before the Revolution (fig. 191).

Of course, the boycott of tea—dubbed "The Badge

191. *Teapot, cup, and saucer*, c. 1750–75, pot: W 24 cm. Overglaze enamels, fine export. Gift of Miss Eleanor Hassam. Courtesy of the Essex Institute.

of Slavery" and called a "noxious" or "poisonous Herb" and "that pernicious Weed"—as well as of china imported from England was not restricted to New England. In Philadelphia in 1774, the following poem appeared:

A Lady's Adieu to her Tea Table

Farewel [sic] the Tea Board, with its gaudy Equipage,
Of Cups and Saucers, Cream Bucket, Sugar Tongs,
The pretty Tea Chest also, lately stor'd
With Hyson, Congo, and best Double Find.
Full many a joyous Moment have I sat by ye,
Hearing the Girls tattle, the Old Maids talk scandel,
And the spruce Coxcomb laugh at—maybe—Nothing.
No more shall I dish out the once lov'd Liquor,
Though now detestable,
Because I'm taught (and I believe it true)
Its use will fasten slavish chains upon my Country,
And LIBERTY's the Godess [sic] I would choose
To reign triumphant in AMERICA.[50]

THE DUTCH AND FRENCH TRADERS

Though Holland had nearly monopolized the trade in china to northern Europe and the colonies in the seventeenth century, the Dutch East India Company did not import china to the Netherlands in the period 1700–1730, though private traders were quite free to do so.[51] What arrived included large amounts of Japanese wares, because the Dutch had exclusive trading privileges with Japan. They brought Japanese wares to Guangzhou, Amoy, Ningpo, Patani, Tongking, and Batavia. (A recent study indicates the quantity of porcelain exported from Nagasaki in this period was more than previously thought.)[52] It is probable, then, that at least some of the Japanese ware coming to England and the colonies was brought by the Dutch. Records also show that the English were supplying the Dutch with Chinese porcelain and other Chinese goods in the first three decades of the eighteenth century. Thus the two markets—as opposed to the two companies—remained as intimate and interconnected as they had in the previous century. Not until 1729 did the Dutch East India Company gain direct trading privileges with the Chinese at Guangzhou, alongside the English, continuing until 1795. It may be assumed that whenever they had surpluses at home, they sold it to the English, not unlike the American coastal exchange.

Of porcelain importers to America, the Dutch and English rightly receive the most attention, but the French also supplied their own colonies. By the 1670s, their explorers were claiming land for Nouvelle France via the St. Lawrence River, through the Great Lakes, and down the Mississippi, opening up the northern and midwest areas of the continent and eventually the territory of Louisiane. By the 1750s there was considerable activity and some settlement.

Strings of forts had been established along major waterways; the western fur trade was in French hands; and even grain and tobacco from the Illinois River country were being collected for trade north and south. In the 1720s, the lead mines of Missouri were being worked by 700 men. From Louisbourg in the northern part of Nova Scotia to New Orleans, the military, missionaries, and explorers established their own European outpost in the New World.[53] These Frenchmen were distinct from French immigrants to East Coast cities who had arrived beginning in the mid-seventeenth century and became native in an English environment. The name of Faneuil in Boston symbolizes them all (fig. 192). Benjamin and Andrew Faneuil were French Huguenots, who first came to Westchester County in 1690, founding New Rochelle.

In 1701, the year after Benjamin's son Peter was born, the family moved to Boston and prospered in business.

What porcelains might immigrants to the French territories as opposed to English cities have brought with them or ordered? In 1755, there were an estimated 45,000 French in Canada and 7,000 in Louisiana, excluding the military and blacks.[54] The French Compagnie des Indes would have been their chief porcelain source. Like the British East India Company, it had been several companies in the seventeenth century and combined in 1719. Regular shipments of wares, however, did not begin before 1722. That was well after two notable voyages in 1700 and 1703 of the ship *Amphitrite*, which pioneered as the first native vessel to bring back a quantity of porcelains, some of them quite fine, for sales at home.[55] When commercial shipments began, the cargoes were unloaded at Brest, Port-Louis, or Lorient, and sold in the markets of Nantes, Paris, Lyons, Tours, Bordeaux, Rennes, Orleans, La Rochelle, and Saint-Malo. Even though the Compagnie's activities came to an end in 1770 and revived in 1785 only to close again in 1790, private French trade continued.[56] The French thus had their own supply throughout the eighteenth century, though it was much less than the Dutch and English. According to a rough estimate of the total shipping of the East India Companies from the sixteenth to the nineteenth centuries, France had only 16 percent of the number of English or American sailings.[57]

In the New World, archaeology has uncovered a rare sprinkling of seventeenth-century porcelains associated with the French, but not surprisingly, most of the pieces date to within a forty-year period, 1720–60, before the British began carving away at Nouvelle France, eventually to claim it in 1761. Some of the porcelain occasionally came directly from China to North America in ships of the Compagnie, which had offices in Montreal, Quebec City, Trois Rivières, and

192. *Plate*, c. 1720–30, D 28.6 cm. Underglaze blue, associated with Benjamin Faneuil, fine domestic/export. Gift of Mrs. Richard W. Hall. Courtesy of the Society for the Preservation of New England Antiquities.

Louisbourg.[58] There was a brief hiatus during the Seven Years' War, yet in French sites of the period, a sizable amount of export has been found of a wide range in quality, from reasonably fine to rough.[59] A limited written record in archaic French supplements the shard finds and corrects an impression given by archaeology alone.

Three sites are worth a closer look. The first, the fortress of Louisbourg in Cape Breton, Nova Scotia, was occupied by the French and British in alternating periods: French, 1713–45; British, 1745–49; French again, 1749–58; and finally British, 1748–68.[60] The site is unusual in that it was virtually undisturbed for two centuries; a small amount of porcelain in comparison to other ceramics was found; and the whole is still to be completely studied. However, the find represents a wide variety, most of it between the years 1730 and 1768, thus spanning all four periods. Blue-and-white typical of the 1730s and 1740s predominates, including "Swatow" ware and some with Islamic motifs. Of the polychromes, Chinese "Imari," iron-red, gold-red, green or celadon, and brown ("Batavian") ware were deposited. Exceptions to this standard china are a few possible pieces that may be Kangxi, one gray and gilt piece, and another of celadon with blue-and-white in reserve.[61]

193. *Goblet*, c. 1700–25, H 13.4 cm. Underglaze blue, above-average export. Courtesy of the trustees of the British Museum.

Alongside the inventory information available for the earlier French period, however, the archaeological evidence tells an incomplete story. In 1740, the goods of an engineer, Jean-Baptiste Decouagne, worth 950 livres, included two goblets of porcelain (fig. 193) and a fruit dish, mustard dish, and a pepperbox that may have been china as well. (The French are said to have introduced the custom of serving fruit in porcelain, no doubt to preserve its flavor.[62]) Four years later, the wealthiest estate on record, worth 22,610 livres, of the acting governor of Cape Breton, Commandant Duquesnal, lists an enormous amount of porcelain. Seventy-five percent was blue-and-white, and the remainder was gilt. All was varied in form: coffee and tea services, butter dishes, salad bowls, and a collection of 348 china plates (fig. 194 and 195). No doubt this variety is not represented by the archaeology because the French probably took their most valuable ceramics home in 1745 and 1758.[63] They clearly indicate, however, that among the upper and upper-middle classes at Louisbourg were some of the best wares available to the French for the period.

At Fort Ligonier, Pennsylvania, built in 1758, 582 pieces of porcelain have been found. Strategic in the French and Indian War, the fort has yielded fragments of cups, saucers, and large bowls, chiefly blue-and-white but also in red and gilt. A few pieces have a brown rim, similar to those found on the upper Hudson of the same period (fig. 196).[64] Contemporary with the shards found at Fort Ligonier is the porcelain found in the 1760 shipwreck of the *Le Michault* on Chaleur Bay, south of the Gaspé Peninsula on the Gulf of St. Lawrence. The ship was scuttled to prevent capture by the British, and the entire cargo of china was preserved, broken or whole. Dating from a decade before, its 1,480 pieces of open-stock china include: 640 bowls, 344 saucers, 200 handleless teacups, 148 plates and soup plates, 119 coffee cups, 7 pitchers, and 6 teapots. Sixty percent of these porcelains are underglaze blue, and the remaining 40 percent are divided be-

194. *Plate*, c. 1730–50, D 22.9 cm. Underglaze blue, common export. Courtesy of Dr. Wesley Gallup.

195. *Saucer dish*, c. 1740–60, D 13.9 cm. Overglaze enamels, fine export. Courtesy of Dr. Wesley Gallup.

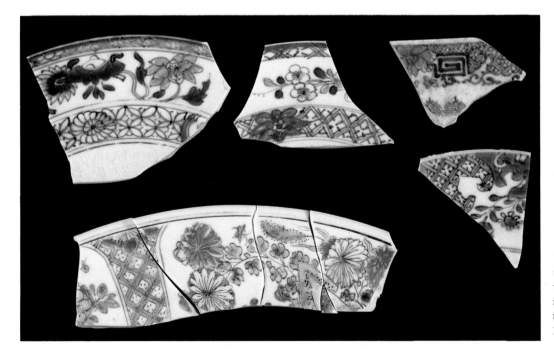

196. *Shards*, contemporary with those from Ft. Ligonier, Pennsylvania, c. 1725–75, from Clermont, home of the Livingstons on the Hudson River. Courtesy of Dennis L. Wentworth.

197. *Cup and bowl* (reconstructed) from ship *Le Machault* (1760), c. 1755–59, cup: D 11.0 cm, bowl: D 26.5 cm. Underglaze blue, above-average domestic/export. Courtesy of Parks Canada.

198. *Plates, pot, and coffee cup* from *Le Machault* (1760), c. 1755–59. Underglaze blue, common export. Courtesy of Parks Canada.

tween Chinese "Imari," iron-red, gold-red, and gilt ware. As with other shipwreck porcelains, the overglaze enamels and gilt suffered underwater making the designs faint on the surviving shards (fig. 197–199).[65]

Another part-French, part-British settlement but different in scope from Louisbourg was Fort Michilimackinac, in what is now the northern tip of Michigan overlooking the Straits of Mackinac. Built in 1715 on the frontier 450 miles from Montreal, the fort became a major fur-trading center and military outpost. Along

with traders, soldiers, and priests were 150 farmer-artisans, English fur traders, and shopkeepers. Before the 1760s the English influence was present, in middle-class merchants such as John Askin and Ezekial Solomon. Like the French officers, they brought sophisticated tastes to this wilderness, accounting for some of the five thousand shards of porcelain, some fine ware, found on the site. Most of it, however, is dated to 1760–80, the years of British occupation.[66]

In Canada under British rule, the same sorts of por-

199. *Coffee and tea cups with saucers* from *Le Machault* (1760), c. 1755–59, coffee cup (handled): D 7.5 cm. Extra plate, cup and saucer similar to shards from the ship. All average to above-average export. Gold-red landscape plate, private collection. Gilt floral cup and saucer, courtesy of Parks Canada.

200. *Urn* (one of a pair), c. 1795–1800, H 38.1 cm. Overglaze enamels, sepia medallion with profiles of Louis XVI and Marie Antoinette at urn base. Gift of the Lansing family. Courtesy of the Albany Institute of History and Art.

celains as were found at Michilimackinac would have been imported on the Atlantic coast. French descendants, intermarried with the English or not, would have bought the British product by force of supply from England. In Montreal, a good case in point is a late-eighteenth-century set of urns (fig. 200). In their oval medallions are hidden profiles of Louis XVI (1754–93) and Marie Antoinette (1755–93), thus the design is French inspired. They are not unique,[67] however, and were probably imported by the British, or possibly the Americans. Their original owner was a native of Montreal, Charlotte La Saussaye (b. 1740), daughter of Philippe Dagneau Donville de La Saussaye and Madelein Raimbault. The Dagneaus had once been part of the French royal circle. Charlotte La Saussaye married General Moses Hazen in Montreal in 1770, well before these urns, which postdate the French king and queen, were made. They are an echo of the royalist loyalties remaining among the French in their now-English territory.[68]

MEXICANS AND YANKEES IN THE WEST

Meanwhile on the West Coast, by the last quarter of the eighteenth century, the Spanish had at last penetrated California, having already been established in what is now Arizona, Texas, and New Mexico for over 150 years. In California, the Spanish established missions, presidios, and, by the nineteenth century, ranchos in four presidial districts: San Francisco, Monterey, Santa Barbara, and San Diego, with ports of the same names. Though the Manila galleons were required by law to stop at Monterey en route to Mexico to take on food and water after the long transpacific run, many ships did not: the promise of high profit in Mexico was worth the fine imposed. Trade in Monterey with the missions or any private person was strictly forbidden. In this atmosphere, some smuggling took place, but probably a small amount in comparison to a later period when high duties made the risk worth it.[69] Normally, goods from the Far East would have come a circuitous route from Acapulco to Mexico City to Guadalajara, to San Blas, a port established by the Mexican navy to supply Alta California in the years 1768–98.[70] But scattered documents show some Chinese wares were shipped directly to San Blas from the Philippines.

Two transports annually from San Blas brought iron and manufactured goods, including some luxuries. One went to San Francisco and Monterey; the other to Santa Barbara and San Diego, which was the first port to be settled in 1769, receiving a supply ship the following year. An inventory of objects at the San Diego Presidio for 1777 and 1778 indicates that the small garrison there had a minimum of tableware: only three dozen plates of Pueblaware, eighteen pewter plates, four metal drinking cups, and two each of large and small candlesticks and iron frying pans.[71] The community also had ten *pozuelos*, oil jars meant to be sunk into the ground, six from Puebla and four from China.[72]

While *memorias* (lists of supplies) of the 1780s show other China goods, especially silk, coming to San Diego,[73] the first possible chinaware arrived in 1795 in the name of the commandante: an assortment of plates, cups, and *pozuelos*, twenty-five to the case.[74] Of course, the wares could have been from Puebla, but the Presidio's porcelain fragments of over a thousand pieces unearthed today demand an explanation. Of these 1,197 Chinese shards,[75] not surprisingly most are blue-and-white. The earliest is represented by a notched, octagonal plate with a typical landscape of pavilions, people, prunus trees, and sampans; a honeycomb diaper inner border; and a complex, wide outer border of the 1750–75 period. Most of the blue-and-white, especially the "Canton" ware and other enameled or enameled-and-gilt wares are of a period after 1790. By this time, the Presidio had about three hundred personnel plus dependents[76] and was ready to order stock-in-trade porcelains in a little quantity. One fragment of exceptional quality is a plate decorated with large Chinese figures that cover the base and extend up the cavetto to a border of small sepia vistas in reserve and a tight, red scroll border, similar to the dish in figure 201. It predates "Rose Mandarin" ware and is earlier, as a style, than the first china that could have come to the Presidio in 1770. Figures 202 and 203 are two such plates; the border of 203 is a particular favorite of the Spanish.[77]

In the Old Town Excavation, San Diego, in areas where there were houses and a hotel, six whole pieces and ninety-five fragments of china have been found, most from the 1785–1830 period.[78] The San Diego Mission, the first in California, also has a number of Chinese shards from the early days, but not as many as have been found at or near the Carmel Mission (San Carlos Borromeo de Carmelo), the second mission to be established; it moved from Monterey to Carmel in 1771, a year after its founding. This initial contact with Monterey, where some Manila galleons stopped for supplies, helps explain why a few porcelains date from this period, although others are later. The

201. *Dish*, c. 1750–75, D 12.0 cm. Overglaze enamels, fine export. Courtesy of the Peabody Museum.

202. *Plate*, c. 1740–60, D 28.0 cm. Overglaze enamels, rare shell lattice cornucopia border, first-class export. Courtesy of the Peabody Museum.

shards, collected by Harry Downie, curator of the mission until his death in 1980, are uncounted but are on display in a glass cylinder divided according to ceramic type (Mexican and European are also represented). Two or three whole pieces survive, most notably a blue-and-white plate of the mid-to-late-eighteenth century and a pair of early-nineteenth-century vases with scalloped lips, painted in gold-red and other polychrome enamels. These last, with Chinese silk hangings, decorate one of the altars. (Silks were often used for vestments as well as hangings, and many Chinese examples are on display in Carmel and other missions.) Chinese chairs and a huge, chest-height Chinese metal locker at the Carmel Mission are

substantial reminders of the China trade during the Spanish era.

Of the other missions, twenty-one in all, La Purisima Concepción had blue-and-white shards, excavated in 1963. They are something of a mystery: they had broken yet apparently not when buried. Perhaps they were discovered and vandalized; one tureen's finial was neatly sliced out.

The La Concepción history explains their presence. Under the leadership of Father Mariano Payeras, one of the ablest Franciscans, the missionary stocked a store with "china, sugar, fine cloths, and other commodities" from San Blas, which were exchanged for mission products in barter trade. Payeras eventually became Father Presidente of the California missions (1815–20) and in 1819 was named commissary prefect, the highest office among California Franciscans, thus he might have owned some of the best objects supplied by San Blas.[79] The buried china may have been smuggled goods, entombed to be protected, then uncovered, at which point some was broken and reburied. La Concepción is near a cove where smugglers often operated in the early-nineteenth century.

Other missions have handfuls of china shards, for example, San Juan Capistrano,[80] and San Luis Rey de Francia, where a single piece of a blue-and-white dish is on display, decorated with degenerate Arabic script in a pattern familiar to export areas in Southeast Asia. Exhibited with it is a quantity of Chinese embroidered silk vestments (see fig. 295). Very few other mission inventories now deposited at the Santa Barbara Mission Archival Library refer to Chinese objects, thus three listings stand out.

The 1834 inventory of Soledad Mission specifies "Jarres en China" worth 0.4 reals as part of the furnishings of a padre's quarters. One would not expect luxuries in the private rooms of the clergy, and certainly these jars were inexpensive. The second item, the Santa Cruz Mission list for 1834–35 (unfinished and in dollars due to Yankee traders), enumerates one

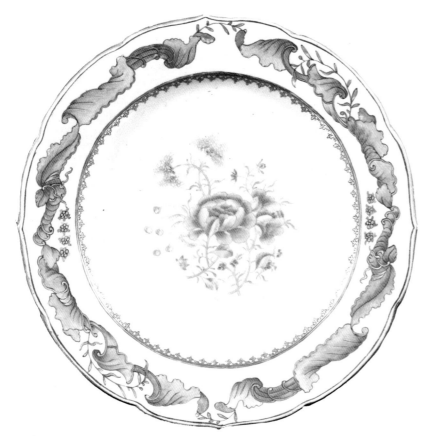

203. *Plate*, c. 1745–65, D 22.9 cm. Overglaze gold-red and gilt, first-class export. Courtesy of the Peabody Museum.

large and three small table services, the first at $1.40, the second altogether at $1.20, noted with ten lacquered imported chairs ($25.00) and one easy chair of Chinese cane ($10.00).[81] Almost ten years later at the Santa Clara Mission, an inventory reveals a chocolate pot with sugar bowl and creamer all "*de China*" worth one real. The set is listed just below an identical one of an unspecified ceramic, but four times as valuable.[82]

As of 1986, it may safely be said that only a few, if any, significant porcelains beyond the commonest types came into California under Mexican rule. By the time revolution broke out (1811–20), times were unsettled and the supply ships' arrival chancy. The Americans, English, and other Europeans were responsible for bringing later porcelains to the West Coast, before the mid-nineteenth century. Their story will be told in chapter 6, on the China trade to the United States and Canada. A final glimpse of the late-eighteenth-century porcelain trade to North America emphasizes the international sources of wares, even after our Revolution, and includes the return of the first American ship from Guangzhou in 1785. Two years afterward, James Huyman of Boston, a Hollander whose shop was called the "Dutch store," advertised tea, spices, fabrics, and rich supplies of porcelain "Just Imported in the *Doggersbank*, Captain Lemmel Tobey, From Amsterdam."[83] The Dutch, second to the British at the century's beginning, capped its end; they were welcome in America when the British, of course, were not. By its decoration, the cup in figure 204 symbolizes the competition among France, England, and Spain (to which Holland should be

204. *Coffee cup*, c. 1790, D 6.6 cm. Overglaze enamels: a unicorn and lion (England and Spain) pursue a deer (Corsica); motto: HUYE OPROBIO DEL MUNDO ("Flee the insults of the world"); superior export. Private collection.

added) for the hundred years. This state of affairs would swiftly shift in the last decade of the eighteenth century as America turned to direct trade with China for her own high pleasure and profit.

CHAPTER 5

A Shared Dutch and English Style

From the start, Mexican merchants and private individuals in New Spain had a direct role in ordering specific forms and decorations of export porcelain from Manila. Somewhat in contrast, early Dutch and English settlers on the East Coast of North America were at first dependent on their own East India companies for defining the market, then by the turn of the eighteenth century, a knowledgeable clientele among them were placing personal orders and had a grass-roots effect upon the choices of company gross loads (see Preface, pp. 9–12). Because the two companies overlapped in time, trade routes, and ports, they also relied on each other in decorative matters. Holland, first of the two to pioneer in porcelain buying in the East, provided England with models of business procedures and stylistic preferences. Later, the English sold porcelains in Dutch ports in Europe and in her former New World colonies.

Even so, both countries often deferred to France in aesthetic taste, as did most of Europe. When the French Compagnie des Indes entered the trade early in the eighteenth century, Gallic decorative preferences were quickly introduced, especially the French choice of polychrome wares before blue-and-white.[1] A good example of a shift to French taste, even in blue, is the appearance of a deeper, richer hue—"Mazarín blue"—often with a fine-line gilt decoration (see fig. 82). The color was a favorite of Cardinal Jules Mazarín (1602–61), a noted collector of late Ming porcelain, among other treasures. An even more central factor was the presence of Père d'Entrecolles in Jingdezhen. As a keen porcelain scholar, connoisseur, and consultant to Chinese and Western buyers alike, he had an untold effect on the orders of significant nationals. Yet the French served a much smaller market than did the Dutch and English, who also had a larger consumer group in the middle class. Their trade, then, was distinctly different not only from that of France but also Mexico.

All Western buyers first purchased wares that were largely oriental. Increasingly, they began to be supplied with pieces fitting occidental taste. Again Chinese porcelain production showed its time-tested flexibility in rapidly meeting foreign demand. As Volker has pointed out, by the 1630s and possibly earlier, the Dutch sent wooden or metalwork models to be followed by the Chinese for both form and decoration.

Period ship papers, English or Dutch, often mention "patterns," but they are not illustrated. Rough sketches are the rare exception, and then only from the eighteenth century.[2]

By comparing the porcelains themselves to known prototypes in metal, wood, or ceramic, however, the nature of the new Western taste in export ware is evident. Of the ceramics, not surprisingly, delftware was among the first of the models. Later china shows hints of the factories at Nevers, Lille, Rouen, and eventually of Montpellier and Moustiers. And from England, examples from Bow, Chelsea, Battersea, Worcester, Wedgwood, and Staffordshire went out for the Chinese to imitate, or if the imitations did not measure up, to compete. Joining these were pieces from Meissen in Saxony and Marieberg, Sweden, as well as majolica (earthenware) from Hispanic centers such as Alcora and Talavera.

As for decorations, every source imaginable found its way onto porcelain: the ceramics just noted, and others; engravings of paintings; bookplates; official documents; coins; card counters; textiles, embroidered or printed; and finally, a number of original designs specifically invented for the China trade market (to be considered in this chapter). Many of these Western designs incorporated Chinese elements, or the Chinese painter inadvertently gave away its origin. Good examples are the common rendering of Western faces with Asian features, or in another category, the English, then American, use of Chinese emblems associated with the scholar in the quadrant design that composes the "FitzHugh" style (fig. 341). The blend of elements is international and almost endless, unlike any other ceramic, making export ware doubly valuable well beyond, or sometimes despite, its aesthetic worth.

FORMS

From a much shorter period of time and geared to a less affluent society than that of New Spain, the porcelains reaching the Dutch and English colonies of North America had a decided utilitarian slant. Unlike Mexico, no splendid architecture, ecclesiastical or domestic, awaited the arrival of large jars and vases in Virginia, New England, or New Netherland. Embellishment was possible, as seen from the collections of De Lange and Van Varick, but it was limited to interiors that were intimate and precious, not spacious and grand as in Mexico. The china was scaled to fit their rooms, and monumental wares, such as the size-one jars of Mexico, would simply have had no place.

The Spanish had just as keen an interest as the Dutch in dictating specific new forms and decorations from the Chinese. Legaspi's reports in the sixteenth century from the Philippines indicate that Spain was beginning to take such initiatives. After all, her neighbors, the Portuguese, had led the way in ordering wares to suit European requirements early in the sixteenth century. Nonetheless, the only known, continuous documentation of such intent is from papers of the Dutch East India Company.

As early as 1608, the Dutch were asking for one thousand saltcellars that year "if they [the Chinese] can make them" as well as "200 large dishes of 2 1/2 span diameter, fine."[3] The commoner wares, such as butter and fruit dishes as well as a variety of cup shapes, including "beer-and-bread cups," would have found their way to North America. The Dutch had shipped coffee cups to Gamron, Persia, in 1635 and to Mocha at the mouth of the Red Sea in 1640[4] but did not start ordering them for Holland until an unspecified later time, about 1650–60. Multipieced condiment dishes were also available as early in 1617,[5] but they would have been unusual as a form in demand in

don auction. This one has an American pedigree; its exceptionally well-rendered painting derives from engravings of Swedish castles of the late-seventeenth and early-eighteenth centuries.[11] The original owner apparently was Major Pierce Butler (d. 1822), who in 1771 married Mary (''Polly'') Middleton, of the Middleton dynasty of Charleston, South Carolina. Later, after generations of contact between Charleston and Philadelphia families summering in Newport, the bowl entered the Philadelphia Cadwalader family, probably when one of the daughters of Eliza Middleton married George Cadwalader.[12] Although this bowl is of unusual quality, hard-drinking America would have had other, humbler, uncovered bowls that predate this one and differ from it only in commoner decoration.

London auctions of 1703 and 1704 of large, trial quantities of porcelain indicate what probably also reached America soon afterward in lesser amount. Between the two years, the differing forms bear witness to the company's experimental orderings and also the particular wares available in each of the three ports open to the English before 1710: Amoy and Chusan as well as Guangzhou.[13] A comparison of the 1703 and 1704 transactions at the company's ''candle'' (bids were received until a small piece of candle went out), shows only £6,208 in the first year, or roughly a third of 1704's, £20,815, which was the highest figure for the half century.

The difference in forms in each year confirms an experimental period, and to some extent, the different sources of the porcelain. Until trade was regularized at Guangzhou shortly after 1710, Chusan and Amoy also supplied the company's ships. Amoy, for example, supplied the *Dashwood* with the following china in 1701: along with the usual items—cups (for tea, coffee, chocolate, and custard), saucers, salvers, plates, dishes, bowls, basins, bottles, cans, mugs, and jars— were other, less-well-known practical pieces and the purely ornamental. Of the first sort were inkstands

and sand boxes (fig. 210), sucking bottles (for infants), bird and incense pots, cruets, and pipes. Of the purely decorative besides jars and beakers were wall flowerpots, ''Sancta Marias'' (or Guanyin goddesses), ''Pulpits and Padres'' (in two pieces), images (probably small oriental figures), painted men (fig. 211), wrestlers, dogs (fig. 212), lions, rabbits, buffaloes, horses, parrots, cocks, and undefined ''beasts.'' In another part of the *Dashwood*'s cargo were other figurines including monsters (fig. 213).[14] Coming from Amoy, these figurines were probably from the famous kilns producing white wares in Dehua in the same province of Fujian as the island port.

This potpourri of the practical and decorative is decidedly different from the china sold in 1704 from the ships *Aurengzeb, Union*, and *Fleet*. (The first two had arrived in 1702; the last in 1703, but their wares were apparently not sold, at least completely, until 1704.[15]) The china from the *Aurengzeb*, also from Amoy, was all predominantly tableware of a variety of decoration: blue-and-white, red and gold, enameled or ''painted,'' blue and gold, ''blue with white squares'' (probably diaper-patterned borders), cream colored, cream colored and blue, cream colored and painted, and brown. The wares from the *Union*, from Chusan, included a few more luxury items, such as longnecked fine bottles, ''Chimney Flower-pots,'' garden pots, rowlwagons (cylindrical vases usually with a flat lip), large- and narrow-necked beakers, hubblebubbles (or water pipes), ''Sancta Marias,'' and jars with covers. However, there were fewer pieces of each form than in the quantity cargo of the *Aurengzeb*. The *Fleet*, which had loaded at Guangzhou, offered lions, birds, elephants (fig. 214), two sorts of double ''josses'' (Chinese deities), and painted bowls and plates. All three ships brought back some Japanese porcelain as well, though not in great quantity.[16]

The early loads met an uncertain demand. But China's restriction of trade to Guangzhou alone by 1710

210. *Box with inkwell and sander*, c. 1700–20, L 27.0 cm. Underglaze blue, average export. Courtesy of the trustees of the British Museum.

211. *Figurine*, man with monkey, c. 1700–10, H 30.5 cm. Overglaze enamels, above-average export. Courtesy of the Victoria and Albert Museum.

212. *Hounds* (pair), not identical, c. 1700–15, H 16.5 cm. Overglaze enamels, fine export. Private collection.

213. *Fo lion with figures* (one of a pair), c.1700–10, H 21.3 cm. Cream-white, listed in a Van Cortlandt family inventory of 1774, above-average export. Courtesy of Sleepy Hollow Restorations.

helped England to standardize her shipments at the same time as sufficient market knowledge had been gained. By 1712, when the *Loyal Blisse* was sent out, a tested demand gave a gauge both of the quantity and type of ware that would sell well. Because of its unusual detail, her officers' instructions are worth quoting in full:

214. *Elephant* (one of a pair), c. 1700–10, L 22.2 cm. White, black lines simulate hide, above-average export. Private collection.

215. *Cup and saucer,* c. 1700–20, cup: D 8.9 cm, saucer: D 13.3 cm. Molded (''quilted'') white, underglaze blue, stock export, now rare. Courtesy of the Society for the Preservation of New England Antiquities.

No. 1. Flat Dishes to be Seven in a Nest some plain and some quil'd [quilted or raised by molding] (fig. 215) of various Patterns but all Blue and the smallest of the Patterns to be the least Three hundred Next Vizt. of the Plain Two Hundred
Ditto Quil'd One Hundred. . . . . .300 Nest

No. 2. Boats—Three in a Nest the Pattern to be the least but variety of Paints and Sprigs or running work instead of blue Strip's in the border with a pretty deal of Scarlet, Four Thousand Vizt. Colloured Two Thousand Ditto Blue Two Thousand 4,000

No. 3. Canasters of this Size but different paint Four Thousand Vizt. colour'd Two Thousand & Ditto blue.
Two Thousand 4,000

No. 4. Handle Chocolatetts [*sic*] [fig. 216], upright of these two sorts Twenty Thousand Vizt. of the biggest blue and white of different Flowers Ten thousand, Ditto the smaller Sort wth brown Edges Ten Thousand. 20,000

No. 5. Ditto—in Collours and Gold Ten thousand but with a border inside with gold Edges & variety of patterns Ten thousand of Ditto Lesser Sort. 20,000

No. 6. Milk Potts the largest, Collour'd and Gold Two Thousand and Ditto blue and white Two Thousand 4,000

Ditto—the second Size, Two thousand Collour'd & blue & white 2,000

Ditto—the third Size, Two thousand Collour'd & blue and white half of each rib'd or quil'd & the other half plain . . . .'. .2,000

No. 7. Milk Potts the Glass pattern One thousand Collor'd and Ditto blue and white One thousand. 2,000

Ditto of bigger Size One Thousand Colloured and Ditto blue and white One Thousand . .2,000

No. 8. Tea Potts Blue and white Two thou-
          sand. 2,000
          Collour'd Ditto Two thousand 2,000
          Ditto Lesser Sort of each One thou-
          sand. 2,000

No. 9. Plates in Collours and Gold with much Scarlet,
         gold edge with variety of Patterns Ten Thou-
         sand 10,000 Dishes of the same work one Size
         bigger than the Plate,
          One thousand 10,000
          one Ditto bigger than that One Thou-
          sand. 1,000
          one Ditto bigger than that One Thou-
          sand. 1,000
          one Ditto bigger than that One Thou-
          sand. 1,000

No. 10. Plates and Dishes, blue and white the same
         Quantity and Sorts

No. 11. Scollop Shells Six in a Nest in Collours variety
         of paints and much Scarlet but with a small flat
         edge One thousand nests (fig. 239) 1,000

         Ditto blue and white with variety of Paint &
         ca[?] One Thousand nests. 1,000

No. 12. Cups in collours sorts to be painted after the
         Japan pattern as these or such like Twenty
         Thousand 20,000
         Sawcers—Ditto Twenty Thousand 20,000

No. 13. Cups—Blue and white the same Size with edge
         brown different Patterns Thirty Thou-
         sand 30,000

         Sawcers—Ditto Thirty Thousand. 30,000

         Cups—a Size bigger, of different patterns
         Twenty Thousand 20,000

         Sawcers—Ditto Twenty Thousand 20,000

         Do Size bigger than the last of different Pat-
         terns of Cups & Sawcers each Twenty Thou-
         sand 40,000

No. 14. Slop Basons a pint & half each variety of paint

216. *Chocolate cups*, c. 1700–20, H 16.2 cm. Underglaze blue,
above-average export. Courtesy of the trustees of the British
Museum.

         half rib'd half plain, blue & white Five Thou-
         sand. 5,000

         Ditto Basons in Collours Three Thou-
         sand. 3,000

No. 15. Dishes—Five in a Nest the Pattern the least to
         be painted of variety of Colours & paints Four
         hundred Nests . . . . .400 Nest

No. 16 Sugar Potts with Covers Two in a Nest the
         Pattern to be the least Two Thousand
         Nests 2,000

No. 17. Deep Square Small Dishes or patty pans ac-
         cording to the Pattern in Tin for the Tea Potts
         to Stand on & to be Painted and collour'd as
         the Tea Potts, Blue and white Two Thou-
         sand. 2,000

         Ditto in Collours Two Thousand 2,000

As item No. 17 indicates, the supercargoes were provided with "patterns" (models) to give an exact guide.
If they could not be matched, then the company's instructions were to buy what approximated them and
to bring the patterns back "That Wee may see how

217. *Bowls* (pair), c. 1720–40, both: D 14.9 cm ("sneaker" size). Overglaze enamels, average polychrome export. Courtesy of Norman Herreshoff.

218. *Coffeepot*, Japanese, Arita, c. 1680, H 27.5 cm. Low hole to take a metal spout, underglaze blue, fine export. Courtesy of the Ashmolean Museum.

219. *Porringer*, c. 1715–25, D (with handle) 18.3 cm. Overglaze enamels, possibly painted in Japan. Courtesy of the trustees of the British Museum.

220. *Teapots with matching cups*, c. 1710–20, pots: H 18.7 cm, cups with covers: H 10.5 cm. Bamboo-shaped ("Fujian") cup handles, "mirror" (underglaze) black with worn overglaze gilt. Courtesy of the trustees of the British Museum.

you have comply'd with them.'' Further, they were told that if any Japanese junks were at Guangzhou with ''Japan earthenware'' (china), some of the required sorts could be bought from them, but none of the large objects ''such as Jars, Beakers or great dishes or Bowls,'' presumably because they were not selling.[17]

The precision with which the company now ordered china indicates the exact types popular in England, and, by extension, America as well. ''Scarlet'' in the *Loyal Blisse* orders refers to iron-red, not the gold-red or rose-pink discussed in chapter 1, which were not available in quantity until the 1720s at the earliest. Interestingly, the reference in entry no. 12 to Japanese models confirms an early date for Chinese ''Imari,'' which began to be produced in the mid-to-late-seventeenth century, but was now imported in larger quantity (see fig. 186).

In an auction of 1721, an even greater difference seems to have occurred. Several ships' wares arriving from Guangzhou a few years preceding the sale,[18] show a proliferation of practical forms from the earlier lists. Along with the usual tablewares were now milk pots, sneakers (small bowls for punch, popular about 1710–40; see fig. 217), knife handles, voiders (large plates for sweetmeats), soup dishes, cisterns, sweetmeat saucers, castors, spoon boats, and mazarines (small dishes put in the middle of a large dish for ragout or fricassees; also for tarts). Chinaware had been expanded beyond the tea table to serve a quantity of foods. These new pieces were in large, sometimes huge lots: cups and saucers from one ship alone numbered 77, 336 pieces. A load of over 5,000 Japanese cups and saucers also came in along with more than 300 other Japanese teacups and saucers, chocolate cups with covers, dishes, plates, and pots (fig. 218).

But the greatest quantity of porcelain was coarse ware, specifically coffee cups, no doubt ordered for coffeehouses. Over 11,600 of such cups, with or without brown rims or blue rims, were sold. In the same category were 4,600 coarse blue-and-white porringers, with brown or white edges and either blue or no rim decoration (fig. 219). Chipped or broken pieces also had their value; they could readily be mended, sometimes with silver lips.

Of the whole lot, blue-and-white was the most popular color; followed by enameled or ''painted'' wares, and last, no doubt because of price, the gilded wares: blue, black, red, and less often, white. The gold-decorated pieces were much less numerous, some less than ten in each shipment, and often not more than twenty or thirty (fig. 220). Not surprisingly, they were objects for serving tea, but also ribbed basins, cisterns, candlesticks, and rowlwagons.[19]

SERVICES

The tea service made its appearance in the early-eighteenth century about the same time as the table service was regularized, at least in the English colonies. Much earlier, scattered references indicate that only a few of the wealthy or prominent had such porcelain sets, and they were not of a definite number or form. One of the first-known services ''*de China*'' was in Spain, originally a gift to an Aragonese, Doña María Juana de Ribas y Silva, from the Emperor Charles V (King Charles I of Spain, 1500–1558). This service included four dozen large plates, a dozen platters, six pitchers, two dozen porringers, eight salvers with a dozen pedestalled salvers, all in a rich, well-executed style of the same legendary scenes.[20] The service, notable for its uniform decoration at this early date, was atypical, for a single individual not a mass market. Similarly, a dinner service bought in 1604 in Amsterdam by Henry IV of France was probably composed

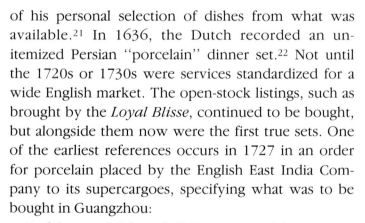

221. *Plate*, c. 1730–50, D 22.9 cm. Underglaze blue, average stock design. Courtesy of Mr. and Mrs. Lewis Rumford II.

222. *Plate*, c. 1730–40, D 22.8 cm. Underglaze blue, first-quality export. Courtesy of Mr. and Mrs. Lewis Rumford II.

of his personal selection of dishes from what was available.[21] In 1636, the Dutch recorded an unitemized Persian ''porcelain'' dinner set.[22] Not until the 1720s or 1730s were services standardized for a wide English market. The open-stock listings, such as brought by the *Loyal Blisse*, continued to be bought, but alongside them now were the first true sets. One of the earliest references occurs in 1727 in an order for porcelain placed by the English East India Company to its supercargoes, specifying what was to be bought in Guangzhou:

> Useful sorts as Dishes of All Sizes in Sets of the same shape *as now used in Silver and Pewter here* [my italics], plates in proportion to the Dishes of the same Painted Figure if possible to be procured, other plates of different Paint and Figures a large Quantity, Tea Cups, Saucers, Tea Pots, Basins, and Sugar Dishes, Coffee Cups, blew and white chiefly, Chocolate Cups with or without handles, Bowls of all Sorts and Sizes none exceeding one Gallon, small Sneakers and any other pretty useful things you can meet with.[23]

Metal forms, then, not only suggested shapes but also the size and number of objects in a set, according to this order. In addition, the decoration was to be uniform within each set; the notation above indicated the novelty of such an ensemble. A few years later, a 1734 order placed with the Hong merchant Quiqua for blue-and-white sets regularized the service: 121 pieces consisting of a large dish, two sets of two progressively smaller dishes each, then two sets of four smaller dishes each, eight ''sallate'' (salad) dishes (fig. 221), and a hundred plates. The same order included a slight variation for enameled sets ''each set 21 Dishes sorted as above & 60 Plates.''[24] Perhaps the French had originally devised these services or merely ordered their decoration. The English order of 1734 just quoted ambiguously referred to the French and their ''direction''; ''The setts of Dishes and Plates were made after the particular Direction of the French last Year, & the blue-and-white especially seem to have had a good deal of care bestowed on them'' (fig. 222).[25]

In fact, the English wished to conclude their business speedily before the French supercargoes arrived for the season and tried to prevent their purchase.

This combination of a few graduated dishes along with sixty to one hundred plates appears to have been the first basic sort of dinner service one might order. Over the next fifty years or so, sets of various sizes, with various pieces, appeared. Soup bowls, salad plates, sauceboats, and tureens joined the dinner and other plates as necessities.[26] By the 1770s, the dinner service as well as breakfast and tea sets were standardized. Hot-water plates, double-bottomed and spouted, had taken a place within them (fig. 223). Salad dishes were now specified as deep and square, thus bowls, joining the flat dishes to serve salad. Their presence indicated that the cruet set (fig. 224), imported to London on its own in the 1720s, if not listed as part of a dinner set, was nonetheless used with it. (In 1759, in Charleston, cruets and cruet stands were advertised.)[27]

By mid-century the now-established dinner service had accessory pieces added from time to time. An advertisement of 1776 in Philadelphia gives some idea of these additions, with old forms joining the ensemble: sauce tureens, pickle shells, mustard pots, butter tubs, artichoke cups, icepails, and beef plates (the well-and-tree sort, see fig. 348). Of other forms not associated with the dining table per se, this advertisement is also illuminating: spittoons, oval baking dishes, pattypans, mugs, jugs, many-sized jars and beakers, myrtle pots and stands, images, groups (of figurines, presumably), urns, chandeliers, a variety of flower vases, bottles, basins, and chamberpots. Their decoration was blue-and-white, enameled or "rich enamelled," possibly meaning gilded.[28]

Tureens were known in other ceramics by the late-seventeenth century, but in export ware, references to them do not appear until just before mid-eighteenth century. Semantics may help explain why; the covered bowls and stands (see figs. 208 and 209)

223. *Hot-water dish*, c. 1740–60, D 22.9 cm. Underglaze blue, above-average export. Courtesy of Norman Herreshoff.

224. *Cruet set*, c. 1740–50, L 20 cm. Blue and white scenes of tea production, first-class export. Courtesy of the Fries Museum.

225. *Tureen*, c. 1740–60, H 28.6 cm. Underglaze blue, overglaze enamels, from the estate of Emily Verplanck Johnstone of Staten Island, above-average export, rare. Courtesy of Mrs. Peter Milliken.

226. *Tureen and stand*, c. 1730–50, tureen: H 29.2 cm. Finial replaced, overglaze enamels, owned by the Otis family of Boston, first-class export. Courtesy of the Society for the Preservation of New England Antiquities.

227. *Dutch junk and plate*, junk: c. 1730, H 30.5 cm, plate: c. 1756–60, D 22.9 cm. Overglaze enamels, first-class export. Courtesy of Dr. Wesley Gallup.

listed in English East India Company records early in the century may be considered tureens. The English word *tureen*, derived from the French *terrine*, is first recorded in 1706, but it may not have come into common usage for some time.

The tureens in figures 225 and 226 have histories in New York and Boston. The bowl in figure 225 was part of the estate of Emily Verplanck Johnstone (1837–1913) of Staten Island.[29] It has a perforated inner liner near the base. The bowl in figure 226 was handed down in the Otis family of Boston. Both tureens are indebted to metal forms with two sorts of fluting; the Otis one is offset by plain banding.[30] The Dutch junk in figure 227 recalls the continuing influence of Dutch taste in the eighteenth century, when English New York collaborated hand-in-glove with the remaining Dutch merchants and their Amsterdam connections. As the fancifully painted sails show, the junk is not Chinese; the Dutch also used their own in Southeast Asia. The Dutch ship *Vryburg* painted on the plate in Canton in 1756, and bearing an authentic national flag, appears with the bow on the left, as does the ship on an identical plate now at the Zeeland Museum, Middelburg, the Netherlands.[31] But on another plate at the Guimet Museum, Paris, the view is reversed and the *Vryburg* sails in the opposite direction.[32] The inscription on all three plates, however, is the same and not reversed. A more common English ship is shown on the large teapot in figure 228. Its standard design would have appeared on the ware of any Western power with the appropriate flag.

The square bottle in figure 229, often called a Dutch bottle (though as noted, it was popular in the Spanish trade), is a development of the seventeenth-century blue-and-white bottles of the same shape. This one, with its gold-red peonies, is an extraordinarily fine specimen, especially with its silver cap. One of the earliest English references to square bottles in London

228. *Teapot*, c. 1750–75, D 22.9 cm. Overglaze enamels, British flag, anonymous ship, good export. Courtesy of the Peabody Museum.

229. *Bottle*, c. 1750, H (with top) 24 cm, 9.5 cm sq. Overglaze enamels, first-class export. Gift of the estate of Mr. Harry T. Peters, Jr. Courtesy of the Peabody Museum.

dates from 1696, when a Richard Chevall bought a quantity of them at 60 pence each from the cargoes of the *Sarah* and the *Dorothy*.[33]

The essence or rosewater bottle with neck tapering to a point was also a late-seventeenth-, early-eighteenth-century import to Holland, England, and, presumably, to the New World. Other small and large bottles with neck variations (bulbous or plain), which may be seen today at the Victoria and Albert Museum and in the Netherlands, were listed in 1696 in the large imports to London (over two thousand rosewater bottles in the sale of two ships' cargoes).[34] In this same sale, spittoons were included (see fig. 173).[35]

Another form whose shape and decoration had gradually evolved was the coffee/chocolate pot (fig. 230). Both beverages might be used in the same pot, but each was introduced to the West at different times. Chocolate, previously noted as an Indian drink,

230. *Coffee/chocolate pot*, c. 1750–75, H 24.8 cm. Overglaze enamels, fine export. Private collection.

was instantly accepted by the Spanish in the sixteenth century, but because of distribution and price it gained slow acceptance elsewhere, including North America. By 1750, however, it had been introduced to all of Europe, becoming a common beverage there and in the colonies, not only for the well-to-do. In 1748 among the Swedes of Pennsylvania, Peter Kalm observed that chocolate as well as tea and coffee were "to be found in the most remote cabins, if not for daily use, yet for visitors."[36] In New York, a thick cup of hot chocolate was a common breakfast drink by mid-eighteenth century, in part because it was recommended as a source of vitamins and as a laxative.[37]

The rococo pot in figure 230, with its rounded body similar to Meissen pots of the 1720s, indicates how richly the form had evolved from the conical blue-and-white examples of the late-seventeenth century (see figs. 155 and 168). The tapered profile was originally Near Eastern, customarily after metal rather than ceramic forms since their appearance in the mid-fifteenth century, following the discovery of coffee in the area (more readily available and preferred to chocolate). Western models could also be in pewter or silver, but were often ceramic, especially delft.[38] These Dutch ceramic examples were probably more frequently sent out to be copied by the Chinese than were their more costly pewter or silver counterparts.

In the last decades of the eighteenth century, the straight-sided pot with round body was succeeded by the lighthouse coffee/chocolate pot and the rarer pistol-handled pot. Often associated with chocolate alone, the pistol-handled pot had straight sides, or, less often, was belly shaped. Like the lighthouse pot, it had handles at right angles to the spout.[39]

Affecting the export forms most in demand, tea and coffee became *the* growth imports to the West in the 1700s, if the records of the English East India Company reflect those in most countries.[40] Tea, especially, became a common English drink by mid-century, the price falling from one pound sterling per pound in the

1700s to only five shillings per pound in 1750. Ten years later, tea accounted for 40 percent of all the company's imports.[41] As an import, coffee had a more mercurial history, rising from 5 percent of imports in 1706 to a high of 24 percent in 1724, then declining after 1730 to a 3–9 percent range.[42] The proportion of tea- over coffeepots reflects these figures, although consumption rates cannot be linked to such data; any sort of pot served any sort of drink.

By 1750, then, tea was queen. The housewife could become sophisticated about the best green, Bohea, Hyson, Congo, or Souchong without ruining her purse. The tea party, a forerunner of the cocktail party, became a central social event, for which young women prepared with the utmost care, at least until the hated tea taxes led some to forswear the practice.[43] The teapot, cup, and caddy in figure 231 indicate typical forms and a very popular brown reserve decoration of the 1720–70 period known in every port city of the East Coast American colonies. A New England dummy board of about 1720, a life-size serving maid, showed two such cups on her tray.[44]

A Charleston, South Carolina, advertisement of 1759, on a long, detailed list of china, included the notation "black, brown and white tea pots."[45] In the late-seventeenth, early-eighteenth centuries, this ware was common. It was often called "Batavian" after Batavia (now Djakarta) and had blue-and-white interior decoration and a plain brown exterior (fig. 150), though the brown varied in shade and luminescence, earning picturesque distinctions: "dead-leaf," "tea dust," "coffee," "café au lait," and "capuchino" (see fig. 119). No doubt "Batavia" ware was the sort of brown china referred to in the Van Varick inventory of 1695 (chapter 3).

Beverage choice affected the cup form, possibly the most common shape in export ware in any era after the dish or plate, thus worthy of a summary view. In the seventeenth century, the West adopted the handleless Chinese wine cup or tea bowl to use for spirits

231. *Brownware* (miscellaneous), 1730–50, teapot: D 23.0 cm. Overglaze enamels, average export. Courtesy of the Essex Institute.

or tea. By the early-eighteenth century, new forms to suit European drinks were introduced: the brandy bowl; the tall, covered, double-handled coffee cup and coffee can; the caudle cup; and the sneaker bowl (see figs. 149, 151, 172, 216 and 217). Contrary to popular impression, handles neither originated in the West in the eighteenth century nor were they confined to coffee cups. From the Tang dynasty before porcelain was on the scene, the Chinese had handled cups in ceramic as well as metal. Handleless cups were simply easier to stack and transport.

Other cup shapes grew with the formation of table services, beginning in the 1730s, gradually becoming common in the late-eighteenth century: breakfast cups (large and handled) and evening cups (small and handleless) for after-dinner tea or coffee. By the nineteenth century, cups within a service had reached an even greater degree of diversity (see figs. 280 and 283). And ceremonial/decorative cups, copied from metalwork, were a latter-day replacement for the goblet as well (compare figs. 207 and 322), but they were the exception. The trend in cup production from the seventeenth to the nineteenth centuries was toward specialization of form according to beverage or time of use and inclusion in sets rather than as single pieces. Open-stock items were, of course, always available.

Finally, though English and Dutch gross shipments were virtually interchangeable, there were some interesting, minor distinctions. English records indicate that more figurines and animals came into London than to Amsterdam, but often such listings refer to "Dutch" men or families.[46] These models were probably in white most of the time; colored examples are rare (compare figs. 24 and 213). (They may include those that arrived white and were then painted, though incoming manifests also included examples already colored.) In no way do these figures reveal their nationality; they are only Western by their dress, with a gloss of the oriental in the rendering of the eyes. "Dutch" was applied by the English in a casual way,

belying the generic nature of these figurines in much the same way as the Guanyin goddesses were labeled "Sancta Marias."

The appearance in Boston of similar images, including animals, testifies to their transshipment to Massachusetts Bay not long after arrival in England. In 1697/98, a Ruth Carter was among the first recorded to have owned an unknown number of "Images." In 1705, Samuel Shrimpton had "5 Alabaster Images" worth £3.15. Ten years later, Sir Charles Hobby, also of the city, owned "2 cheny Lyons & Elephants" valued at £2. Others appearing in the 1720s and 1730s adorned the manteltree (mantel) along with flowerpots and glassware.[47] These dates suggest an ownership of five to ten years at least, indicating that English colonial taste might follow the Dutch example of decades before in New York. That precedence was no doubt the reason why Western figures were easily, though inaccurately labeled "Dutch."

DECORATIONS

As introduction to the developed scheme of export painting, a seemingly insignificant detail may tell the story in microcosm. In figure 232 three illustrations of similar scroll-and-arrowlike motifs are shown. The first, the corner decoration of a Dutch tile (a), or another similar source, appears to have been adopted and altered in a Meissen pattern, which was then faithfully copied by the Chinese painter (b); at the same time it was transformed by, rather than merely copied on, another style of export ware in a common cavetto border (c; see also fig. 221). The copying or melding of European with Eastern motifs by the Chinese in a natural evolution of the original, whether Western or Eastern (including Japanese), is the basic principle of the Chinese export ceramic aesthetic.

That principle took effect shortly after the advent of Westerners in China. The Chinese blue-and-white car-

rackwares, Transitional pieces, and late-seventeenth-century Kangxi porcelains indicate many of the commonest, initially open-stock decorations of the first periods of importation in America (fig. 233). Bridging the seventeenth and eighteenth centuries is the cup and saucer in figure 234. The fluting of this pair accentuates the paneled layout of late-seventeenth-century Kangxi wares. At the same time, it echoes the wide borders of contemporary Japanese-inspired plates (fig. 235), no doubt in order to compete with them. The sketchy willow tree in the central decoration of figure 234 is a forerunner of fuller willows to follow; it is a lesser ware than that represented by the plates in figures 236 and 237. Another early eighteenth-century design, a spotted deer, native to India, is also a typical motif. The cup and saucer of figure 238, of a slightly later date than those of figure 234, are from Salem; the

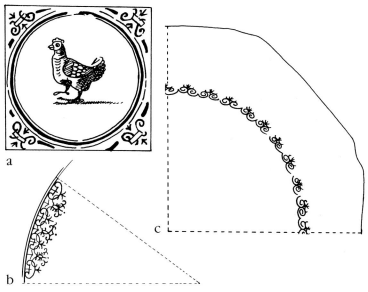

a

b

c

232. *Dutch tile and Chinese export borders*:
a. Tile, 17th century, with corner "ox-heads."
b. Outer border, export plate, c. 1740; gilt lacework from a Meissen prototype, c. 1725–40.
c. Cavetto border, export plate, c. 1735–50.
  (Drawing by Robert Williams)

234. *Cup and saucer*, c. 1690–1710, cup: D 5.7 cm, saucer: D 8.9 cm. Underglaze blue, average export. Courtesy of Mr. and Mrs. Lewis Rumford II.

233. Shelves of transitional underglaze blue, Fries Museum. Courtesy of the Fries Museum.

235. *Plate*, Japanese Imari, 1688–1703, D 31.0 cm. Overglaze enamels, common domestic/export. Courtesy of the Museo Nacional del Virreinato.

236. (far left) *Plate,* c. 1740, D 22.5 cm. Underglaze blue, brown rim, in Canby family since 1803, possibly earlier; fine export. Courtesy of Mr. and Mrs. Lewis Rumford II.

237. (left) *Plate,* c. 1740–50, D 22.8 cm. Overglaze enamels, fine quality willowware. Courtesy of Mr. and Mrs. Lewis Rumford II.

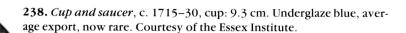

238. *Cup and saucer,* c. 1715–30, cup: 9.3 cm. Underglaze blue, average export, now rare. Courtesy of the Essex Institute.

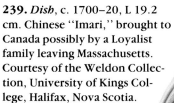

239. *Dish,* c. 1700–20, L 19.2 cm. Chinese "Imari," brought to Canada possibly by a Loyalist family leaving Massachusetts. Courtesy of the Weldon Collection, University of Kings College, Halifax, Nova Scotia.

240. *Charger,* c. 1720–30, D 39.0 cm. Chinese "Imari," owned by Hugh Cargill of Concord, Massachusetts; fine export. Courtesy of the Concord Antiquarian Society.

pair had a twin in a Philadelphia context, beginning about 1720, according to archeological finds.[48]

Writing about the color, thickness, and breakage of such blue-and-whites, an official of the English East India Company noted in 1740 in advice to supercargoes: "most people like a Pale Blue, and the China thin and as there is a great deal more breakage in the Cups than in the Saucers, it will be very proper to buy Eleven hundred Cups to every thousand Saucers."[49] (Given this breakage difference, archaeologists might expect to find more cup than saucer shards.) Plain white ware, for later painting or not, was also imported. In a purchase of 1734 from Tinqua, "200 Setts of white China ware for Tea Tables" was part of the order, though only a very small fraction of the total contract.[50]

Colored wares, including those with gilt trim, were listed in the *Loyal Blisse*'s cargo of 1712. The ship carried twenty thousand "cups in collours sorts to be painted after the Japan pattern." Chinese "Imari" ware is probably the "Japan pattern"—a palette of underglaze blue, overglaze iron-red and gilt, sometimes with green overglaze touches (fig. 239). That they were already familiar to colonial users is suggested by the Van Varick inventory. "Imari" ware is also probably the sort used by William Penn when visiting "Friend Cooper" in Camden, New Jersey. He wrote of a "little Oriental tea set, with decorations in underglaze blue and red," before leaving for England in 1701, never to return to Pennsylvania.[51]

The charger in figure 240, once owned by Hugh Cargill (1739–99) of Concord, Massachusetts, represents a fine example of a well-executed version of the style. The charger in figures 241 and 242, with a New England pedigree in the Russell and Gerry families, is of a commoner type but also painted with finesse. Chinese "Imari" plates of humbler composition and handwork were imported by the thousands to the colonies, in special vogue before the advent of gold-red

241. *Charger*, c. 1720–30, D 41.7 cm. Chinese "Imari," owned by the Russell and Gerry families, fine export. Courtesy of the Peabody Museum.

242. Detail of fig. 241.

243. (far left) *Tureen*, c. 1740–60, H 22.8 cm. Chinese "Imari" palette, fine export, rare. Ex. coll. Mr. and Mrs. Bertram Rowland. Courtesy of the Peabody Museum.

244. (left) *Charger*, c. 1730–40, D 34.3 cm. Overglaze enamels, owned by Jonathan Sayward of York, Maine; fine export. Courtesy of the Society for the Preservation of New England Antiquities.

245. *Plate, tureen, and salt* (same service), c. 1735–50, tureen: L 35.5 cm. Overglaze enamels, descended in the Schuyler and Van Renssalaer families, fine export. Courtesy of the Newark Museum.

246. *Plates*, c. 1740–60, left: D 22.9 cm, right: D 22.9 cm. Overglaze enamels; left: brown rim, owned by Alexander and Elizabeth Schuyler Hamilton. Courtesy of the estate of Mrs. John Church Hamilton, on loan to the Museum of the City of New York.

247. *Sauceboat and stand*, c. 1750, boat: L 19.7 cm. Evolved Chinese ''Imari'' palette, descended in the Van Cortlandt family, the Van Cortlandt Mansion, the Bronx. Courtesy of the National Society of Colonial Dames of the State of New York.

but also slow to taper off, apparently, for some time afterward. In Mexico, large twin jars in this style with *qilin* in underglaze blue still remain in a private collection, matching the fine paintings of the Russell-Gerry charger. The tureen in figure 243 is Chinese ''Imari'' in color, though ungilded, but special in design. It is similar to the cruet set in figure 224, especially with its bold shell border, but the central decoration differs: two Chinese on rafts ferry jars across a river.

Contemporary with Chinese ''Imari'' but heralding the ascendancy of gold-red's popularity is the octagonal charger in figure 244, one of two matching chargers and six plates, once owned by Jonathan Sayward (1713–97) of York, Maine.[52] Its touches of rose in the flowers and butterflies framing the buffalo are slight and exploratory rather than dominant as in wares to come. Though purchased in England in the early 1760s, the piece may have been made thirty or thirty-five years earlier based on its unnotched octagonal shape,[53] asymmetrical design, limited use of the gold-red, and thick, opaque application.[54] Its similarities to known earlier pieces is striking (fig. 245). Other examples of gold-red ware, successors in style to those just

mentioned, with more rose and greater finesse in its application, are the two plates and a boat stand in figures 246 and 247.

Somewhat later in date, the tea service in figure 248 has a thinner, smoother application of the gold-red than do the plates, boat, and stand. This set has a Providence, Rhode Island, history with a note on the reverse of the plate that the whole set came from Surinam in 1757.[55] The set now consists of the objects illustrated plus a covered globular teapot with a spoon tray, a slop bowl, eight tea cups and nine saucers, three coffee cups with handles, and a smaller plate. The 1757 date places this style of ''Mandarin'' ware solidly in mid-century, given the sophistication of the painting, requiring a lead time of at least a decade or more before reaching this polished state (see figs. 201 and 230). It proves the popularity for depictions of Chinese figures well before the ''Rose Mandarin'' designs of the nineteenth century. Beginning as early as the 1650s, that taste developed into the highly popular chinoiserie style, the West's avid adoption of Eastern motifs, including likenesses of the Chinese, for architecture and the decorative arts.

248. *Part of a tea service*, c. 1750,
plate: D 20.6 cm. Overglaze enamels,
from a Providence, R.I., family; fine
export. Private collection.

249. *Tureen*, c. 1760–80, H 19.1 cm. Overglaze enamels, part of a
service associated with Abigail Adams. Courtesy of Adams National
Historic Site.

250. *Plate*, c. 1775, D 22.9 cm. Overglaze enamels, owned by Abigail and John Adams. Courtesy of Adams National Historic Site.

251. *Punch bowl*, c. 1760, D 39.3 cm. Overglaze enamels, owned by Alexander and Elizabeth Schuyler Hamilton. Courtesy of the estate of Mrs. John Church Hamilton, on loan to the Museum of the City of New York.

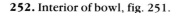

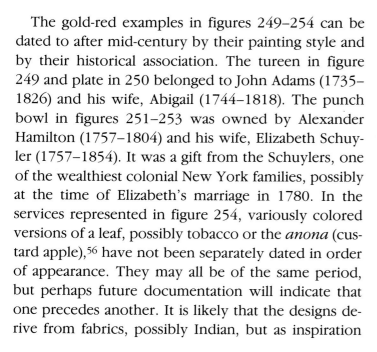

252. Interior of bowl, fig. 251.

253. Detail of border, fig. 251.

The gold-red examples in figures 249–254 can be dated to after mid-century by their painting style and by their historical association. The tureen in figure 249 and plate in 250 belonged to John Adams (1735–1826) and his wife, Abigail (1744–1818). The punch bowl in figures 251–253 was owned by Alexander Hamilton (1757–1804) and his wife, Elizabeth Schuyler (1757–1854). It was a gift from the Schuylers, one of the wealthiest colonial New York families, possibly at the time of Elizabeth's marriage in 1780. In the services represented in figure 254, variously colored versions of a leaf, possibly tobacco or the *anona* (custard apple),[56] have not been separately dated in order of appearance. They may all be of the same period, but perhaps future documentation will indicate that one precedes another. It is likely that the designs derive from fabrics, possibly Indian, but as inspiration for a European artist's invention of a pattern for the ware rather than a textile model itself.[57] Very finely decorated porcelains in gold-red alone, in effect a rose-colored engraving, were known by the 1760s. Their floral style is akin in its detailed brushwork to the later "FitzHugh" plate in figure 229. A similar service of about 1765 was owned by Philip and Maria Van Rensselaer at Cherry Hill in Albany and may be seen there today.[58] The ongoing popularity of blue-and-white designs are represented by figures 255 and 256, co-travelers with the rose-colored wares just described.

Finally, a late eighteenth-century service (represented by the tureen in fig. 257) was made for DeWitt Clinton (1769–1828) and Maria Franklin (1775–1818). The tureen's entwined initials suggest that it was probably made for their wedding in 1796, but the style of

254. Five styles of the so-called "tobacco leaf" design, c. 1750–75. Overglaze enamels, fine export.
Courtesy of Earle D. Vandekar, London.

its decoration echoes earlier wares. The central painting is a finely rendered Chinese landscape with pagodas; gold-red is used sparingly in prunus tree or cloud, and the whole is trimmed with gold fleurs-de-lis. In a special touch, the outer border is painted with the Eight Taoist Immortals. A unique service, nonetheless it parallels wares of about 1740–70 belonging to the Clintons' friends, the Van Renssêlaers of Cherry Hill. Another dinner service of 1740–60, belonging to the Otis family of Boston, has an almost identical landscape, and a tureen originally owned by Alexander Henderson of Dumfries, Virginia, of about 1765–75, is also similar.[59] Probably the Clintons wanted an "old-fashioned" pattern for their wedding china, not an infrequent request from purchasers. The choice of purely Chinese decoration, except for the monogram,

indicates a continuing taste for oriental scenes, even at the height of the vogue for patriotic porcelains in America.

Both DeWitt and Maria Clinton descended from Dutch and English colonial families. Their service epitomizes over a century and a half of the combined taste of West and East in export chinaware. Such a background for the U.S. population at large in 1783 made others alert to the potential of porcelain: with equal rapidity, it could repeat familiar patterns or adapt to new ones. The country's nationalistic, even chauvinistic fervor for individual and civic emblems on china at the end of the eighteenth century gave the Chinese export industry a whole new impetus. At the same time, the last great era of the China trade until today was inaugurated.

255. *Soup dish*, c. 1750–75, D 22.9 cm. Underglaze blue, owned by Mary Webb Updegraff of York, Pennsylvania. Courtesy of Mr. and Mrs. Lewis Rumford II.

256. *Soup dish*, c. 1750–75, D 24.5 cm. Underglaze blue, French design, no mark on base. Courtesy of the Peabody Museum.

257. *Tureen*, c. 1796, L 31.7 cm. Overglaze enamels, wide border with Eight Immortals, cipher DWMC for DeWitt Clinton and Maria Franklin, m. 1796; unique export, gift of Mrs. James Alexander Miller. Courtesy of the Museum of the City of New York.

Trade to the United States and Canada

The American Revolution was a watershed moment for the trade in export porcelains from China to North America. Without it, importation would have shriveled to almost nothing by the early-nineteenth century, as it did in England, and, for the most part, in Canada. The new United States enormously increased the China trade to this continent. Benjamin Franklin used the image of a china vase about to crack when he spoke of the British Empire in 1773. Ten years later, he referred to the now independent thirteen colonies as the vase firmly mended.[1] If not as strong as well-restored china, the country was at least intact in 1783. The Revolution's release of fresh entrepreneurial blood among investors on the East Coast in the post-1783 years gave high promise of concerted trading energy. Risk there was, to be sure, in launching independent voyages to the Far East, but the men who financed the first American ship to China, the *Empress of China*, in 1784–85, had the advantage of knowing a well-established market for China goods existed at home (figs. 258 and 259). They had nothing to lose except the ship itself by piracy, storm, or other misadventure.

OLD CHINA HANDS

Although the backers of the *Empress of China* came from the Middle Atlantic states, and although New York City gradually became the primary port of entry for goods from China, it was New England that first-to-last launched most of the ships, gave models of successful seamanship necessary to long arduous voyages, and provided most of the resident staff in China, who organized a worldwide enterprise. Not only did these agents arrange to supply America with tea, silks, and other luxuries, but they became interconnected with all foreigners trading in China and acted for others who were not, such as the Australians. They were also intimate with the diplomatic community. New England, then, made much of China for the benefit of

258. *Punch bowl*, c. 1784–85, D 38.7 cm; mahogany stand, 46 cm sq. Overglaze enamels; ship appears only on interior, unlike six similar bowls; unique. Gift of Mr. Richard V. Lindabury. Courtesy of the New Jersey State Museum.

259. Interior of fig. 258. Banner: JOHN GREEN/EMPRESS OF CHINA/COMMANDER.

260. *Tureen*, c. 1796, H 21.6 cm. Overglaze enamels; figure of Commerce with anchor, banner: SPERO; part of service for Elias Hasket Derby; unique. Courtesy of the Winterthur Museum.

the whole country and for certain Chinese merchants as well, like the Co-hong leader Houqua. For the Chinese, in matters of language, the association was fortuitous. It was easier for a Chinese to speak English or Pidgin English with a New England accent that allowed one to drop *r*'s, always a problem for the Oriental to pronounce.

The period of the "Old China Trade," wistfully referred to in later days when the going was tougher in China, began with the first ships in Guangzhou in the 1780s; it ended with the Opium Wars of the 1840s, with the opening of new treaty ports to foreign trade, and, by the 1850s, with the advent of steamers in China's coastwise shipping. Huge fortunes were made by the canniest investors and their agents buying goods in China and selling them at home, usually at great profit. The first American millionaires in this country made their fortunes in the China trade. Such a one was Elias Hasket Derby of Salem, whose adventures to

China exceeded all others in the first decade of trade (fig. 260). Derby trained later captains and merchants such as Thomas Handasyd Perkins, Joseph Peabody, Jacob and George Crowninshield, Benjamin Hodges, and Ichabod Nichols. Perkins, a Bostonian, set up a partnership with his brother James; with Derby turning to general enterprise in the Far East, the brothers had no competitor in Guangzhou in the early days. Perkins hired his relatives for work in China and at home, along with his friends and their relatives. An old-China-boy network under Perkins's aegis, involving the Cabots, Lambs, Cushings, Forbeses, and other families, made New Englanders preeminent in the entire Guangzhou exchange. Competition for Perkins eventually came, however, from a fellow New Englander, Samuel Russell of Middletown, Connecticut, and several Rhode Island associates, who took the lead when Perkins's firm closed in 1838. Two years later, Augustine Heard, Sr., of Ipswich, a partner of Russell's, set up a rival house, which he and his nephews operated until the Civil War. The houses of Russell and Heard thus dominated lesser merchants both in China and Boston until after mid-century.

The emphasis on Salem/Boston, interconnected in their China interests from the start, does not eclipse the activity of other ports. In Providence, operating from capital amassed in colonial days, the Brown family—originally operating as Brown, Benson and Ives, then as Brown and Ives—were first in China. Edward Carrington and Company later entered the trade, especially after the War of 1812. Carrington's mansion (fig. 261) boasted many fine porcelains (fig. 262). Some of them were displayed in his dining room, an addition to most wealthy American homes in the Federal Period.[2]

The depression of 1826 set back the port, however, and only in 1831 did trade in Providence resume, with just six ships sailing in the next, and final, decade. In contrast, New York's activity increased after 1826. The city's trade was often dependent upon New

England agents of Russell or Heard, or upon New Englanders, such as Seth, Abiel A., and William H. Low, transplanted to New York and China. John Jacob Astor's early ventures on the Northwest Coast to obtain the furs always in demand in China were over by 1815; and others, such as Thomas H. Smith, were big investors but suffered from the 1826 depression. Still others were more stable: N. L. & G. Griswold; Daniel W. C. Olyphant; Grinnell, Minturn and Company; Minturn and Champlin; and Howland and Aspinwall, along with the Lows, who were important in the 1840s. New York was a natural entrepôt for distribution to areas inland to other coastal towns. The bowl in figure 263 is witness to the city's final preeminence in the trade.

As for ports farther south, Philadelphia stands out. She had sent a ship to China in the spring of 1786 and continued to be active into the late 1830s, carrying the heaviest loads of all the ports, especially in the peak years before the War of 1812. The names of her merchants still resonate in the city: Charles Wharton, Jones and Clark, Robert and Jesse Waln, Samuel Archer, and Stephen Girard, among others. Even so, in the number of ships used in the China trade, Philadelphia and Boston were both behind New York by the 1830s. Nearby Baltimore operated her sporadic exchange as a side issue after welcoming home the ship *Pallas* in 1785, bought in Guangzhou to help bring back the *Empress*'s goods.

Within Philadelphia's range, a Delawarean, John R.

261. Interior, southeast parlor, house of Edward Carrington, built 1810–11, razed 1962. Courtesy of the Rhode Island Historical Society.

262. *Urn* (one of a pair on mantel in fig. 261), c. 1800–10, H 47.6 cm. Overglaze enamels, first-class export, rare. Courtesy of the Rhode Island Historical Society.

263. *Bowl*, c. 1811, D 53.3 cm. Exterior upper border: PRESENTED BY GENERAL JACOB MORTON TO THE CORPORATION OF THE CITY OF NEW YORK, JULY 4, 1812; **unique.** On loan from the City of New York, 1912. Courtesy of the Metropolitan Museum of Art.

Latimer, rose in the exchange toward the end of the "Old China Trade," becoming more than a mere satellite figure, though he began as a common supercargo. In 1815, on order of the Philadelphia merchant William S. Evans, Latimer traded opium for an eighty-one piece tea and coffee service "of a deep blue color with rather a deep gold edging & the initials *APE* upon each piece & the gilding well put on."[3] Like Robert Bennett Forbes of Boston, Latimer finally made his fortune in opium. He became a prominent shipowner, dealing not only with Philadelphia but also with New England and New York. In late 1829, his *Sumatra* carried three hundred boxes of chinaware to Salem, whose own trade to China was on the wane.[4]

In Norfolk, Charleston, Savannah, Mobile, and New Orleans, many trade records were lost in the Civil War. A ship may have left Norfolk for China in 1796; another departed from Charleston for the Far East but it is unknown whether or not she touched at Guangzhou. Apart from the items ordered specially by the Manigaults of Charleston (see chapter 7) and a handful of other southerners, it is safe to assume that most of the China goods reaching American cities south of Philadelphia and Baltimore came via transshipment from New England, or increasingly, from New York.[5] More porcelains were brought back by

East Coast shippers in the fifty years after the Revolution than reached the colonies before, but not immediately. America's fleet, much reduced in the war, had to be rebuilt. Investors had to be recruited, the Guangzhou procedures of trade assimilated, ships outfitted, markets more closely studied. By the 1790s, the machinery was present for the growth (figs. 264–266), and a first high point occurred in 1805–06 when about forty-two American ships were loading at Guangzhou. Between 1790 and 1812, more than four hundred voyages had been made to Guangzhou and back. After the War of 1812, trade increased rapidly toward a second high in 1818–19, with forty-seven American ships registered. Interestingly, the previous year had been a peak for porcelain importation.[6]

Porcelain cargoes varied from year to year and did not necessarily correspond to the number of ships but rather to the supplies in Guangzhou and the anticipated American market. Also, even in these busy years of the trade, porcelain was a small fourth behind much larger shipments of teas, fabrics, and spices in demand at home. However, porcelain's special power was permanency. Today, this ware has outlasted all her more bountiful rivals from China in their day to stand as a supreme symbol of a great era in the East-West exchange.

By the mid-1830s, porcelain in quantity was demoted from even a minor item in the trade to a "sundry," a miscellaneous import. In the 1833–34 season, only 1,322 boxes of chinaware were shipped from Guangzhou to the United States, an amount more than easily handled by the forty-three ships registered in China that year. Still, the mystique of the East died hard, and the quality of the ware, even its imperfections, had grown on buyers in America. While many turned to porcelains from Europe and England, despite high customs duties (see p. 288), a few people still ordered China's or, more commonly, bought what was shipped. And that happened even after the "Old China Trade" was disrupted and gradually disappeared, beginning with the Opium Wars, 1839–42.

The best opium was from India and was the money item sold by the British and Parsees in China. It was in part financed by Americans, who also dealt in a lesser type from Turkey. The drug gave the West the wherewithal to buy its teas, silks, and porcelains. In 1839, the Chinese demanded the confiscation of all opium in Guangzhou in order to stop the trade—fearing the flight of specie from the country as well as the drug's effect on its citizens. In fact, their first fear was unfounded; money was returned by the purchases just mentioned.[7]

The British resisted confiscation with force. Her profits were too great and her demand for tea and silk too strong to accept the new Chinese policy without resistance. China was forced to acquiesce, suffering a permanent loss of face vis-à-vis the West. The Treaty of Nanking in 1842 opened up four new ports: Amoy, Ningpo, Fuzhou, and Shanghai, to which the Americans also had access by the Treaty of Wanghia two years later.[8] Guangzhou would no longer be the focus of the exchange. During the 1850s, Shanghai, building

264. *Urn* (one of a pair), 1803, H 47.6 cm. Overglaze enamels, a variant of the English arms of Leslie-Melville with American flag; unique (compare fig. 262). Private collection.

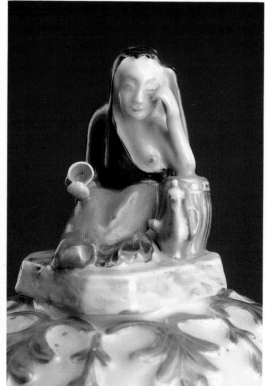

265. (left) Finial of fig. 264, original; see repaired finial in fig. 262.

266. (above) Medallion of fig. 264.

for overseas commerce since 1846, became the chief port serving the West.

Under the gun of foreigners from the outside, the Qing dynasty also suffered internally in the Taiping (The Heavenly Kingdom of Great Peace) Rebellion of 1851–64. This peasant revolt, whose leader brought together aberrant Christian ideas with Confucianism, began in southern China, where the government had just suffered at the hands of the British.[9] During the fifties, their forces swept the Chang Jiang (Yangtze) Valley but were unable to take Beijing. Imperial troops in effect managed a stalemate. Meanwhile, however, the countryside was ravaged and many lives were lost. Jingdezhen was one of the areas partly destroyed.

267. *Vase*, c. 1840–60, H 23.5 cm. Overglaze enamels, American clipper ship, possibly unique. Gift of Frederick S. Colburn. Courtesy of the Art Institute, Chicago.

When rebuilt, its population and production were much reduced.[10]

Concurrent with the first Opium War and the Taiping Rebellion, the American clipper-ship era enjoyed a brief but brilliant existence. Seven years before the British developed their own, the American clippers emerged in the 1840s; their number peaked in the early 1850s, and they virtually disappeared before the Civil War. They were latter-day cousins of the Baltimore clippers, developed for speed in privateering before the Revolution. The ships' names alone spoke of their new power and beauty: *Wings of the Morning, Memnon, Flying Cloud, Sparkling Sun, Pride of America.*[11]

So famous did America's "China Clippers" become that they are often alluded to as *the* ships in the trade; their finely raked lines and multiple masts were the reasons for both their rise and demise. A sharp lift of floor gave the bow a knife edge to cut the seas, and the four masts allowed for plenty of sail. Speed in delivering mail and responding to the demands for high-priority teas was their great virtue, but at the price of strength. In heavy weather, always met in rounding South America's Cape Horn, the strain on the clippers' hulls was enormous; the wind's force, a huge press upon her canvas. After a few long voyages, she could be racked, her seams opened, exposing her cargoes to water damage. Shippers and insurers were wary of the clippers and turned to substitutes: continental rail transport and mail steamers between China and California.[12]

In their heyday, the clippers needed a good deal of ballast to steady such slender, yard-rich vessels. Contrary to popular impression, the ballast was not chinaware. In fact, porcelains had been used to "floor-off" regular ships, protecting teas, fabrics, and spices from getting wet, but never as ballast per se. Only *chow chow* (miscellaneous) chinaware would have been brought back via the clippers. Perhaps the vase in figure 267 was in such a shipment. A clipper's carrying capacity was limited to registered tonnage in dead weight with only a little more in mixed weight and measurement cargo.[13] However, the teas carried by clipper came home in record time—on the average, a hundred days from Guangzhou to New York or Boston. The record was eighty-four days, set by the *Atalanta* of New York.[14]

TWO RIVAL MERCHANTS

A view of the fortunes of the Forbes family in the mid-nineteenth century, especially Robert Bennett Forbes (1804–89), and of Augustine Heard, Sr. (1785–1868), and his nephews, gives an intimate picture of the last period of significant porcelain importation, even though the china was a sundry. Thomas H. Perkins's commission firm had been bought by Samuel Russell of Connecticut in 1838. Russell and Company inherited Perkins's personnel, including the Forbeses, who were direct relations. Robert Bennett Forbes, Perkins's nephew, succeeded his two brothers, Thomas T. and John M. Forbes, in serving as chief officer of Russell's in Guangzhou by 1840. Also, like his brothers, Robert was intimate with Houqua and did business for him abroad in exchange for investment in Russell and Company with commission to himself.

Robert Forbes's story, vividly told in his *Personal Reminiscences*, shows him to be an exemplary "old China hand." Thanks to his Perkins connections, at age thirteen he was a cabin boy, and three years later, third mate. At twenty, he commanded a ship; at twenty-six, he owned the ship he commanded. At twenty-eight, he left the sea for business administered from Boston. But speculating unwisely in a Pennsylvania nail venture and suffering from the depression of 1836, Forbes was forced to return to China, where he sought a "competency," that is, a way to recoup and perhaps exceed his earlier fortune.

Forbes's knowledge of porcelain was as keen as his expertise with the money goods of tea and fabrics. It was his business to know what porcelain was worth and the preferences of those at home. He had first-hand experience with chinaware reserved for the domestic market, as well. Within three months of his return to Guangzhou in 1838, in December, Forbes and others from Russell's were entertained by Mingqua, a Hong merchant, at Mingqua's home. The seemingly endless, hours-long, multicourse dinner that Forbes lavishly described, with only two fifteen-minute breaks to stretch and walk about, exemplifies Chinese hospitality and explains the digestive complaints of the Americans who habitually over-ate out of boredom.

The chinaware on which Mingqua's banquet was served was noted by Forbes as well. To begin, tea appeared *à la chinoise* (i.e., without milk or sugar) in covered porcelain cups with stands, probably similar to that in figure 268. After tea, the cups were repeatedly filled with a warm rice wine, *samshue*, which Forbes later called "vile" and compared to opium in its debilitating effects.[15] The party toasted each other and gamely drained their cups, showing them empty to their drinking partners. "Humpers" (bottoms up), Forbes explained, was orthodox in China on all occasions (and in the 1980s, still is). At each place setting was "a small porcelain saucer highly painted about 3 inches in diameter, a spoon of same material, a small shallow cup & saucer & a porcelain cup or stand to rest the spoon in"; the meal was to be eaten with silver-tipped chopsticks.[16]

"Highly painted" may refer to polychrome figures similar to the contemporary "Rose Mandarin" or

268. *Cup and saucer*, c. 1835, cup (with cover): H 10.2 cm, saucer: D 12.7 cm. Underglaze blue, originally owned by Edward Carrington of Providence, above-average domestic/export. Private collection.

"Rose Canton" china, but the forms were unlike those common to an American table. That was true, too, of dishes on a second "board," literally a slab of wood brought in to replace the first with another series of courses, including one served in an octagonal porcelain quart bowl. Small, octagonal, covered cups contained three more courses, and with these, everyone drank a very strong wine "tasting like a decoction of dried raisins." In addition, a chafing dish with still other choices of delicacies, such as fried frog, surrounded by seven or eight bowls of boiled "something" was on the table. Then, a simple bowl of rice was served to each diner. No sooner was it done than a whole new course appeared: roast pig, leg of mutton, and roast duck—a gift from the host's father! Finally, the meal finished with fruits—fresh, dried, and preserved in syrup—with Forbes, and no doubt others, in extremis.[17]

A quantity of dishes was needed for such a meal, as many or more than those used in the West, but obviously, different. Those differences would have been uppermost in Forbes's mind as he selected gifts of china to send home to his wife, Rose, and close

friends. Still, one of his first china purchases, "a great piece of extravagance," less than a month after Mingqua's banquet, was "$25.00 worth of china such as the Chinese use themselves in rich homes. . . ."[18] Forbes continued:

> Some of the China is superb—the 10 cups one within another cost 2 1/4 dolls—there is a muster of plates which I think are very handsome the six large cost 3 1/4 the six small 2 3/4 for the six—There are two setts of dishes—one of 4 & one of more the latter all match together, that is they fit together & make one large dish with compartments for different kinds of fruits or sweetmeats—the 6 bowls & saucers cost only 1.50—there are no regular sets like the plates—but only plates. I thought these things would do to distribute very sparingly among your most attentive friends.[19]

Rose Forbes, writing in early June, 1839, greatly anticipated the arrival of the chinaware: "I am afraid you knew a weak corner about me when you bought that China—*pretty things* being an infirmity I have to struggle against . . . ," especially before her husband had regained his "competency." Ten days later, however, the china had arrived, some of it broken ("four of the large plates, and a bowl, and some other things"), about which Rose was "dreadfully vexed," but the rest, she wrote, "come in well with our best painted sett and I was very much delighted with them."[20] Of the two plates in figure 269, the blue-and-rose one (right) is the sort of china that pleased wealthy Chinese. One or the other services represented by the plates in figures 270 and 271, both owned by the Forbeses, was possibly the "best painted sett" Rose mentioned. ("Best painted" does not necessarily mean "highly painted.") Figure 272 is a blue-and-white condiment dish, a variation on the sort of multipiece object to which Forbes referred in his January letter.

In late October of 1839, Rose also wrote of an antique vase just arrived: "I am perfectly *delighted* with it—it stands on the book case and is the envy of a good many . . . I like it as well as anything you have sent me—that is saying a good deal. . . .''[21] Perhaps the vase was a cylindrical one of the Kangxi period, which tradition has attributed as a gift from Houqua to Robert's brother, John Murray Forbes. That vase is now at the Peabody Museum in Salem. It is not likely that either of the Forbeses would have mistaken the vase in figure 273, which matches the plate on the right in figure 269, as ''antique.''

Two other references to china occur in Forbes's let-

269. *Plates*, c. 1875–1900, D 19.0 cm, overglaze cabbage-leaf design, common domestic/export; right: c. 1835, D 19.7 cm, overglaze enamels, four *shou* characters in gilt, owned by Robert Bennett Forbes, fine domestic/export. Courtesy of the Peabody Museum.

270. *Dish*, c. 1820–30, L 26.7 cm. Overglaze sepia, owned by Robert Bennett Forbes, unusual monochrome export. Courtesy of the Peabody Museum.

271. *Soup plate*, c. 1820–30, D 25.4 cm. Overglaze enamels, owned by Robert Bennett Forbes, superior export. Courtesy of the Peabody Museum.

272. *Dish* (for condiments), c. 1820–40, D 49.0 cm. Underglaze blue, "Nanking" design, superior export. Courtesy of the Peabody Museum.

273. *Vase* (one of a pair), c. 1835, H 43.2 cm. Overglaze enamels and gilt (see fig. 269), right, owned by Robert Bennett Forbes, fine domestic/export. Courtesy of the Peabody Museum.

ters of 1839. One was a dinner or tea service he contemplated for Ester [Osgood?]. A second was "a Box marked JSCG containing Cuspadores [*sic*] for Copley to whom give my perpetual regards."[22] These personal gifts were hand selected and do not represent large consignments to merchants, a rarity in the remaining Forbes papers. References to such presents are also relatively rare in Robert's correspondence. He could not yet afford to send friends expensive objects, and he was hard at work; when he was not actually trading in tea or fabrics, he was embroiled in the coming Opium War buildup. Earlier business papers of the Forbeses include references to chinaware bought in the 1820s and early 1830s and mention others through the 1870s, both as commercial loads (though not very large) and as private purchases.

Robert Forbes was only thirty-six when he became head of Russell and Company; he served in Guangzhou until 1840. When the Opium Wars broke out in 1839, he benefitted as representative of neutral America and made great profits for the company and himself by supplying the British with Chinese goods. This opportunity lasted only a matter of months, and he soon returned home, where for nine years he and his brother, John, were consignees of shipments from China and joint owners of vessels. In 1849, Robert Forbes returned to China, and during the next eight years, he witnessed two major changes: the shift of the center for foreign trade from Guangzhou to Shanghai, and the experimentation with steamers for the carrying trade along the coast.

Forbes, a "steam enthusiast," had a wooden paddle steamer, *Spark*, built at New York and sent out to be completed at Whampoa for Captain John B. Endicott. Capable of speeds of eleven knots or more, this pioneer vessel was soon put into service between Hongkong, Guangzhou, and Macao. Thomas Hunt and Company of Whampoa, a firm involved in shipbuilding and repairing as well as trade, also entered the early steamer venture in the mid-1850s.[23] According to Hunt's business papers, he carried chinaware among the coastal ports; although he made frequent reference to his china cargoes in the 1860s, the amounts were meager and the designs unspecified, possibly because much of it was white, utilitarian tableware.[24] (Plain white may have been one of the most popular; Augustine Heard, Sr., ordered it before blue-and-white in 1848.)

These two experimenters in steam—Forbes and Hunt—and a handful of others preceded Russell and company in setting up regular steamer service between the coastal ports. Russell's Shanghai Steam Navigation Company (S.S.N.) was started in 1862 and lasted well into the latter part of the nineteenth century, along with many British and eventually Chinese colleagues in steam. A sample ceramic cargo of 1867 shows that the S.S.N. carried a limited amount of fine and coarse chinaware from abroad, as well as five times as much domestic porcelain of both qualities between Shanghai and Tianjin (Tientsin).[25] The China trade overseen by Americans thus changed from one principally involved with shipping on the high seas from East to West to transport of goods and passengers between Chinese ports, including those opened up on the Chang Jiang (Yangtze) River.[26]

Forbes's residency in China in the steamer period of the 1850s put him in the midst of the last years of the Old China Trade. At the same time, his former colleague in Russell's, Augustine Heard, Sr. (with his nephew), was competing in the commission business. The Heard records in the porcelain trade complement Forbes's purchases, giving a fuller view of the limited amounts of, but still-desired wares being bought for America in the 1840s and 1850s. In 1848, one order for a dessert set from Heard, Sr., then resident in the United States, to Augustine Heard, Jr., his nephew, requested the decoration be "painted figures upon a light green ground."[27] Figure 274 is such an example. White was another Heard choice, preferred at least to blue-and-white, as he had specified in an order for

"deep oval or octagon dishes" a few months earlier.[28] Still, blue-and-white might be of first quality and priority. In an order for blue-and-white "FitzHugh" in 1850, Heard, Sr., asked for a dining service, which he noted was "for rich people," indicating an upper-class preference for this pattern. In the same order, six garden seats of a barrel form and "rich colors" were also included.[29]

The same year the senior Heard was annoyed by his inexperienced namesake, who had mistakenly interpreted a request for "pots" as meaning flowerpots. Heard, Sr., had intended a nest of pots of about five per set, the largest about 5 inches high, 4 inches in diameter; the innermost, a little over an inch high. He wanted them of a "whitish ground with figures, chi-

274. *Plate*, c. 1840–50, D 24.5 cm. Overglaze enamels; upper-right: characters *Shengxian* (Chai Shaobing, 1616–70), poet and connoisseur of antiquities; fine domestic/export. Courtesy of the Peabody Museum.

276. *Cup and cover*, period and mark of Tongzhi, 1862–74, matches saucer in fig. 275.

275. *Saucer*, c. 1862–74, D 14.5 cm. Overglaze enamels; in center, Li Taibo (A.D. 701–762), poet of the Tang dynasty; above and below, other historic figures; owned by Augustine Heard, Sr.; above-average domestic/export. Courtesy of the Peabody Museum.

277. (below) *Tea service* (partial), c. 1855–70. Penciled ware; made for owner, Catherine van Rensselaer Bonney, teacher in China, 1856–71; unusual export. Courtesy of Historic Cherry Hill, Albany.

nese inscriptions." Having been sent the flowerpots instead, Heard, Sr., complained, "I am without the pots after having promised them to some half a doz persons, if old Cumchong is alive in the first shop on the right hand side of Old China St. just go in and he will show you what I want & send them by the first opportunity."[30] The style was popular at least among Heard and his friends and may have resembled those in figure 311. The saucer in figure 275 could have been among the "doz largest size cups & saucers with covers ornamented with Chinese figures" that he asked for a few months later.[31] This saucer is large,

and with its cup and cover (fig. 276), part of a set that once belonged to Heard.

Two years later (1852), in a similar order, Heard, Sr., wrote:

> I want two or three doz. of large size cups & saucers with covers, with figures, inscriptions, etc. on them they should be thick and strong I have had same sort twice, but they are too thin. When I came from China I brought some such as I now want. . . . The edge at the cover was flat for an eighth or more of an inch & rested on the edge of the cup instead of going inside the cup.[32]

Heard appears to be describing a bouillon bowl and cover (fig. 277, left). Such a pattern was contemporary with more richly painted gold-red export (fig. 278).

Heard's personal interest in porcelain extended to

278. *Toilet set*, c. 1855–70, "Rose Mandarin" ware: basin, covered bottle, commode, brush box, and soap dish; associated with Catherine van Rensselaer Bonney; common export. Courtesy of Historic Cherry Hill, Albany.

279. *Plates*, c. 1835–50, period and mark (orange-red), Qianlong (1736–95); left: D 21.6 cm, three bats on rim on reverse; right: D 20.3 cm. Overglaze enamels, fine domestic/export. Courtesy of the Peabody Museum.

280. *Greenware* (not a set), c. 1845–55. Shaped dish (nappie): L 26.7 cm. Overglaze enamels on green ground, owned by Robert Bennett Forbes, above-average export. Courtesy of the Peabody Museum.

finding replacements for his friends. Miles Timming had broken an "old China plate bought by his brother at a curiosity shop . . . 14 3/4 to 15 inches in diameter with painted flowers, birds, & beasts on a white ground."[33] A plate of similar style, if not of such size, is in figure 279 (right). Heard might also write to find just the right "FitzHugh" service, blue or green, for the relative of a friend.[34] He would pursue just the right strength (thickness—and frequently the requirement was for thick not thin wares) of a stock pattern. This was often fulfilled by china with a green ground on which birds, butterflies, and flowers in polychrome enamels were prominent (fig. 280).[35] Further exhibiting his interest and nascent connoisseurship in 1856, he wrote to his youngest nephew, Albert, also a procurer of porcelain for him, of the "very curious ware" from Suzhou, which pleased him very much. On the strength of it, he increased from $50 to $100 the amount to be spent on purchases of this sort.[36] Finally, he commented to Albert, "You say that it is more difficult to find curious things at Shanghai than

at Canton, which I suppose is the case, and yet I believe for us rather odd China ware are [sic] found there."[37] Clearly, an American merchant could easily become a china collector, given the means, the curiosity, and in the elder Heard's case, distance from the hustle of trading per se.

Heard and Company did not join in the race to be the first in steam on the China coast. Their activities were over by the end of the Civil War; but others, such as Thomas Hunt and the Russell Company, continued. In the 1860s, Hunt and Company, from their bases in Shanghai and Hongkong, dealt not only in Chinese porcelains but in Western (probably English) earthenware and porcelain as well. The foreign residents of the treaty ports liked to have such familiar wares as well as foodstuffs from home. In fact, in the Hunt records, "blue line," "blue edged," white and gold table services, and earthenware of "French shape" may have outnumbered the Chinese ware.[38] Indefinite references as to type of ceramic make comparisons impossible.

UNITED STATES TRADERS ON THE WEST COAST

Across the Pacific, California, at the end of the eighteenth century, was the setting for still another episode in the China trade. French, English, and American ships had begun to search out the potential of the West Coast. In 1796, the first American vessel, the *Otter*—so named for the sea otter, the chief catch along the Pacific coast and in great demand for its fur in China—arrived at Santa Cruz, then was off Carmel before stopping in Monterey for a week. She was a Boston vessel, en route to Hawaii and Guangzhou before returning to New England.[39]

The *Otter* and three other American vessels in the late 1790s (the *Garland*, *Eliza*, and *Betsy*) stopped at the coast on their way to the Far East. They were not importing Chinese goods except perhaps an infinitesi-

mal, unknown amount left over from supplies originally destined for New England.[40] By the first years of the nineteenth century, American ships were touching on the coast before and after crossing the Pacific to Guangzhou. Thus, the *Hazard* and the *Lelia Byrd*, in their multiport meanderings in 1803–05 beginning in Liverpool and Hamburg respectively, set a pattern of meeting numerous markets, including those of China and California.[41] Most of the owners of these ships were from Boston, putting a lasting Yankee stamp upon activities in California as business went through several phases on the coast.

During the Spanish period, a royal decree officially prohibited foreigners from trade. Unofficially, however, bartering was carried on for otter skins in return for manufactured products. The latter were always in short supply, and the government was not always powerful enough to stop clandestine exchanges, including those with the missions.[42] Even so, the limited number of buyers and sellers meant that little porcelain changed hands. There were only about two thousand *gente de razón* in all of Spanish California in 1800–10,[43] and a mere twenty-four vessels were on the coast in 1800–09, though some of them touched ports several times.[44] By 1803, the Yankees began to free themselves from barter by contracting with the Russians, who had settled in Sitka in 1799, to hunt the otter for equal shares. This scheme marked a new stage of independence from the Spanish and more activity among the Americans.

Still, only a handful of ships went to Guangzhou with furs, and few returned with China goods for California.[45] Also, recording cargoes was unusual, because the trade was illicit. One exception was the *Mercury*, Captain George Washington Eayrs. For seven years, 1806–13, this ship was in the Pacific, stopping first in southern California, then Hawaii, then Guangzhou. Recrossing the ocean in 1808, it arrived on the Northwest coast, then traded far down the California coast, returning north to the Columbia River and on to Sitka.

Again it descended the coast, stopping at several places on the way to Santa Barbara. From there it sailed for Guangzhou a second time in 1811, perhaps stopping in Hawaii en route. Returning to Sitka, it went to and from there to northern and southern California, with a final cruise south along the coast, where it was finally seized by the Spanish and taken in at Santa Barbara.[46]

During these voyages, Eayrs both bartered with the Spanish and contracted with the Russians, taking care to trade not at any of the major ports but rather out of range of Spanish surveillance at places such as San Luis Obispo, San Buenaventura, San Gabriel, San Juan Capistrano, San Miguel, and Rosario, where he was welcomed by padres and rancheros alike. He also stopped at ranchos like the Ortegas's at Refugio, a famous contraband center west of Santa Barbara.[47]

On his first trip to China, Eayrs evidently picked up some chinaware along with silks and crepes. His account books show that he sold pitchers and a punch bowl, probably Chinese export.[48] When he returned from his second Guangzhou voyage, he sold to the mission at San Luis Obispo goods valued at $1,385, some of which were undoubtedly oriental. He had earlier supplied the new Russian settlement at Fort

281. *Platter with strainer*, c. 1810, D 45.0 cm. Overglaze enamels. Fine export. Courtesy of the Peabody Museum.

Ross with some of his fresh cargo from China: the usual silks, rice, pepper, and mother-of-pearl.[49] Some of these wares lasted until his ship was inventoried after its confiscation in 1813. Along with silks and other fabrics, the *Mercury* carried seventy-two bouillon cups, seventy-two flowered plates, twelve flowered platters (see fig. 281), coffeepots, tureens and cups, and various kinds of dishes as well as four large and finely decorated earthen water jars.[50] The *Mercury*'s supplies are a sample of the wares so prized by a product-lean frontier society.

The *Mercury*'s days in China and California bridged the end of the Spanish and the beginning of the Mexican periods on the West Coast. The years of revolution, 1811–20, were ones of uncertainty, lack of supplies from New Spain, and scarcity of money. The dearth of manufactured goods was felt even more.[51] Yankee shippers took quick advantage of this opportunity. In the 1810–19 period, fifty-two ships, twenty-four of which were U.S. vessels, touched the coast, many of them either from China or Hawaii.[52] These voyages gradually established a fresh pattern, so that by 1822 a new era in the California–China trade was underway.

The Northwest fur trade dwindled, and the focus turned south. A great circular route—which came to be called the "Spanish Main"—developed between China and California, interconnected by Hawaii and other calls in the South Pacific. In the years after the War of 1812, otter skins gradually were succeeded by other hides and tallow produced by California rancheros. Supplies to them of manufactured goods from Guangzhou had this sure advantage: their price was lower than anywhere else. Some Atlantic Coast goods were also included,[53] among which might be export china first shipped to the East Coast. For example, in 1823, a small box of Chinese porcelain containing plates sent by Blanchard and Dorr of Boston arrived for sale in San Francisco to the mission and other buyers.[54]

First Marshall and Wildes, then Bryant, Sturgis and Company, both of Boston, were leaders in the new trading pattern. The latter sent out the *Mentor*, Captain Goerge Newell, in 1824, which made an exceedingly speedy, four-month voyage from Guangzhou to Monterey, to sell $1,800 worth of goods to the mission, presidio, and other buyers. Newell also sold to the Russians at Bodega and Monterey before going on to Mazatlán.[55] The following year, the *Nile*, Captain Robert Bennett Forbes, with Newell as supercargo, left Guangzhou for Hawaii and California. No porcelain was on board their first voyage in January 1825. In June, on another ship, the following wares, no doubt of various qualities, were loaded in Guangzhou "for a voyage to the Pacific Ocean," almost certainly Hawaii and California:

50	Boxes of China Ware ea a Tea Sett of 42 ps.	$1.60	80
20	" do do ea a dinner Sett 172 ps.	16.—	320
5	" ea a Tea Sett of 52 ps.	7.—	55
2	" each are 12 Cuspadores @	.75	9
2	" 20 is 40 pr Candle Stands	.75	30
1	" 100 Fruit bowls	.60	6
1	" 10 doz Chocolate bowls & saucers	.10	10[56]

No one shipment of porcelain to California was "typical," and this one was experimental, carrying wares much like those in figures 281 and 282. However, the size of the vessel was somewhat standard. A brigantine was in keeping with the importers' best experience: better to have small ships with a limited amount of goods, which could be quickly sold, than to have large ships and surplus wares.

Sales were often small, as Newell discovered with the *Nile* goods, although, he noted, they "nett a very good profit."[57] Limited demand among a *gente de razón* of only 3,270 in 1820 and 4,250 ten years later[58] is also reflected in an 1827 shipment. The brig *Mary Esther* carried six crates each of blue-and-white china plates and cups and saucers (fig. 283) as well as eight crates of pitchers, mugs, and chamberpots. Only

282. *Candlesticks* (pair), c. 1820–30, H 17.8 cm. Underglaze blue "Canton" ware, average export, now rare. Courtesy of Norman Herreshoff.

284. *Plate*, c. 1825–50, D 22.8 cm. Underglaze blue, common export. Private collection.

283. *"Canton" ware* (not a set), c. 1825–35, dish: L 25.4 cm. Underglaze blue, willow pattern, owned by Robert Bennett Forbes, common export. Courtesy of the Peabody Museum.

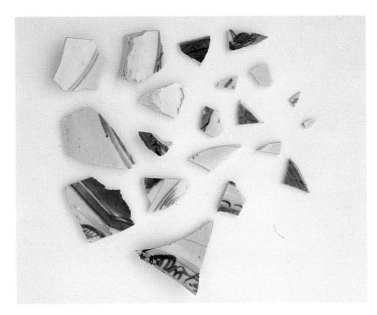

285. *Shards* from the priest's house, Old Plaza Church, downtown Los Angeles, c. 1819–21. ''Canton,'' ''Four Seasons'' (see fig. 303), and enameled ware. Courtesy of the Northridge Archaeological Research Center, Northridge, California, and El Pueblo de Los Angeles State Historic Park.

half of the total was to be sold in California; the other half was destined for Acapulco, Mazatlán, and San Blas (fig. 284).[59] Perhaps porcelains similar to the ones carried by the *Mary Esther* are represented by blue-and-white and polychrome shards from a large trash pit beneath the priest's house of the Old Plaza Church, Los Angeles (fig. 285). The refuse was probably thrown in the pit and compacted before the house was built, thus giving a rough date of about 1819–21 to the deposit. The porcelain's original owners are unknown; the pit was used jointly by several households, a mixture of Spanish and Indian settlers in the Pueblo de Los Angeles. The proportion of porcelain to majolica and mission (brownware) is 1 to 20 to 200 pieces. The apparent prevalence of missionware in such quantities may be because it was a coarser earthenware, more roughly used in storage and cooking than the finer, more carefully handled tableware.[60]

In the 1830s, six vessels—four brigantines, a schooner, and a barkentine—sailed directly from Honolulu to California with porcelains, documenting new energy in the China trade. A robust market was reported in San Franciso in 1834 by Alfred Robinson, supercargo for Bryant and Sturgis: ''The California trade at present is brisk and we have a good demand for Goods of every description, each year approach-

286. *Jar*, c. 1815–30, H 66.0 cm. Underglaze blue, brass-bound with lock, first-class export. Courtesy of the Essex Institute.

287. *Plate*, c. 1830, D 21.2 cm. Overglaze enamels, owned by Frederick Hall Bradlee and Lucretia Wainwright of Boston (m. 1831), fine export. Courtesy of the Peabody Museum.

288. *Plate*, c. 1820–30, D 24.1 cm. Overglaze enamels and gilt; four Chinese "Auspicious Figures" with emblems of the "Hundred Antiquities"; monogram NPH for Nathaniel Perez Hamlen of Boston; fine export. Courtesy of a descendant, Mr. Devlen Hamlen.

289. *Plate*, c. 1825–50, D 25.0 cm. Overglaze enamels, fine export. Courtesy of the Peabody Museum.

ing to a greater consumption. . . ."[61] Two years later, Robinson profiled the San Diego market: "Fancy articles generally sell well. . . . they are fond of using in this Country anything that in style is new rich & shewy. . . ."[62] The jar in figure 286, familiar to Hispanic taste, would have been in this category.

Porcelains, at their best, are always "new rich & shewy." The pieces from the six ships' cargoes thus had healthy markets whether in northern or southern California. The *Crusader* (1832) carried a case containing 6 each of large, second- and third-size plates; 12 each of "Rose pattern" (fig. 287) and "Antiquities" soup plates (fig. 288); 12 "Rose pattern" plates (fig. 289); 144 "Lustre" (no doubt, English) mugs of two different patterns; 288 blue mugs, also of two patterns (probably blue-and-white); 36 coffee cups and saucers of three patterns; 24 "China teas" (teacups) of two patterns; 6 each of large and small flowerpots; 24 deep covered dishes and 48 shallow covered dishes

(fig. 290); 48 gravy boats and ladles of two patterns; and 24 "Globe Lanthorns" (lanterns). In another case were unidentified ceramics, which were doubtless English wares: "Scroll Dishes," "Punty Plates" (decorated with a hollow circle or oval), "Gothic" and "Thistle Octagon Dishes," "Diamond pattern Salts," handled "Shell Compotia," "Wafer Boxes," and a "Toilet Inkstand" in three pieces. Of the two cases, the quantity of Western ware was roughly double that from the East.[63] The second voyage of the *Crusader* in 1833 brought only a handful more ceramics, and their types, except for one Japanese sugar bowl, is uncertain.[64]

Two other vessels, the *Harriet Blanchard* (1833) and the *Loriot* (1833–34), also imported domestic ceramics. The *Avon* (1834) had a modest amount of miscellaneous ware, including 3 tea sets, 84 first-size and 102 second-size plates, 36 white mugs, 20 colored mugs, 42 pint bowls, 24 each first- and second-size soup plates, and 24 tea plates.[65] Obviously, this list was as minimal and open-stock as was the *Crusader*'s, indicating that Chinese porcelain, even when taste was high for luxury items, was as much a "sundry" on the West Coast of America as it was on the East.

Each vessel's load reflected the supercargo's guess about what would sell. Sometimes various types of ceramics would be in separate but small boxes, as appeared in the invoice of merchandise on board the *Iolani* (1835). And in the "Larboard Locker" of this ship was a combination of ceramics, either one of each type or only a few objects: white, "blue edge," "red" (possibly Ixhing), and "blue" pieces along with "6 green figured Tea Sets," no doubt stylistically similar to the "Rose Mandarin" and "Rose Canton" pieces in figures 274 and 299. (Green and Rose dominate this ware, thus the possibility of alternate period names for it.)[66] China so lumped together was easily denoted as "crockery," a general term, used by the West Coast shippers, that no doubt sometimes meant porcelain. Thus the *Clementine* (1836–37) and the *Don Quixote* (1836) were carrying at least some chinaware, as the

documents show, when casks of crockery in the former and "a large quantity of splendid crockery" in the latter were noted.[67]

Of the *Clementine*'s 1836 cargo, two cases of crockery contained 300 first- to fourth-size plates all of a "green fig'd" pattern, and 21 soup plates of the same design (fig. 291). It also held 270 first- to fourth-size plates and 2 deep dishes in a "Steamboat pattern."[68] The green-figured design might have been Chinese export ware (see figs. 269, 274 or 280), but the steamboat pattern was probably English. Two small plate shards with steamboats labeled "British America," dating from about 1835–45, have been found in Monterey on the site of Nathan Spear's house and store. Spear was the importer of the *Clementine*'s goods.[69] (The only known steamboat depicted on export porcelain is one showing the ship *Philadelphia*, which operated on the East Coast between Chesapeake Bay and the Delaware River, an unlikely pattern to be found in the West among former New Englanders.)[70]

Nathan Spear was an example of Yankee shopkeeping that matched Yankee seafaring in the China trade.

290. *Dish*, c. 1830, L 23.0 cm. Overglaze sepia and gilt birds, butterflies, flowers, and fruits ("bbff"). Courtesy of the Peabody Museum.

291. *Plate and cup*, c. 1830–50. Plate: D 24.1 cm. Overglaze enamels, owned by Robert Bennett Forbes, above-average export. Courtesy of the Peabody Museum.

Several New Englanders, such as Alpheus B. Thompson of Oahu and Santa Barbara, had moved West, married into Spanish families, and prospered. Among others were Francis Branch, William Dana, William Gale, Elias Grimes, William Hartnell, William Hinckley, Samuel Prentice, and David Spence.[71] Spear's predecessor on the same property in Monterey was a former Englishman, John B. R. Cooper. In 1823, Cooper came west as the captain of the *Rover*, a Boston ship sold to the government of California before she made a trip to Guangzhou.[72] He settled in Monterey about 1828 in what is now known as the Cooper-Molera Adobe. Four years later, John Coffin Jones bought the western half of Cooper's property, which he sold in 1835 to Spear. Spear, a Bostonian and shipmate with Cooper on the *Rover*, twice traveled to Hawaii and learned the Pacific market before opening a shop in Monterey in 1832. On his half of the Cooper property, he continued shopkeeping, and when he opened a branch in San Francisco in 1838, he put William Warren in charge of the Monterey store. Seven years later, Spear sold out to Manuel Diaz, a Mexican merchant, whose widow occupied the house until the turn of the century.[73] The property has, therefore, been relatively undisturbed.

This adobe complex plays an important part in the porcelain story of the 1820s to 1840s in California. Spear's accounts document porcelain imported in the ship cargoes just given. And these lists probably refer to the very porcelains represented by the export shards found on the site, which date from the Cooper-Spear eras. The combination of documents and objects is rare. Further, even before reconstruction of the shards, a good many are larger than average (figs. 292–297). Typical of the most common blue-and-white imported, they supplemented supplies of English wares; the latter was much more numerous by both shard and written record. Pieces similar to those

292. *Plate* (reconstructed), c. 1825, from Cooper-Molera Adobe, Monterey. Underglaze blue, rough domestic/export. Courtesy of the California Department of Parks and Recreation (CDPR).

293. *Plate* (reconstructed), c. 1825, same site as fig. 292. Underglaze blue and copper-red, rough domestic/export, compare fig. 289. Courtesy of CDPR.

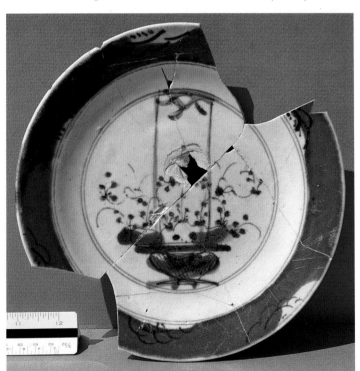

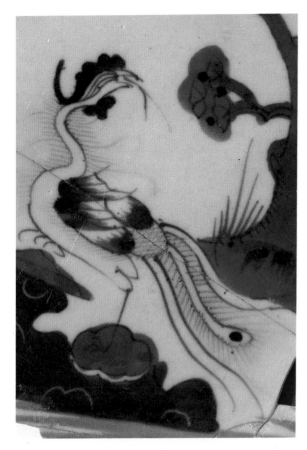

294. (left) Detail, *plate shard*, c. 1825, same site as fig. 292. Underglaze blue and copper-red, close-up of phoenix, rough domestic/export. Courtesy of CDPR.

295. (above) *Cup and plate shards*, c. 1825–35. Underglaze blue, abstracted Arabic script and design, rough domestic/export. Cup from Wrightington Adobe Site, Old Town, San Diego. Courtesy of CDPR.

296. *Platter shards*, 1830–40. Underglaze blue, "Canton" ware, average export. Courtesy of CDPR.

297. *Plate shards*, c. 1825–40. Underglaze blue, "Canton" ware, rough export. Courtesy of CDPR.

298. *Pitchers*, c. 1825–50. Five "Rose Mandarin," one "Rose Medallion"; top left: H 25.0 cm. Courtesy of Mrs. Cleveland Alma Porter and the Peabody Museum.

in figures 292–295, like earlier examples in Mexico, have also been found in Southeast Asia.[74]

The lineage of the cup and plate shards in figure 295 can be traced to Arabic script, first introduced to Chinese porcelain in the fifteenth century. Here they have devolved to mere decorative, totally unreadable elements. Such shards have been found at the Mission San Luis Rey de Francia, at many other places throughout the Pacific Basin, and even at Louisbourg, Nova Scotia.[75]

The 1840s, the last decade of Mexican rule in California, saw a dwindling supply of porcelains. Shipping records indicate that fewer vessels that touched at Guangzhou also traded in California after the 1830s,

though they may have kept up the Hawaiian connection.[76] The Opium Wars of the early 1840s and the opening of new treaty ports broke the Old China Trade patterns, as we have seen. No doubt the taste for English wares made up for any reduction in export pieces. Still, the cargo of the *Alert* in 1840, which came by way of Boston, included what were probably Chinese porcelains: 60 cup-and-saucer sets of "painted Teas," 121 "fancy Chambers," 504 "fancy Painted bowls," 240 "fancy qt. bowls," and 54 "painted pitchers," along with other, clearly English ceramics (fig. 298).[77]

The next year, however, Henry Delano Fitch, a famous West Coast seacaptain and supercargo in the

China trade, bought a mere eighteen "Chinese mugs" for $3.75 total.[78] His purchase was a telling note on the reduced availability and popularity of Chinese export echoing the length of the coast. Such a falling off of porcelain in the late Mexican period is confirmed by the ceramic shards found on the Sepulveda Rancho. José Andrés Sepulveda made an estate from the San Capistrano Mission property and lived there from 1837 to 1864. Of the shards found on his property from the time of his ownership, 50 percent were English, 7 percent local Indian, 4 percent Mexican, 3 percent Chinese, 2 percent American, 2 percent French, and 1 percent Scottish.[79]

In 1848, California entered the Union, and, simultaneously, the Gold Rush began. The next year, the first Chinese immigrants, largely from the Guangzhou area, began to arrive. They were initially welcomed as servants, diggers in the gold and silver mines, and eventually, railroad workers. By 1853, there were approximately four thousand Chinese, with increases every year thereafter. Despite the return of some to China, gradually "Chinatowns" developed in San Francisco, Stockton, and Sacramento.[80] Growing antipathy to the Chinese as foreign competitive labor did not prevent some Chinese from establishing import–export wholesale businesses in San Francisco with retail outlets throughout California and the West. Through them, bulk items such as rice, tea, and dry goods, including textiles and porcelain, were imported.[81] One observer of San Francisco in the 1850s remembered the Chinese door-to-door peddlers who brought "bright silks, ivory fans, lacquer boxes, pale green tea-cups of 'Canton Medallion,' and carved sandalwood that scented everything." Though the porcelains in figure 299 descended in New England families, they were contemporary with those just described (see also fig. 280). Subsequently, such peddlers were outlawed by a Chinese merchants' association. But shoppers could still buy "Canton china that found its way into San Francisco dining-rooms" on Dupont

299. *Cup and saucer, dish, teapot,* cup and saucer: c.1850–70; dish: c. 1830, D 24.8 cm, "Mandarin" pattern with unusual border; pot: c. 1850–70, W 19.05 cm, good quality export. Private collection; teapot, courtesy of Norman Herreshoff.

Street downtown.[82] The pieces in figure 300 were from the Carrington family of Providence, Rhode Island, but interchangeable with china for the wealthy in California.

These wares were now increasingly brought in large ships to serve a growing population of transplanted easterners. For example, the *Rhone* arrived in San Francisco in the summer of 1849 direct from Guangzhou with goods bought by Wetmore and Company, New England consigners there. The *Rhone*'s cargo, sold at public auction, consisted of a large quantity of *chow-chow* goods familiar from generations past, most of it Chinese. There was little or no tea but a great supply of silk goods, furniture, lacquerware, portraits, paintings on ivory, engravings— including "Views of San Francisco and its Vicinity"— silverware, paper hangings, locked boxes and trunks, tortoiseshell combs, fans, and sweetmeats; also "Chi-

naware, in complete Tea and dinner Sets, each set packed separately; complete set of Cups, Saucers, and Plates; Toilet Sets, Etc." As it had done for other China merchandise, the Gold Rush could only increase demand for a well-established market in porcelains.[83] The taste for Chinese porcelain among "Anglos" thus continued into the Chinese immigrant era, although French and English porcelains may have been preferred. The latter were offered for sale by a number of crockery and glassware shops advertising in San Francisco in 1850.[84] Among these dealers were some who imported "from the Pacific." One commission merchant, B. Frederick Moses, advertised himself as an "Importer of China Goods," but he was the exception.[85] He would have been supplied not by the Chinese but by agents in Guangzhou, such as Russell and Company, who, in 1850, shipped S. H. Williams and Company of the city a small amount of miscellaneous

300. *Cups and saucer* (from one service), c. 1825–50, saucer: D 15.9 cm. Left to right: cups for custard, breakfast, and two types for tea. Overglaze enamels, owned by the Carrington family of Providence, stock pattern, above-average export. Private collection.

301. *Plate*, c. 1850–75, D 25.4 cm. Underglaze blue and copper-red carp, rough domestic/export. Author's collection.

302. *Plate*, c. 1820–60, D 28.3 cm. Underglaze blue and copper-red carp; prototype of fig. 301, better executed; above-average domestic/export. Courtesy of the Victoria and Albert Museum.

porcelain (washbowls, flower vases, cuspidors, and punch bowls).[86]

Joining export porcelain was much commoner ware imported largely for the overseas Chinese immigrants, who for a half century after their arrival in 1850, took it with them to mining, railroad, fishing, and lumbering areas. Later, this type of ware, which included earthenware and stoneware as well as porcelain, served urban Chinese in the food, laundry, agricultural, and merchandizing business, or in domestic service. Such china was much rougher than the usual export porcelain and differed in typical design (figs. 301–304). Dating from the Gold Rush to the twentieth

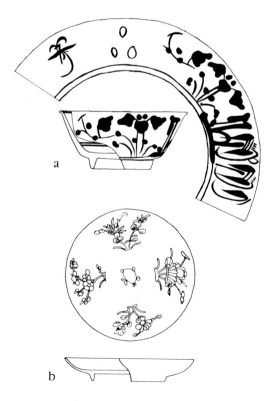

303. *Overseas Chinese ware*, c. 1850–90. a.: ''Three Circles and Dragonfly'' stoneware, underglaze dark blue or green-gray.
b.: ''Four Seasons'' green porcelain, overglaze enamels on green ground. Drawings by Paul G. Chace, archaeologist, Escondido, California.

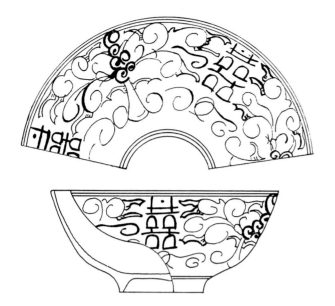

century, its nature—for the Chinese domestic market—and design variations are a subject unto itself. Appendix D lists selected areas where shards of this porcelain have been excavated. Presumably, they were made in or near the Guangzhou area, or in Guangdong Province, from which most of the immigrants came.

In the mainstream export story, transpacific steamers continued to bring small amounts of chinaware on demand to America in the last part of the nineteenth century. The whole export trade of China was much diminished from its apex a century before. Still, some objects of quality were produced. Their existence is due to a complex of contradictory factors, some explained previously in this book, others new. Before 1800, European, English, and American buyers often turned to their own porcelains, now of better quality and less costly than they once were, if still not as cheap as the Chinese, nor as exotic and quaint. By the 1830s, this preference was well established. (Some customers sent blank Western ware to China to be decorated in the export style, the reverse of an earlier practice.)[87]

On the Chinese side, imperial support of the porce-

lain industry lapsed in the Jiaqing period (1796–1820), and declined by the time of Daoguang (1821–50). In the era of his successor, Xianfeng (1851–61), Jingdezhen was almost totally destroyed by the Taiping rebels in 1853. Not until Tongzhi (1862–75) was there a revival.[88]

During the same period, the U.S. Congress began to protect its own potteries, gradually increasing the customs duties on chinaware from abroad. From 10 percent *ad valorem* duty in 1789, to 12.5 percent a year later, the rate rose to 20 percent in 1816, 30 percent in 1842, 35 percent in 1862, 40 percent two years later, then to 60 percent in 1883. This rate held until 1894 when it dropped to 35 percent for three years, to rise back to 60 percent in 1897. It remained at this level up until 1909.[89] Like the British duty scale of the late-eighteenth century, the American customs rates of the nineteenth century ensured that Chinese export wares, even though their quality might be acceptable, would have to be underpriced to compete with English and European porcelains. Also, by 1891 the marks, "China" or "Made in China" were required on all Chinese porcelains (see appendix A).

Yet competing aspects of the China trade kept demand and quality from falling off completely, before and after the Taiping troubles. With the rejuvenation of Jingdezhen, in 1864 the production list of imperial wares—and by extension, export as well—showed an impressive comeback.[90] In part, Western merchants, such as those of the Russell and Thomas Hunt companies, and other countries' business houses, doubtless had some influence, as had their predecessors several dynasties before (see chapter 1). Shanghai was a bustling business center for foreigners, as noted, and the Tongzhi period was one of looking to the West, at least in order to bolster a national consciousness.[91]

Despite a loss of political prestige among foreigners after the Opium Wars, China still exercised a certain mystique as a distant, little-known culture, and her products drew an exotic appeal with the virtue of fine craftsmanship. To own porcelain from the land of its origin had been and remained a status symbol, especially among the wealthy who could afford better pieces. Export ware of the last half of the nineteenth century, though less plentiful than its predecessors, represents a residual respect for China. It also continued to embody Western demands in its form and to some extent in its decoration, though the latter was more often Chinese with only details supplied from the West. The valence of values in export thus retained its historic hybrid nature.

On the West Coast, near the end of the imperial dynasties, a different sort of porcelain buying began in San Francisco in 1890, when the firm of Vickery, Atkins and Torrey began to sell antique imperial, or imperial-quality Chinese porcelains.[92] It was the first time on the West Coast that such wares had been available even for viewing: there were no public museums at the time.[93] The success of this store led others, most notably A. L. Gump, to begin importing Chinese and Japanese goods, for the first time seriously competing with Chinatown's Guangzhou merchants, although they served a lesser clientele.[94] This classical porcelain market, unlike the China trade of the early-nineteenth century, was not one for the middle-to-upper class, but rather principally for the wealthy. The merchandise itself was not originally made for export. It was imperial ware now free of the emperor's restraint, following the British and French invasion of Beijing in 1860.

TRADE TO CANADA

Canada, still part of the British Empire and not independent until 1867, had a dramatically different history of importing Chinese porcelains than did the United States. Earthenwares far outnumbered porcelains, which were reserved largely for those who could afford luxury ceramics, such as Simon McTavish, chief fur dealer and one of the richest men in Montreal.[95] Also, the East India wares, which were as plentiful in Canada as in the United States in the late-eighteenth century, tapered off in the nineteenth, according to period advertisements. They were replaced by Staffordshire china, especially porcelains of Copeland and Minton.[96]

Still, there is written evidence and some remaining objects to show the sort of Chinese export being bought in Canada. For example, from a collection of general ceramics brought to Canada, formed about 1860–70 by Mrs. John W. Weldon, 20 percent was export, mostly practical tablewares. Evidently, the better pieces were carried from England by settlers to Nova Scotia in the 1830s. Other pieces were among the possessions of Loyalists from New England, leaving the American colonies after the Revolution. Two objects were found in the West Indies, a Transitional bottle and a Chinese "Imari" shell (see fig. 239).[97]

Stock patterns in Canada, mostly blue-and-white, were virtually identical to those purchased farther south. Certain polychrome designs were also popular from Canada to Florida (fig. 305). In unusual patterns, however, blue-and-white might upstage polychromes, as in the plate decorated with vases (fig. 306), owned by Edward Black Greenshields (b. 1850) of Montreal.[98] Of the rare special-order wares, armorials are the single known genre, similar in form and border decoration to others common to Europe, England, and America. Yet they are quite rare in themselves. Of the personal armorials, only two are known for certain (not counting a mid-eighteenth-century service

305. (above) *Plate*, c. 1750–75, D 21.6 cm. Overglaze enamels; originally from Wilmington, Delaware; stock pattern; fine export. Courtesy of Mr. and Mrs. Lewis Rumford II.

306. (above right) *Plate*, c. 1875–1900, D 25.0 cm. Mark on base, *yu* (jade). Underglaze blue, owned by Edward Black Greenshields of Montreal, unusual fine export. Courtesy of Elizabeth Collard.

307. *Tureen and stand*, c. 1790–1810, D 25.0 cm. Overglaze enamels, inexact arms of Mackenzie of Seaforth (only known Mackenzie arms); motto: LUCEO NON URO (''I shine, not burn''); probably made for Roderick McKenzie [*sic*] (1761?–1844) of Terrebonne, Canada. Courtesy of the Canadiana Department, Royal Ontario Museum.

for Philip Durell, a British Naval officer at Louisbourg): that of the Mackenzie arms (fig. 307) and another of an Ontario family, bearing only its crest.[99] A third, of the McGillivray family, has been reported but not seen.[100] The plate in figures 308 and 309 with the arms of an unidentified, possibly Canadian company correspond in their celebration of commerce to others in Europe and America (see fig. 365).[101]

In western Canada, certain posts of the North West Company have yielded shards of common export ware (see appendix D). On the coast, the Hudson Bay Company, incorporating the North West Company in 1821, established Fort Vancouver three years later as the headquarters and depot of its Western Department, that is, Columbia and New Caledonia. The HBC

extended itself considerably, especially with a fleet of four or five barques, sloops, and one steamer. It supplied the Russian American Fur Company in southwestern Alaska, maintained a mercantile store in San Francisco, and sent fur trappers as far south as Utah and California's central valley. In Hawaii, the company kept a store and dealt with Boston–China trade ships. With this network, it is not surprising that Chinese porcelains—the only porcelain among several types of British earthenware—have been found at Fort Vancouver, identical to those in California.[102]

These porcelains are less than 1 percent of the total ceramic find. In this proportion, they may be less than other yields on the coast, but they combine with the California evidence to show a pattern of importation

308. *Plate*, c. 1790–1800. D 24.8 cm. Underglaze blue "Nanking" border; unidentified coat of arms: may or may not be Canadian; above-average export. Bequest of Mrs. J. Insley Blair. Courtesy of the New York Historical Society.

309. Detail of fig. 308. Quarterly field, azure and gules: mink, salmon, crayfish, whale; crest: ship on world; figures of Commerce and Indian with bow and beaver; motto: COMMERCIO LIBERALI CRESCUIUS.

310. *Vase* (one of a pair), c. 1840–50, H 63.5 cm. Overglaze enamels, first-class export. Gift of Mrs. Richard S. Russell. Courtesy of the Essex Institute.

of common wares that holds for the whole West Coast. First in quantity was the "Canton" willow design. "Nanking" was second. No "FitzHugh" was found, a sign that luxury wares were scarce, also clear from the fact that 90 percent of the ware was blue-and-white with only a few polychrome fragments.[103] All of the ware date from approximately the late 1820s to 1840s. No written records of porcelains purchased for the HBC are known, but various teas, Guangzhou beads, pure Chinese vermilion, and China ink appear on the company's invoices and in its inventories.[104] However, archaeology is recent and only partial; other types may emerge.

The Canadian Gold Rush of the 1850s led to a great influx of men and supplies to the West, so that soon such major settlements as Victoria, New Westminster, and even Vancouver Island had a great variety of crockery and glassware.[105] Chinese ornaments and fancy vases were advertised in the 1860s, as were Chinese spittoons. In fact, direct trade with China from Canada's West Coast was considerable; in 1863, Chinese goods purchased amounted to $45,434, but again, in proportion to teas and textiles, the china—encumbered with heavy duties—would have been a miscellaneous, not a major item. One of the more prominent Victoria firms carrying Chinese porcelains were the auctioneers, J. P. Davies and Company. They, with others, built upon earlier contacts for such merchandise imported not only straight from China but also via Hawaii and San Francisco.[106]

Late-nineteenth-century commerce with China continued on both coasts to some extent. In 1880, Thomas J. Potter, an auctioneer from Montreal, advertised Chinese vases, "quaint" teacups, rice bowls, and platters—"A Rare and Beautiful Collection direct from China."[107] Figures 310 and 311 illustrate the difference in general quality between early and late wares, despite the commercial rhetoric of Potter and others. On the East Coast, direct China-Canada trade had ap-

311. *Assorted "Rose" ware*, 1856–70. Pair of vases, punch bowl (one of two), two sets of nesting boxes, two mugs. Associated with Catherine van Rensselaer Bonney of Albany, in China 1856–71. Courtesy of Cherry Hill, Albany.

parently continued from earlier in the century. An advertisement in 1837 listed "Elegant China" with a large amount of tea that had arrived "by the *Clifton*, from Canton" at Saint John. Although doubtless a small quantity, it was probably Chinese.[108] In Canada, as elsewhere in the West, the appeal of Chinese (and Japanese) wares leapt the customs barriers for those whose taste for the oriental "real thing" first and last determined choice.

A Style for the United States

The vigorous entry of the United States into the China trade in 1784 brought fresh demand in North America for export ware. During the colonial period, Dutch and English tastes prevailed, but now with the emergence of a proud republican spirit and independent entrepreneurship freed from the restrictions of an East India company, a shift in taste occurred. Export porcelain was made new for America. The forms might follow previous models, but there were clear native preferences. In contrast, decorations, especially symbols of personal and national self-esteem, made the ware unlike any other. Or if not wholly new, Americans might redefine old patterns or define afresh; for example, "Nanking"—an older blue-and-white landscape style—now often gilded, was distinguished from "Canton," similar but rougher blue-and-white without gilding. To follow the country's array of major choices is to see its self-images in the chinaware.

FORMS

After the Revolution, tea drinking resumed apace, perhaps never having fallen off except in the Boston area. The tea service in figure 312 shows the principal objects used along the East Coast in the 1790s. The lighthouse coffee- or chocolate pot, which was part of a full tea service; drum teapot; helmet pitcher; and covered, rounded sugar pot are standard silhouettes of their day. So too is the double-curved teacup, larger than its predecessors, to facilitate cheaper, quantity tea drinking. The curved spout of the coffeepot might be interchangeable with the straight one of the teapot; indeed, on other services, they are reversed (compare figs. 312 and 313). Often these services bore keyholelike vignettes of local landscapes, more often taken from prints in contemporary periodicals than sketched by those who ordered them (fig. 314). Teacup and pitcher handles differed from the crossed strap handles ending in fern leaves of the larger pieces, the latter based upon English Leedsware prototypes. Another pitcher, or milk-pot form, is in figures 315

312. *Tea set* (partial), c. 1790–1810, coffee/chocolate pot: H 25 cm. Overglaze sepia, dark brown, and gilt; gift of Miss Miriam Shaw and Francis Shaw, Jr.; superior export. Courtesy of the Essex Institute.

313. *Tea set* (partial), c. 1802, coffee/chocolate pot, H 24.8 cm. Overglaze sepia, black, and gilt; gift to Elizabeth Roberts and James Canby of Wilmington, Delaware (m. 1803); fine export. Courtesy of Mr. and Mrs. Lewis Rumford II.

314. Detail of landscape vignette in fig. 313, possibly a Philadelphia residence.

and 316, this one from a tea service of John Adams, painted appropriately with a well-executed eagle and his monogram all in gilt. At this moment in the export trade, European and especially English pottery and porcelain were the models dictating American taste at Canton.

Of uncommon forms, two stand out: the monteith (fig. 317) and the condiment set (fig. 318). Since the early-eighteenth century, porcelain monteiths had been made, though apparently not in quantity.[1] Used to cool wineglasses, more monteiths may have existed in their day than now, as satellites to dinner services,

at least by the late-eighteenth century, with decoration identical to the whole set, following the example of the French porcelain from Sèvres. In figure 317 is such a one from Salem with a typical sepia vignette of a landscape view, possibly identifiable. No doubt it was derived from a periodical whose oval or circular engravings were convenient patterns for a painter at Guangzhou to follow. Identical in shape to this monteith is a pair of them with the arms of the Clement family of Philadelphia, now at the Nantucket Historical Society.[2]

In contrast to this historic form, the condiment set

315. *Milk pot*, c. 1790, H 14.6 cm. Clear glaze on white, overglaze gilt; part of John Adams's tea service; fine export. Courtesy of Adams National Historic Site.

316. Detail of eagle with JA, in fig. 315.

317. *Monteith*, c. 1790–1800, L 30.5 cm. Overglaze black, sepia and gilt; gift of Mrs. H. P. Sturgis; fine export, rare. Courtesy of the Essex Institute.

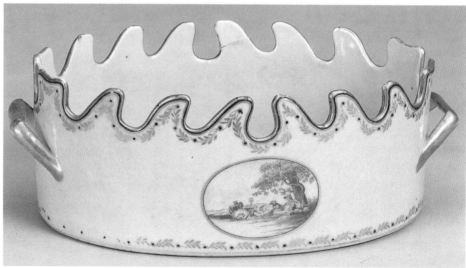

318. *Condiment set and covered dish*, c. 1790–1800, left: 36.5 cm, right: L 31.7 cm. Overglaze blue and gilt, owned by John Brown, fine export. Courtesy of the Rhode Island Historical Society.

was not in great demand in America before her own captains and supercargoes became familiar with the cuisine of the Far East in the late-eighteenth century. In this category, the Browns of Providence were among the first. John Brown (1736–1803) owned the set in figure 318 (left) consisting of a small dish atop a shaft, itself fitting onto a platter that holds six shell-shaped smaller dishes. It was more fragile than lower-shafted examples (see fig. 272). The carefully pierced border, overglaze blue and gilt painting, and fine body make this piece first-class. The shallow, covered vegetable dish to its right, painted with the same urn filled with flowers, indicates that this condiment set was also part of a larger dinner service.

True to the classical nature of Federalist tastes, the urn design echoes the urn shape used in more decorative chinaware than ever before. In contrast to a century earlier, when even a porcelain teacup was a rarity in America, china merely for decoration appeared in reasonable quantity in the 1780s and later. Two urns of this classical period have been illustrated before (figs. 262 and 264). Still a more unusual urn is represented by the pair in figure 319, whose Greek key handles vie for attention with the acanthus-leaf cover and base. These urns have been associated with the

319. *Urns* (pair), c. 1800, H 44.4 cm. Overglaze blue and gilt, associated with the Montgomery family of Philadelphia, gift of Mrs. Angus W. Morrison; superior export. Courtesy of Gunston Hall, the National Society of the Colonial Dames of America.

320. *Cups* (pair), c. 1800, H c. 24 cm. Overglaze gold-red flowers, lime-green leaves, gilt, pseudo-armorial mantle; monogram TSS for descendant of Isaac Sears (1730–86), Boston merchant in U.S.-China trade; fine export.

321. *Garniture set*, c. 1780–90, ovoids: H 29.5 cm, beakers: H 23.5 cm. Underglaze blue and gilt; ''best Nanking'' ware for Elizabeth Roberts and James Canby of Wilmington, Delaware (m. 1803); fine export. Courtesy of Mr. and Mrs. Lewis Rumford II.

Montgomery family of Philadelphia.[3] Two large covered urns, like slenderized punch bowls on stems, possibly for drinking and possibly unique, are known to have belonged to two Providence owners: one was John Brown's and still survives in his former house, now the Rhode Island Historical Society; another is at the Winterthur Museum, Delaware. Urn-shaped loving cups with covers from the Sears family of Boston sit on bell-shaped bases and exhibit pseudo armorials with a Sears monogram (fig. 320).

Linked to urns as mantelpiece furniture are garniture sets. The group in figure 321 is high-quality blue-and-white in the ''Nanking'' style, unusual for still having the covers to all three baluster forms and much of its gilt trim. In New York in 1774—and doubtless soon afterward elsewhere in the colonies—such

"Nanking" sets were undergoing a stylistic transformation. Frederick Rhinelander, a major ceramic and glassware importer, bought two sorts of "Nankeen Jars & Beakers" from his London agents that year, paying nearly twice the price for those of "New Shape" as he did for those already known—fifteen versus eight shillings.[4] As in the figures 321 and 322, the older forms of the typical five-piece garniture had round bodies: three beakers or roll wagon shapes, and two baluster, lidded vases. These forms were continued into the early-nineteenth century. The "new" sets were probably, from a bird's-eye view, ovoid (for an example, see figs. 323 and 324), curvilinear in profile, and lobe-molded with three pieces of baluster shape, two of gourd form. These were more difficult to make, thus more expensive, and probably not as plentiful as the traditional style.

322. Detail of an ovoid piece in fig. 321.

323. (above) *Vase* (one of a pair, both part of a garniture set), c. 1790–1810, H 49.5 cm. Overglaze enamels, "cane basket" ground in Meissen style, owned by Edward Carrington, superior export. Private collection.

324. (above right) Handle to vase in fig. 323.

325. *Goblets* (pair), c. 1795–1812, H 13.9 cm. Overglaze enamels, eagle identical to ownership certificate (1803) of New York ship *Elizabeth*, bequest of Hope Brown Russell, superior export, rare. Courtesy of Museum of Art, Rhode Island School of Design.

326. (above left) *Bowl*, c. 1800–15, H 12.4 cm. Overglaze blue, green, and gilt in French or Swiss cornflower; from a service owned by the Middletons of Charleston, S.C.; fine export, rare. Private collection.

327. (above right) Detail of decoration in fig. 326.

328. (below) *Tea and dinner service* (partial) *with jug*, c. 1825–35; platter: L 43.0 cm. Overglaze enamels; tea pieces: medallion with cipher DAP for David A. Pingree (1795–1863), gift of Mrs. John F. Fulton; platter and leaf dish: gift of Mr. Stephen Wheatland; jug: with HMB in medallion, gift of Hope W. (Mrs. Francis) Brown; first-class export. Courtesy of the Essex Institute.

More useful but still predominantly decorative, the handsome pair of urn-shaped goblets in figure 325 are noteworthy for their form, derived from glass and not often a substitute for it. Their bold eagles make them very American, eagles identical to those found on form copies of ship papers, thus readily accessible to the Guangzhou enamelers.[5]

Metal forms in the nineteenth century, as in the last, gave models to the export industry. A clear example is the fluted bowl in figures 326 and 327 from the Middleton family of Charleston. The cornflower design, pristine and precise, is as carefully rendered as if done by the French enameler whose work was being copied. (Such a spray is similar to the single blue corn-

flowers on a service for the Winthrops of Boston, also a copy of French porcelain on export ware.[6]) Like the monteith, which usually cooled wine glasses but could have alternate uses, bowls of this shape were more frequently used for fruit and as a centerpiece; this one is of the same design as a dinner service.

A tea and dinner service of the 1820s and 1830s is represented by the sepia "FitzHugh" set in figure 328. A glance indicates the new French-style forms, which followed the War of 1812 and other temporary estrangements from the British. The border pattern in the Empire style also follows French taste. Of the same period, with a decided hybrid East-West flavor, is the dinner service in figure 329. The water-buffalo

329. *Dinner service pieces*, c. 1825–35, tureen: H 36.2 cm. Overglaze enamels; water buffalo: Chinese form; others: Western; owned by the Forbeses of New York, gift of Mrs. Henry D. Sharpe; first-class export. Courtesy of the Rhode Island Historical Society.

330. *Coffee- and teapots,* c. 1835–70, rear center: H 24.5 cm. Overglaze enamels; "Mandarin" decorated: pre-1850; "Medallion" (with reserves): post-1850; above-average export. Courtesy of Mrs. Alma Cleveland Porter and the Peabody Museum.

331. *Ewers* (pair), c. 1830–50, H 26.8 cm. Overglaze enamels, owned by the Cadwalader family of Philadelphia, fine export. Courtesy of Matthew and Elizabeth Sharpe.

tureen dominates conventional serving ware, including two egg cups, also French in style. Though bought by the Forbeses of New York, this service was not personalized; its winged cartouche was left blank.[7] These services, stunning in both form and painting, were nonetheless produced during a time when porcelain importation was on the wane: competition from European and English ceramics coincided with the decline of the Qing dynasty and its support of the Jingdezhen industry, and adverse tariffs were increasing.

Despite these handicaps, certain standards were still met, and later pieces are worthy of study and collection. Hybrid shapes or exclusively Western ones continued into the next decades of the nineteenth century. The pots and pitchers of figure 330 typify much more common forms. Earlier styles in pot profiles—for example, the small globular teapot (lower right)—are mixed with new ones like the large coffeepot (rear center). The Western strapwork handles of the late-eighteenth century appear along with the Eastern, phoenix-shaped one of the coffeepot (left), a nineteenth-century version of an historic Chinese handle, itself influenced by Near Eastern models. In contrast, the pairs of ewers in figure 331, once in the Cadwalader family of Philadelphia, echo only Western styles and their metal prototypes in the close fluting of their bodies. While the grape-and-leaf pattern is a venerable Greek and Roman border motif, absorbed into the Chinese aesthetic, the use of it here is much more expansive, covering as it does most of the body. The lamp base in figure 332 also derives from a metal, probably pewter prototype. Its fine body and careful painting indicate the quality of work possible to the nineteenth-century potter.

One of the most popular imported forms of the nineteenth century was the garden seat (figs. 333 and 334). Along with ornamental vases, it well represents the miscellaneous, purely luxurious category to which porcelain was now tending as it was imported to America and Canada. Simpler ones in blue-and-white and polychrome had been imported from the late-eighteenth century, but the demand increased as the century continued, while it decreased for other forms—for example, tableware, in favor of European and English china. In 1850, this seat and five mates were made in China in 1850–52 for Louis Manigault (1828–99) of Charleston. (Manigault was then working for Russell and Company under Robert Bennett Forbes.) The seat bears a unique identification: the

332. *Lamp base*, c. 1850, H 20.6 cm. Underglaze blue, above-average export. Courtesy of the Peabody Museum.

333. *Seat* (one of a pair), 1850, H 46.2 cm. Overglaze enamels, gilt brass-imitation nails, crest of Manigault arms, initials LM backward; fine export. Courtesy of the Reverend Emmet Gribbin.

334. Detail of reverse of fig. 333, panel above cash in Chinese: "*man-yi-gou*," phonetic spelling of Manigault from part of French tricolor flown in Guangzhou on special occasions by Louis Manigault.

335. *Vase* (one of a pair), c. 1855–60, H 87 cm. Overglaze enamels, probably bought in 1858 by Admiral Samuel Francis du Pont; gift of Mrs. Rodney Layton; above-average export. Courtesy of the Winterthur Museum.

336. *Tureen*, c. 1865, L 33 cm. Overglaze enamels, pewter handles, first-class export. Private collection. Courtesy of Richard R. Forster III.

crest of the Manigault arms (to be discussed on p. 207): an Indian, or aborigine, with LM backward below it. On the opposite side in a rectangle in the same place as the crest, are the Chinese characters *man-yi-gou*, the *gou* pronounced "go," a phonetic spelling of Manigault.[8] Manigault's invoices and description of the purchase of these seats make them among the best-documented porcelains of the nineteenth century:

> In Canton the Chinaware is painted and rebaked. Frequently in the rebaking process, the Chinaware cracks. I bought a little supply . . . from one of the largest merchants, Po-hing, at 10 Pa My Hay St. He has every variety of jars, vases, etc. I did not like to go into his shop as I was always tempted to purchase. I bought, amongst other things, Six Chinaware Seats with my name in Chinese on one side, and crest and initials on the other. These seats were painted expressly for me; in the baking one was cracked. Po-hing, knowing that he could do nothing with it gave it to me as a Cumsha & painted

another. All these things have been sent home pr. Oxnard.[9]

Admiral Samuel Francis du Pont, in China in mid-century, also owned a rather chaste garden seat for the period, pale green with white relief decoration, which he bought in 1853.[10] Another equally popular form of the same period, samples of which du Pont also purchased, was the floor-size vase; some were three to even five and six feet high. Often their busy coloring overwhelmed their decoration. The one in figure 335, believed to have been one bought by du Pont in 1858, is not the largest; therefore, it might have had a stand. Du Pont ordered stands in several pairs. One, made of earthenware or stoneware, is painted a mottled blue-and-white; standing four feet high, it would have been taller than this vase. The admiral sailed with a French porcelain service (in lieu of one from China) aboard his ship, the *Minnesota*, when he left for Guangzhou in 1857.[11]

Other forms that represent the *chow-chow* nature of the porcelains available in the last quarter of the nineteenth century are listed in the catalog of the Philadelphia Exhibition of 1876. Shanghai merchants had presumably sent those wares they thought would be most in demand in the United States. Among them were some tea and dinner services (no breakfast sets), but many more vases, jars, flowerpots (including "bough pots" with perforated covers), fruit stands, garden seats, toilet sets, a variety of boxes, umbrella and hatstands, ashtrays (or "cigar holders"), cuspidors, toys, ornaments, figures, animals (all with stands), pairs of lions and elephants, candlesticks, and, in one case, a pair of urinals in the form of a cat.[12] If these urinals were like an earlier one now at the Winterthur Museum, the cat's head was the container's lid.[13]

Another animal form, the sleeping-duck tureen in figure 336, is covered with careful incisions skillfully imitating delicate feathers. Its stylized wave-painted base is an appropriate ground above the scroll feet, which match the duck's bill and help to unify the whole. Not the least of the tureen's charms are its finely wrought pewter handles.

DECORATIONS

One reason blue-and-white appealed to the West from the seventeenth century on was its depiction of China, its land, people, flowers, birds, and insects. The exotic, complex painting opened a window into a mysterious and distant land. Also, most of the underglaze blue wares were useful. The simplicity of the color scheme, added to objects that were usually the most practical of the whole range of form, made blue-and-whites constantly in demand even after the advent of enamels and gold-red. In part, their appeal was their price: "Canton" and "Nanking" wares were comparatively cheap and plentiful, especially after the Revolution, although the best "Nanking" could be more expensive than polychrome pieces. Their differences, and their distinction from "FitzHugh," have been detailed in the author's earlier book about American wares.[14] The pudding dishes in figure 337 are a good example of the "Canton" border, and the plate

337. *Dishes* (obverse, reverse), c. 1825–35, D 25.4 cm. Underglaze blue, "Canton" pudding dishes, common export. The Van Cortlandt Mansion Museum, the Bronx. Courtesy of the National Society of Colonial Dames of the State of New York.

in figure 338, of "Nanking." The terms "*Canton*" and "*Nanking*" repeatedly appear in period documents, distinguishing respectively, a common versus a better-quality blue-and-white.

How they acquired their names is easier to answer in the case of "Nanking" than of "Canton." Presumably both were potted and painted in underglaze blue at Jingdezhen and sent south by sea or overland. Those coming by way of Nanjing (formerly Nanking) and then by coastal junks to Guangzhou were the better wares and may have taken longer (see figs. 339 and 340). Though stock items, nonetheless they may have required special order. Those blue-and-whites available off the shelf in Guangzhou, less good and

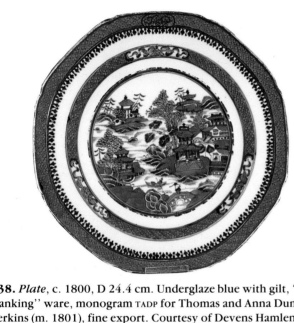

338. *Plate*, c. 1800, D 24.4 cm. Underglaze blue with gilt, "best Nanking" ware, monogram TADP for Thomas and Anna Dummer Perkins (m. 1801), fine export. Courtesy of Devens Hamlen.

339. *Tureen*, c. 1780, L 30.3 cm. Underglaze blue, "Nanking" ware; owned by the grandmother of Henry David Thoreau, Jane Burns Thoreau (m. 1781, d. 1796/97); above-average export. Courtesy of the Concord Antiquarian Society.

340. *Stand* to tureen in fig. 339.

341. *Pattypan*, c. 1815–30, D 12.9 cm. Underglaze blue, four-part border, common export. The Van Cortlandt Mansion Museum, the Bronx. Courtesy of the National Society of Colonial Dames of the State of New York.

cheaper, could easily have acquired that port as a label. Also, "Canton" may have been made at potteries nearby,[15] but that possibility has not been confirmed. (In the records, "Nankeen" is often confused with "Nanking"; the former is a kind of cotton cloth often used in the West for men's breeches.) As early as the last quarter of the eighteenth century, "Nanking" is mentioned (spelled "Nanquin"), as in the 1776 advertisement of a Philadelphia China merchant.[16] However, as with the British, it may have been a general term for blue-and-white of any sort in the eighteenth century. Before then, Americans had little firsthand experience of trade at Guangzhou and could not distinguish between "Nanking" and "Canton"—cities or chinaware.

H. Crosby Forbes states that about half of the known blue-and-whites have borders other than "Canton," "Nanking," and "FitzHugh." Nonetheless, the historic nature of the terms and their brevity still makes them useful, especially because they denote wares of three different qualities. According to Forbes, the other blue-and-white borders derive from traditional Chinese motifs or geometric patterns (fig. 341), which are combined in great complexity or which may recur: the volute, feather-edge, diaper, or the butterfly-scroll-and-double-lozenge, fungus of immortality, and cell-and-key borders.[17] Perhaps the pattern books that gave the painters models for these designs—beyond the ones that are known, such as the *Mustard Seed Garden Manual of Painting*, 1679–1701—will someday surface to help name them.

In a few instances, certain cavetto borders are nearly always linked with the same central landscape (see fig. 338). Only in recent years has there been an effort to distinguish the apparently endless scenes of "hills" and "streams." (The two Chinese characters for these words together mean any kind of landscape.) Forbes has categorized these views of the late-eighteenth and nineteenth centuries in great detail. He classifies them, I to III, in decreasing order of rarity.

Designs are then named according to their principal motif: floral, the most common; figural; and scenic, which divides further into cityscape; right-oriented designs with or without a bridge; such designs with people and a bridge; and the less-common, left-oriented designs of seven sorts.[18] There is more work to be done in identifying other types, backward and forward in time, but Forbes has made a good, workable start.

"FitzHugh" is often a blue-and-white pattern, thus in the same family as "Canton" and "Nanking." But more expensive and thus for the wealthy, it is invariably of even better quality than "Nanking." Also, as figure 342 indicates, it may appear in different enamel colors or gilt, sometimes two in combination. In America, a style developed that was originally English. Both countries preferred the same four quadrant decorations of symbols associated with the Chinese scholar's skills: calligraphy, painting, chess, and music. However, in the United States, the center of that four-part grouping more often has a substitute for the mythical beast, the *qilin*. In its place may be an eagle, coat of arms, monogram, or vignette. Also, the English ware does not have the American variation in color, which are, in order of rarity beginning with the most common, underglaze blue, overglaze green, orange-red, brown or sepia, yellow, rose-pink, black, blue enamel (as opposed to underglaze blue), lavender, gray, and gilt.[19] Not surprisingly, considering its origins among officers of the English East India Company in the late-eighteenth century, no Mexican "FitzHugh" objects are known. Though there must have been examples in Canada, none are now identified.

Apart from standard blue-and-white patterns, patriotic porcelains announcing America's new nationalism burst forth in the first decades after the U.S.-China trade began. Chief among these were those porcelains with exact or variant versions of the U.S. seal (1782), featuring an eagle. The number of changes on this mo-

342. Examples of "FitzHugh" overglaze enamels or gilt, c. 1800–50. Courtesy of the Peabody Museum.

tif seem to be somewhat open-ended; another eagle occasionally appears which adds to an earlier total variously counted from fifteen[20] to twenty-three.[21] However, probably not more than twenty-five or thirty will finally come to light. The bird—sometimes more like a skinny chicken—appeared in many postures, wings high or low, but the decoration on the double-handled cup in figures 343 and 344 best approximates the U.S. seal.

Also derived from the seal was the eagle on china that bore the badge of the Society of the Cincinnati (fig. 345). The Cincinnati porcelain, restricted to certain Revolutionary officers, now has among its survivors nine tea sets, three dinner services, and two punch bowls, all made within the period 1785–1800.[22] As the years passed, vigorous spread-winged eagles gained favor (figs. 346–348), either alone or centered in "FitzHugh"-style quadrant frames (fig. 349).

Besides the eagle, American flags bedecked standard ships, which had earlier flown English or European colors, now transformed by the stars and stripes.

344. Detail of fig. 343.

346. (below) *Plates*, c. 1825–35, right: D 24.8 cm. Overglaze enamels, eagle design, gift from the Chinese government to John C. Calhoun, Vice President (1825–37); left: soup plate, D 24.4 cm, overglaze pseudo-armorial with CMJ for Thomas Ap Catesby and Mary Walker Jones (m. 1823); first-class export. Courtesy of Dr. Wesley Gallup.

343. *Cup and saucer*, c. 1790–1800, cup: D 6.9 cm, saucer: D 14.2 cm. Overglaze enamels, U.S. seal (1782), gift of Mr. Harry T. Peters, fine export. Courtesy of the Peabody Museum.

345. *Coffee/chocolate pot*, c. 1790, H 22.9 cm. Overglaze enamels; emblem of the Society of the Cincinnati, Major General Henry Knox (1750–1809), founder; HKL for Henry and Lucy Knox. Gift of de Lancey Kountze (Yale, 1899). Courtesy of Yale University Art Gallery.

347. Close-up of typical eagle pattern, c. 1810–20. Overglaze enamels, finely painted. Courtesy of Dr. Wesley Gallup.

348. *Dish*, c. 1820, D 28.3 cm. Overglaze enamels; exterior: Western couple and carriage; interior: eagle with "FitzHugh" border; fine export. Courtesy of the Henry Ford Museum and the Edison Institute.

349. *Platter*, c. 1810–20, L 43.2 cm. Overglaze "FitzHugh" molded server ("well-and-tree"); associated with John R. Stockton, senator, then congressman from New Jersey; first-class export. Courtesy of the Old Barracks Association, Trenton.

350. *Tureen*, c. 1820–40, L 31.0 cm. Overglaze enamels and gilt (later retouched); AMERICA OF SALEM, possibly a Salem ship; fine export. Courtesy of the Dietrich Brothers Americana Corporation. On loan to the Diplomatic Reception Rooms, U.S. Department of State.

351. *Bowl*, c. 1790–1800, D 28.7 cm. Overglaze enamels, bust of Washington with emblem of the Society of the Cincinnati, unique export. Courtesy of the Historical Society of Pennsylvania.

Models for these ships were generic ones copied from ships's documents, newspapers, or less often, prints, and were popular especially with the men who sailed to the Far East. However, the tureen in figure 350 is an exception. It is labeled with a banner reading AMERICA OF SALEM; a ship of Jacob Crowninshield's, perhaps the vessel itself, anchored downriver from Guangzhou at Whampoa, and posed for its own painting. Marine scenes, of particular ships in storm or battle, also were popular.

One figure's likeness stood out above all others to puff up the new nation—George Washington (1732–99). Export so painted was not intended for his possession (though he and Martha owned a sizable amount)[23] but to commemorate his role in the Revolution and to celebrate his presidency (fig. 351). Upon his death, designs from prints or paintings of Mount Vernon (fig. 352) and of Washington's grave, as well as prints of his bust, continued to honor him as a semi-god.

Three years before Washington died, A. E. Van Braam Houckgeest (1739–1801), a Dutch merchant living in Philadelphia and familiar with the Guangzhou market, presented Martha Washington (1731–1802) with a unique tea service, including saucers with raised centers and double-handled, covered cups for chocolate.[24] The set had been brought back on the *Lady Louisa*; its manifest read "A Box of China for Lady Washington."[25] Its decoration, filled with national symbols, probably expressed Houckgeest's enthusiasm for his new American citizenship as much as did his gift to the first lady. The rising sun of the republic radiates outward to a fifteen-link chain with the names of the states in each, and a wreath signifying peace surrounds the cipher MW, the whole encircled with a snake biting its tail, an ancient symbol of eternity (fig. 353).[26]

The Washingtons owned a certain quantity of china

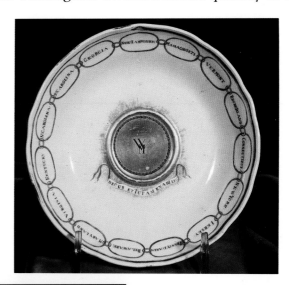

352. (left) *Butter tub and stand*, c. 1800–10, stand: L 18.1 cm. Overglaze enamels, view of Mount Vernon, superior export. Private collection.

353. (above) *Saucer*, c. 1795, D 16 cm. Overglaze enamels and gilt; DECUS ET TUTATMENT AB ILLO ("Honor and defense come from it"), MW for Martha Washington; gift of Mrs. Elizabeth Renshaw; unique export. Courtesy of Diplomatic Reception Rooms, U.S. Department of State.

well before the Revolution. In 1757 they had received a large china order as cargo of the *Salley*, which had sailed from England up the Rappahannock. Included in this purchase was "1 compleat sett fine Image china,"[27] probably similar to the pieces in figure 248. Nine years later, the Washingtons received another complete china set "of fine blue and white" of eleven long dishes, twenty-four plates, twelve soup plates, a tureen and stand, four sauceboats and four salts.[28] It was Washington, too, who received one of the first Cincinnati services, distinguished by the figure of Fame trumpeting her possession of the insignia of the society.[29] The 1810 inventory of Mt. Vernon showed that whether the "New Room," "Front Parlour," "Small Room" or "Closet," chinaware was in each. The "New Room" contained two sideboards, each with an "Image & China flower Pot" and "5 China Jarrs."[30]

For presidential porcelain, the Washingtons set a precedent that continued to the twentieth century. Among their successors who owned such ware, bearing appropriate personal identification, were John Adams (with Abigail, a great collector of ceramics), Jefferson, Monroe, Buchanan, Tyler, Grant, and Franklin Delano Roosevelt. Roosevelt's maternal grandfather, Warren Delano, had been in Guangzhou with Russell and Company (c. 1840–70). Porcelains from the Delanos, largely "Rose" wares and blue-and-white but including two nineteenth-century ornamental vases, one black and one green, are now at FDR's restored home in Hyde Park, New York.[31]

Some of the states had their coats of arms reproduced on porcelains in vestigial loyalty to their former colony.[32] New York and Pennsylvania both did so. Many more are known for New York, whose arms were based upon late-sixteenth-century Dutch government seals. These arms have variants in the central decorations and were made in the period 1790–

354. Oil on panel, *Still Life with Strawberries*, 40 cm × 56 cm, American, 1822, Raphaelle Peale (1774–1825). Sugarbowl vignette of Commerce with anchor and distant ships. Courtesy of Mr. and Mrs. Robert C. Graham, Graham Gallery, New York.

355. *Punch bowl*, c. 1821–25, D 27.9 cm. Overglaze enamels, eagle with trumpet, IN GOD WE HOPE (seal of Newport, R.I., 1821), owned by John Jay (1745–1829), first-class export. Gift of Mrs. George P. Morse. Courtesy of the Diplomatic Reception Rooms, U.S. Department of State.

356. *Punch bowl*, c. 1870, D 41.3 cm. Overglaze enamels, almost complete seal of Illinois of 1868, possibly unique. Courtesy of the Bayou Bend Collection, Museum of Fine Art, Houston.

1810.[33] New Jersey is reported to have china with its arms as well, but no examples are known. Though an anchor with the word HOPE and a classical female figure leaning against it, as on the sugar bowl in the Peale painting (fig. 354), have been called the arms of Rhode Island, no exact copy of the true arms has been found. The figure probably represents Commerce, and is commonly part of both British and American naval iconography, thus cannot be convincingly linked to Rhode Island.

Regional loyalty within Rhode Island may have led to another sort of civic armorial ware. The port of Newport's seal, adopted in 1821, is an eagle perched on a trumpet with a banner in its beak reading IN GOD WE HOPE.[34] It is in every way identical to the one on the punch bowl in figure 355, once belonging to John Jay (1745–1829). Though Jay was from New York State, a Providence ship bearing his name went to China in 1794. In the same year, Jay, long active in America's foreign affairs, successfully concluded a treaty with Great Britain, averting war. America's mercantile class appreciated his efforts to stabilize international trade. Perhaps admirers in Newport, like those in Providence, eventually honored him with this bowl, simultaneously celebrating their port.

Two other state arms were produced later in the century, this time announcing national unity with the

eagle, rather than recalling a former colonial identity. One is on a punch bowl for Illinois, based upon the state's seal adopted in 1868 (fig. 356).[35] Another is on a number of plates, possibly for New Mexico (fig. 357).

In the effort to identify porcelains as American and personal, private citizens also chose custom decora-

357. *Plate*, c. 1915 or later, D 29.2 cm. Underglaze blue; eagle with three arrows in left claw, major element of New Mexico's seal of 1913; Chinese inscription *zheng dian* (?). Courtesy of the Ottema–Kingman Foundation, the Princessehof Museum.

359. Detail of hunt vignette in fig. 358.

360. End of inscription, FOR JOHN SEAWELL OF GLOUCESTER COUNTY VIRGINIA, in fig. 358.

358. *Punch bowl*, c. 1780–90, D 40.6 cm. Overglaze enamels; three sepia vignettes of the hunt, racecourse, and steeplechase; for John Seawell, Gloucester County, Virginia; first-class, special-order export. Courtesy of P. Hairston Seawell of Virginia.

tion. Though men of political, naval, or military rank often ordered porcelains to display their power and status, others did so to celebrate a family history. One recipient of a punch bowl with his name on it was John Seawell, a descendant of a long line of John Seawells in Virginia since the 1630s (figs. 358–360). It was a gift from English agents, merchants at Gloucester Point, but possibly made to Seawell's specifications. According to tradition, it was shipped aboard the *York* with a pair of hounds, fit company for the one in sepia standing guard over a dead hare in one of three vignettes on the bowl (fig. 359). Spaced between the three is the inscription in gilt FOR JOHN SEAWELL OF GLOUCESTER COUNTY VIRGINIA, originally repeated but now overpainted around the outer rim, done no doubt in Virginia. The decoration and the inscription is a private celebration of lineage, which by the nature of the form, was to be used publicly. Countless bowls with Masonic emblems, often personalized, even with a full name, such as RICHARD GRIDLEY (the bowl now at the Bostonian Society), fulfilled the same private/public announcement.

Women too put their mark upon the chinaware, usually in a more modest way. Figure 361 shows a cup and saucer from a tea service belonging to Abijah Arden (1759–1832), possibly designed by her but probably ordered by her brother, John Arden, and their nephew, Frederick Babcock, partners in an importing business at Front Street and Old Slip in downtown New York. The cipher AA is identical to that on Arden mother-of-pearl card chips ("loos"), probably the model for the Guangzhou painter of this unusual service.[36] In a Wilmington collection made before 1890 is a documented cup and saucer, which is listed by its owner, Elizabeth C. Canby, as having been "designed by Catharine Roberts for [her, E. C. C.] in 1803 and

361. *Cup and saucer*, 1815–30, cup: D 8.6 cm. Overglaze gilt, saw-tooth border, tasseled and ribboned swags in French Empire style; AA for Abijah Arden (1759–1832) of New York; fine export, rare. Courtesy of Mrs. Peter Milliken.

362. *Jug*, c. 1780–1800, H 21.9 cm. Overglaze enamel rococo arms of Hancock, descended in Hancock family of Boston, fine export. Courtesy of the Bostonian Society.

sent for to China." They bear a well-done, simple floral border in gold-red.[37]

Much more flamboyant and commonplace were the armorial porcelains mentioned in chapter 1, although before or after the Revolution, American armorials on porcelain are rare.[38] Made in the colonial period, the jug in figure 362 bears the arms of the Hancock family of Boston, reputedly initiated in 1735 by Thomas Hancock, uncle of John Hancock (1737–93). (The coat of arms is a variant of the English arms, with a rococo cartouche instead of a shield, but otherwise the same elements.) The jug descended in the family of John's sister, Mary.[39] Possibly, however, it was part of "a long Sett of Table China," which was described as "very handsome" and sent to John Hancock from London in 1770, presumably on order. In its box was a smaller box containing a "Tea Table Sett" for John's aunt.[40] Among other extant Hancock papers of either Thomas or John, however, there are very few references to chinaware, even though Thomas Hancock's name appears on the county list of 1755 of shopkeepers dealing in tea, coffee, and chinaware.[41]

In New York State after the Revolution, another armorial service is firmly dated to 1804–05 (figs. 363 and 364). In the first year, Gerrit Wessel Van Schaick (1758–1816) of Albany received a tea set of 88 pieces for $40.00 and a dinner set of 160 pieces for $80.00. Both were bought for him by John Jacob Astor, the New York China trade magnate and a notorious misspeller of English, not his native tongue. Astor warned him, "Chinia is higher in Canton than it was last year which may be one reason why yours may cost more than you exspect."[42] It was, in fact, 20–25 percent higher than previously, as Astor told him in a following letter, making the total bill $172.60 with 10 percent insurance, 3 percent commission at Canton, 7 percent interest, and 18 percent duty. Perhaps because some of the plates were broken, or because he placed another order, Van Schaick received a second group of porcelains in 1805. They were miscellaneous pieces, probably supplements to the previous year's porcelains, and included a coffeepot and cake and pickle dishes.[43]

Another New York armorial, unusual in identifying a man's occupation rather than his own arms, appears on the twin covered jugs of figure 365. The owner,

363. *Plate*, 1804 or 1805. D 24.5 cm. Overglaze enamels and gilt; crest of the Van Schaick family from rococo arms of John Gerse Van Schaick's bookplate; part of tea set of Gerrit Wessel Van Schaick (1758–1816) of Albany. Courtesy of the Albany Institute of History and Art.

364. (above) Detail of crest in fig. 363.

365. *Jugs* (pair), c. 1790–1810, H 28 cm (11 in). Overglaze enamels; arms of the Bakers' Guild, New York; beneath gilded spout, TB for Tucker Brown, chief flour inspector, Port of New York; fine export. On loan to the Peabody Museum. Courtesy of Lt. Col. Michael M. Sheedy III.

366. *Table service* (partial), c. 1820–23. Brown and black ''FitzHugh'' with coat of arms of Charles Izard Manigault (1795–1874); PROSPICERE QUAM ULCISCI (''It is better to anticipate than to avenge''). Courtesy of Mrs. Isaac Northrup.

Tucker Brown, was the chief flour inspector for the port of New York. His monogram is inconspicuously placed beneath the jug's spout so as not to compete with the arms of the Bakers' Guild, prominently displayed on the body. For Brown, his organization apparently deserved first identity.

In Charleston, several decades later, the Manigault family lends a French Huguenot and southern slant to the armorial picture (fig. 366). This service belonged to Charles Izard Manigault (1795–1874), who had been in China for almost six years, 1817–23, when he had it made. The arms are slightly different from those

367. *Coffee can*, c. 1820–23, H and D 6.4 cm. Brown and black "FitzHugh" with post-1820 Manigault crest, with GHM for Gabriel Henry Manigault (1788–1834), brother of Charles Manigault. Courtesy of the Reeves Collection, Washington and Lee University.

devised for a bookplate by Charles's father, Peter Manigault (1731–73), made while he was studying law in London in 1754. Then they appeared in a rococo cartouche: three gold-hooded, belled, red falcons on a blue field, placed two and one without a crest but with the motto below, PROSPICERE QUAM ULCISCI (It is better to anticipate than to avenge).[44]

When Charles was in the Far East, he went to Botany Bay, Australia, in 1820, and finding a first-class engraver—a forger sent out as a convict—he had a bookplate engraved with the arms, which by that time had been altered. The elaborate cartouche had been slimmed down to a classical shield, and an American Indian with eagle-feather headdress had replaced the crest. The Australian engraver was instructed to make two more changes: a half-moon above the falcons, to signify that Charles was a second son, and ostrich plumes of the Australian aborigines for the Indian's eagle feathers. Possibly the plumes were the engraver's idea. This new bookplate was the model for the Chinese painter of Charles's brown "FitzHugh" service.[45]

(The service was made at the same time for Charles's older brother, Gabriel Henry Manigault; see fig. 367).

As with the Van Schaick service, nineteenth-century armorials tended to shrink to crests alone, possibly in favor of more democratic sentiments. A generic crest, nuptial birds, became a favorite even for distinguished citizens such as Bishop William White (1748–1836) of

368. *Cup and saucer*, c. 1790, cup: D 8.6 cm, saucer: D 13.9 cm. Overglaze blue and gilt; crest of two birds, common anonymous armorial motif; owned by the Reverend William White (1748–1836); above-average export. Courtesy of Mr. and Mrs. Lewis Rumford II.

369. *Plate*, 1830–50, D 20.1 cm. Rare "Rose Mandarin" with unidentified crest, associated with a family of Newburyport, Maine; fine export. Private collection.

370. Detail of crest in fig. 369. Swan above crown within buckled belt; OPTIMUS EST QUI MINIMIS URGETUR ("Happy is he who is least harried").

Philadelphia (fig. 368). The practice continued into the next stylistic period, as illustrated in figures 369 and 370, a "Mandarin" plate. Only a handful of such armorials are known, most merely with initials or monograms, not arms or crest.[46] Among the former is one of importance, a plate representing a service made for Ulysses S. Grant in 1868 (fig. 371). It reflects the prestige that porcelain from China continued to enjoy at the White House in the nineteenth century, if not everywhere in America.

Such light attention has been given nineteenth-century export wares that John Quentin Feller's recent catalog and two articles on "Canton Rose" wares are welcome. While they carry forward the work begun by Carl L. Crossman in the late 1960s, two cautions should be raised. The names of these wares originated in the nineteenth century and should be in

371. *Soup dish*, 1868, D 20.5 cm. Overglaze enamels on gilt; in medallion, USG for Ulysses S. Grant (1822–1885), elected president 1868, when this service bought for Grant; first-class export. Gift of Edith Grant Griffiths. Courtesy of the Peabody Museum.

372. *Soup dish*, c. 1830, D 25.3 cm. Overglaze enamels; Chinese *shou* characters on border, right: two scholars, left: warrior; owned by Mary Jane Derby (1807–92) of Salem (m. Ephraim Peabody, 1832). Courtesy of the Peabody Museum.

quotes so to signify. The pre-1850 "Mandarin" and post-1850 "Medallion" styles were not so called in their day, but rather "rich" or "highly painted." In documents of the period, this author has seen "Rose patterned" used only once. Also, "Canton Rose" wares were not the only, possibly not even the most-popular, porcelains of the nineteenth century; they were merely the most gaudy. Among the cognoscenti, "rose" wares were ordered (figs. 372–374), but as just noted and in chapter 6, so were others in the post–1835 period: green figural; blue, green, and brown "FitzHugh"; and white wares with Chinese figures and inscriptions (fig. 375). To these should be added the orange-red and overglaze blue "Sacred Bird" wares (fig. 376), the "hundred butterflies" pattern (fig.

373. *Punch bowl*, 1832, D 50.8 cm. Overglaze enamels; FROM/ THE COMMANDER AND WARD ROOM OFFICERS/ OF THE/ U.S. SHIP PEACOCK/ TO/ DWIGHT BOYDEN—TREMONT HOUSE/ BOSTON 1832; unique. Gift of Dwight Boyden, 1924. Courtesy of the Bostonian Society.

374. Interior of fig. 373, view of the foreign hongs (factories) at Guangzhou.

375. *Cups and saucers*, c. 1862–74, circular saucer: 16.5 cm. Overglaze enamels, Tang poet Li Po and others, from the Edward Carrington House, Providence. Private collection.

376. *Cup, saucer, plate*, c. 1830–50, plate: D 24.7 cm. Overglaze enamels and gilt, unidentified MES monogram. Courtesy of the Peabody Museum.

377. *Plate and stand*, left: c. 1870–90, D 23.8 cm. Overglaze enamels, "Hundred Butterflies" stock pattern; right: c. 1810–25, L 27.9 cm, overglaze gold-red and gilt, owned by Stephen van Rensselaer (1764–1839); fine export. Courtesy of Dr. Wesley Gallup.

378. *Plate*, c. 1870–90, D 24.1 cm. Overglaze enamels; owned by Brooks Adams (1848–1927), great-grandson of John Adams. Courtesy of the Adams National Historic Site.

379. *Vase*, c. 1870–90, H 25.7 cm. Overglaze polychrome and gilt, signers of the Declaration of Independence. Courtesy of Dr. Wesley Gallup.

377), and those like a red-and-green double-dragon plate (fig. 378) of John Adams's great-grandson, Brooks Adams (1848–1927). None falls into the category of "Canton Rose."

Comparing the earlier demand for U.S. and private symbols with later ware indicates that as demand for

porcelain declined, so too did requests for the reproduction of dominant national or individual emblems. Increasingly, purely Chinese decorations prevailed. Still, ingrained tastes had an effect. Two polychrome pieces illustrate wares with national symbols continuing into the late-nineteenth and early-twentieth centuries. The first is a vase with the signers of the Declaration of Independence, all looking quite oriental thanks to the cultural conditioning of the Chinese painter (fig. 379). It represents a variety of forms with the same decoration, many of which are today at the Winterthur Museum. The scene derives from a painting by John Trumbell, *The Declaration of Independence*, later reproduced in engravings by Asher B. Durand and Edward Hicks, doubtless used by the Chinese painter.[47] With several sources, it is not surprising that remaining pieces vary from one to another slightly, probably indicating a time difference in their making over the last half of the nineteenth century. Perhaps some of this ware was made to help commemorate the centennial of the Declaration in Philadelphia in 1876. A punch bowl now at the White House, bearing a reserve of seven men and the banner

THE SURRENDER OF BURGOYNE, also dates from this era and represents a national nostalgia at the centennial in the same way as do the Declaration pieces.

A late example of international ties is a platter bearing the crossed flags of China and America (fig. 380). The former is the national flag of the Republic of China, in the period 1912–28. One could expect a certain time lag between the adoption of the flag and the appearance of the porcelain, perhaps a year. Like the goblet (see fig. 38), this platter celebrates the collaboration of Sino-American business interests, but it also probably acknowledges the American source of the republican spirit behind the Chinese Revolution of 1911.

Neither the Declaration of Independence pieces nor those with the two countries' flags are of the best clay or workmanship. As noted, the Qing dynasty's sup-

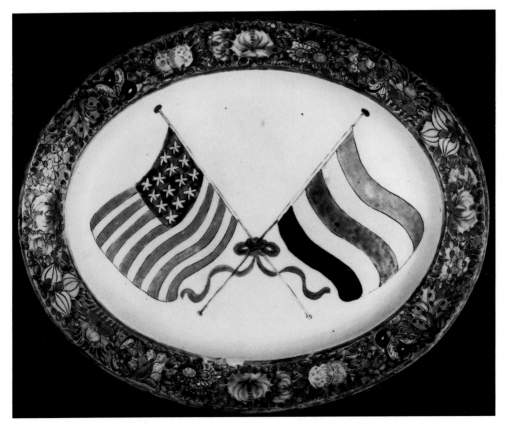

380. *Platter*, c. 1912–28, L 33.7 cm. Overglaze enamels; flags of the United States and the Republic of China, 1912–28, striped iron-red, yellow, blue, white and black; average export, now rare. Gift of Mr. and Mrs. Joseph D. Shein. Courtesy of the Diplomatic Reception Rooms, U.S. Department of State.

port of Jingdezhen had considerably declined from internal weakness, foreign intervention since the Opium Wars, the want of foreign demand, and the West's protective tariff policies. Yet the Chinese potter could not fail to continue producing worthy pieces. The blue-and-white plate in figure 381 is marked and is of the period of Xuantong (1909–11), the last Qing emperor (fig. 382). In export porcelain's effective end, though potting still continued at Jingdezhen, is the echo of its first importation to the United States. This piece was brought back from China in 1909 by Edward M. Raymond, a Salem man.[48] At the close of over four hundred years of supplying the West, which began with blue-and-white as well as greenware, China was still doing so, though in much less quantity. Supply and demand had both radically declined.

In the 1980s, after a virtual hiatus of seventy years, the situation is now ripe for a resumption of trade in quality export porcelain in traditional and contemporary styles. Unfortunately at present, motley and ornate cheap wares now flood foreign shops for the most part, especially Chinatowns in the United States. Much better sorts are currently available in Jingdezhen at the Jingdezhen Museum, the Ceramic Institute, and the Jian Guo Porcelain Factory outlet. Through the proper Chinese channels, foreign demand could stimulate more production of these fine pieces. Once again, both China and the West might enjoy the pleasures of timeless shapes, symbolic-decorative paintings, and reasonable profits—the enduring virtues of export porcelain. With a distinguished history and new tastes stimulating both buyer and potter, the China trade in china might well surpass its former glory.

381. *Plate*, period and mark of Xuantong (1909–11), D 27.1 cm. Underglaze blue; gift of Edward M. Raymond, 1909; fine domestic/ export. Courtesy of the Essex Institute.

382. Reverse of fig. 381, mark of Xuantong (1909–11).

Marks

Marks on export wares have a meaning beyond simple identification of Chinese conventional signs in certain periods. Emblematic of international attitudes, they also indicate the way in which China and foreigners assessed each other; they are measures of mutual appreciation or contempt between the trading nations. By shape and decoration, the objects themselves show shifting mutual appraisals of East and West, not simply by the dominance of one style over the other but in a complex mixture of technical and aesthetic factors. The bottom markings make an additional statement. Even the blank, unglazed bases of export ware give mute testimony to how one country viewed the other. That blankness has usually been associated with imperial disdain toward "barbarians" outside the Celestial Kingdom. But in fact, it probably means that in the eighteenth century, the West was satisfied with its own orders and did not look for Chinese signs of quality or symbolic intent.

Even among porcelain collectors, marks are not often associated with export wares. The assumption has been that almost all marks on porcelains, except the crudest, were reserved for quality pieces intended for the emperor and his court. When the subject is export, then, not much attention has been paid to the range of marks known on porcelains. Such marks include: those dating the ware to a sixty-year cycle; imperial wares with their *nianhao* (an emperor's reign period) in characters or seals; those designating the hall, studio, workshop or, more rarely, the potter who made the piece; those commending an object (often comparing it to jade) or offering good wishes; and others derived from Buddhism, Taoism, and more primitive religious beliefs symbolic of longevity, marital bliss, or another value (see figs. 383 and 384).

Well before the custom of marking porcelains became specific and regular, however, export wares were made alongside porcelains reserved for the court, as noted in chapter 1. Then in the fourteenth century, when *nianhao* delimited imperial porcelains, overseas buyers came to value such marks. Subsequent export pieces may bear almost all the types of marks just listed; most of the range is well represented in a single collection at the Fort Jesus Museum, Mombasa, Kenya.[1]

As early as the Tang dynasty (A.D. 618–707), a single character signifying "official" ware sometimes appeared on a piece.[2] A few such pieces doubtless reached wealthy clients in the Tang's far-flung trading areas: Japan to the east, Indonesia to the south, and Iran, Iraq, and Egypt to the west.[3] Very early, too, the Chinese would have recognized the value of the mark for any market and put them on lesser pieces in either good or careless imitation. From the start, then, some marked wares—imperial or export—may be assumed to have been sold abroad, especially because only a few pieces of imperial ware would have been considered national treasures, which, along with the more highly prized gold, silver, and pewter vessels, were not allowed out of the country on pain of imprisonment.

"Pain of imprisonment" became "pain of death" in the Ming dynasty. Then began a period of isolationism typical of Chinese policy toward outsiders until the past decade. Wares made for the emperor were so marked and were not to be used by any but his court. The emperor Hongwu (1368–98) began the *nianhao* custom of putting his four-character mark on the bottom of a piece in underglaze blue with a double circle enclosure. Successors followed suit, using either four or six characters (fig. 385). (These characters appear most often in two lines, but also in three lines of two characters, or in a single line—all read left to right.) During this time, until the eighteenth century, they were in underglaze blue, usually on the bottom, but occasionally on the lip or body of a piece. In the eighteenth century, during Yongzheng, marks first appeared in red (and sometimes in gold), a practice that became more

383. *Eight Precious Objects (ba bao)*

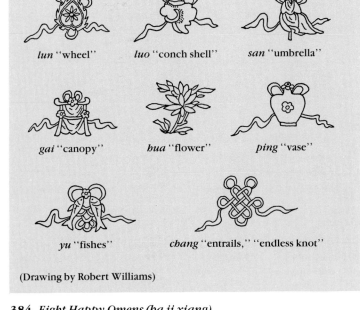

384. *Eight Happy Omens (ba ji xiang)*

common than underglaze blue in the nineteenth century. Marking with the *nianhao* was followed until the death of the last Chinese "emperor," Hung-hsien, in 1916. (Actually, this former prime minister died before becoming emperor, but he ordered porcelains manufactured with his *nianhao*.)[4]

However, despite the Ming intent of enforcing exclusivity, if not of court quality, wares with the reign mark found their way abroad, shown by a number of examples of Ming- and Qing-marked wares in both the Ardebil Collection and the Topkapi Museum.[5] Perhaps they were gifts of high Chinese officials or imitations of imperial wares sold by unscrupulous dealers. Copying earlier periods was a discipline expected of the novice potter/painter as an act of veneration for the achievements of the past and as an exhibition of "vitality." Initially it was not an attempt to dupe the foreign or domestic buyer, but became so by those who recognized the easy profits to be had for such wares. As Volker has noted, "Potters in the Far East have played fast and loose with such marks to please their customers."[6]

Such "playing" could be with *nianhao* as well as with lesser marks, but usually the calligraphy of the copied

mark is much more casual than the official mark. Often the seal style is so sloppy as to become meaningless. However, readable or not, any sort of mark could raise the price. As Hobson noted, the marks of periods whose pieces are rarest—Xuande (1426–35) and Chenghua (1465–87)—are the most frequently copied in later periods, beginning in the sixteenth century (see figs. 2 and 3). By the reign of Kangxi (1662–1722), they were used more often than that emperor's *nianhao*. Furthermore, even later pieces, stylistically different from Xuande and Chenghua, may bear the marks of those periods.[7] For these and other reasons, marks are the least trustworthy aspect of a piece. Shape and probable use; style of decoration; colors and color range; signs of age and wear; and now, at some trouble and expense, thermoluminescent and magnetic analysis may help to date a piece within at least a fifty-year range.[8] Because marks *may* be authentic, however, they cannot be ignored, and even when they mean nothing, some have become so abstract that their very unreadability seems to add to their value as it increases their mystery.

As the marked pieces in Iran and Turkey prove, the habit of exporting marked wares began before the West

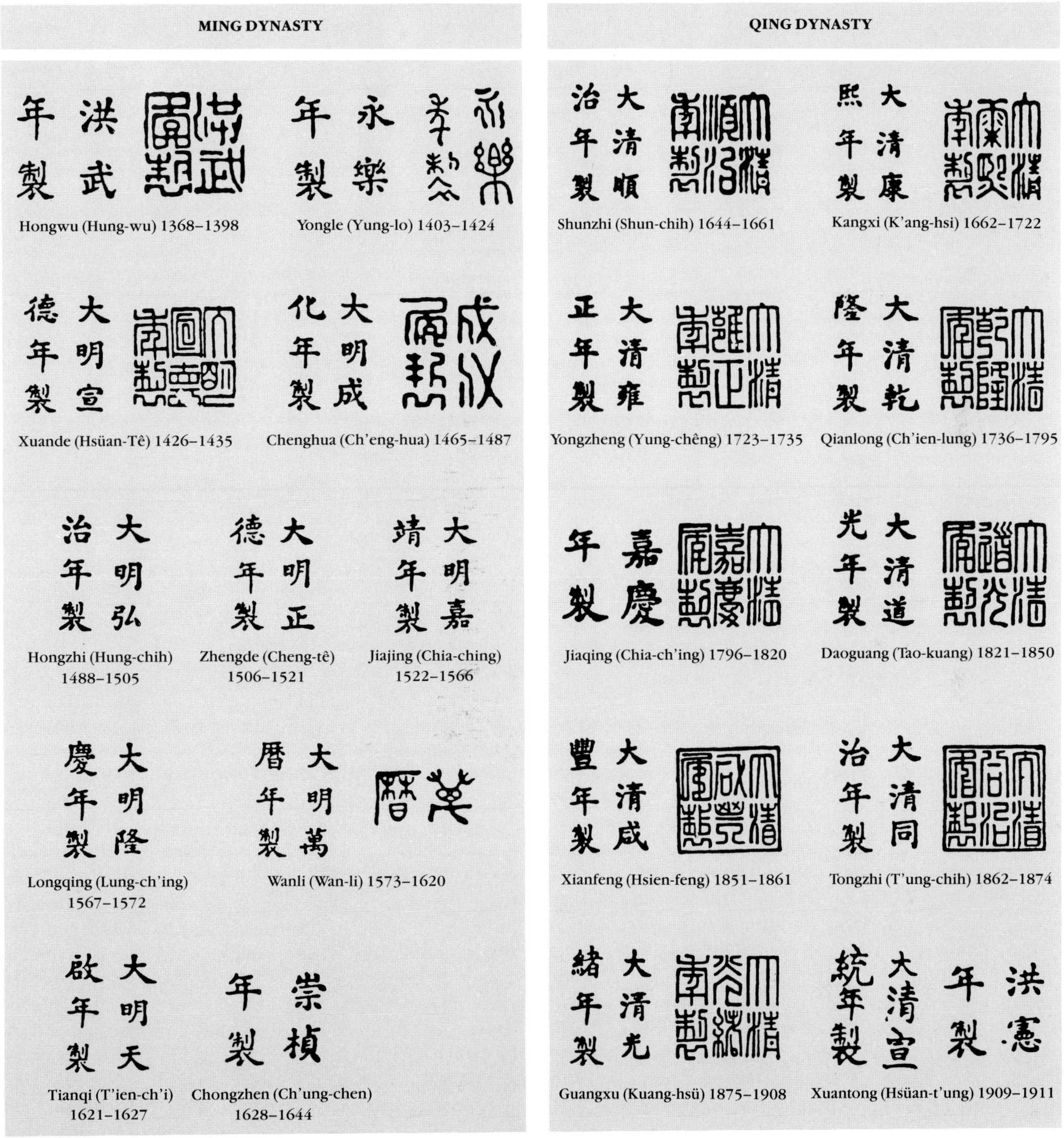

MING DYNASTY
洪武年製
Hongwu (Hung-wu) 1368–1398
永樂年製
Yongle (Yung-lo) 1403–1424
大明宣德年製
Xuande (Hsüan-Tê) 1426–1435
大明成化年製
Chenghua (Ch'eng-hua) 1465–1487
大明弘治年製
Hongzhi (Hung-chih) 1488–1505
大明正德年製
Zhengde (Cheng-tê) 1506–1521
大明嘉靖年製
Jiajing (Chia-ching) 1522–1566
大明隆慶年製
Longqing (Lung-ch'ing) 1567–1572
大明萬曆年製
Wanli (Wan-li) 1573–1620
大明天啟年製
Tianqi (T'ien-ch'i) 1621–1627
崇禎年製
Chongzhen (Ch'ung-chen) 1628–1644
QING DYNASTY
大清順治年製
Shunzhi (Shun-chih) 1644–1661
大清康熙年製
Kangxi (K'ang-hsi) 1662–1722
大清雍正年製
Yongzheng (Yung-chêng) 1723–1735
大清乾隆年製
Qianlong (Ch'ien-lung) 1736–1795
嘉慶年製
Jiaqing (Chia-ch'ing) 1796–1820
大清道光年製
Daoguang (Tao-kuang) 1821–1850
大清咸豐年製
Xianfeng (Hsien-feng) 1851–1861
大清同治年製
Tongzhi (T'ung-chih) 1862–1874
大清光緒年製
Guangxu (Kuang-hsü) 1875–1908
大清宣統年製
洪憲年製
Xuantong (Hsüan-t'ung) 1909–1911

385. *Ming and Qing Dynasty Marks*

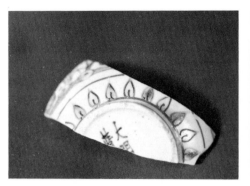

386. *Shard*, c. 1550–66, exterior base of a small bowl (compare figs. 115 and 116), Mexico City subway excavations.

387. *Shards*, c. 1550–66; right: interior of a small bowl, underglaze blue on convex center; left: exterior of similar bowl, overglaze yellow and green. Partial underglaze blue mark, *fu kuei jia chi*; Mexico City subway excavations.

388. *Shard*, c. 1590–94, base of a thin, pure white, small bowl. Underglaze blue mark, *yu tang jia qi*, associated with the galleon *San Agustin* (1595), Drake's Bay. Courtesy of the Archaeological Research Facility Collection, University of California, Berkeley.

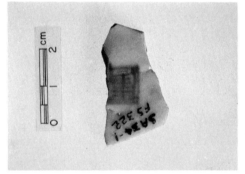

389. (far left) *Shard*, c. 1590–1600, base of an unidentified vessel from a well filled in 1600. Part of *fu* mark ("good wishes," or "good luck"). Courtesy of the Florida State Museum.

390. (left) *Shard*, c. 1550–66, exterior of a small bowl in underglaze blue extract waterweed design. Underglaze blue mark, *fu* (compare fig. 389.) Mexico City subway excavations.

ordered large quantities of porcelains. Then as early as 1605, the Dutch East India Company's records show that fine porcelains were "most desired when they have a blue mark drawn like a character on the bottom."[9] Five years later, among a large load of porcelains "of the finest kind" to be sold on the Coromandel Coast, the company's instructions specified that all should have "under the bottom a blue seal, for about this they [their customers] are very particular."[10] It is worth noting that the first mention of "a character" is singular, thus in this case not a *nianhao*, and that the "blue seal" is unspecified. A plural reference appears in 1640: "the cups with Chinese characters on the bottom are called '*paytaght*' [in Persian, *paitakht*, or royal residence, that is, for the emperor's court] at Mocha and they are favored and in demand above the others"[11] (fig. 386). These sorts of wares were not first-class but were nonetheless marked for the em-

peror *and* exported in the same way as they had been to the Middle East. The practice of allowing second-rate *nianhao* wares out of the country meant that when the Dutch turned to Japan to acquire fine wares, beginning about 1657, they might order, as they did in 1659, five thousand cups "wholly snow white with six Japanese letters on the foot below."[12] Chinese, rather than "Japanese," was meant. As Volker has pointed out, Japanese porcelains have four, not six characters, and the models were obviously Chinese.[13]

With this long-established precedent for marked export wares, it is not surprising that shards and whole pieces have turned up in North America. Those marked and of the Jiajing period are the earliest known (figs. 386 and 387). Another shard, doubtless Wanli, is from the *San Agustin*, a Spanish galleon wrecked in 1595 about four hundred yards off Drakes Bay, north of San Francisco. It is

luo "conch shell"

ding "cauldron"

ruyi tou "head of 'as-you-like-it' scepter"

chang "entrails" "endless knot"

wan "swastika"

xiefang li wan "swastika in a lozenge"

fangsheng "double lozenge"

he "stork"

yutu "the Jade Hare —the moon"

yutu "the Jade Hare —the moon"

yutu "the Jade Hare —the moon"

ai ye "artemesia leaf"

lingzhi "magic fungus"

fu "blessings"

Line drawings from several sources and examples from shards: Hobson, Linsingh-Scheurleer, Pope, Williamsburg, Drake's Bay

(Drawing by Amy McNair)

391. *Kangxi Period Symbols*

one of six bowls of a quality apart from all shards recovered in the area, one of two showing surf abrasion, thus associated with the *San Agustin*, and the only one of all the porcelains that is marked. It bears a four-character inscription, "Beautiful Vessel of the Jade Hall" (fig. 388).[14] Another, also probably Wanli, is the shard in figure 389 unearthed from a well in St. Augustine, Florida; the city was a Spanish possession at the time. The shard's very abstract mark may be derived from the seal, *fu kuei jia chi* ("fine vase for the rich and honorable"), a travesty of its original intent, given the poor quality of both the shard and the mark (compare figs. 389 and 390).

Besides the cup illustrated in figures 137 and 138, the author knows of Transitional wares in North America that have come to light. The single find is probably promise of more to come, though never as many as those of the reign of Kangxi (1662–1722), when importation was regular and frequent. Also, during Kangxi, conventional signs were much more common, even among imperial wares, than the *nianhao* or any hallmark, greeting, or good wishes. In 1677, the district magistrate of Jingdezhen proscribed the reign mark from appearing on porcelains lest by breakage the emperor's name be defiled. For a time, then, substitutes in the form of well-known symbols (fig. 391) appeared within the usual two concentric circles in underglaze blue (figs. 392 and 393), or the space was left empty.[15] Yet this practice could happen in any reign, and in modern times was deliberately done to imitate Kangxi pieces. The symbols might appear on the edge of a piece without any circles (fig. 394). Despite this substitution, Ming marks, especially those of the fifteenth century, are common on Kangxi wares. The Kangxi mark itself, probably used in the late part of the reign, is rather rare (fig. 395).

The Ming mark of Chenghua was often imitated in Kangxi,[16] thus the shard in figure 396 from Virginia fits a well-established pattern from its context date. Still other examples of Kangxi marks are those in figures 397 and 398 with the date of 1715, the year they went down with their ship off the Florida coast. The tradition of marking export with swift suggestions of symbols or sayings thus continued until the early eighteenth century, and in some cases, later. The same mark as in figure 396 appears on blue-and-white wares retrieved from a mid-eighteenth-century shipwreck at Table Bay, South Africa; the wares

392. Ding-*like* (incense-burner) *mark*, c. 1690–1720, on base of underglaze blue; overglaze brown saucer. Courtesy of the Henry Francis du Pont Winterthur Museum.

393. *Saucer base*, c. 1690–1700, D 16.5 cm. Underglaze blue fish in two circles (obverse: overglaze iron-red and gilt, early willow pattern, see fig. 118). Private collection, Mexico City.

394. *Bowl under-rim detail*, c. 1685–1700, D 28.9 cm. Underglaze blue, fungus with grass (obverse: landscape with Japanese Imari–style wide border, see fig. 106). Private collection, Mexico City.

395. *Dish base*, c. 1680, D 27.3 cm. Grooved base, underglaze blue mark of Kangxi (1662–1722). Private collection, Mexico City.

396. *Shard base*, c. 1690–1710. Mark of Chenghua (1465–87), found on the Drummond Plantation. Courtesy of the Virginia Research Center.

397. *Cup base*, c. 1713, D 8.6 cm. Underglaze blue, recovered from The San José, (1715). For obverse, see Fig. 109.

398. *Bowl base*, c. 1713, D 12.1 cm. Underglaze blue mark, *yi*? ("appropriate; suitable for progeny").

399. *Cup and saucer*, c. 1700–20. Octagonal, overglaze light-brown ground; on base, underglaze blue mark, *yi* ("happiness"), different from fig. 398. Courtesy of the Fries Museum, Leeuwarden.

400. *Shard*, c. 1700–20, octagonal, cup base. Underglaze blue mark, conch shell in two circles, Mexico City subway excavations.

are now at the British Museum. From fragmentary evidence of marked shards recovered in Williamsburg, Virginia, in known and unknown contexts, which fit the Kangxi period stylistically and historically, one may say that such wares were not uncommon in North America, although not enough data is now available to give a percentage (see fig. 393).[17] (The variety of marks in Kangxi derives not only from the 1677 prohibition against use of the *nianhao* but also from artistic variations in rendering characters and symbols [compare figs. 399 and 400]. This unsurprising individuality makes even the commonest symbol, like the sacred fungus [*ling-chih*, see fig. 394] look quite different from one hand to another.)

After Yongzheng, marks on exported wares are less and less frequent. Perhaps the growing demand for objects of Western shape with Western decoration replaced the desire to have a seal of approval, however meaningless or indecipherable it might be by its own slapdash execution on an inferior piece. Such a mark, formerly more exotic than significant, was now essentially irrelevant to the finished export product. Quality, pure and simple, was the major requirement. Many references to quality in both Dutch and English records testify to the premium put on fine porcelains. While imperial ware or that of imperial quality might be coveted and perhaps exported (fig. 401), West-

ern demand was satisfied with its own orders when they were well done and well packed. This was the case especially with armorials, which were another sort of mark of their own. At their best, in terms of potting and painting, they were the top of the line in faithful execution if not originality. They were, of course, in the category of special-order porcelains, *chine de commande*.

National signs, such as that of the English East India Company (fig. 402) and those reflecting America's patriotic pride, apparent well beyond the 1780s and 1790s (figs. 403 and 404), were another sort of mark that eclipsed Chinese signs on export. This type includes an unusual dinner set with "Canton in China, 24th Jany 1971," in English script on the bottom.[18] Porcelains of this sort probably led everyone, Chinese and foreign, to make a sharper distinction between those wares bearing the *nianhao* or other marks and the export pieces. However, such individual or national emblems on the body of the ware died out with the decline in the Western market. This trend, underway by the 1830s, continued into the nineteenth century, despite the revival of Jingdezhen in the 1860s after the Taiping Rebellion. Also, with the sacking by the British and French of the Summer Palace in Beijing in 1860, a number of imperial porcelains began to reach the West in greater numbers. If one wished a quality

401. *Plates* (identical), obverse and reverse, c. 1715–25, D 21.6 cm. Overglaze enamels, underglaze blue mark in double square, *cai hua tang zhi*, ("Made for the Hall of Beautiful Paintings"); first-class imperial Ex. coll., kitchener. Private collection.

402. *Stand*, c. 1790, L 22.2 cm. Pierced border, overglaze enamels, arms of the English East India Company, part of a service owned by the governor of Bombay, fine export. Courtesy of Dr. Wesley Gallup.

403. *Vase*, c. 1850–75, H 31.8 cm. Overglaze enamels, figure of Liberty, above-average export, rare. Bequest of estate of Mr. Harry T. Peters, Jr. Courtesy of the Peabody Museum.

404. Detail of fig. 403.

405. *Cups and sauceboat*, c. 1870–90, sauceboat: L 18.4 cm. Overglaze enamels and gilt, descended in the Morgan family of Worcester. Courtesy of Professor and Mrs. Charles M. Morgan.

piece made for the emperor, not merely the same mark executed poorly, it was possible to have it at a price.

At the same time, on export wares an occasional mark occurred. In figure 405, a handled cup is the single form in this dinner set imported into Massachusetts about 1875–80 to be marked (fig. 406). After 1891, U.S. Customs required "China" or "Made in China" on the base of pieces. These words may be either in blue or red, the latter stamped on the bottom as in figure 407. In contrast to other marks, this one was merely commercial, not a measure of either quality or prestige. Finally, by the end of the imperial reigns, export ware would again bear the *nianhao*, as the plate in figs. 381 and 382 of 1909 clearly show.

406. (far left) Detail of mark on cup (fig. 405) base in overglaze red.

407. (left) *Dish base*, c. 1895–1900, L 37.1 cm. Overglaze enamels; mark of Guangzu (1875-1908); associated with the J. Gray Bolton family of Philadelphia, above-average export. Author's collection.

APPENDIX B

Gilt Porcelains

As described in chapter 2, gilded wares had long been produced in China before their arrival to North America in the first cargoes of export at Acapulco. Even though gilt is the first painting to wear, the technique employed was for permanence. On a glazed piece, the gold—mixed with lead carbonate—was combined with gum and applied with a brush. Then it was fired in a "muffle," or small enameler's kiln, at a lower temperature (in the high 600s° C) than the first firing (about 1200° C). A sure fix was obtained by mixing garlic juice with the gold.[1] A method of gilding with oil, which omitted a second firing, was fruit-less; the gold inevitably wore off.[2]

The experiments of a twentieth-century Japanese potter, Kenkichi Tomimoto, help explain the process of gilding and reveal the properties of gold that allow it to adhere better to red enamel than to any other color. To fuse gold with red enamel, Tomimoto found, required higher temperatures than for other enamels, thus making a surer bond. Examples of red-and-gold Chinese porcelains compared to blue-and-gold or green-and-gold dramatically confirm his findings.[3]

Even blue-and-white porcelain, usually left ungilded, has been occasionally embellished in the Yongle and Xuande periods well before Jiajing. The Peking and Taibei Palace Museums each have blue-and-white bowls with gilding, but despite their mention in historical records, such wares are now rare. For one thing, the gold easily wore off.[4] Also, the best blue-and-white porcelain, that of Jingdezhen, was considered of greater worth than most gilded ware, according to the Jesuit missionary Père d'Entrecolles.[5] Often, enameling and gilding could cover defects in the porcelain; the underglaze blue, applied before firing, could not.[6] Like the official kilns in Jiajing, the private factories also gilded polychrome and monochrome porcelains.[7] If the blue-and-white export was gilded and it wore off, then it could be retouched in Europe; plain pieces could be embellished from scratch. Repairs, however, were routinely made in gold or with silver or brass staples. The twentieth-century gold repairs to the cups and saucers in figure 182 thus follow long historical precedent.

APPENDIX C

Shipwrecks

Some of the best finds of historic porcelains have been recovered from shipwrecks. The objects are often whole and closely dated, more so than their on-shore counterparts. Packed in clay, straw, matting, pepper or other foodstuffs like sago, they were cushioned against breakage. Overglaze enamels or gilt may disappear after long immersion in salt water, but the worst injury to underglaze blue is surface abrasion. Below, references to reports listed more fully in the Bibliography are in parentheses by author and date.

1323–31. Junk, Chinese. Off Sinan, near Mokpo, 320 miles southwest of Seoul, Korea; Yuan dynasty (1279–1369): greenware (celadon) and whitish blue (*qingbai*)—cups, plates, bowls, jars. (Keith 1979; Ayers 1984)

1579. *Golden Hind.* English ship with Spanish treasure. Drake's Bay, California: 77 shards (shards recovered on shore; see appendix D, "Archaeological Sites," and 1595 in this list). (Shangraw and Von der Porten 1981; Von der Porten 1984)

1588. *Trinidad Valencera.* Spanish. Kinnagoe Bay, County Donegal, Northern Ireland: 3 shards (2 Wanli), 1 intact bowl, typical of late-Ming crude wares. (Martin 1979)

1594. *San Pedro.* Spanish. Bermuda: 1 underglaze blue cup. (Benchley 1971)

1595. *San Agustin.* Spanish. Drake's Bay, California (see appendix D, "Archaeological Sites"). (Shangraw and Von der Porten 1981)

1613. *Witte Leeuw.* Dutch. James Bay, St. Helena: Wanli and other late-Ming dynasty whole porcelains—bowls, dishes, wine cups, pitchers, jars, drinking pots. (Sténuit 1978; Muckelroy 1980)

1622. *Nuestra Señora de Atocha.* Spanish. Off Florida coast: cargo, discovered in 1985, under analysis.

1641. *Concepción.* Spanish. Abrojos of the Florida Straits: 1 underglaze blue cup, dish fragments; pottery shards. (Earle 1980)

c. 1645. Junk, Chinese in Dutch employ. South China Sea, 19.7 miles off Singapore: 60,000–70,000 pieces (30,000 recovered) underglaze blue carrack and Transitional wares; green, white, blue and yellow ware. (Sheaf 1984, 1985; Green 1984)

1647. *Sacramento.* Portuguese. Port Elizabeth, South Africa: Ming underglaze blue. (Muckelroy 1980)

1656. *Nuestra Señora de la Maravellas.* Spanish. Little Bahama Bank: underglaze blue (Metropolitan Museum of Art has 4 shards from this wreck). (Letter to author, Valenstein 1979)

1668. *Sacramentos.* Portuguese. Bay of All Saints, Bahia, Brazil: early Kangxi—2 fragments of underglaze blue; 1 polychrome drug jar (*albarello*). (De Mello 1979)

1692. Earthquake, followed by tidal wave; several Manila galleons lost, not specified. Port Royal, Jamaica: Dehua figurine of Guanyin with child (fig. 112); porcelain shards. (Marx 1968, 1971; Link 1960)

1697. *Santo António de Tanná.* Portuguese. Fort Jesus, Mombasa, Kenya: large, eroded polychrome shallow bowls, two with underglaze blue mark of fungus in double circles (compare fig. 394); in underglaze blue, 1 high-quality bowl with six-character mark of Chenghua; 1 large high-quality shallow bowl (unusual decoration); small plates or shallow bowls; small bowls. (Piercy 1978; Kirkman 1972; Sassoon 1981)

1715. "Plate Fleet." Spanish. East of Cape Canaveral, near Sebastian Inlet, Florida: 28 Kangxi intact cups—underglaze blue, white with tracing of former decorative border; darkened ox-blood (*sang de boeuf*), 1 "China aster" intact bowl (figs. 397 and 398, examples). (Hahn 1980; *Treasure of the Spanish Main* 1967; Wagner 1965)

1724. *Guadalupe y Tolosa.* Spanish. Dominican Republic, Samana Bay: unspecified ceramics. (Peterson 1979)

1724. *Slot ter Hooge.* Dutch. Porto Santo (now Port do Guilherme), Madeira Islands: fragments of a porcelain plate. (Sténuit 1975; Muckelroy 1980)

1727. *Zeewijk.* Dutch. Western Australia: unspecified porcelain shards. (Muckelroy 1980)

1730–60. Civic Centre ship. Dutch. Cape Town, South Africa: fragments of 3 Guangdong bowls. (Lightley 1976)

1733. *San José y las Animas.* Spanish. Straits of Florida: 362 shards; underglaze blue and a few polychrome plates, cups, case bottles, bowls; square "Dutch bottle," underglaze blue, overglaze enamels eroded, silver overglaze. (Logan 1977; Saltus 1972)

1737. Unnamed Portuguese vessel. Returning from Goa: Chinese figurines; underglaze blue lidded bowl; underglaze blue rectangular caddy with lid; six-lobed tea caddy on scroll base with lid; brown-glazed lid to bowl with four leaf reserves (overglaze enamels eroded). (Letter to author, Mathewson 1982)

1740. *Svecia.* Swedish. Orkney Island, off North Ronaldsey, England: Yongzheng underglaze blue shards. (Muckelroy 1980)

1743. *Hollandia.* Dutch. Isles of Scilly off Cornwall: unspecified Chinese shards. (Muckelroy 1980)

1745. *Göteborg.* Swedish. Gothenburg Harbor, Sweden: quantity of intact underglaze blue plates and bowls. (Roth 1965)

1751. European merchant ship, probably Dutch. "The Nanking Cargo," so-called for its majority of blue-and-white landscape pieces in over 100,000 underglaze blue, overglaze brown, and Chinese "Imari" tablewares; some figurines. (Sheaf 1986; see Jorg, pp. 196–97)

1760. *Le Machault.* French. Gaspé Peninsula, Quebec: see appendix D, "Archaeological Sites." (Whate 1980; Peterson 1977)

1762. *Santissima Trinidad.* Spanish. Three weeks out of Manila, bound for Acapulco: cargo unknown. (Letter to author, Mathewson 1982)

1763. *Jonge Thomas.* Dutch. Table Bay, South Africa: underglaze blue shards, some at the British Museum. (Hyde 1954)

1775. *Royal Savage.* British. Richelieu River, Fort St. Jean, Canada: shards date 1770–1830, most from 1800–1825, thus not from ship but probably from dumpsite. (Ship raised by Americans, renamed USS *Yankee* in 1776.) (Theoret 1976)

1776. *Niew Rhoon.* Dutch. Capetown, South Africa: Guangdong bowls. (Muckelroy 1980)

1778. HMS *Orpheus.* English. Narragansett Bay off Portsmouth, Rhode Island: underglaze blue plate and saucer fragments. (Montgomery 1984)

1779. *Valentine.* British. Sark, Channel Islands: unspecified shards. (Muckelroy 1980)

1781. Cornwallis Cave wreck. Origin unknown. Yorktown, Virginia: Unspecified shards. (Johnson 1978)

1810–11 or 1816–20. Point Cloates wreck (unnamed vessel; may be one of two possibilities). American. Western Australia: underglaze blue shards. (Henderson 1980)

1850. *Frolic.* American. Off Point Cabrillo, California: a quantity of rough underglaze blue and heavy stoneware. (*Daily Alta California,* 5 Aug. 1850; Layton 1984)

Archaeological Sites

Archaeology has uncovered many porcelain shards in North America, but digs are sometimes incomplete, and not all excavations have published reports. Nonetheless, this list overviews the current evidence, beginning with Canada, the Caribbean and Mexico, then moving to the United States. For each item, the first date approximates the start of occupation; however, shards may be of an earlier date. The end date, the year the site was abandoned, is the last possible date of deposit. The numbers and types of export wares are listed with author/date references to sources.

CANADA

1730–68. Louisbourg, Nova Scotia. Fortress of Louisbourg: most typical of 1730s and 1740s; a few Kangxi; underglaze blue including "Swatow" ware, Islamic motifs, Chinese "Imari," iron-red, gold-red, green, brown, and incised; Japanese export. (Lunn 1972; letter to author, Crépeau 1982)

1750–60. Chaleur Bay, mouth of Restigouche River, Shipwreck of *Le Machault*, sunk 1760: c. 1480 intact objects, underglaze blue (60 percent), Chinese "Imari," iron-red with and without gilt, gold-red, brown. (Letter to author, Whate 1981)

1786–1813. North West Company posts—Pine Island, Fort George, Terre Blanche (none associated with posts of the Hudson Bay Company), North Saskatchewan: 21 shards (9 percent of all ceramics). Underglaze blue "Canton" and "Nanking," penciled Greek key. (Nicks 1969)

1796–1829. Fort St. Joseph: small number of shards from limited total ceramic find. Fluted bowl, underglaze blue, penciled Greek key. (Whate 1980)

1799–1821. North West Company Rocky Mountain House, North Saskatchewan River: 16 shards, among them those of a small bowl (c. D 16 cm, H 6 cm) with penciled Greek key inner border. (Steer and Rogers 1978)

1824–45. Fort Vancouver, Hudson Bay Company, Vancouver: less than 1 percent of total ceramic find, "Canton" and "Nanking," green. (Ross 1976)

THE CARIBBEAN AND MEXICO

1503–40 (formally abandoned 1576). Puerto Real, Haiti: small fragments of grayish underglaze blue. (Letter to author, Fairbanks 1981)

1519–1671. Panama La Vieja, Panama: 141 shards, mostly underglaze blue; 17 pieces of a vase or wine ewer molded in the shape of a phoenix with clouds in relief, applied feathers, probably Jiajing or Wanli. (Baker 1969)

c. 1550–early 1800s. STC (subway) excavations, Mexico City: a quantity of Ming dishes, plates, cups, bowls, and jars of a large range but predominantly underglaze blue (Jingdezhen and "Swatow"), overglaze green, iron-red, Dehua white, and gilt. Little or no greenware (celadon)—too commonplace a color for Hispanic taste familiar with green lead glazes dating from Roman times. Qing pieces: same form types and colors as Ming with the addition of gold-red and black; some Japanese shards from 1700s. (Cervantes 1977 and 1982; Lister and Lister, *Historical Archaeology* and *El Palacio*, both 1974)

c. 1550–early 1800s. El Templo Mayor, Mexico City: in quantity similar to STC excavations just listed. (Cervantes 1982)

prob. 1550–early 1800s (but no date given). Puebla State, Mexico: underglaze blue, overglaze polychrome. By the 1630s, Puebla potters were copying Chinese shapes and motifs. (Letter to author, Cervantes 1983; Lister and Lister, *El Palacio*, 1974)

prob. 1550–early 1800s (but no date given). Michoacán State, Mexico: underglaze blue, overglaze polychrome. (Letter to author, Cervantes 1983)

c. 1655–89. Port Royal, Jamaica: a quantity of shards of utilitarian pieces, largely underglaze blue; of the polychromes, red and green dominate. (Letter to author, Aarons 1983)

c. 1700–1850. New Seville and Drax Hall, Jamaica: similar to Port Royal site. (Aarons 1983)

c. 1730–1850. Spanish Town and New Montpelier, Jamaica: similar to Port Royal site. (Aarons 1983)

THE UNITED STATES
South
FLORIDA

c. 1570–late 1700s. St. Augustine (various sites): 2 percent of ceramic finds regardless of period or economic status of inhabitants, Spanish or British; presumably tablewares though shards are quite small, fine underglaze blue or grayish of late 1500s–early 1600s; Transitional wares not yet identified; Chinese "Imari," iron-red and gilt, iron-red. (Letter to author, Deagan 1982)

c. 1633–1704. San Francisco de Oconee Mission, 26 miles southeast of Tallahassee: 2 shards. (Smith 1955)

c. 1675–1725. Higgs sites, offshore island between Indian River and the Atlantic, south of Sebastian Inlet (a pirate rendezvous): small number of quality pieces, tablewares, and screen slab typical of Transitional and Kangxi underglaze blue; also, Kangxi polychrome and gilded fragments, one of a powder-blue and gilt jar (see similar shard, fig. 82). (Aga-Oglu 1955)

c. 1689–1940. Fort Castillo de San Marcos and the Dragoon Lot, St. Augustine: small quantity, but some fine, all blue-and-white; tablewares, possibly a vase. (Aga-Oglu 1955)

c. 1722–56. Santa Rosa, Pensacola: 207 shards, 2 Kangxi, 1 Kangxi shard with Ming mark. (Florida State University, *Notes in Anthropology*, 1965)

c. 1764–80. Spaulding's Lower Store, Indian Trading Post, south of Palatka on St. John's River: 330 shards; tablewares of white, underglaze blue, polychrome; some Japanese underglaze blue. (Lewis 1969; Aga-Oglu 1955)

n.d. Rookery Mound on the Shark River, Monroe County: small quantity found on the surface, average underglaze blue. (Goggin 1950)

GEORGIA

c. 1736–50. Fort Frederica and Frederica (town): from two houses, underglaze blue, Chinese "Imari," gold-red; some Japanese. (Aga-Oglu 1955; letter to author, Fairbanks 1983)

c. 1794–1866. Cannon's Point Plantation, Saint Simon's Island: from slave cabin—7 shards "Canton"; from overseer's house— 29 "Canton," 1 gilt. (South 1977)

SOUTH CAROLINA

c. 1566–86. Santa Elena, Parris Island: small quantity Ming underglaze blue, including large shard with crayfish design and spout to a blue-and-white ewer similar to figure 88. More shards in domestic Santa Elena dwellings than at Fort San Felipe. (South 1979, 1980; letter to author, South 1984)

c. 1685–1800s. Charleston County: 20 sites, 10 each dating from the 1600s and 1700s, unspecified number and type of Chinese porcelain. (South and Hartley 1980)

1714–82. Green Grove Plantation, Kinloch Site, Charleston County. Structure A: 460 shards, primarily underglaze blue, 6 percent of total ceramic find. Structure B: 200 shards, 24 percent of total ceramic find. (Carrillo 1980)

1780–81. Clarendon County: 20 shards, 12 from stockade, 8 from outside (3 percent of total ceramic find). (South and Hartley 1980)

late 1700s–early 1800s. Middleton Place, northwest of Charleston: 4 underglaze blue shards, 1 with gilt; cornflower plate shard, may be Chinese rather than French (see figs. 326 and 327). (Haskell 1981)

VIRGINIA

Unless otherwise noted, it may be assumed that shards from the early 1600s in Virginia are almost all underglaze blue, with the later Qing fragments following the common types indicated in chapter 6. Following listed objects are not whole, but, rather, identifiable.

c. 1607–98. Jamestown: several hundred shards of Ming and Qing dynasties from 30 sites in 19 structures belonging to middle and lower-income settlers. (Letter to author, Haskett 1979)

c. 1618–1820. Governor's Land, James City County, near Jamestown.
c. 1618–1625, The "Maine": 6 wine cups, 1 small bowl.
c. 1648–1820, Drummond/Harris Plantation: 1600s—4 small cups (bowls), 1 unidentified rim, "Swatow"; 1700s—48 tea cups, 44 saucers, 13 punch bowls, 13 plates, 2 teapots, 1 teapot stand, 1 lid to tea caddy, 2 milk pots, 1 platter, 1 sauceboat, 2 cans, and unidentified objects or miscellaneous bowls. (Letter to author, Outlaw 1983)

c. 1620–1800. Kingsmill Properties, James City County, near Williamsburg.
c. 1620–50, Kingsmill Tenement: 1 wine cup, 1 tray with compartments (possibly from isolated c. 1680–1710 deposit at this site).
c. 1640–90, Pettus Plantation (Littleton): 2 small bowls.
c. 1690–1740, Tutter's Neck: late 1600s cup.
c. 1700–1790, Bray Plantation (same site as Pettus Plantation): 3 punch bowls, 6 teacups (bowls), 3 plates, 2 saucers.
1725–75, Kingsmill Quarter: 9 plates, 2 soup plates, 7 teacups (bowls), 6 saucers, 6 small bowls, 4 punch bowls, 2 cans, 1 each— platter, tea caddy lid, mug.
1770–1800, North Quarter: 3 teacups (bowls), 2 plates, 1 bowl, 1 brown saucer. (Letter to author, Outlaw 1983; for Tutter's Neck—I. N. Hume 1968)

late 1600s–1815. College Landing, Williamsburg: late 1600s—3 fragments; late-1760s deposit—15 teacups (bowls), 10 saucers, 3 plates, 2 cans, 1 bowl; c. 1750–1815—6 plates, 4 bowls, 3 teacups. (Letter to author, Outlaw 1983).

c. 1700–1810. Colonial Williamsburg.
c. 1700. Hubard site: 1 cup, exterior green, yellow, dark brown, interior underglaze blue. (Records of Colonial Williamsburg, courtesy of John Austin)
c. 1720–60. Peyton-Randolph site: total of 221 shards; in underglaze blue—9 plates, 3 saucers, 3 low bowls, 2 large bowls, 1 teacup, 1 handled cup; 79 overglaze, in iron-red—1 handled cup, 1 saucer; in polychrome—2 teacups, 2 saucers, 2 plates, 2 large bowls, 1 low bowl, 1 molded dish, 1 soup plate. (Letters to author, Marley Brown III 1984; William E. Pittman 1984)
1743–60. Wetherburn Tavern, Williamsburg: tablewares of blue-and-white, overglaze polychrome similar to "white flowered china" listed in Henry Wetherburn's 1760 inventory. (I. N. Hume 1969; A. N. Hume 1970)
c. 1790–1810. Coke-Garrett site: fluted teacups, polychrome floral decoration; handle: single-strap with fern endings. (Records of Colonial Williamsburg, courtesy of John Austin)

1763–72 (when artifacts discarded). Rosewell site, Gloucester County: shards of 35 objects, most underglaze blue, a few polychrome and gilt, one fragment of Dehua white figurine. (I. N. Hume 1962)

1700s–early 1800s. Flowerdew Hundred Plantation, Prince George County: a quantity of typical period shards, work in progress. University of California at Berkeley. (Telephone conversation with Deetz 1983).

late 1700s–early 1800s. Monticello: Jefferson porcelains; "Canton," "Nanking," "FitzHugh" in underglaze blue; polychrome "Altar of Love" pattern (Palmer 1976, p. 90); mustard pot of "artichoke pattern"; other unidentified patterns. (Letter to author, Sanford 1983)

late 1700s–early 1800s. Alexandria: quality underglaze blue—1 platter with "Dutch folly" ("go-down," or warehouse) on Pearl River near Canton; "Canton" (crude and fine); 1 Chinese "Imari" shard; polychrome teawares, overglaze black and gold water bottle and canister, 1 coffee cup with American eagle. (Magid 1982; letter to author, Magid 1983)

early 1800s. Taylor-Whittle House, Norfolk: "Canton" and "FitzHugh" underglaze blue, polychrome. (Foss 1974)

c. 1820. Deer Chase, Middlesex County: fire damaged—12 saucers (4 fluted), 4 teacups, 10 small plates, 1 teapot with lid, strap handles, 1 helmet creamer. (Letter to author, Outlaw 1983)

Middle Atlantic

DELAWARE, PENNSYLVANIA, AND NEW JERSEY

1643. New Gothenburg, Prinzhof (house of Johan Printz, governor of New Sweden), Great Tinicum Island, 12 miles north of Wilmington on Delaware River, Delaware; *no* porcelain found. (Becker 1979)

1722–1810. Dover, Delaware: 1722–1807—the State House; 1739–1800—the Liston House; c. 1810—the Robinson House. Analysis incomplete, but fine-quality polychrome shards, especially from the Liston House. (Letter to author, Wise 1979)

c. 1740–65; 1785–1815. Franklin's Court, Philadelphia: 80 vessels (8.1 percent of total ceramics), over 75 percent teawares, 12.5 percent various-sized bowls, 3 plates and miscellaneous shards; most of underglaze blue in early period; later, principally polychrome with gilt and possibly silver; 1 shard "Canton." (Cosans 1974; Liggett 1973)

c. 1740–1800. New Market, Philadelphia: 1740–65—underglaze blue and polychrome with gilt; late 1700s—more polychrome. (Liggett 1978)

c. 1750–75. Bishop William White House, Philadelphia: underglaze blue "Nanking" platter shards. (Independence National Historical Park 1961)

c. 1750–1820. Between Second and Front Streets (E-W), and Ionic and Sansome Streets (N-S), Area F, Philadelphia: 2 percent underglaze blue, 40 reconstructed vessels, .01 percent polychrome (of total ceramics). (Letters to author, Giannini 1979, 1984)

c. 1750–1820. Deshler-Morris House, with Franklin Court and Bishop White House, Philadelphia: 1–5 percent porcelain of total ceramics. (Letter to author, Giannini 1984)

1758–66. Ft. Ligonier, Pennsylvania: 582 shards, most underglaze blue; a few iron-red and gilt; some with brown rims; 1 punchbowl shard, another large bowl with dragon decoration. (Grimm 1970)

1761–1830s. Hudibras Tavern, Princeton, New Jersey: unspecified porcelains found. (Baker and Thorbahn 1977)

1790–1825. Mendenhall House, Wilmington, Delaware: underglaze blue heavy bowls, fluted saucer with floral sprig. (Letter to author, Fleming 1980)

1800–1820. McIlvaine House, 315–317 Walnut Street (built 1791–93), Philadelphia: .09 percent of total ceramics (c. 1440 shards). (Letter to author, Giannini 1984)

NEW YORK

c. 1637–1810. Stadt Huys Block, 7 Hanover Square, and 64 Pearl Street, New York City. 1600s—2 small Transitional underglaze blue fragments; c. 1720–65—overglaze polychrome; 1785–95—special-order wares from a china shop. (Author's examination 1983; letters to author, Janowitz 1983; Howard 1984)

c. 1650/60–1800s. Fort Orange, Albany (abandoned only for a short period in the 1750s and 1760s; in the 1790s, site of the mansion of Simeon DeWitt, surveyor general of New York): Transitional underglaze blue to "Canton" and "Nanking"; Chinese "Imari," iron-red and gilt. (Letter to author, Huey 1980)

c. 1650s–1910. Schuyler Flats, north of Albany on the Hudson: c. 1600–1620—3 underglaze blue fragments of 2 carrack bowls; 1700–1720—2 bowls and molded saucer; c. 1730—small plate or saucer. (Howard 1984)

1670s or 1680s. Philipse Manor, Hudson River, north of Getty Square, Yonkers: Transitional underglaze blue, two almost intact bowls, D 11.4 cm (Howard 1984)

c. 1728–77. Clermont (ancestral home of the Livingstons, built 1730, burned 1777 by a British raid) Germantown: underglaze blue: 1700–1720—marked bowl, mug or chocolate cup, plate, hexagonal salt, base of Dehua white figurine (2 attached feet); 1730–1735—plate fragments; 1740—shards from dinner service. Overglaze polychrome: c. 1720—red/green punch bowl; c. 1730—gold-red coffee cup; c. 1740—Chinese "Imari" dish; c. 1760—underglaze blue teacup with overglaze enamels; c. 1765—gold-red, iron-red and sepia jug and teapot; c. 1775—teabowl with floral swags, trellis. (Letters to author, Wentworth 1979 and 1980; Howard 1984)

1753–1800s. Vereberg Tavern, Albany County: 1700s—23 shards underglaze blue, 2 polychrome; c. late 1700s and late 1800s—56 underglaze blue, 23 polychrome. (Feister 1975)

1756–73. Crown Point Barracks, Lake Champlain: small number of underglaze blue shards from soldiers', not officers' quarters. (Howard 1984)

1758–81. Fort Stanwix, Rome: 827 shards; 183 undecorated (possible blank parts of painted ones), 570 underglaze blue, 10 iron-red, 63 polychrome. (Hanson and Hsu 1975)

1763–1860s. Johnson Hall, 14 miles north of Mohawk River, near Saratoga: underglaze blue: 1610–20 Wanli bowl; 1620–30 Wanli dish; c. 1666 early-Kangxi bowl; c. 1680 fine-line fragment; 1735–45 saucer, almost intact. Overglaze black-penciled, possibly eroded enamels on 1 plate fragment. (Howard 1984)

New England

CONNECTICUT

c. 1660–1830. Ebenezer Grosvenor Homestead, Pomfret: 8 underglaze blue cup and bowl shards; bowl later than cup. (Baker 1978b)

MAINE

1692–1760. Pemaquid (occupied since 1625; fort built 1692): 161 shards. (Camp 1975)

c. 1755. Tate House, Portland: 1 underglaze blue teacup; a few shards brown ("Batavia") ware. (Source unknown)

MASSACHUSETTS

c. 1700–1870. Narbonne House, Salem: 1700–57—10 shards; 1757–80—59 shards; 1780–1820—745 shards; 1820–70—141 shards. Teacups, saucers, few large bowls, 1 thick base of tureen or punch-bowl; underglaze blue, iron-red, polychrome and gilt. (Moran 1982)

early 1700s. Paul Revere Houselot, Boston: unspecified amount of porcelain. (Elia 1983)

c. 1720–50. Bostonian Hotel, Boston: few shards of saucers and plates; underglaze blue with and without gilt; Chinese "Imari." (Montgomery 1984)

c. 1740s–1850s. Wright Tavern, Concord: 1 percent of total ceramics. (Baker and Thornbahn 1977)

c. 1775–1908. Josiah Nelson House, Lincoln: 8 shards—6 underglaze blue, 2 polychrome. (Abel 1966)

c. 1789–1845. Black Lucy's Garden, Andover: 2 percent of total ceramics. (Baker 1978a)

c. 1790–1800. Wilson Farm, Dover: 1 saucer shard, puce husk design (unusual), normally overglaze blue and gold. (Montgomery 1984)

1700s. Dr. Thomas Williams House, Deerfield: 1 semiwhole underglaze blue tea bowl. (Blades 1976)

NEW HAMPSHIRE

c. 1750–1825. Hart-Shortridge House, Portsmouth: 2 teacups, 1 underglaze blue, the other polychrome; 1 "Canton" plate. (Montgomery 1984)

RHODE ISLAND

1700s. South Main Street, Providence: 104 shards, most underglaze blue; few Chinese "Imari." (Stachiw and Margolis 1974)

VERMONT

1800s. Green House and Store, Windsor: fragment "Canton" cup and plate (letter to author, Montgomery 1983)

Midwest

MICHIGAN

c. 1715–80. Fort Michilimackinac, southeast of Mackinac City: 5000 shards; 1715–61—French occupation, very few tiny shards; 1760–80—British occupation, most underglaze blue, many polychrome tea pieces or punch bowls, a few tea bowls and saucers with exterior brown, interior underglaze blue. (Miller 1970; Stone 1970; Peterson 1982)

West

ARIZONA

c. 1640–1819. Awatovi: 104 European ceramics, 3 shards underglaze blue, 1 is 1600s. (Montgomery et al. 1949)

c. 1750–1850. Tubac Presidio: 39 shards underglaze blue; 42 polychrome, 9 iron-red, 85 unclassified white. (Shenk and Teague 1975)

1859–1903. Johnny Ward's Ranch, southwest of Patagona. 369 total ceramic shards; 2 of poor-quality Chinese cup, white-blue glaze. (Fontana and Greenleaf 1962)

c. 1862–73. Tucson Urban Renewal site: underglaze blue—carp plate, 1 teacup; polychrome—5 intact wine cups, 4 plates, 7 saucers, 2 shards with overglaze fowl; greenware—unspecified number of rice bowls, tea and wine cups, small saucers; "Swatow" bowls in pale blue and green; rice-grain bowls and saucers; miscellaneous porcelains. (Olsen 1978)

c. 1885–1915. Papago Reservation: 191 porcelain shards, Japanese red and brown edges with decals, Chinese pale blue and green (similar to Tucson pieces above), underglaze blue and white. (Teague 1980)

CALIFORNIA

1579. Drake's Estero, Drake's Bay, Point Reyes Peninsula, Francis Drake's expedition of the *Golden Hind*: 77 shards, underglaze blue Wanli, most high-quality carrackware, not surf-abraded. (Shangraw and Von der Porten 1981)

1595. Limantour Spit, Drake's Bay, Point Reyes Peninsula, wreck of Sebastian Rodriguez Cermeno's *San Agustin*: 158 underglaze blue Wanli, Fukien provincial, "Swatow" and lesser carrack, most surf-abraded. (Shangraw and Von der Porten 1981)

1769–1833. Presidio Chapel site, San Diego: 1197 shards, most tablewares underglaze blue, including "Canton" and "Nanking;" polychrome and gilt, 1 "Swatow" fragment; Japanese pieces. (Krase 1979)

1769–1830. Presidio Gateway, San Diego: 677 shards, 92.6 percent export (54.1 percent of total ceramics); 30.8 percent underglaze blue, 7.7 percent polychrome. (Letter to author, Barbolla-Roland 1984)

1771–1882? Mission San Antonio de Padua, near Jolon: 10 shards, 8 polychrome, 2 "Canton." (Hoover and Costello 1979)

1772–1830? Mission San Luis Obispo de Tolosa, north of Santa Barbara: "Cantonese trade pottery" from 3 midden areas. (Donald M. Howard, quoted in Heizer 1978)

1776 and 1805. Soldiers' Barracks, San Antonio: Chinese porcelains found in each building of separate dates. (Letter to author, Hoover 1981)

1776–1821? Mission San Juan Capistrano, Orange County: small unreported number of shards. (Magalousis 1981)

1784–1830. Old Town site, San Diego: 93 total—75 miscellaneous shards, 10 "Canton," 2 "Nanking," 5 greenware, 1 "Swatow." (Schulz 1982)

1791–1835. Soledad Mission, near Monterey: "Cantonese porcelain trade wares" with other ceramics and "glass trade beads." (Heizer 1978)

1795–1984. Fort Guijarros site, Ballast Point, Point Loma, San Diego: 22 shards—2 overglaze enamels with gold-red, 2 with gilt; 8 underglaze blue; 10 white. (Krase 1985)

1798–1865. Mission San Luis Rey, between San Juan Capistrano and San Diego: no tally of total; underglaze blue shards, 1 saucer with abstract Arabic calligraphy (compare fig. 295). (Letter to author, Hermes 1980; author's visit, 1980)

c. 1800–1830. Rancho Vejar Adobe, Walnut, south of Los Angeles: 74 shards—52 "Nanking," 6 "Canton," 8 miscellaneous underglaze blue, 6 polychrome, 2 greenware. (Krase 1981)

1815–25. Avila Adobe, Los Angeles. Eight underglaze blue "Canton" plates, D 8 to 9 inches, almost new condition. (Telephone conversation with Franklin Fenenga 1985)

1815–35. Ontiveros Adobe, Santa Fe Springs, east end of Los Angeles County: large, important find, tightly dated—"Canton," "Nanking," "Swatow," "Rose Medallion," white, brown-glazed stoneware. (Greenwood, ed. 1982)

1819–21. Plaza Church site, Los Angeles: "Canton," "Four Seasons," unidentified polychrome. (Letter to author, Edberg 1982)

c. 1820–30. Mission La Purísima Concepción: underglaze blue, two groups, one finer than the other. (Deetz 1962–64)

1820–45. Cooper-Molera Adobe, Monterey: (largest deposit in pit dated 1828–33)—underglaze blue "Canton," abstract Arabic calligraphy, underglaze copper-red and blue phoenix or bird pattern (see figures 292–297). (Felton and Motz 1984)

c. 1822. Plaza Church site, Los Angeles: unreported number of export shards, also a baptismal font (L 33.6 cm, W 30.5 cm) made from polychrome (?) bowl plastered to wall, now at Santa Barbara Presidio. (Conversation with author, Richard Whitehead, librarian, Santa Barbara Mission, 1980)

1837–64. Sepulveda Rancho, on San Juan Capistrano Mission site: 3 percent of total ceramics, Chinese (50 percent English). (Robert Schuyler in Heizer 1978)

1840–50. Bandini-Cota Adobe, Prado Dam, Riverside County: small collection—"Canton," Dehua white, green jars. (Greenwood, ed. 1983a)

1850–70. Bear Valley: assorted overseas Chinese wares—bowls of double-happiness emblem (limited to 1850–70 period), of plants/3 circles/character, "Four Seasons"; 15 greenware cups; 4 teapots. (Evans 1980)

1850–70. Central California sites associated with Chinese Gold Rush miners, on Stanislaus River, along Mother Lode in Stanislaus and Tuolumne Counties: "Canton," "Swatow," "Four Seasons," Dehua white (decorated over and underglaze), greenware. (Greenwood, ed. 1983b)

c. 1850–1900. Benecia, Calistoga, Napa, Sierra Nevada foothills, Puget Sound (Washington), British Columbia: assorted overseas Chinese wares (a few fine, most rough)—underglaze blue bamboo, floral and abstract, some with green glaze, "Swatow," white. (Quellmalz 1972)

c. 1850–1900. San Clemente Island sites, 50 miles west of San Diego: 9 underglaze blue— 6 "longevity," 3 miscellaneous patterns; 1 large brown-glazed stoneware jar. (Krase 1978)

1860s–1906. San Buenaventura Mission Plaza Project, Ventura: 115 underglaze-blue shards—77 "Canton," 1 shaped into scraper; 27 polychrome, 17 greenware, 10 "Swatow," and 30 underglaze (color not specified). (Greenwood 1975)

1865–69. Donner Summit: assorted overseas Chinese wares—1019 shards, bowls identical to Bear Valley above; greenware teacups;

"Four Seasons" bowls, saucedish, teacups, and unidentifiable shards; teapots. (Evans 1980)

1883–88. Harmony, in Death Valley: 7 percent of all ceramics, 42 shards—underglaze blue "Canton," underglaze blue, green, white. (Shenk and Teague 1977)

c. 1900 Riverside: assorted overseas Chinese wares—51 total vessels, same types as at Bear Valley and Donner Summit. (Evans 1980)

c. 1907. Chinatown site, Ventura: assorted overseas Chinese wares similar to last listing—125 (stoneware and porcelain) total vessels; included 4 "Red Dragon" soup spoons, "Red Bird/Cherry [prunus] Tree" bowls and other decorations. (Chace, in Greenwood, ed., 1976)

n.d. Islands off coast—Santa Catalina, San Nicholas, and San Miguel: collection of Ralph Glidden formed 1915–30. Shards from Catalina Museum, c. 1815–30: underglaze-blue strap handle, "Canton," polychrome floral along with stoneware; English, Mexican and Spanish ceramics. (Memo to Krase from Moore 1981; letter from Krase 1982)

IDAHO

1862–1900. Idaho City site: assorted overseas Chinese wares—177 total vessels similar to last twelve listings, most underglaze blue; "Three Circles and Longevity," ginger jar and food jar. (Jones et al. 1979)

1865–85. Boise Basin site, near Idaho City: assorted overseas Chinese wares—total number not given, similar to Idaho City wares. (Wylie 1980)

1878–1920. Boise Redevelopment Project, former Chinatown: 110 total vessels typical overseas Chinese wares, in underglaze blue, "Three Circles and Longevity" and "Peach and Plum" bowls. Four other Boise sites: 21 shards plain, green, polychrome, and unidentified. (Jones et al. 1980)

NEVADA

1860–1890. Virginia City: assorted overseas Chinese wares—503 vessels similar to last twelve listings for California. (Evans 1980)

NEW MEXICO

early 1600s. Bandolier's Puaray, 15 miles north of Albuquerque: 1 underglaze blue shard with scroll design. (Archives, Laboratory of Anthropology, Museum of New Mexico 1985)

c. 1610–1750. Palace of the Governors, Santa Fe: 31 shards, most underglaze blue, 2 of small cup (bowl) with gilt possibly Ming; 1 (unspecified decoration) made into scraper tool; 2 polychrome may be Japanese. (Kolner, report draft, n.d. in letter to author, Weber 1982; Snow 1974)

Selected Museums and Collections in the West

THE AMERICAS

CANADA

Halifax:
  Weldon Collection, University of King's College
Louisbourg:
  Fortress of Louisbourg
Ottawa:
  Archaeological Research Division, Parks Canada
Toronto:
  Royal Ontario Museum

MEXICO

Mexico City:
  Castillo de Chapultepec, Museo Nacional de Historia
  Museo Isidro Fabela
  Museo Franz Mayer
Tepotzotlán:
  Museo Nacional del Virreinato
Puebla:
  Museo Bello
  Museo José Luis Bello Zetina
  Museo Regional del Estado
  Museo Regional Michoacano, Morelia

PERU

Lima:
  Museo Nacional de Historia
  Instituto Cultural Peruano-Chino
  Iglesia San Pedro
  Iglesia San Francisco

UNITED STATES

Albany, N.Y.:
  Albany Institute of History and Art
  Historic Cherry Hill
Boston, Mass. Area:
  Essex Institute, Salem
  Peabody Museum (including the China Trade Museum, formerly in Milton), Salem
  Museum of Fine Arts, Boston
Charleston, S.C.:
  Charleston Museum
  Middleton Plantation
Chicago, Ill.:
  The Art Institute
Cleveland, Ohio:
  The Cleveland Museum of Art
  The Western Reserve Historical Society
Dearborn, Mich.:
  The Edison Institute, the Henry Ford Museum
Detroit, Mich.:
  Detroit Institute of Arts
Indianapolis, Ind.:
  Indianapolis Museum of Art
Kansas City, Mo.:
  Nelson-Atkins Museum of Art
Newark, N.J.:
  The Newark Museum
New Haven, Conn.:
  New Haven Colony Historical Society
Newport, R.I.:
  The Preservation Society of Newport County
New York, N.Y.:
  The Brooklyn Museum
  Cooper-Hewitt Museum
  The Metropolitan Museum of Art
  Museum of the City of New York
  New-York Historical Society
Norfolk, Va.:
  The Chrysler Museum
Philadelphia, Pa.:
  Philadelphia Museum of Art
  Historical Society of Pennsylvania
Phoenix, Ariz.:
  Phoenix Art Museum
Princeton, N.J.:
  Princeton University Art Museum
Providence, R.I.:
  Rhode Island Historical Society
Richmond, Va.:
  The Virginia Museum
San Francisco, Calif.:
  The Asian Art Museum
Washington, D.C.:
  Smithsonian Institution
  Freer Gallery of Art
  National Museum of American History
Williamsburg, Va.:
  Colonial Williamsburg Foundation
Winston-Salem, N.C.:
  Museum of Early Southern Decorative Arts
Winterthur, Del.:
  Henry Francis du Pont Winterthur Museum

EUROPE AND GREAT BRITAIN

ENGLAND

Bristol:
  City of Bristol Museum and Art Gallery
Cambridge:
  Fitzwilliam Museum
Durham:
  Gulbenkian Museum
London:
  British Museum
  Victoria and Albert Museum
Oxford:
  Ashmolean Museum

IRELAND

Dublin:
  National Museum of Ireland

DENMARK

Copenhagen:
  Nationalmuseet

FRANCE

Paris:
  Fondation Custodia, Institut Néerlandais
  Musée Guimet
  Musée des Arts Décoratifs
  Musée du Louvre
  Musée National de Céramique

GERMANY

Dresden:
  Zwingermuseum, Porzellansammlung
Hamburg:
  Museum für Kunst und Gewerbe
Munich:
  Bayerisches Nationalmuseum
West Berlin:
  Kunstgewerbemuseum

HOLLAND

Amsterdam:
  Rijksmuseum
  Amersterdams Historisch Museum
Groningen:
  Groninger Museum
Leeuwarden:
  Fries Museum
  Gemeentelijk Museum Het Princessehof
The Hague:
  Gemeentemuseum

PORTUGAL

Lisbon:
  Calouste Gulbenkian Museum
  Fundaçao Ricardo Espirito Santo
  Museu do Ultramar e Ethnografico

SPAIN

Madrid:
  Inspección General de Museos del Patimonio Nacional, Palacio de Oriente
  Museo Nacional de Artes Decorativas
  Museo de Arqueologia Nacional
Valencia:
  Museo Nacional de Cerámica

SWEDEN

Göteborg:
  Göteborgs Historiska Museet
Stockholm:
  Nationalmuseum
  Ostasiatiska Museet

Glossary

Two principal sources for the definitions that follow are Yule and Burnell, *Hobson-Jobson* (HJ), and the *Oxford English Dictionary* (OED). Others among several of importance are Barber, *The Ceramic Collector's Glossary*; Boger, *Dictionary of World Pottery and Porcelain*; Castillo, *University of Chicago Spanish-English, English-Spanish Dictionary*; Drepper, *Dictionary of American Antiques*; Medley, *The Chinese Potter*; and Volker, *Porcelain and the Dutch East India Company, 1602–1682*.

Albarello. A twelfth-century Persian jar used for medicinal drugs. The word derives from the Arabic for bamboo, a section of which the jar resembles (between two nodules are slightly concave walls, varying in degree with the piece). Though albarellos usually had lids, often they were lost and their flared lips were used for tying parchment covers. In Mexico, a jar of the same shape is called a *canilla* (a slender leg or calf).

Artichoke. An Anglo-American misnomer for a painted or incised pattern of lotus leaves, either rounded and staggered or pointed.

Atole. A Mexican drink of pap consistency made of cornmeal.

Baby or babyes. An Anglo-American word from the mid-sixteenth century for dolls, puppets, or small figurines.

"Batavia" ware. Brown overglaze ware, often with reserves of overglaze enamels, so called for the Dutch port of Batavia (now Djakarta) where many were transshipped to the West.

Beaufet. A wooden corner cupboard designed for ceramic display, often with three scalloped shelves, rounded and shell-shaped top frame, fluted pillar sides, brass eagle or ball finials, and a paned door (also, *bofet*, *beaufat*, or buffet).

Bisquit. An unglazed ceramic object, once fired, usually at 950–1100° C, but higher for vitrification to occur.

Blanc de Chine. French, smooth, creamy-white glazed ware with no underglaze or overglaze decoration, made at Dehua (Fukian Province) and Jingdezhen, especially models of the Guanyin goddess. Appliquéd cups and figurines are often in *blanc de Chine*.

Burnt (ware). Fired ware, especially when solid fuels are used, e.g., wood or coal. (*a*) Specific reference to "burnt" probably refers to gilded ware fired a second or, sometimes, third time; such gilding

408. *Babyes* (two boys), c. 1690–1720, H 12.0 cm. Underglaze blue aprons, "chow-chow," above-average export. Courtesy of the Groninger Museum, Groningen, the Netherlands.

409. *Cup* (burnt), c. 1790, D 8.6 cm. Overglaze gilt, S W PENNOCK for Sarah Wistar Pennock. Courtesy of Mr. and Mrs. Lewis Rumford II.

and firing would have been done in the Guangzhou area or after importation in Europe, England, or America; thus it had been known to have received an additional "burning": 1752 Chambers's *Cyclopedia*—"burnt in an oven apart." The definition of "unburnt ware," gilded but unfired, supports this meaning. N.B. Burnt ware in a list with gilded ware may signify the former was gilded after exportation. (*b*) For some, "burnt" may have referred to a brownish yellow or sienna color, which is often found on export ware, also requiring a second firing.

Caddy. See *Tea caddy*.

Camaïeu. A painting technique using a single color in two or three tones, especially in blue, sienna, or brown. It is distinct from *grisaille*, which is gray or grayish and may use many tones.

Canton (Guangzhou). (*a*) A city in Guangdong Province, the single port open to Westerners on the China coast from 1710 to the 1840s. (*b*) "Canton" refers to a crude type of blue-and-white, which may have the same central design as "Nanking" ware (see *Nanking*") but which has a different border and rarely is gilded. As a term, "*Canton*" apparently arose in the late-eighteenth century, particularly among Americans, possibly because it was made at kilns near Guangzhou as well as being exported there. For the English, "Canton Rose" refers to gold-red, nineteenth-century chinaware.

Carolus dollar. A coin, minted in Mexico in the period 1772–89, worth 8 reals and therefore called "pieces of eight." "Carolus" refers to Charles III, King of Spain (1759–1788). On the dollar's obverse; CAROLUS.III.DEI.GRATIA 1772; reverse: crowned, simplified arms of Spain in a shield between the two pillars of Hercules. (The ancient Greeks believed that Hercules had split the once-single rock of Gibraltar.) Each pillar bears a ribbon PLUS ULTRA; on margin, HISPAN.ET.IND.REX; mint mark for Mexico City; 8R (eight reals); and F.M., assayer's initials. These dollars became standard in the international China trade by the eighteenth century.

Carrack. A Portuguese vessel that gave its name to brittle export underglaze blue ware, when such ware was found aboard carracks captured by the Dutch in the early-seventeenth century. In Dutch, *kraakporselein*. Carrack dates from c. 1550 to c. 1650, overlapping with Transitional ware.

Cavetto. The bowl or depression in the center of a bowl or plate; hence, the cavetto border is at the outer edge of that area, often within the curve of the object.

Celadon. French, in ceramics, referring to a glaze color from deep brown to a variety of greens to yellow, but normally in the green range. In eighteenth-century France, the term denoted a pale willow-green named for Celadon, hero of D'Urfés's drama *Astrée*, whose costume was this color. Now increasingly called greenware.

Charger. A large round serving dish, originally a silver-and-pewter piece duplicated in porcelain and other ceramics.

Cheroot (a roll of tobacco). A cigar truncated at both ends, as Indian

and Manila cigars. Ashtrays of porcelain for cheroots are probably the leaf-shaped dishes with large round depressions at one end in which to place the cigar.

China. (*a*) The origin of the name is still debated. It may derive from the first emperor to unite China, Qin Shi Huangdi, in office 221–220 B.C. In the West by the first century A.D., the word *Thin*, meaning "the country," came into use, possibly derived from the dynastic name, Qin. Marco Polo called the country Chin in the late-thirteenth century, but not until the early-sixteenth century did Westerners call it China. (*b*) **Chinaware** or **china dishes** became shortened to simply *china*. As early as 851 B.C., a Middle Eastern traveler reported: "There is in China a very fine clay with which they make vases transparent like bottles; water can be seen inside of them. These vases are made of clay." (*HJ*) The Persians called such objects, *chini*. By 1350, they were known as "china-ware." (Also see *Porcelain*.) Spanish: *china, porcelana, loza*; Dutch: *porselein, kameraad, vriendlin*; French: *chine, porcelaine*. In English, different spellings indicate a range of pronunciation: chiney, cheny, cheney, chenea, chaney, cheenie.

China clay (kaolin). A white clay, a quartz derivative, difficult if not impossible to work by itself but which gives plasticity to the porcelain paste in combination with petuntse (See *China stone*). The word *Kaolin* is a corruption of *kao-ling* or "High Ridge," the mountains near Jingdezhen, which were formerly the major source of the material. Now it is obtained farther afield in Jiangxi Province.

China root. A once-famous drug of the same species as sarsaparilla, used specifically to cure gout. By the early-twentieth century, it was out of use in English-speaking countries, though still popular in China and India. In shipping lists, china root may be confused with china ware, both sometimes being denoted "china" in bulk amounts.

China stone (petuntse). A felspathic stone (silicate of alumina), ground; like china clay (kaolin), a quartz derivative. Mixed with kaolin to give porcelain its hardness and translucency. Also a component of hard, felspathic glazes. Petuntse, "white briquettes," refers to prepared china stone, ground and shaped in brick form.

Chine de commande. French, special export porcelain made to order for Western customers.

Chinese "Imari." The combination of underglaze blue, overglaze iron-red, and often gilt in ware made in China in the Japanese, or Imari, style, so called from the port of export of Japanese ceramics (see chap. 1, p.33). The Chinese were attempting to recoup a market in export ware captured by the Japanese during the mid-Transitional period, c. 1660–80. In the West, this ware continued to be popular from the late-seventeenth to the mid-eighteenth centuries.

Chiñita. Spanish, in Mexico, a shard of Chinese porcelain, used as small change.

Chow-chow. A Pidgin English term of many uses, originally referring to food (chow) and indicating a mixture of trifles. Its use as a measure of value was wide ranging and sometimes ironic, e.g., a no. 1 chow-chow item was totally worthless; but applied to food, indicated the best. A chow-chow cargo was an assorted one (miscellaneous and of varying qualities); a general shop was also a chow-chow; and a factory, or hong, where several countries traded was a chow-chow factory.

Christian ware. Porcelain decorated with Christian symbols or scenes of Christ's life in underglaze blue, overglaze fine-line black (to imitate engravings), and overglaze polychromes. Long called Jesuit-ware in reference to the Jesuits' pioneering missionary and technological roles in China, this ware also had markets among other Catholic orders in the Far East and with converts in China and Japan. In Japan, it served as a reminder of the faith after the Shogunate's persecution of Christians in the seventeenth century.

Ci. Chinese, pinyin term for either stoneware or porcelain (See *Stoneware* and *Porcelain*).

Cobalt blue. A mineral ore used in painting porcelain under the glaze. Before firing, it appears dark green, then dries to black; afterward, to various shades of blue. In the eighth century (Tang dynasty), it was probably imported into China from the Middle East as glass bricks. The Chinese altered the Persian word for it, *sulimānī*, to *sumani* and other similar terms. In the early-sixteenth century, it became known as "Mohammedan blue," perhaps to distinguish it from the native Chinese ore consistently used by then, following its appearance in the mid-fifteenth century. Chinese cobalt ore, "asbolite," contains more manganese and less cobalt than the Near Eastern mineral; the latter may also have traces of arsenic. Only laboratory tests for the amounts of manganese and arsenic in a specimen, not the tone of blue, determine the difference between the two ores.

Coffee. A term possibly derived from the Arabic *gahwah*, originally a word for wine, or perhaps from Kaffa, a district of South Ethiopia (then Abyssinia), where the coffee plant apparently first appeared. Coffee is believed to have been introduced in Aden in the mid-fifteenth century by a sheik who had discovered it on the African coast. Its use spread north to Mecca, Cairo, Damascus, Aleppo, and finally Constantinople, where the first coffeehouse appeared in 1554. In 1573, it was reported being served in china cups, but probably poured from metalwork vessels, the first coffeepots. By the early seventeenth century, coffee drinking was commonplace in Turkey and Persia, thirty years before its introduction in England.

Copper-red. An oxide of copper applied under the glaze to obtain a number of colors, not only red, in a reducing atmosphere. By the Zhengde period (1506–21), the technique had deteriorated and was abandoned until the late-seventeenth century, when it appeared rather differently. Its replacement was overglaze iron-red, which continued after copper-red's reintroduction.

Cowrie (*Cypraeidae moneta*). A small white shell whose hardness, translucency, and gloss reminded Westerners of chinaware. Because the profile of the cowrie was like a piglet (*porcelletta* in Italian), the cowrie *and* chinaware might be called porcelain. In use as currency in China from the fourteenth century B.C., it remained the monetary unit even after copper coins, some shaped like the cowrie, were introduced in the fourth century B.C. Cowrie currency was standard in South Asia, India, and Africa, in some places until the nineteenth century. Because of its similarity to the mystical egg, the seat of life, and because of its undershape, like the female genitalia, a sexual magic was attached to the shell, perhaps imputed to porcelain as well (see chap. 2, n. 12). In 1704/05, the English ship *Kent* carried both chinaware and cowries in its outward cargo from Guangzhou (Morse, vol. 1, 144).

Crackle. A cracking of the glaze resulting from a deliberate cooling of the glaze at a different rate from the body. Aesthetically pleasing, a special effect may be obtained by applying fine-ground iron oxide to the cracks, another thin layer of glaze, and firing the piece a second time. "Crazing" is the unintentional appearance of very fine cracks in

410. *Bowl*, c. 1750–70, D 10.8 cm. Overglaze enamels, crackled glaze, gift of David Lewis to Catharine Lewis in 1774, unusual export. Courtesy of Mr. and Mrs. Lewis Rumford II.

the glaze, which occurs from imperfect balance in its ingredients or from burial and aging, and is not to be confused with intentional crackle.

Cutwork or lattice-work (*linglang*). A type of openwork in a number of trellis patterns, often not completely through the vessel, and often unglazed (*bisquit*). Objects of this technique date from the Wanli period (1573–1620).

Delftware. See *Majolica*.

Doucai (*tou-ts'ai*). Chinese, a decorative technique of "dove-tailed" or "contrasted" colors: an underglazed-blue outline with areas of translucent overglaze enamels in a precise, delicate technique. The first pieces so decorated are believed to date from Chenghua (1465–87) and are small in size (compare to *Wucai*).

Earthenware. A varicolored clay ranging from coarse to fine, fired at low temperature, 800–1150° C. Because it is porous, it must be glazed at low temperature to become impermeable. At higher temperatures, the whole object melts. In pinyin, *tao*.

Encre de Chine. See *Grisaille*.

Faïence. See *Majolica*.

Famille rose. A nineteenth-century French term, introduced by the collector-author Albert Jacquemart, to describe the spectrum of pink shades on porcelain. These shades are produced by the introduction of a small amount of gold chloride with a white oxide of arsenic to the overglaze palette of metallic oxides in the red range. Today in the People's Republic of China it is called gold-red and joins copper and iron-red in this study as a substitute for the chemically less precise *famille rose*. The addition of the arsenic white oxide in varying amounts to the gold chloride gave not only various rose hues but when combined with other colors produced the "soft" or "pastel" shades. Gold-red and white oxide used in this double way, for a range of reds and to produce pastels, came from Western enameled ware, according to the Chinese themselves. Thus *famille rose* may be translated as either *yangcai*, foreign colors, or *yuancai*, pastel enamels. (*Famille verte, famille jaune,* and *famille noire,* also Jacquemart's terms, have not received as much attention as *famille rose,* probably because the Chinese had developed these colors on their own. But they too may soon be called by either their chemical common names or by color, as they are in the People's Republic of China.)

"FitzHugh." An Anglo-American design for dinner or tea services, incorporating four symbols associated with the Chinese scholar in the central decoration and often a standard "Nanking" border or a complex quadrant border of butterfly, pomegranate, fish roe, and scrolls. Decorated in underglaze blue or overglaze enamels or gilt, sometimes in several combinations. An expensive export for the wealthiest.

Fo dog. See *Lion of Fo*.

Gente de razón. A Spanish term for the *gapuchines* and the *criollos*, the two upper classes of Mexican society, first buyers of export ware in Mexico and California under Mexican rule.

Glaze. A glassy, transparent, usually thin protective covering to ceramics. A glaze may be low fired, usually with a lead flux (thus called a lead glaze), or high fired and fluxed with alkalines, e.g., potassium, sodium, and calcium (thus called an alkaline glaze); the bridge temperature, 1150–1250° C, is between the two. Colors may be mixed with the glaze, painted on the unfired vessel before glazing, or painted over the glaze and refired.

Goglet (guglet or gurglet). An Anglo-Indian word for a long-necked vessel for water, often made of porous earthenware, allowing evaporation to cool the water. *Gurglet* is an onomatopoeic term, named after the noise of water poured from the vessel.

Gold-red. A contemporary term used today in the People's Republic of China to denote the range of reds achieved by the use of gold chloride as an overglaze color. White oxide added to it in varying amounts accounts for its shades. In this study, it is a substitute for the nineteenth-century French term, *"Famille Rose,"* indicating the chemical nature of the red, as in copper and iron-red (See also *"Famille Rose"*).

411. *Jar*, c. 1730–50, H 34.3 cm. Overglaze gold-red in the leaf reserve and on scrolled turquoise ground, orange/yellow lappets on shoulders and base, carved replacement lid probably Mexican, fine export. Private collection.

412. *Teapot*, c. 1730–40, H 12.7 cm. Chinese "Imari," descended from Rebecca Wistar. Courtesy of Mr. and Mrs. Lewis Rumford II.

Grisaille. French, monochrome painting in gray with many tones; on porcelain, combined with fine black lines. In Renaissance painting, such grays were used to achieve modeling effects and often to imitate sculpture. On Chinese porcelain, *grisaille*, more loosely defined, is executed with a fine-hair brush with or without shades of gray and is used to imitate engravings. Also called *encre de Chine* or penciled decoration.

Guanyin. A Chinese diety often reproduced for export in Dehua or Jingdezhen as a decorative object. She is the Buddhist goddess of fertility, and may hold a child, thus was sometimes mistaken by early Westerners in China as the Roman Catholic Madonna. But there is no evidence that she was so Christianized for serious worship in East or West.

Hubble-bubble (Fr. Hubbel de Bubbel). A popular, onomatopoeic name for the hookah, or water pipe, sometimes made from kendis, earthenware or porcelain, and also from silver or glass. The tobacco was cut fine and mixed to a pulp with molasses and water; spices, herbs, or fruit might also have been added. This mixture was placed with charcoal balls and lit. Smoke passed into a lower chamber filled with water (discolored by it) up to a small spout from which a tube (reed or cane) allowed one to inhale. A cool, "wholsom" (1616) smoke was believed the result (*HJ*). Hookah smoking was popular in Calcutta among the English after dinner, including the women; but by the late-nineteenth century, few used it.

India-China. A name for export porcelain during the colonial period and after in North America, so called from its transport from the East Indies. The term is applied to different colored wares, as in "Green India-China," etc. By the early-nineteenth century, it had fallen into disuse, but even today, some remember the term being used, especially in the southern United States.

Iron-red. An oxide of iron painted over the glaze, producing an orange-red after firing, in contrast to the highly volatile copper-red, applied under the glaze and fired at a higher temperature (also compare *Gold-red*). Iron-red is the red used in the Chinese "Imari" combination of colors (See *Chinese "Imari"*).

Jesuit ware. See *Christian ware*.

Joss. An idol. A corruption of the Portuguese *Deos* (god). The term developed in Chinese ports in Pidgin English, then was used in the West as if it were a Chinese word. In Chinese homes, a joss image, e.g., a figure of Guanyin, was customarily on the family altar.

Kaolin. See *China clay*.

Kendi (gorgelet). A Southeast Asian water bottle with a mammalian spout; the latter became smaller during the eighteenth century. It was also convertible to a "hubble-bubble" (See *Hubble-bubble*).

Kentledge. Pig iron used as permanent ballast. Chinaware was not used as ballast per se, but rather to floor off a ship and provide protection for sea-damageable cargoes like tea and spices.

Kinran-de. A Japanese term (meaning gold-brocade style) for fine export—which may have been brought to countries other than Japan—with gold and enamel decoration, dating from the sixteenth century. The style may derive from Turkish textiles or from oriental lacquerware.

Lang lizen. A Dutch term for the elongated female figures on late-Ming, early-Qing export wares. In English, "Long Elizas."

Lebrillo. In Spain and Mexico, a large earthenware washbasin or tub. In Puebla, Mexico, lebrillos were made in imitation of Chinese blue-and-white wares beginning in the seventeenth century.

Lion of Fo. Guardian lion for the Buddha (Fo), often used as a decorative finial on export porcelain. In Chinese art, usually found in pairs. In the West, formerly called a "Fo dog."

Lowestoft. A misnomer used until the 1960s. It correctly refers to wares made in England in the Chinese or English style at Lowestoft, an English pottery town, beginning in the eighteenth century. Some blank Chinese export wares were also painted here, as they were in other places, but the term should not be applied as a general term to export from China.

Majolica. A fine-quality earthenware with a white, tin glaze, often decorated with metallic oxides in polychrome. Its name derives from the island of Majorca, called Majolica in the Middle Ages, where the style is believed to have originated. Tin-glazed earthenware is called majolica in the Hispanic world and Italy, faïence in France, and Delft in Holland, each place producing an easily distinguished style.

Mancerina. In Spain and Mexico, a cup-holder with attached saucer. The saucer is often shell-shaped. The Marqués de Mancera, the twenty-third viceroy of New Spain from 1664 to 1673, suffered from palsy and apparently gave his name to this form. It was copied in Chinese export porcelain.

Mandarin ware. Export porcelain with Chinese figures of the mandarin class dating from the sixteenth century on, but first appearing in quantity on export ware in the mid-eighteenth century. It continued to be popular into the nineteenth century, when Rose Mandarin ware was in vogue until about 1850.

Martaban. A port in Burma whose name has been generally given to a type of stoneware jar, varying in height, used for shipping edibles. Many are made throughout Southeast Asia, including China, and specific names of other locales are more accurate. The Dutch probably popularized the term.

Mazarine. A deep dish or plate, or a small dish put in the middle of a large one for ragout or fricassees; also a small tart filled with sweetmeats.

Mazarine blue. A shade of deep rich blue on late-seventeenth- and early-eighteenth-century export porcelain, often with gilt (inevitably most wore off). Possibly the name derives from Cardinal Mazariń, prime minister of France (1601–62), or less likely, the Duchesse de Mazariń (d. Chelsea, 1699).

Meissen ware. The first porcelain made in quantity in Europe at Meissen, northwest of Dresden (the first was a short-lived venture of the Medicis in Florence in 1575). Discovered in 1708, Meissen (softpaste, then hard-paste) porcelain was developed in a royal porcelain factory (1710–1868) by J. F. Böttger under the patronage of Elector Frederick Augustus I (Augustus II of Poland). Augustus's ceramic collection, including many pieces of Chinese export ware, may still be seen in Dresden. Also known as Dresden ware, Meissen is most famous for its figurines.

Mission ware. A common, brown-glazed, heavy earthenware shaped into cooking and utilitarian forms, largely by Indian potters instructed at the Spanish missions in California in the late-eighteenth and early-nineteenth centuries.

Nankeen. A fawn-colored fabric of natural cotton woven in China and India and popular for men's breeches.

"Nanking" (*Nanjing*). The capital of Jiangsu Province on the China coast. Eighteenth-century foreigners gave the city's name to a fine underglaze blue-and-white porcelain: the port was a way station between its production at Jingdezhen to its sale at Guangzhou (Canton), 2,127 km (1,322 mi.) south. "Nanking" ware was of better quality than its cousin, "Canton" blue-and-white, often gilded when the latter was not. By the third quarter of the eighteenth century, the term was established, well before "Canton" appeared in the records.

Nappy. (Old and Middle English—nap or bowl). A shallow open serving dish, sometimes shaped with a flat lip as handle.

Nianhao. Chinese, the imperial reign mark on porcelain, usually in underglaze blue until the eighteenth and nineteenth centuries, when it began to be applied in overglaze red or, less often, in gold.

Pattypan. A pan in which patty shells were baked. Also, the shell itself.

Penciled ware. See *Grisaille*.

Petuntse. See *China stone*.

Picul. In China and the East, a measure of weight equal to 100 catties, or about 133 1/3 lbs.

Porcelain. A term applied to chinaware by the West, derived from the Italian *porcelletta* (little pig) for the shape of the cowrie shell whose surface is similar to china. It is composed of two related ingredients, both forms of decomposed granite, china clay (kaolin) and china stone (petuntse). Kaolin, though itself not plastic, causes the petuntse to be more easily worked. Porcelain ranges from pure white to pale gray in color and is fired higher than earthenware, 1280° C and above, fusing and becoming glasslike, sonorous, and translucent. For aesthetic reasons, it is often covered with a felspathic glaze, fired in the first firing at high temperature (above 1200° C) for underglaze colors, and lesser temperatures for overglaze enamels (c. 800–900° C) and gilding (c. 600–700° C). Two or three firings may be necessary for a complete decoration (See *Burnt*).

Chinese porcelain is both hard and soft paste. European porcelain was, at first, soft paste (beg. 1575, Florence, Medici), a mix of clay and ground glass, requiring a lower, "softer" firing temperature (c. 1200° C). Hard paste (beg. c. 1708, Meissen, Saxony) eventually became more popular. It was produced in quantity at St. Cloud and Chelsea in the eighteenth century. Soft-paste porcelain may be cut with a file; hard paste cannot. The former also becomes permanently dirty; hard paste may be washed clean. Bone china (beg. 1800, Spode, England) is made by adding calcined bones to hard-paste clay. It does not chip as readily as hard-paste porcelain. See also *Soft-paste porcelain*.

Pozuelo. Spanish, a large Chinese storage jar of earthenware or stoneware, listed in the first records of the Spanish presidios in California, thus common in Mexico then and earlier. Meant to be sunk in the ground, pozuelos were often denoted as oil jars. No doubt they resembled the Martaban jars so common in the Southeast Asia trade (See fig. 43).

Punch. Origin obscure, but possibly from an Indian or English source. A beverage composed of a base of hot milk, tea, or water, flavored with sugar, spices, and citrus (usually lemon), and a liquor. This last

413. *Platter*, c. 1790–1810, L 54.5 cm. Underglaze blue "Nanking" pattern, unusually large and finely painted. Courtesy of the Peabody Museum.

414. *Bowl*, c. 1750, D 31.2 cm. Overglaze enamels in iron-red, gold-red, and gilt, from the Kip family of New York, gift of Robert Swartwout Talmage, fine export. Courtesy of the Museum of the City of New York.

often gave its name to the punch, e.g., arrack, brandy, claret, gin, rum, whiskey, wine.

Qilin (ch'i-lin). Chinese, a mythical beast, sometimes called the Chinese unicorn, with features of both the lion and horse with many variations. A popular motif on late-Ming export ware.

Qingbai (or *yingching*). Chinese, the thin bluish or greenish glaze on white porcelain attributable to a small iron content in the glaze.

"Quilted" ware. An eighteenth-century English term to describe the intricate, molded ground of some types of export ware, resembling stuffed quiltwork.

Rice-grain ware. Porcelain punched with patterns whose unit is a rice-grain shape. The perforations are filled with glaze, and thus are more transparent than the rest of the piece. Popular for export from the second quarter of the nineteenth century, the style had been known centuries earlier in Near Eastern ceramics.

415. *Bowls in stands*, c. 1875, left: H 8.9 cm, fluted, overglaze enamels; right: H 10.2 cm, rice-grain, underglaze blue, both average ware. Courtesy of Mr. and Mrs. Lewis Rumford II.

Rolwagon. A Dutch term denoting a cylindrical vase, usually with a flat lip. In the late-seventeenth century, the Dutch began to use rolwagons with vases in sets of three, five, or seven pieces to decorate cabinets and mantels.

Rouge-de-fer. See *Iron-red*.

Ruyi (*Ju-i*, in Chinese, "as you wish"). A scepter in the stylized form of a lotus flower and stalk, given as a token of esteem and good wishes; also a decorative motif often appearing on borders of export ware derived from the head of the *ruyi* scepter (See fig. 391).

Sago. A powdery starch obtained from the trunk of the sago palm, used in Asia as a food thickener, textile stiffener, and packing material, as was pepper, for porcelain.

Sneaker. A large cup, or small basin, with a saucer and cover. In America, a "sneak-cup" was one who wanted less punch than the average, a "despicable creature" who shrank from "his convivial duties." Alice Morse Earle, *China Collecting in America* (New York: Charles Scribner's Sons, 1892), 237–38.

"Soft-Paste" porcelain. Something of a misnomer derived more from the appearance of the glaze rather than the exact nature of the body. Produced in the Yongzheng era (1723–35), this ware has a softer-looking glaze. Though steatite, or soapstone, which is slippery, may replace the kaolin, "soft-paste" ware is generally very hard. It is more porous, however, than hard-paste porcelain, and thus stains easily. Usually small objects with a thin glaze tending to craze are "soft-paste" porcelain (See *Porcelain*).

Stoneware. A multicolored clay of varying quality but harder than earthenware, fired at 1200–1300° C, at which temperature it sinters and fuses. It is already impermeable and requires no glaze, but one is often applied for aesthetic reasons.

"Swatow" ware. Export ware made near and named for the port of Shantou (Swatow), Guangdong Province, often in underglaze blue but also with overglaze enamels in distinctive designs.

Tablewares. The principal objects made for export. In England in the

seventeenth century, the following definitions of wares, probably derived from metal forms, were applied to ceramics (in the same way that metalwork services were prototypes for the form and size of ceramic ones). The sizes, given where possible, refer to pewter plates and dishes of the mid-eighteenth century or to surviving examples. (From Randle Holme, *The Academy of Armory* (1688) and *The Compleat Appraiser* (1770), as quoted in Beaudry et al., "Vessel Typology," 1983, see Bibliography.)

Dish: a generic and specific term (10 3/4″ to 28″).

Platter: usually large, though sometimes small, oval.

Plate: (7 3/4″ to 9 3/4″).

Flesh and broth dishes: (H. 1″ to 2″).

Middling and sallet [salad] dishes: smaller than plates, but probably larger than saucers.

Saucer: a small plate.

Basin: "almost half round in the concave," used for dining or washing.

Tael. The historic Chinese name for 1 oz. of silver; also a weight, 1 1/3 oz. avdp. Until the late-nineteenth century, worth about $1.50.

Tallow. Animal fat used for candles or as a protective smear on ships' bottoms, masts, and elsewhere; an item in the west-coast China trade of the early-nineteenth century.

Tea. From the Chinese *Te* (*cha*), pronounced first "tay," then "tee" in English; though pronunciation of the two overlap, the change occurred between 1720 and 1750. Probably very early, tea was known in China, though the first mention of it is in the fourth century A.D. Types imported to the West: black (Bohea, a fashionable tea from the early eighteenth century on; Campoy, Congou, Oolong, Pekoe, Pouchong, and Souchong) and green (Hyson, Young Hyson—picked when the leaves were half opened before the spring rains—and Twankay).

Tea caddy. A box used for the daily use of tea, probably derived from the term *catty*, a weight equivalent to 1 1/3 lbs., the amount roughly contained in such a box.

416. *Tea caddy and tray*, c. 1700, tray: 13.3 cm sq., caddy: H 10.6 cm. Overglaze enamels with arms of Higginson, owned by Nathaniel Higginson, governor of Madras. Courtesy of the Essex Institute, Salem.

Tibor. Spanish, "a large Chinese jar."

Transitional ware. Porcelain, both imperial and export, made during the period of transition between the Ming and Qing dynasties, c. 1620–80, a period when the kilns at Jingdezhen were under less imperial control and new designs of a freer nature developed in the hands of the private potter. From 1657 to the early 1680s, little fine ware was exported.

Tulip. A flower popular in Turkish decorative arts, presumably borrowed by the Dutch in the seventeenth century to become an important motif on Transitional blue-and-white. Via Vienna, the tulip was introduced to Holland between 1573 and 1587, becoming a craze by 1630. The Dutch also traded porcelains in Turkish ports in the early-seventeenth century and may have seen faiences decorated with tulips in the style of earlier examples on Turkish faïence (See fig. 87).

Twifler. Colloquial for "trifler"; a dish used to make and serve trifle, a light pudding. A trifle was also the name of a pie dish.

Underglaze. Painting applied to the unfired, unglazed body of an object, e.g., cobalt blue or copper red. After firing, it is better preserved than overglaze enamels.

Wucai. Chinese, five-colored ware (underglaze blue, overglaze red, green, yellow, and black, sometimes with turquoise). Outlined in overglaze black, dark brown, or red, and usually appearing on large forms, it is distinct from contemporary *ducai* decoration, which is more delicate and most often on small objects, especially in the sixteenth century.

417. *Jar*, c. 1583–1620, H 34 cm. *Wucai* decoration in the "Hundred Bats" design; gift of Mr. Harry T. Peters, Jr.; above-average domestic/export. Courtesy of the Peabody Museum.

Concordance

CHAPTER 1

1. *Cowrie shells*, two egg-shaped, one simple. L 8.4 cm, 7.9 cm, and 2.54 cm (3⁵⁄₁₆ in, 3¹⁄₈ in, and 1 in). Since they resemble the profile of a piglet, medieval Italians called them *porcelletta* or *porcellana*. Author's collection.

2. *Saucer*, Xuande mark, 1426–35, probably Yongzheng period, 1723–35. D 14.76 cm (5¹³⁄₁₆ in). *Doucai*: peach tree with trunk shaped in character *shou*, signifying longevity, with fungus to left and right. Imperial quality. Author's collection.

3. Reverse of Fig. 2, showing Xuande *nianhao*.

4. *Jar*, Wanli, 1573–1620. H 34 cm (13³⁄₈ in). Underglaze blue in four horizontal bands. Top to bottom: narrow scrollwork, four white floral reserves on blue latticework with *ruyi*-headed dividers, moonlit scene with peacock and peony dominant, stylized lotus leaf, white-on-blue base border. Fine domestic/export. Private collection, Mexico City.

5. An artisan throws a pot, 1982, Jian Guo Porcelain Factory, Jingdezhen. At this factory, preindustrial techniques are simulated at each stage of the production of porcelain.

6. A painter applies a circular line on a vase neck with the help of a wheel, 1982, Jian Guo Factory, Jingdezhen.

7. A master painter retraces cobalt blue on a previously sketched design, 1982, Jian Guo Porcelain Factory, Jingdezhen.

8. *Ewer*, Wanli, late sixteenth century. H 19.5 cm (7³⁄₈ in). From petal-point rim, neck tapers to six-lobed body with S-shaped, branch-painted spout ending in leaf sprays attached to body. Dark underglaze blue birds on prunus blossoms under crescent moon on each side of neck and by leaf and key-fret borders. Below latter, panels of chrysanthemums. Average export. Courtesy of the Ashmolean Museum (1978.1935).

9. *Kendi*, Wanli, c. 1600–20. H 19.4 cm (7⁵⁄₈ in). Underglaze blue in dotted and floral panels on mammalian spout and body. Tapering neck with stylized plantain leaves sharply narrowed at rim. Common Southeast Asian form; average domestic/export. Private collection, Mexico City.

10. *Bottle*. Transitional Period, probably Chongzhen, 1628–44. H 39.2 cm (15³⁄₈ in). Underglaze blue mark on base: flowerhead (lotus?). On the knobbed neck, the first signs of special order underglaze blue and white: a stylized tulip, adopted from Turkey by the Dutch, with open-scrolled leaves; the latter motif repeated on shoulder border with central floret. On the body, an entire narrative: one side, a warrior with supporters and chariot; the other, a pastoral scene of herdsman with cattle. Bought by Robert G. Haliburton, a Canadian, in St. Thomas in the 1870s, descendant of Loyalists transplanted from New England to Nova Scotia in 1761. Fine export. Courtesy of the Weldon Collection, University of King's College, Halifax (W.113).

11. *Plate*, Kangxi, 1662–1722. D 20.3 cm (8 in). Underglaze blue, twelve panels of formalized flowers, the "China aster," outlined by a foliate blue line paralleling the rim. In the center, four flowers define a whorled cross; fifth flower in middle. Juxtaposed whorls, common on middle to late sixteenth-century Islamic ceramics; a pointed palmette leaf appeared on the same ceramics three centuries earlier. Standard design in a wide quality range. Average domestic/export. Private collection, Mexico City.

12. *Jar*, Kangxi, 1662–1722. H 45 cm (17³⁄₄ in). Underglaze blue alternately blue on white or white on blue: dominant peony scroll on white body and lid; blue lid edge in half-prunus blossom; white neck; blue *ruyi* shoulder border; finally, blue lotus-leaf base. Fo-lion finial. Masque ears (for rattan rope), additional blue accents, the only utilitarian vestige to a decorative piece. Fine domestic/export. Private collection, Mexico City.

13. *Cup and saucer*, late Kangxi or Yongzheng, c. 1715–30. Cup: (holds ¾ cup), H 7.9 cm, D 7.6 cm (3⅛ in, 3 in). Saucer: D 14.6 cm, H 2.54 cm (5¾ in., 1 in). Tall, handleless cup with deep, smooth-surfaced saucer, in underglaze blue, iron-red, and gilt; brown edge. Feathery, willowlike leaves identical to formalized sprays on thirteenth-century Iranian ceramics. Average Chinese "Imari" ware. Courtesy of the Peabody Museum (1977.97.15a/b).

14. *Saucer*, Yongzheng, c. 1725. D 11.9 cm, H 2.8 cm (4¹¹/₁₆ in, 1 in). Underglaze blue interior, brown exterior, formerly called "Batavia" ware. Common, underglaze blue line drawing and wash. Interior border, early version of tighter motif, possibly derived from the corners of Dutch tiles (see fig. 232). Stock export, now rare. Bequest of Mrs. L. P. Dean. Courtesy of the Society for the Preservation of New England Antiquities (1920.161).

15. *Dish* (with cover), Kangxi, c. 1700. H 24.1 cm, D 27.3 cm (9½ in, 10¾ in). *Doucai*: double-domed dish, interior divided in three sections: in half, one side halved again. Exterior divided into three scenes in dominant overglaze green with red, yellow, brown, and black. 1. A European ship and Chinese junk. 2. Westerners on foot explore or fight (with gun and sword), ignoring a mounted Chinaman stalking a deer. 3. More Westerners with dog walk near a walled church with bell tower. Perhaps unique; fine export. Courtesy of the Victoria and Albert Museum (1920.161).

16. *Vase* (part of a garniture set), late Kangxi c. 1710–22. H 38.1 cm (15 in). Overglaze enamels in iron-red, black, and gilt overglaze enamels. Deep neck, shoulder, and base wave borders; a four-clawed dragon chases a blazing pearl and his tail. Well-modeled Fo-lion finial. Fine domestic/export. Private collection, Mexico City.

17. *Jar*, Yongzheng, 1723–35. H 84 cm (33 in). Overglaze enamels of Chinese "Imari" palette with gold-red and overglaze blue. Westerner with Oriental wife and child, possible the Dutch Governor of Indonesia, Dierderik Durvan, in office 1676–1740, or one of many merchants with such a family. Eroded, blue karst (limestone) finial similar to Japanese finials of the Genroku Era (1688–1703). Fine, special-order export, possibly unique. Museo Nacional del Virreinato, Mexico.

18. *Jar*, Yongzheng/Qianlong, c. 1735–40. H 50.8 cm (20 in). Overglaze enamels: black ground; tightly scrolled, leafed greenery with trios of chrysanthemums in blue, white, and rose; superimposed, panel with bird amid lotus with touch of turquoise. Fine domestic/export. Private collection, Mexico City.

19. Detail of fig. 18, well-modeled and painted Fo-lion finial, pawing gold brocade ball.

20. *Tureen*, Qianlong, c. 1750–75. H 22.2 cm, L 26.6 cm (8¾ in, 10½ in). Round tureen with minor fluting and crown-shaped finial based on metal form; part of a service possibly ordered by Don Ignacio Leonel Gómez de Cervantes (1762–1813). The Cervantes arms: on blue field, two gold deer, a banner gules, EX ANTIQUS, eight green spears (compare figs. 54 and 62). Boar's head handles, single Chinese feature. Fine export. Private collection, Mexico City.

21. *Teapot and mug*, Qianlong, c. 1740–50. Pot: H 13.5 cm, OW 19.5 cm (5⁵/₁₆ in, 7⅝ in); mug: 12.3 cm, OW 9 cm (4¾ in, 3½ in). Coat of arms of Fauntleroy (1633): gules three infants' heads crined or. Crest: fleur de lis or between two wings expanded azure. Possibly ordered by William Fauntleroy (1684–1757), grandson of Moore Fauntleroy (1616–1665), the first Fauntleroy to immigrate to Vir-

ginia about 1643. By family tradition, most of this set broke when dropped on the dock during its unloading from England. Fine English export. Courtesy of Mrs. Bertram C. Harrison and Miss Janet Fauntleroy Taylor.

22. *Soup bowl*, Jiaqing, c. 1810–20. D 20.5 cm, H 4.7 cm (10 in, 1⅞ in). In overglaze pastel enamels, a cicada and dragonflies among tiger lilies. Cicada, symbol of life renewed after death, appropriate for the unidentified owner, whose Spanish arms, initials, and insignia of an archbishop (a green hat with 1, 2, 3, and 4 knots to his tassles) break a border of peach, pomegranate, and peonies amid exotic birds. Fine Spanish export. Courtesy of the Peabody Museum (1977.53).

23. Detail of fig. 22.

24. *Soup bowl*, Jiaqing, c. 1800. D 24.7 cm, H 3.81 cm (9¾ in, 1½ in). Sepia vignette with "Monticello" and "Thomas Jefferson" in contemporary script probably from a periodical print, often oval or round. Outer four borders in red, beige, black, and gold with black and gilt leaf repeat; cavetto border, a dotted sawtooth in black on beige with thin red and gilt inner line. Fine American export. Courtesy of Dr. Wesley Gallup.

25. Detail of fig. 24.

26. *Figurine*, seated woman, Qianlong, c. 1750–75. H 22.4 cm (8¾ in). Overglaze enamels: well-modeled woman in gray-black brocade on low-backed red chair with a *pipa*, an ancient lutelike instrument in yellow. Tiny bound feet, a sign of her high rank. Fine domestic/export. Courtesy of the Trustees of the British Museum. (1935 12-20 1).

27. *Twin boy figurines*, the Merry Spirits of Union and Harmony (*he he er xian*), associated with the god of longevity, *Shou Lao*, Kangxi, c. 1700–20. H 27.6 cm (10⅞ in). Overglaze enamels in red, green, black, and yellow, carrying lotus in pots or a broom, popular images in the West. Associated with Chinese merchants, especially potters, ironically most of them not of first quality. Domestic/export. Courtesy of the Franz Mayer Collection, Mexico City.

28. *Plate*, Qianlong, c. 1740–60. D 23.1 cm, H 1.9 cm (9⅛ in, ¾ in). *Doucai*, a typical landscape. Thick white and gold-red enameling in relief to other colors. Displayed on wall or mantel like a painting. Above-average export, now rare. Courtesy of Norman Herreshoff.

29. *Dish*, Jiaqing, c. 1820. D 27.5 cm (10¾ in). Overglaze gold-red and gilt FitzHugh design. Unidentified central vignette in sepia and gilt of horse and shay before neoclassical building. Undulating cavetto border in gilt. Superior export. Courtesy of the Peabody Museum (1981.54).

30. *Saucers*, Qianlong, c. 1790. Both, D 13.0 cm (5⅛ in). Overglaze enamels: left, three Europeans in a Chinese shop with porcelains on a street just behind the foreign factories, visible in saucer on right. On foreground islands, "go-downs," or factory warehouses. Perspective rendered by acquired eye rather than formal training. Fine export. Courtesy of Dr. Wesley Gallup.

31. *Saucer*, mark and reign of Qianlong, c. 1736–50. D 17.4 cm (6¹³/₁₆ in). "Eggshell" thin with everted lip; ruby-red on reverse, sides only. A European couple with child in partial Chinese dress seated Oriental-style amid porcelain jars. Between the couple, a dish of finger-citron and peaches and a vase of peonies. Before them, two

bottles and a European goblet and jug. Shadowing technique to achieve modeling in the Western mode, probably by a Chinese painter instructed in Western techniques. One of four similar plates with variations. Imperial ware. Courtesy of the Baur Collection, Geneva (A 608).

32. *Sugarbowl*, Qianlong, c. 1790. H 13.9 cm (5½ in). Overglaze enamels on typical Western form, a composite armorial from top: left to right, elements of the English, Prussian, and (below) Dutch royal arms (English arms used in the reign of William of Orange, 1533–1587), a unique expression of unity among major powers trading with China, possibly to commemorate the Triple Alliance of 1788. No obvious Chinese elements. Fine export. Private collection, U.S.A.

33–37. *Gouaches* from a series of twenty-four untitled drawings on porcelain production by a Guangzhou artist, c. 1825. On Chinese paper, each c. 38.5 × 53 cm. Descriptive titles: 1. Potters at work. 2. Potters and molds. 3. Painters and inspector (close-up). 4. Glaziers with ware drying. 5. Chinese and European traders in a factory at Guangzhou. The brown morocco album in which these watercolors are bound bears the bookplate of Charles John, 5th Baron Dimsdale (1801–72), Meesdon Manor, and the library shelf mark 10A. It descended in the family to the present owner. Courtesy of the Peabody Museum, Salem (1983.8).

38. *Goglet*, Daoguang, c. 1845. H 31.1 cm (12¼ in). Overglazed enamels on Chinese form with elaborate elephant-head handles; overglaze emblem of Sino-American cooperation after the Opium Wars: U.S. eagle grasps both Chinese and American flags. Unique American export. Courtesy of the Henry Francis du Pont Winterthur Museum (66.641).

39. *Bottle*, Japanese Arita, late seventeenth century. H 12.0 cm, W 8.8 cm, D 6.3 cm (4¾ in, 3½ in, 2½ in). Figure in underglaze blue with large hat and walking stick; on opposite side, birds on branches and overglaze enameled flowers. Mark on bottom: overglaze red chrysanthemum. Silver top, probably Mexican. Above-average export. Private collection, Mexico City.

40. "*Korean Fo Dogs*" (pair), male and female, Japanese Imari, Kanbun Era (1661–72). H 19.36 cm (7⅝ in). Derived from the Chinese Fo lion, Japanese counterparts are frequently large, highly colorful (to symbolize their power), and sometimes gilded; often they are part of temple decoration. Above-average. Private collection, Mexico City.

41. *Sugarbowl*, Japanese Imari, c. 1690. H 9.5 cm, OW 15.9 cm, (3¾ in, 6¼ in). Deep-necked, bellied form with molded animal-mask handles. Underglaze blue and overglaze red and green enamels in large and small chrysanthemum patterns with fine-line gilt trim. On neck, alternating *ruyi* and half-prunus blossom. Average export. Private collection, Mexico City.

CHAPTER 2

42. *Box*, c. 1803 (1802 painted on the lid). D 6.1 cm, H 3.2 cm (2⅜in , 1¼ in). A 1785 version of its model, a Carolus dollar (8-real piece), Mexico City. This Carolus dollar was minted in the period 1772–89 in the reign of Charles III, King of Spain (1759–1788). The decoration was taken from a coin minted in the reign of Charles IV,

but reads CAROLUS III, garbled by the Chinese painter, from the original Carolus dollar, 1772. Above-average export. Courtesy of Dr. Wesley Gallup.

43. *Jar* (stoneware), Qianlong/Jiaqing, c. 1773–1810. H 41.2 cm, D 29.7 cm (16³⁄₁₆ in, 11⁷⁄₁₆ in). Medium brown glaze over six panels, set in after molding: two scrolls, two chrysanthemums, a bust of Charles III, a right hand; four small ears for rattan rope. A type often called "Martaban" (a Burma port where many such pots were exported), found in a Philippine mountain province in the early twentieth century. Average utilitarian export, now rare. Courtesy of the Field Museum of Natural History, Chicago (H 524, No. 252394).

44. Detail of a panel on jar in fig. 43, a bust of Charles III, taken from a Carolus dollar (see fig. 42) in circulation well after its first minting in 1772.

45. Detail of a panel on jar in fig. 43, Arabic "Fatimah's Hand," so-called in Europe, with European ruff. Open right hand with five (a magic number) outstretched fingers thought to be protection from the "evil eye," a common Arab superstition adopted among some Christians and Moslems.

46. *Vase* (one of a pair), Yongzheng/Qianlong, c. 1730–50. H. 132.5 cm (4 ft 3 in). Size "no. 1" for the Spanish, and larger than jars of any market, including the Chinese. Flat-domed lid with Fo lions, attenuated body. The polychrome phoenix in a garden is the epitome of quality painting and a model for lesser jars. In Europe, vases of this size were often called "soldier vases" from the exchange of a collection of them for a regiment of soldiers by Augustus II, Elector of Saxony and King of Poland (1670–1733); his collection of export ware (10,000 Chinese and 9,000 Japanese objects) was the largest in Europe. In nineteenth-century Mexico, the lion finials were often removed by revolutionaries mistaking Chinese for Spanish royal lions. First-class export. Courtesy of Mr. Arthur A. Houghton, Jr.

47. Detail of phoenix in fig. 46.

48. Oil on canvas, Spanish, *La Plaza Mayor de México* (1695) by Cristobal de Villalpando. 2.12 m × 2.66 m (6 ft 11 in × 8 ft 8 in). View south with Mt. Popocateptl in distance; cathedral on left, government buildings on far side, and shops to right, near canal and causeways. Walled "Parian," a small city, in lower right with elaborate portico (one of eight doorways), canopied stalls, a small plaza with fountain, and galleries north and south. Other rows of stalls beyond. Courtesy of Colonel Paul Methuen, Bath, England.

49. *Jar*, Wanli, c. 1575–1600. H 38.1 cm. (15 in). Hexagonal, underglaze blue in panels: emblems of Spanish monarchy under Philip II (1556–98), crowned bicephal eagles, one on shoulder, another on body (earliest known date for such an eagle, c. 1559 in choir stall, Brujas Cathedral, Spain). Chinese designs on others: phoenixes, elephants, saddled horses, lions, birds. Base border: white on blue stylized lotus. Possibly unique export. Private collection, Mexico City.

50. Reverse of fig. 49.

51. *Jar* (one of a pair), Qianlong, c. 1750–75. H 106 cm (3 ft, 5 in). Size "no. 1" in Spanish terms, high-domed lid; Fo-lion finial (restored). Overglaze polychrome: gadrooned classical urn with peonies, carnations, lilies, and tulip from an unidentified print, possibly French or Dutch. Deep shoulder lappet: blue ground with

checkered and scrolled design with red, yellow, and gilt border; base cartouche in same colors, female mask on shell. First-class special-order export. Private collection, Mexico City.

52. Detail of fig. 51, arms of Fernando de Valdés y Tamón in cartouche with mask.

53. *Vase* (earthenware), c. 1625–50, Puebla, Mexico. H. 16.6 cm (10½ in). Underglaze blue with familiar Chinese-style borders and central deer amid tree peonies. Ex. coll. Francisco Pérez de Salazar. Private collection, Mexico City.

54. *Jar*, Qianlong, c. 1760–80. H 66.0 cm, OW 43.2 cm (2 ft 2 in, 1 ft 5 in). Size "no. 2." Polychrome scroll, festoon and floral design of European origin with bicephal eagle beneath crown, armorial device of the Conde de Santiago de Calimaya (Don Ignacio Leonel Gómez de Cervantes), Mexico (compare figs. 20 and 62). Floral and paneled borders at neck and base. First-class special-order export, unique. Private collection, Mexico City.

55. Detail of arms on fig. 54.

56. *Bottle*, Kangxi/Yongzheng, c. 1715–40. H 22.5 cm, W 7.9 cm square (8⅞ in, 3⅛ in). Unthreaded neck (black top, twentieth century), rounded corners. Underglaze blue, overglaze red, green, and gilt. Often called Geneva (gin) or Dutch bottle. Private collection, Mexico City.

57. *Kendi*, Kangxi, c. 1680–1700. H 12.1 cm, 16.5 cm (4¾ in, 6½ in). Neck lost at base, smoothed and painted, probably in Mexico. "Swatow"-type, overglaze red, green, turquoise, yellow, white; iron-red overpainting on shoulder and around reserved phoenix. Above-average export, rare. Private collection, Mexico City.

58. *Albarello*, Yongzheng, c. 1725–35. H 22.2 cm (8¾ in). Bamboo-section shape. Overglaze polychrome scrollwork borders on neck and base; half-circles at neck; heart-shaped reserve, blank for a label, pierced by two arrows (compare fig. 49), suspended: possibly a buckle. Hat with three tassles, sign of lesser prelate of an urban church or cathedral. Floral and leaf surrounding design. Above-average export. Courtesy of the Victoria and Albert Museum (FE.3-1976).

59. *Mancerina*, Qianlong, c. 1750. D 23 cm, H (cup) c. 5 cm (9 in, c. 2 in). Shell-shaped saucer, attached saw-tooth, perforated cup holder. Overglaze polychrome and gilt panels, floral and fruit motifs. The form is sometimes found with the cup removed. Fine export. Courtesy of the Museo Nacional del Virreinato (54470).

60. *Mancerina* (majolica), c. 1730–49, Alcora, Spain. D 17.8 cm (7 in), H (cup) 6.6 cm (2⅝ in). Shell-shaped saucer, attached smooth-edged, perforated cup. Underglaze blue, yellow, and red: six classical busts, crowned yellow eagle on red at shell base. In orange, signed Ferrer (Vicente Ferrer, working dates: 1727–43 or 49). Courtesy of the Victoria and Albert Museum (c. 80-1951).

61. *Basin*, Qianlong, c. 1740–60. D 63.5 cm, H 17.8 cm (2 ft 1 in; 7 in). Mask-head handles. Overglaze iron-red and gilt scroll and floral border. Stylized lotus-leaf lower border. Fine export, rare. Private collection, Mexico City.

62. *Tureen*, Qianlong, c. 1760–80. H 41.3 cm, OL 31.7 cm (16¼ in, 12½ in). Realistic molded goose probably based on a Strasbourg faience model. Overglaze polychrome and gilt fantasy painting, originally with stand. Arms of Don Ignacio Leonel Gómez de Cervantes on center back (compare figs. 20 and 54). First-class export, coloring unique. Private collection, Mexico City.

63. Detail of head in fig. 62.

64. Detail of feathers in fig. 62.

65. *Tureen*, Qianlong, c. 1775–1800. L 48.3 cm, H (at tail) 25.4 cm (19 in, 10 in). Realistic molding in carp form with arms of Gálvez in medallion near mouth. Original ceramic lid replaced by one of Mexican silver with incised scales. Fine export. Private collection, Mexico City.

66. Detail of arms of Don Matias de Gálvez y Gallardo, Viceroy of New Spain, 1783–84, on a plate (identical to the arms on the tureen in fig. 65). Courtesy of the Mayer Collection, Mexico.

67. *Stand*, c. 1760–80. L 48.3 cm, W 43.2 cm, H 4.4 cm (19 in, 16½ in, 1¾ in). Overglaze enamels, boar's head with basket. Fine export, possibly unique (compare fig. 68). Private collection, Mexico City.

68. *Tureens and Stands*, c. 1760–80. L (tureens) W 38.3 cm, H 20 cm. Overglaze enamels, on right: unidentified Spanish arms. Fine export. Courtesy of Earle D. Vandekar.

69. *Stand*, c. 1760–80, L 48.3 cm, W 43.2 cm, H 4.4 cm (19 in, 17 in, 1¾ in). In overglaze enamels, a condor or turkey vulture with iridescent feathers, native only to North America. Originally, with a tureen, part of a set. Fine export, possibly unique. Private collection, Mexico City.

70. *Sconce*, Qianlong, c. 1750. L (without silver shell) 27.9 cm (11 in). Angular, foliate edge; raised molded lotus and scroll, overglaze iron-red and gilt ground. Silver shell on top, cup on base and edging of central oval, probably Mexican. Fine export, rare. Courtesy of the Mayer Collection, Mexico City.

71. *Dishliner*, Yongzheng/Qianlong, c. 1720–40. L 23.2 cm, W 17.1 cm, H 3.5 cm (9⅛ in, 6¾ in, 1⅜ in). Punched, scalloped rim with fluted sides to conform to metal container, probably silver. Overglaze iron-red and green: four reserves on green and black-scroll ground, two with birds, two with tree shrews; in well, stylized chrysanthemum. On reverse: near well, eight iron-red floral sprays, green hawthorne and narrow, cracked-ice outer border. Above-average export. Private collection, Mexico City.

72. *Figurine*, Westerner with dog, Kangxi/Yongzheng. c. 1715–30. H 15.2 cm, L 10.2 cm, 4.1 cm (6 in, 4 in, 1⅝ in). Molded figurine on raised base in overglaze green-gray and orange-brown. Man with sack and, originally, a staff, right leg once rested on now-missing support; dog turned to see master. Above-average export, rare. Private collection, Mexico City.

73. *Pair of cocks*, Qianlong, c. 1740–60. H 39.7 cm (15⅞ in). Mirror-twin, molded cocks. Overglaze iron-red combs on brown base. Fine export. Courtesy of the Mayer Collection, Mexico City.

74. *Shaving bowl*, Qianlong, c. 1740–50. L 33.6 cm, H 7.6 cm (13¼ in, 3 in). Oval, smooth rim scooped for neck. Overglaze gold-red and polychrome; outer borders: lattice and flowers; Westerner with trumpet in rocky landscape, peonies; inner border: linked whorl pairs with rayed arc. Above-average quality, unusual painting. Private collection, Mexico City.

75. *Flowerpot* (one of a pair), Qianlong, c. 1740–50. H 17.1 cm, W (with handles) 24.1 cm (6¾ in, 9½ in). Modeled on metal form, four-scalloped, banded rim, body fluting continues through foot, handles attached at rim. Overglaze iron-red and gilt lilies, florets, and leaves. Foot border: linked whorl pairs with rayed arc. Fine export. Private collection, Mexico City.

76. *Pieces for a tea/coffee/dinner service*, Qianlong/Jiaqing, c. 1790–

1800. H (left to right): cruetstand, 8.9 cm; chocolate pot, 20.3 cm, sugarbowl, 14.0 cm; pitcher, 19.1 cm (3½ in, 8 in, 5½ in, 7½ in). Classical forms with different finials. Molded bosses outline border of overglaze gold-red, green, black-line, and gilt. Fine export. Private collection, Mexico City.

77. *Sauceboat on stand*, Qianlong/Jiaqing, c. 1790–1800. L 36.8 cm, OH 17.75 cm (14½ in, 7 in). Same service as fig. 76. Private collection, Mexico City.

78. *Tureen*, Qianlong/Jiaqing, c. 1790–1800, H. 35.5 cm, L (base) 58.4 cm (14 in, 23 in). Same service as fig. 76. Private collection, Mexico City.

79. *Dish cover*, Qianlong/Jiaqing, c. 1790–1800. H 18.4 cm, square side 19.1 cm (7¼ in, 7½ in). Same service as fig. 76. Courtesy of the Mayer Collection, Mexico City.

80. *Pair of bowls*, Jiajing/Wanli, c. 1550–1600. D 10.2 cm (4 in). White porcelain with overglaze gilt scroll and stylized chrysanthemum. Fine domestic/export. Courtesy of the Percival David Foundation, University of London (A464, A465).

81. *Ewer*, Jiajing, 1522–66. H 21.1 cm (8⅛ in). Mark on base within double-lined square: *fu kuei jia chi* ("fine vase for the rich and honorable"). Overglaze enamels red, green, and gilt. Flat-domed, pear-shaped with S-scroll spout and handle; open circle thumb rest for chain to attach to lid. Typical lotus, scroll, plaintain, and meander borders; lattice ground to inverted heart-shaped reserve with gilt phoenixes and flowers. *Kinran-de* ware, made for export at private kilns near Jingdezhen. Superior export. Courtesy of the Idemitsu Museum of Arts, Tokyo.

82. *Shard*, late Kangxi/early Yongzheng, c. 1700–1725, Mexico City. 6.66 cm × 9.20 cm (2⅝ × 3⅝ in). Mexico City excavations. Private collection.

83. *Three shards*, clockwise from left: carrack with deer, carrack with figure (compare fig. 10), "Chinese aster" design, Mexico City. First two, Wanli, c. 1600; last, Kangxi, c. 1700–20. Largest shard: 9.52 × 9.52 cm (3¾ × 3¾ in). Mexico City excavations. Private collection.

84. *Bowl*, Wanli, c. 1590–1610. D 12.5 cm, H 6.0 cm (4¹⁵/₁₆ in, 2⅜ in). Rounded sides and everted rim with underglaze blue figures, alternately three Chinese women and three children. Common export. Courtesy of the Rijksmuseum, Amsterdam (RAK 1971-2).

85. *Dish*, ninth century, Nishapur, Iran. D 19.7 cm (7¹³/₁₆ in), H 7.3 cm (1¹³/₁₆ in). Underglaze brownish black, green, and yellow design. Central medallion with six oval reserves in cavetto border. Background crosshatching imitates Near Eastern metalwork fields or textiles. Compositionally, a distant but possible model for late sixteenth, early seventeenth carrackware (compare figs. 92 and 94). Museum für Kunst and Gewerbe, Hamburg. After Jakobsen, pl. 1, p. 37 (see Bibliography, "Books"). [Drawing: Robert Williams]

86. *Bowl*, thirteenth century, Kasan, Iran. D 21 cm. Underglaze blue and black (compare figs. 11 and 13). Kunstgewerbemuseum, Kohn; after Klein, p. 169 (see Bibliography, "Books"). [Drawing: Robert Williams]

87. *Dish*, c. 1530–40, Isnik, Turkey. D 26.7 cm (10½ in). Underglaze blue (compare figs. 157, 206, and 207). Victoria and Albert Museum; after Lane, pl. 30, pp. 51–52 (see Bibliography, "Books"). [Drawing: Robert Williams]

88. *Ewer*, Kangxi, c. 1685–1700. OH 28.6 cm (11¼ in). Deep under-

glaze blue, almost identical to early fifteenth-century prototype (Pope, *Ardebil*, pl. 54). Form may derive from a Persian source. Cloud-painted support for spout, lotus, and peony motifs: all Chinese elements. Fine domestic/export. Private collection, Mexico City.

89. *Dish*, Jiajing/Wanli, c. 1550–70. D 21.2 cm, H 4.4 cm (8⅜ in, 1¾ in). Foliate rim; *ruyi*-molded cavetto with central underglaze blue of a Buddhist flaming wheel, fungus, fly whisk, and swastika within six alternating borders of fish scale and swastika. Common export. Private collection, Mexico City.

90. *Dish*, Jiajing/Wanli, c. 1560–80. D 19.68 cm, H 3.8 cm (7¾ in, 1½ in). Underglaze blue, thin border of waterweeds and lotus, spotted doe and buck under pine tree in moonlight. On reverse: two birds on branches. Fine domestic/export. Private collection, Mexico City.

91. Detail of fig. 90.

92. *Cup*, Wanli, c. 1585–1620. H 8 cm, D 15 cm (3⅛ in, 5 in). Foliate rim, eight panels in underglaze blue on exterior and interior. Panels alternate: bird or bamboo shoots, divided by pendants of simplified circles (Buddha's jewels). In center bottom: singing bird under the moon. Common domestic/export. Several were recovered with the *White Lion* (1613). Private collection, Mexico City.

93. *Shard*, dish, Wanli, c. 1590–1620. D 19.05 cm, H 3.49 cm (17½ in, 1⅜ in). Flat edge "Swatow" ware; standard underglaze blue pattern: "Phoenix Standing in a Garden." Common domestic/export. Mexico City excavations. Private collection.

94. *Dish*, Wanli, c. 1605–25. D 47.6 cm, H 7.9 cm (18¾ in, 3⅜ in). Foliate rim with eight-pointed underglaze blue circle reserves, four with sacred emblems alternate with four of stylized peaches. Octagonal, star-shaped medallion with *ruyi* heads and alternating ogival panels of four each: swastika and fish-scale motifs. In center: by pool, bird amid flowers and tree peony. On reverse: eight swiftly painted panels, each with flower. Similar to dishes on the *White Lion* (1613). Common domestic/export. Private collection, Mexico City.

95. Detail of fig. 94.

96. *Bottles*, Wanli, c. 1610–20. Left: H 27.94 cm (11 in); right: H 26.7 cm (10½ in). left: garlic-bud mouth with *ruyi* collar, neck with lotus leaves. On pear-shaped body: *qilin*, lotus, and one of Eight Trigrams. Right: slender neck with Buddha's jewels in six panels, hexagonal division on body, *qilin* alternates with stylized flowers. Similar to others from the *White Lion* (1613). Above-average domestic/export. Courtesy of the Mayer Collection, Mexico City.

97. *Kendi*, Wanli, c. 1612. H 17.0 cm (6⁹/₁₆ in). Elephant-shaped with broken neck. Underglaze blue on body simulates cloth with reserved flowers on swastika ground. Attached bells and whisks on neck and rump. A similar kendi was listed in the collection of Philip II, king of Spain (1556–1598); this one is from the *White Lion* (1613). Courtesy of Rijksmuseum, Amsterdam, the National Geographic Society, and Bates Littlehales.

98. *Jar*, Wanli, c. 1600–20. H 15.5 cm, D 17.1 cm (6⅛ in, 6¾ in). Molded eight-lobed jar with underglaze blue persimmons among tendrilled vines. Key-fret borders on neck and base with pointed overlapping triangles on top and bottom borders. Average domestic/export. Private collection, Mexico City.

99. *Jar (chocolatero)*, Wanli, c. 1590–1620. H (with lid, without key)

27 cm (10³/8 in). Fitted in Mexico with a hinged iron lid with key, an underglaze blue jar with four reserve panels of flowers on latticework, floral and *ruyi* borders. Common domestic/export, now rare. Private collection, Mexico City.

100. *Bowl*, Wanli, c. 1600–1620. D 35.5 cm, H 16.5 cm (14 in, 6¹/2 in). On a pierced (*linglang*), swastika ground, six underglaze blue circular reserves, three each: the imperial dragon and phoenix, emblems of the emperor and empress. Interior center: circular medallion with tree peony. Interior border: feathered scroll. Above-average domestic/export. Private collection, Mexico City.

101. *Pot*, Wanli, c. 1612. H 19.0 cm (7¹/2 in) S-shaped spout with handle joined at shoulders; underglaze blue six panels diverge from molding: alternating peonies with emblems (shown, an artemesia leaf and fly whisk). Used for wine in China; for tea, punch, chocolate, coffee, *pulque*, or other beverage in the West. Common domestic/export. Recovered from the *White Lion* (1613). Courtesy of the Rijksmuseum, Amsterdam, the National Geographic Society, and Robert Sténuit.

102. *Plate*, Jiajing/Wanli, c. 1560–80. D 26 cm, H 3.5 cm (10¹/4 in, 1³/8 in). Underglaze blue with wide border: six stylized floret reserves on two types of diaper; six white on blue cranes within ogival reserve. On reverse: two borders divided by blue line: four asymmetrical floral motifs in each. Fine domestic/export. Private collection, Mexico City.

103. Oil on canvas, *Still Life with Fruit and Pottery*, Spanish, by Juan Zurbarán (1620–d. before 1664). 36.3 cm × 62.8 cm (14¹/4 in × 24³/4 in). Three cups, a pot, and low dish of Transitional underglaze blue porcelain, c. 1635–50. Courtesy of the Cincinnati Art Museum (1939.52).

104. *Beakers*, Transitional, c. 1640–80. H 5.5 cm, D (top) 6.6 cm (3⁷/8 in, 2⁵/8 in). Each with five panels in underglaze blue with birds in flowering branches. Stylized feather border on inside lip; stylized wave base border. Common export. Private collection, Mexico City.

105. *Urinals* (pair: male and female), early Kangxi, c. 1680s. Left: H 14.6 cm, L 24.13 cm, W 10.7 cm (5³/4 in, 9¹/2 in, 4¹/4 in); right: H 15.8 cm, L 20.3 cm, W 10.7 cm (6¹/4 in, 8 in, 4¹/4 in). Identical underglaze blue painting of a major landscape scene, lotus leaf, and fungus bowl/neck decorations. Common export, now rare. Private collection, Mexico City.

106. *Bowl*, Kangxi, c. 1685–1710. D 28.8 cm, H 5.08 cm (11³/8 in, 2 in). Mark on base: fungus (see fig. 374). Broad border in Japanese style: sixteen panels of four repeating views (deer, honeycomb, and two different peonies) frame two islands with pagodas and pine and prunus trees. Above-average domestic/export. Private collection, Mexico City.

107. Detail of fig. 106, spotted deer.

108. *Cup and dish* (not a pair). Kangxi, c. 1685–1710. Cup: H 7.6 cm, D 8.6 cm (3 in, 3³/8 in). Saucer: D 12.7 cm, H 2.5 cm (5 in, 1 in). The Crucifixion, probably from a woodblock print. Not a pair but both identically marked on base: cross in square parens within double blue circles. On saucer base: two sets of branches. Common Christian domestic/export. Courtesy of Dr. Wesley Gallup.

109. *Bowl*, Kangxi, c. 1714. D 12.1 cm, H 6.4 cm (4³/4 in, 2¹/2 in). Eight-paneled underglaze blue and white with stylized chrysanthemums, the "Chinese aster." Recovered from the *San José* (1715).

Average export. Courtesy of Dr. Charles Fairbank, University of Florida.

110. *Platter*, Qianlong, c. 1750–70. L 41.9 cm (16¹/2 in). Scalloped foliate rim with underglaze blue fish-scale and cash border, scalloped and feathered inner border. Cavetto border, latticework strip with four reserves; center: peony bouquet with four sprays. Above-average export. Courtesy of the Mayer Collection, Mexico City.

111. *Cup* with silver cover, Kangxi, c. 1690–1710. H 12.0 cm (4¹¹/16 in). Dehua white molded cup with lacy silver cover and handles, probably Mexican. Cup average; silverwork superior. Ex. coll. Francisco Pérez de Salazar. Private collection, Mexico City.

112. *Guanyin with child* (headless), Kangxi, c. 1690. Dehua white, recovered off Port Royal, Jamaica. Two-thirds of the city was submerged by the earthquake of 1692, according to a letter published in England, an enlargement of which lies under the figurine. Above-average domestic/export. Courtesy of the National Geographic Society and David L. Arnold.

113. *Westernized Guanyin with child*, Qianlong or Jiaqing, late 1700s/early 1800s. H 48.89 cm (19¹/4 in) Dehua white. The head was replaced with one of Western features for the export market. Average domestic/export, rare. Courtesy of the Victoria and Albert Museum.

114. *Shards*, Wanli, 1573–1620, Mexico City excavations. Private collection.

115. Base of fig. 116 with mark.

116. *Bowl*, Wanli, c. 1580–1600. D 9.18 cm, H 5.3 cm (3⁵/8 in, 2 in). Exterior: overglaze enamels in red and green with ball, whisk, jewels, and double lozenge. Interior: central medallion in underglaze blue on convex base, border of latticework. Mark on base, indecipherable. Courtesy of the Princessehof Museum, Leeuwarden (GRV 1929/162).

117. *Vase*, Wanli, c. 1600–1620. H 22.8 cm (9 in). Underglaze blue and overglaze red and green, two reserves of red flowers on a fish-scale ground, stylized leaves and scrolls. Average polychrome domestic/export. Private collection, Mexico City.

118. *Dish*, Kangxi/Yongzheng, c. 1715–30. D 16.5 cm (6¹/2 in). Overglaze iron-red and gilt willow tree and peony; stylized lotus and leaf outer border. Above-average domestic/export. Private collection, Mexico City.

119. *Tureen*, Kangxi/Yongzheng, c. 1715–30. H 17.1 cm, OW (with handles) 24.13 cm (6³/4 in, 9¹/2 in). Molded pumpkin, relief leaf, leaf handles, stem finial. Raised green ogival reserve spans lid and body: overglaze iron-red, gilt, and brown phoenix, bird and peonies on terrace with rocks. Fine export. Private collection, Mexico City.

120. *Beakers* (pair), Yongzheng/Qianlong, c. 1730–40. H 11.1 cm, D 8.9 cm (4³/8 in, D 3¹/2 in). Overglaze black, gold-red, turquoise, yellow; four floral reserves on each; diaper inner lip border. Fine export. Private collection, Mexico City.

121. *Charger*, Qianlong, c. 1750. D 38.1 cm (15 in). Overglaze gold-red and polychrome enamels; white-on-white six-panel floral outer border; inner border, a carefully rendered scroll motif with alternating fleur-de-lis and dot above abutted scrolls. Central decoration, a precise painting of two cocks on karst rocks amid peony trees. First-class export. Private collection, Mexico City.

122. *Plates*, Qianlong, c. 1730–40. Left and right: D 22.9 cm, H 2.5 cm

(9 in, 1 in); center: D 20.9 cm, H 3.8 cm (8¼ in, 1½ in). Left: the Adoration of the Shepherds. Right: the Resurrection. From unidentified engravings, both in gold-red, polychrome; border similar to Viennese *Laub- und Bandelwerk* (du Paquier factory): strapwork, trellised cartouches, cornucopia, flowers, and leaves. Center: the Crucifixion with John and Mary, decorated in the Netherlands. Painted in either the East or the West, the human body is anatomically inaccurate. Above-average export. Courtesy of Dr. Wesley Gallup.

123. *Stand*, Qianlong, c. 1760–80. L 48.3 cm, W 40.6 cm, H 4.4 cm (19 in, 16½ in, 1¾ in). Foliate, fluted edge with overglaze line, dot, and fleur-de-lis outer and inner borders. Overglaze polychrome chicken with basket in center, probably identical to tureen to which stand originally belonged (see Howard and Ayers, II, p. 592). Model, possibly in faience from Strasbourg. First-class export, maybe unique (compare figs. 67 and 69). Private collection, Mexico City.

124. Detail of center of fig. 123.

125. *Plate*, Qianlong, c. 1740, D 26.3 cm, H 3.2 cm (10⅜ in, 1¼ in). Penciled and gilt Viennese-style strapwork border (compare fig. 122) with arms of the Ovando family (1734). In gilt, clockwise from top, OBANDO ["B" for "V"], at 1, 3, 5, 7, 9, 11 o'clock. First-class export. Private collection, Mexico City.

126. Detail of Ovando arms, fig. 125.

127. *Plates*, Yongzheng/Qianlong, c. 1730–50. Left: D 23.2 cm, H 2.5 cm (9⅛ in, 1 in); right: D 24.4 cm, H 1.9 cm (9⅝ in, 3/4 in). Both scalloped-edged but of different treatments; left: border of two European (Viennese?) designs alternating three times; right: raised band from metalwork prototype. Left: unidentified arms; right: arms of Ahedo family. First-class export. Private collection, U.S.A.

128. *Pitcher*, Qianlong, c. 1790. H 13.3 cm, OW 12.1 cm (5¼ in, 4¾ in). Probably modeled on Spanish metalwork, banded neck, low pear-shaped body, slim spout, loop handle. Overglaze iron-red, green and gilt dot and stylized leaf borders. Arms of Mexico City inscribed: .EN.SU.EXALTACION.AL.TRONO.LA .CIUDAD.DE.MEXICO.EN.27.DE. DICIEMBRE.DE.1789. To commemorate the ascension of Charles IV (1788–1808) to the Spanish throne. Courtesy of Dr. Wesley Gallup.

129. Detail of saucer, Qianlong, c. 1790. Overglaze polychrome medallion. Arms of the Consulado of Mexico City, its shield flanked by symbols of its power, maritime trade. Left: figure of Mercury (for speed), right: a galleon. Inscribed: A.SU.PROCLAMACION.EL.CONSULA-DO.DE.MEXICO.ANO.DE.1789. CIL [Gil] at base for designer of the medal (a model for the medallion), Jeronimo Antonio Gil (1732–1798), Spanish engraver. Private collection, Mexico City.

130. *Plates*, Qianlong, c. 1790. Left to right: D 26.4 cm, H 2.5 cm; D 30.5 cm, H 3.2 cm; D 20.6 cm, H 2.2 cm (10⅜ in, 1 in; 12 in, 1¼ in; 9⅛ in, 7/8 in). Same foliate rim on each, different chaste classical borders. Left: arms of the city of Puebla, inscribed: EN.SU.FE-LIS.PROCDAMACIOM [sic].LA CIUDAD.DE.LOS.ANGELES.A.17.DE.ENERO.DE.1790. For Charles IV's ascension to the throne of Spain. (Inner Latin inscription also in error.) CIL for Gil, the engraver (compare fig. 129). Center: seal of the Royal Academy of San Carlos (now, Palacio de las Bellas Artes); Gil, a director; inscribed: IN.SOLEM.INAUG.MEX.ACAD. EXC.CUR.AN.1790. Right: seal of Valladolid, inscribed: PROCLANADO.EN.LA. CUDAD[sic].DE.VALLADOLID.DE.MICHOACAN.1781. Inner: PRO.SU.ALEREZ.

R.D.JOSE.BERNARDO.EONCERRADA (Forcerrada), Royal Lieutenant of Valladolid (now Morelia). (Forcerrada's portrait in center.) Private collection, U.S.A.

131. *Cup*, seal identical to plate on right in figure 130, c. 1790; first-class export. Courtesy of Franz Mayer Collection, Mexico City.

132. *Risco fountain*, begun c. 1739–40. Casa de Don Isidro Fabela, Plaza de San Jacinto, San Angel, Mexico City.

133. Detail of fig. 132.

CHAPTER 3

134. *Box*, Jiajing, 1522–66. H 7.6 cm, 13.6 cm square (2¹⁵/16 in, 5½ in square). Mark: *chuan xia bian yong* ("seal box for use as required"). Polychrome cover with an official hearing disputants; behind him, symbolic scroll with salmon swimming upstream; borders of lotus and peony scrolls in reserve on red or green. Inside, a *qilin*. Fine domestic/export. Courtesy of the Trustees of the British Museum (1936 10–12 193).

135. *Cup* (60 percent reconstructed), Wanli, c. 1610. D 4.5 cm, H 3.7 cm (1¹¹/16 in, 1⅜ in). Underglaze blue with overlapped leaf design; beneath, deteriorated whorls (compare *White Lion* cup, Van der Pijl-Ketel, p. 144). Above-average domestic/export. Courtesy of Colonial National Historic Park, Yorktown, Virginia.

136. *Cup shards*, left: carrack, Wanli, c. 1615; right, cup shard, Kangxi, c. 1685–1700. Shards found on the Drummond/Harris Plantation, the Governor's Land near Jamestown, occupied c. 1648–1820. William Drummond, the first governor of North Carolina, was from Virginia. Average to above-average domestic/export. Courtesy of the Virginia Research Center, Yorktown, Virginia.

137. *Cup*, Chongzhen, c. 1628–44. D 9.3 cm, H 6.9 cm, (3¹¹/16 in, 2¾ in). Mark on base, see fig. 138. Underglaze blue landscape scene. Double blue lines at rim and on high foot. Found near the Chiswell-Bucktrout House. Above-average domestic/export. Courtesy of Colonial Williamsburg (1404-2. H.6).

138. Detail of base mark on fig. 137. Transliteration of hallmark: *Jigutang* ("Hall of Investigating Antiquity"). Hallmark of Gao Chengyan (1603–1648), a famous bibliophile and poet, also a prominent official from Jiaxing (between Shanghai and Hangzhou).

139. *Cup shard*, Transitional, Chongzhen/Shunzhi, c. 1640–60. Underglaze blue scrollwork, rim paneling. Recovered from "Littleton," Kingsmill Properties on the north side of the James River near Williamsburg, James City County. Colonel Thomas Pettus (d. by 1669), prominent colonist, owner of the property in the period 1648–60. His son, Captain Thomas Pettus (d. 1691), inherited "Littleton"; both associated with this shard. *Bowl shard*, Kangxi, c. 1690–1720. Underglaze blue stylized lotus spray. Associated with Captain Pettus and his successor, James Bray II, a wealthy landowner, burgess, and justice of the peace in James City County, and his two children, Elizabeth Bray Allen and Thomas Bray. Courtesy of the Virginia Research Center, Yorktown, Virginia.

140. *Plate*, Qianlong, c. 1740–60. Underglaze blue and eroded overglaze enamels showing black with traces of gilt in morning glory and insect pattern. Typical outer and cavetto borders of the middle-eighteenth century. Associated with Thomas Bray's son, James Bray III, and his sister, Elizabeth Bray Johnson. All above-

average domestic/export or export. Courtesy of the Virginia Research Center, Yorktown, Virginia.

141. *Bottle* (square), Transitional, early Kangxi, c. 1665. H 31.4 cm, W 11.2 cm (12¼ in, 4¼ in). Sloped from silver screw top. Underglaze blue, two views of mandarins in a landscape. Above-average export. Courtesy of the Ashmolean Museum (1978.863).

142. *Tankard*, Transitional, Shunzhi/Kangxi, c. 1645–65. H 22.65 cm, D 8.2 cm (8⅘ in, 3⅕ in). Underglaze blue landscape scene with scholar and attendant. Lip border roughly approximates open-leaf motif. Lower border, lappets; base slightly concave. Above-average to good export. Courtesy of the Ashmolean Museum (1978.802).

143. *Dish*, Transitional, Chongzhen, c. 1630–40. D 20.9 cm, H 4 cm (8⅕ in, 1½ in). Underglaze blue, five horses beneath a moon and a poem. Exterior: four crude whorls; slightly convex glazed base. Average export piece, now rare. Courtesy of the Ashmolean Museum (1978.2037).

144. *Shards* (reconstructed), edge of vessel, Transitional, Chongzhen/Shunzhi, c. 1650–60. Underglaze blue border in open-scroll leaf motif. Found on the site of a well-to-do trader at Ft. Orange (now Albany), New York. Above-average export. Courtesy of Paul Huey, senior archaeologist, New York State Parks and Recreation, Waterford, New York.

145. *Mustard pots* and *salt*, left to right: matching Japanese mustard pot and salt, *ko-Imari* (Old Imari), c. 1680. Pot H 11.4 cm (4⅖ in)., salt H 6.4 cm, D 9 cm (2½ in, 3½ in). Chinese mustard pot, Transitional, Shunzhi/early Kangxi, c. 1645–65. Tall-footed Chinese pot in underglaze blue: attendant hands hat to official in moonlit landscape with rocks and banana tree. Floral meander, curved lappet borders on the body. Handle border: open-scroll leaf. Rim left unglazed for metalwork lid. Convex glaze base. Later Japanese pot and salt copy Chinese prototypes. Japanese objects: fine; Chinese pot: average. Courtesy of the Ashmolean Museum (1978.419, 1978.427, 1978.821).

146. *Dish*, Transitional, Chongzhen/Shunzhi, c. 1640–60. D 37.5 cm (14.7 in). Overglaze red and green enamels imitate underglaze blue carrack prototype. Flattened edge of eight panels: alternating sacred symbols and fruit. Foliate star medallion with eight *ruyi* heads bordering typical honeycomb, cash, and interlocking Y reserves. Center: one large vase of flowers, two smaller on either side. Purchased in Japan in 1959; if original to Japan, then available for the Manila trade. Fine export. Courtesy of the Ottema–Kingma Foundation, the Princessehof Museum (OKS. 1959.56).

147. *Beaker*, Transitional, early Kangxi, c. 1660–75. H 51 cm, D 21.5 cm, (20 in, 8⅖ in). Underglaze blue with overglaze polychrome enamels. Three sections, top to bottom: mounted scholar with retinue looks back at lady on balcony, boys at play, two peach sprays. "Cracked ice" lip border with brown rim. Superior domestic/export. Courtesy of the Ashmolean Museum (1978.1807).

148. *Teapots*, right: both porcelain, Kangxi, c. 1685–1700; on left, Ixing red stoneware, Qianlong or Jiaqing, c. 1736–1820. Ixing, H 11.3 cm, D 15.2 cm (4⅖ in, 5⅞ in); Dehua white, H 21.2 cm, D 18.6 cm (8⁵⁄₁₆ in, 7⁵⁄₁₆ in); polychrome, H 10.3 cm, D 15.7 cm (4 in, 6⅕ in). Left to right: Ixing, unpainted and unglazed. Incised mark of appreciation, probably *ju*, ("complete"). Hexagonal De-

hua molded pot with handle attached at shoulders. Overglaze red, green, and blue enamels on raised lotus leaves; white body with green spout, handle, and lid; lotus finial. Courtesy of the Trustees of the British Museum (F 878, polychrome pot).

149. *Bowl* (mounted in silver), Transitional, Tianqi/Chongzhen, c. 1630. H 8.5 cm, OW 19.2 cm (3⁵⁄₁₆ in, 7½ in). Silver mount marked A 1632 MS, for Leeuwarder silversmith Minne Sickes. Leeuwarder inventories of 1600–1625 list such mounted cups. Called "brandy bowls" in Holland. Treasured, this one is probably similar to the one in the Van Varick inventory, New York, 1695. Courtesy of the Fries Museum, Leeuwarden, the Netherlands.

150. *Bowls*, right: Kangxi, c. 1690. H and D 6.6 cm (2⅝ in with cover); left: Qianlong, c. 1740. H 4.1 cm, D 6.9 cm (1⅝ in, 2¾ in). Right with cover; underglaze blue on interior and in reserves on exterior; brown ground. Left: overglaze enamels, including blue, in leaf reserves on brown exterior; inside, same enamels on white. Common export, now rare. Nos. 196 and 108, Elizabeth C. Canby catalogue. Courtesy of Mr. and Mrs. Lewis Rumford II.

151. *Cups*, Kangxi, c. 1685–1710. Left to right: H 6.4 cm, 6.7 cm, 6.4 cm (2½ in, 2⅗ in, 2½ in). Can with handle in overglaze red, green, blue; octagonal cup with figures in red, blue, and turquoise; Dehua cup. Single cups rather than sets, with or without saucers, used for tea in late-seventeenth- and early-eighteenth-century homes in Europe, England, and America; compare Van Varick inventory. Courtesy of the Trustees of the British Museum (F534, F30, F891).

152. *Lion whistle*, Kangxi, c. 1690–1720. H 12.3 cm (4⅖ in). Dehua white, molded lion of Fo (Buddha) seated on prunus-decorated pedestal with right paw on brocade ball. Common domestic/export. Courtesy of the Groninger Museum, the Netherlands.

153. *Figurines*, two Chinese scholars, Kangxi, c. 1690–1710. Both H c. 14.0 cm (5½ in). Three-color ware of mandarins popular in the West as representatives of the exotic East. Common domestic/export. Courtesy of the Trustees of the British Museum (F502, F503).

154. *Plate*, Kangxi, 1672. D 27.3 cm, H 5 cm (10¹¹⁄₁₆ in, 1¼ in). Underglaze blue and red, two women on a walled terrace in the moonlight. Mark on base, underglaze blue in two rows of eight characters: *Kangxi renzi Zonghe tang zhi* (The renzi year of the Kangxi reign [1672], made in the Zhonghe Hall ("Central Harmony")) (Forbidden City). Collection of F. Lugt. Courtesy of the Fondation Custodia, Paris.

155. *Coffee/chocolate pot*, Kangxi, c. 1690–1710. H 28.0 cm (11 in). Octagonal shape, domed lid with lion finial from a silver or Delft model. Bent end to straight spout attached with a C-shape bracket, loop handle, three ball feet. Underglaze blue rendering of seminaked figures in a hunt, mounted men in pastoral scene with buildings and trees. Europa and the bull in deep cartouche-apron. Above-average export, one of five known examples. Courtesy of the Victoria and Albert Museum (C.71 & A-1963).

156. *Plate*, Wanli, c. 1585–1600. D 38.1 cm, H 7.3 cm (15 in, 2⅞ in). Smooth rim with painted foliate edge to eight panels of white reserves on underglaze blue, separated by narrow panels of jewels; three birds in waterweed and rockscape. No exact parallel on the *White Lion* (1613). Private collection, Mexico City.

157. *Basin*, Transitional, Chongzhen/Shunzhi, c. 1635–60. D 35 cm, H

14.5 cm (13²/₅ in, 5¹¹/₁₆ in). Underglaze dark blue, six foliate panels with scrollwork frames divided by floral-and-leaf repeat. Inside center: two scenes, one above another, with European houses but Chinese figures in sampan, same combination of Orientals in Western setting of the panels. Above-average Dutch export. Courtesy of the Ottema–Kingman Foundation, the Princessehof Museum (OKS 1982.74).

158. *Bowl*, Wanli, c. 1612. D c. 21 cm, H c. 5.8 cm (8¹/₄ in, 2³/₁₆ in). Underglaze blue flat-edge bowl, quadrant design of two masks and two fans on opposite edges. Four dividing panels of streamers. Center: a butterfly and grasshopper on a rock with tree peony. From the *White Lion* (1613). Average export. Courtesy of the Rijksmuseum, the National Geographic Society, and Robert Sténuit.

159. Shelves of carrack, Wanli, 1573–1620. Cups, dishes, plates, and bowls. Courtesy of the Princessehof Museum.

160. *Dishes*, Japanese porcelain, middle to late seventeenth-century, early enameled wares. Left: c. 1670–80, D 32.8 cm, H 5.5 cm (12¹/₄ in, 2¹/₈ in). Overglaze enamels in red, blue, green, yellow, and black. Chinese carrack-inspired center design of peonies in vase on swastika-fenced terrace. Asymmetrical prunus sprouting from rocks on edges. Center: middle to late seventeenth-century, *ko-Imari*, D 13.8 cm, H 2.1 cm (5³/₈ in, ³/₄ in). Single chrysanthemum in center; four floral reserves on two diaper grounds. Base: single spur mark; square *fuku* mark in red. Right: c. 1660–70, D 32.5 cm, H 7.3 cm (12¹¹/₁₆ in, 2³/₄ in) Chinese carrack-inspired, eight-paneled flat edge: alternating single flower and emblem. Sharp octagonal central medallion with geese in pond. Base with five spur marks, chatter marks, seal mark in red. Above-average export. Courtesy of the Ashmolean Museum (1978.680, 1978.682, 1978.413).

161. Shelves of Transitional ware, c. 1620–80. Courtesy of the Princessehof Museum.

162. Detail, vase on lower left shelf in fig. 161.

163. *Plate*, Kangxi, c. 1685–1700. D 38.1 cm (15 in). Underglaze blue, foliate edge of open lotus in twelve panels on edge and center. Floral motifs, lattice ground. *Ruyi* heads surround central medallion. Fine domestic/export. Private collection, Mexico City.

164. *"Puzzle" jugs* (pair), Kangxi, c. 1690–1710. H 23.4 cm, D 10.8 cm (9¹/₄ in, 4¹/₄ in). From domed, knobbed lid to base, continuous hexagonal shape. Overglaze enamels in red, yellow, aubergine, and green. Reed-painted handles. Panels and borders not exact. Puzzle jugs, dating from an English source (1569), have hollow handles and a hollow band near the lip. When the jug is turned sideways, the liquid travels the tubes, bypassing the perforated neck. Unusual in their day, now quite rare. Courtesy of the Newark Museum (41.924 A-D).

CHAPTER 4

165. *Dish*, Kangxi, c. 1710–20. D 38.7 cm (15¹/₄ in). Foliate edge, paneled with arms of Magellan, now Mechlin: on crowned shield gules and or, the bicephal eagle of Spain. One in a series of armorials of Dutch, English, and French provinces or cities. "Amsteldam," for the river Amstel which flows through Amsterdam. *Figurine*:

Kangxi, c. 1700–1715, H 22.2 cm (8³/₄ in). Probably a Frenchman in high court fashion of Louis XIV, king 1643–1715. *Mug*: Kangxi, c. 1720. H 12.6 (4¹⁵/₁₆ in). Arms of Penn: probably made for William Penn's son, Thomas of Stoke Park, Buckinghamshire (m. 1751 Lady Juliana Fermor, d. 1775). *Teapot*: Yongzheng, c. 1735. H 11.4 cm (4³/₈ in). Arms of Hanbury with Comyn in pretence; made for John Hanbury (1700–1758), Quaker tobacco merchant of Maryland and Virginia, a director of the South Sea Co. Fine export. Courtesy of Dr. Wesley Gallup.

166. *Cup and saucer*, left: Yongzheng/Qianlong, c. 1730–40. Cup: H 3.1 cm, D 6.3 cm (1¹/₄ in, 2¹/₂ in); saucer: D 10.5 cm (4¹/₁₆ in). Mark on cup base in overglaze gold-red: voc (Vereenigde Oostindische Compagnie). Arms of the Dutch East India Company from coin minted in 1728. *Dish*, center: c. 1740. D 22.9 cm (9 in). Capetown, Table Bay, South Africa (Dutch since 1652), with Dutch ships. Outer border, copy of Meissen porcelain; cavetto border, gilt scroll and brown lappet. *Cups*, right: c. 1750–70, H 6 cm, D 5.4 cm (2³/₈ in, 2¹/₈ in). Typical gold-red, fish-scale fill in floral swag border. Dish, superior; cups and saucer, above-average export. Private collection, U.S.A.

167. *Plate*, Kangxi, c. 1690–1710. D 35.3 cm (13.9 in). Mark: underglaze blue *nianhao* of Kangxi. Edgeless plate in Chinese style with no export features. Underglaze blue waves beneath four underglaze copper-red carp and twelve lotus blossoms with half-lotus border. Fine domestic/export. Private collection, the Netherlands.

168. *Coffee/chocolate pot*, Kangxi, c. 1690–1720. H 29.2 cm, OW 19.7 cm (11¹/₂ in, 5¹/₄ in). Nineteenth-century Dutch silver mounts, possibly replacements. Underglaze blue peonies with tulips near spout on high-domed tapered pot. Curved spout with bird/reptile head similar to spouts on Turkish gilt-copper ewers; script-shaped handle reminiscent of Arabic characters. "Mahometan coffee" and "Popish Spanish Chocolate" so identified in 1705 in London (OED). From the 1660s, both coffee and chocolate were in the city's public houses. A blend of Middle East, Western and Chinese features. Fine export, now rare. Courtesy of the Newark Museum (67.381).

169. *Tea service* (partial), Yongzheng, c. 1730–35. *Teapot*, H 11.1 cm (4³/₈ in). Smooth, thin body. Left to right: tea canister, milk pot, teapot, slop bowl, teacup and saucer, spoon tray, coffee cup and saucer (coffee also served in teapots). Overglaze black-line ("penciled") and gilt in unidentified Western design. Owned by Hendrik and Catharine de Peyster Rutgers (m. 1732). Rutgers (1712–1779), a prominent merchant; his wife (b. 1711), from a wealthy, office-holding family. Fine English colonial export. Ex. coll. Waldron Phoenix Belknap, Jr. Courtesy of the Museum of the City of New York. (58.12.21 a-v).

170. *Plate*, Kangxi, c. 1710–25. D 22.2 cm (8³/₄ in). Underglaze blue with gilt. Three asymmetrical floral circles on a thin border around a central medallion of landscape with house and moon. Cavetto border: early form of standard, midcentury design. Outer border: four floral reserves on blue with gilt lotus ground. Formerly associated with Jacob Leisler, in New Amsterdam from 1660 until his death in 1691, but form and decoration postdate Leisler. Fine export. Courtesy of the Museum of the City of New York. (43.406).

171. *Cup and saucer*, Yongzheng, c. 1730–35. Cup D 6.4 cm, H 3.5 cm (2¹/₂ in, 1³/₈ in); saucer D 10.5 cm, H 1.9 cm (4¹/₈ in, ³/₄ in). Under-

glaze blue line and wash drawing, four ogival panels with boys at play on whorled ground. In 1740, owned by David and Mary Lefevre Deshler (m. 1739), No. 11, Elizabeth C. Canby catalogue. Average domestic/export. Courtesy of Mr. and Mrs. Lewis Rumford II.

172. *Cups and saucers* (pair), Qianlong, c. 1740–45. Cups D 8.3 cm, H 7.0 cm (3 1/4 in, 2 3/4 in); saucers D 12.7 cm, H 3.5 cm (5 in, 1 3/8 in). Chinese "Imari," almost identical two medallions, two ogival reserves each with floral ground, brown rims. Listed as "caudle cups," dated 1745, owned by Anna Clifford, great-grandmother of E. C. Canby. No. 55, Elizabeth C. Canby catalogue. Above-average export. Courtesy of Mr. and Mrs. Lewis Rumford II.

173. *Spittoon*, Kangxi/Yongzheng, c. 1720–25. H 7 cm, top edge 12.5 × 11 cm, (2 3/4 in and 5 in × 4 1/2 in). Underglaze blue octagonal body with square, notched large lip, loop handle. Indians tend and harvest tobacco leaves ("Indian" or "sot" weeds); Westerners smoke long clay pipes. Based on a dated Delft model, 1721, no Oriental features except for the style of rendering bodies and faces. Above-average export, now rare. Courtesy Ottema–Kingman Foundation, Princessehof Museum, Leeuwarden (OKS 1979-34).

174. Bird's eye view of rim in fig. 173.

175. *Cup and saucer*, Japanese, early eighteenth century. Cup D 6.9 cm, H 3.2 cm (2 3/4 in, 1 1/4 in); saucer D 10.2 cm, H 2.5 cm (4 in, 1 in). Underglaze blue stylized eroded rock and peony design. Bought in Portsmouth, N.H., in 1878. No. 256, Elizabeth C. Canby catalogue. Common export, now rare. Courtesy of Mr. and Mrs. Lewis Rumford II.

176. *Bowl*, Yongzheng, c. 1715–30. D 23.2 cm, H 10.2 cm (9 1/8 in, 4 in). Underglaze blue landscape design overpainted ("clobbered") in enamels sometime later, probably in the Netherlands; red and green flower basket of Chinese style and inner border in a hybrid East-West style. Owned by Lt. Gov. George Brown of R.I. Above-average export. Gift of Mr. Robert Dunn. Courtesy of the Rhode Island Historical Society (1951-4-1).

177. *Teapots* (illustrating form's growth and westernization), left: Kangxi/Yongzheng, c. 1715–30. H 14.6 cm, OW 16.5 cm (5 3/4 in, 6 1/2 in); capacity 1 1/4 cups. Hexagonal shape with fish handle, animal spout. Overglaze enamels in black, red, yellow, green, and blue. Right: Qianlong, c. 1740–50. H 14.6 cm, OW 16.5 cm (5 3/4 in, 6 1/2 in); capacity 2 1/2 cups. Stand: L 14.3 cm, H 1.9 cm (5 5/8 in, 3/4 in). Finely penciled black butterfly and flowers, probably from a Western print, touch of overglaze enamel on neck and lid borders. Fine export. Gift of Mr. Harry T. Peters, Jr. Courtesy of the Peabody Museum (1977.2.24AB, 1300.70AB).

178. *Plate*, Yongzheng/Qianlong, c. 1725–45. D 23.2 cm, H 3.2 cm (9 1/8 in, 1 1/4 in). Underglaze blue lotus and tree peony. Cavetto: three reserves on latticework ground; edge: three peony with prunus sprays. Said to have been purchased from William Gooch, governor of Virginia (1727–49, when he left for England), by the Page family, formerly of Rosewell. Average export, now scarce. Courtesy of Ms. Page Warden. (C79-271).

179. *Platter*, Qianlong, c. 1736–50. L 27.3 cm, W 18.4 cm, H 1.9 cm (10 3/4 in, 7 1/4 in, 3/4 in). On octagonal, notched form, underglaze blue spotted buck and doe gambol on island; two of the "three friends," pine and bamboo, nearby; the third, the prunus, with pagoda in right background. Cavetto border of symmetrical scrolls and rayed half circles; outer border of stylized bell flowers and paired leaves. Once owned by Thomas Nelson, governor of Virginia (1781). Average export, now scarce. Courtesy of the Virginia HIstorical Society (C71627, also G967.16c).

180. *Dish*, Kangxi/Yongzheng, c. 1715–30. D 21.6 cm, H 3.5 cm (8 1/2 in, 1 3/8 in). *Doucai*: central bird, insect, floral and rock; tulip-shaped red line of outer border possibly "clobbered" in the Netherlands; scalloped edge. Above-average export. Gift of Mr. Harry T. Peters, Jr. Courtesy of the Peabody Museum (1977.56.22).

181. *Cup and saucer*, Yongzheng, c. 1725–40. Cup: D 7.3 cm, H 4.1 cm (2 7/8 in, 1 5/8 in); saucer: D 11.7 cm, H 2.2 cm (4 5/8 in, 7/8 in). Overglaze iron-red and gilt butterfly amid peonies with scalloped, dotted outer border. No. 142 in Elizabeth C. Canby catalogue. Above-average export. Courtesy of Mr. and Mrs. Lewis Rumford II.

182. *Cups and saucers* (nearly identical), Yongzheng/Qianlong, c. 1725–40. Left: cup D 6.3 cm, H 3.5 cm (2 7/16 in, 1 3/8 in); saucer, D 10.7 cm, H 1.7 cm (4 3/16 in, 11/16 in); right: cup D 6.4 cm, H 3.7 cm (2 1/2 in, 1 7/16 in); saucer 10.6 cm, 1.8 cm (4 1/8 in, 11/16 in). Close but not identical in either size or painting, underglaze blue island scenes with pagodas, men in sampans, and fishermen on shore. Descended in families from Plymouth and Essex counties, Massachusetts, and southern New Hampshire. Gilt repair, twentieth century. Average export, now rare. Courtesy of Mr. Winslow Ames.

183. *Plate*, Yongzheng/Qianlong, c. 1725–40. D 23.4 cm, H 2.54 cm (9 1/4 in, 1 in). Flat edge with no border, underglaze blue bird on bamboo, chrysanthemums and rock. Overglaze gilt and red bird, grasshopper and butterflies with similar touches in grass. Fine quality export. Ex. coll. G. R. Curwen. Courtesy of the Essex Institute (338).

184. *Coffee and tea cups with saucer* (part of a tea service), Yongzheng/Qianlong, c. 1720–40. Coffee cup with handle D and H 6 cm (2 3/8 in); saucer D 12 cm, H 2.54 cm (4 3/4 in, 1 in); teacup D 7.5 cm, H 3.8 cm. (2 15/16 in, 1 1/2 in). Incised underglaze leaf pattern in "artichoke" or "lotus" design. Leaf in gilt, red-edge outline with central butterfly in scalloped, staggered petals. Fine domestic/export. Courtesy of Norman Herreshoff.

185. *Platter*, Yongzheng/Qianlong, c. 1725–40. D 31.1 cm, H 2.9 cm (12 1/4 in, 1 1/8 in). Scalloped, foliate brown rim, flat borderless edge, overglaze enamels in gold-red, yellow, green, blue, and turquoise. Above-average export. Private collection, U.S.A.

186. *Cups and saucers*, Yongzheng/Qianlong, c. 1730–40. Left: cup, D 6.6 cm, H 3.5 cm (2 5/8 in, 1 3/8 in); saucer D 10.5 cm, H 1.6 cm (4 1/8 in, 5/8 in). Center: cup D 6.4 cm H 6.8 cm (2 1/2 in, 1 1/2 in); saucer D 10.5 cm, H 1.9 cm (4 1/8 in, 3/4 in). Right: cup D 6.3 cm, H 3.5 cm (2 1/2 in, 1 3/8 in); saucer 10.2 cm, 1.9 cm (4 in, 3/4 in). Center cup and saucer of older Chinese "Imari" palette; other two sets in gold-red, commonly available after the late 1720s. Nos. 139, 274, and 145 in Elizabeth C. Canby's catalogue. Fine stock-pattern export. Courtesy of Mr. and Mrs. Lewis Rumford II.

187. *Shards* (reconstructed): slop bowl, two coffee cups, one teacup, one plate. Yongzheng/Qianlong, c. 1720–40. Polychrome and gilt. Associated with the Milner family, predecessors of the Heywards. From the Heyward–Washington House, Charleston, S.C. Fine export. Courtesy of the Charleston Museum.

188. *Bowl* (reconstructed), Qianlong, c. 1740–60. Underglaze blue large bowl. Fish roe, honeycomb, floral inner border; reserves with flowers and butterflies on exterior. Associated with the Milner and Heyward families. From the Heyward–Washington House, Charleston, S.C. Above-average export. Courtesy of the Charleston Museum.

189. *Plates*, Yongzheng, c. 1725–35. Left: D 31.8 cm, H 3.5 cm (12½ in, 1⅜ in). In overglaze gold-red, white oxide, blue, green, yellow, brown, and black, well-painted quadrant border in stylized peony, crane, prunus, and lappet motifs on whorled ground. In center: Chinese basket of same flowers plus morning and moon glories (blue and white convolvulus); brown rim. First owned by Miss Susan Ingersoll of Salem. Right: D 22.0 cm, H 2.5 cm (8⅝ in, 1 in). Octagonal plate with two complementary, black-lined quadrant borders: brown whorled lappet with prunus; pastel rose and aqua latticework with a pendant, ribboned scroll. In center: peonies and pair of birds. Superior domestic/export. Ex. coll. George R. Curwen. Courtesy of the Essex Institute (304, 309).

190. *Sauceboat with stand*, Qianlong, c. 1745–65. Boat OL 21.6 cm, OH 10.8 cm (8½ in, 4¼ in); stand L 18.4 cm, W 13.3 cm (7¼ in, 5¼ in). Scalloped, loop-handled boat with same deep outer and cavetto borders as leaf-shaped stand with typical landscape. Part of a dinner service first owned by the Ropes family, Ropes Mansion, Salem. Common pattern, above-average export. Courtesy of the Essex Institute (R188-188a).

191. *Teapot, cup, and saucer*, Qianlong, c. 1750–75. Pot: H 13.3 cm, W 24 cm (5³⁄₁₆ in, 9⅜ in). Lobed body with raised moldings on curved spout and handle; flat, fluted lid. Cup D 7.9 cm, H 4.6 cm (3¹⁄₁₆ in, 1¾ in); saucer D 12.5 cm (4⅞ in). Foliate edges define fluted sides. Thin body finely painted in overglaze gold-red, green, yellow, and gilt in three borders: bamboo, ribbon, floral swag. In center, cornucopia-shaped basket with rose and morning glory. Almost entirely Western except for bamboo border; possibly in imitation of Chantilly porcelain. Fine export. Gift of Miss Elinor Hassam. Courtesy of the Essex Institute (124, 660).

192. *Plate*, Kangxi/Yongzheng, c. 1720–30. D 28.6 cm, H 3.5 cm (11¼ in, 1⅜ in). Underglaze blue outer border of white prunus on blue with four reserves of landscape and scholar's items; cavetto of elaborate double scroll and rayed half disk alternating with double loops. In center, spotted deer near natural rock table beneath tree, peony, pine, and bamboo. Possibly unique design; fine domestic/export. Associated with Benjamin Faneuil, father of Peter Faneuil of Faneuil Hall. Gift of Mrs. Richard W. Hall. Courtesy of the Society for the Preservation of New England Antiquities (1958.27).

193. *Goblet*, Kangxi/Yongzheng, c. 1700–25. H 13.4 cm (5¼ in). Tapered body, knobbed base, slightly convex broad foot. Underglaze blue meander border and typical early eighteenth century motifs: floral sprays and eroded rock. Probably from a Western glass model. Above-average export. Courtesy of the Trustees of the British Museum (F1583).

194. *Plate*, Yongzheng/Qianlong, c. 1730–50. D 22.9 cm, H 2.2 cm (9 in, ⅞ in). Underglaze blue in delicate lines of three trees on a rocky landscape with structure to left. Cavetto border: fleur-de-lis; outer border; stock diaper; brown rim. Common export. Courtesy of Dr. Wesley Gallup.

195. *Saucer dish*, Qianlong, c. 1740–60. D 13.9 cm, H 3.5 cm (5½ in, 1⅜ in). Overglaze polychrome pastoral of courtiers amid ruins as shepherd and shepherdess with sheep. Outer border, floral garland. From a print of a painting in the style of or by Francois Boucher (1703–1770), court painter to Louis XV. Fine export. Courtesy of Dr. Wesley Gallup.

196. *Shards* (contemporary with those from Ft. Ligonier, Pennsylvania), Yongzheng/Qianlong, c. 1725–75. From Clermont, the ancestral Livingston home overlooking the Hudson River, built 1730, destroyed by the British in 1777. Underglaze blue and overglaze polychrome. Note brown-rimmed shard in upper left. Courtesy of Dennis L. Wentworth.

197. *Cup and bowl* (reconstructed) from ship *Le Machault* (1760), Qianlong, c. 1755–59. Cup: D 11 cm, H 5.5 cm (4¼ in, 2⅛ in). Deep, underglaze blue border of grape and vine tendrils, florets, bamboo. Bowl: D 26.5 cm, H 11 cm (10⅜ in, 4¼ in). In underglaze blue, a seated lady on terrace with tuft of grass, possibly from fungus, with two children playing beneath a willow. Above-average domestic/export. Courtesy of Parks Canada.

198. *Plates, milk pot, and coffee cup* from *Le Machault* (1760). Qianlong, c. 1755–59. Plate D 23.0 cm (9 in); pot: H 12.0 cm (4⅖ in); cup H 7.6 cm (3 in). Underglaze blue in typical sizes and decorations for the period. Common export. Courtesy of Parks Canada.

199. *Coffee and tea cups with saucers* from *Le Michault* (1760), c. 1755–59. Left to right: coffee cup and saucer; teacup and saucer from the ship. Plate, cup, and saucer similar in decoration to shards from the ship, Qianlong, c. 1745–65. *Michault* shards: Brown ware, coffee cup with handle D 7.5 cm, H 8 cm (2⅞ in, 3¹⁄₁₆ in), saucer D 14 cm, H 2.5 cm (5½ in, 1 in), gold-red tea ware, cup D 7 cm, H 4.5 cm (2¹¹⁄₁₆ in, 1¹¹⁄₁₆ in), saucer D 12 cm, H 2 cm (4¹¹⁄₁₆ in, ¹¹⁄₁₆ in). Average to above-average export. Gold-red landscape plate, private collection. Other gilt floral cup and saucer, courtesy of Parks Canada.

200. *Urn* (one of a pair), Qianlong/Jiaching, c. 1795–1800. H 38.1 cm (15 in). Pistol-handled from a Wedgwood prototype, itself traceable to Swedish and Italian antecedents. Overglaze blue, red and gilt highlight two raised sepia medallions. One side: "L'Urne Mysterieuse" (Paris print, 1973) with profiles of Louis XVI (king of France 1774–92) and Marie Antoinette in space at urn's base; also images of the dauphin and Madame Royale. Opposite side: a temple in trees. The pair has a French-Canadian history (see text and footnotes). Gift of Gertrude, Anna, and Cooper Nott Lansing in memory of their parents. Courtesy of the Albany Institute of History and Art.

201. *Dish*, Qianlong, c. 1750–75. D 12 cm, H 3cm (4¹¹⁄₁₆ in, 1⅛ in). In overglaze polychrome, group on a terrace entertained by a female *pipa* player. Narrow outer border of single honeycombs with wide inner border of eight reserves. Called "highly painted" or "highly colored" ware; continuous with nineteenth-century "mandarin" ware as a style. Fine export. Courtesy of the Peabody Museum, Salem.

202. *Plate*, Qianlong, c. 1740–60. D 28 cm (11 in). In overglaze enamels, a bold shell, cornucopia, and lattic border derived from the West but with no known exact source. Three variants are known, one in blue-and-white or blue-and-white with iron–red (fig. 243), a more attenuated one associated with Spain (fig. 203)

and on examples with Spanish arms, and a similar one with Dutch arms. In the center, a pair of cocks near karst rocks and a peony tree. Above-average export. Courtesy of the Peabody Museum (1980.63.2).

203. Plate, Qianlong, c. 1745–65. D 22.9 (9 in). Overglaze gold with gilt rococo scrollwork and shells. In center, a floral bouquet. The border pattern is associated with Spain for its appearance on a service with Spanish arms. Fine export. Courtesy of the Peabody Museum (1978.21.3).

204. Coffee cup, Qianlong, c. 1790. D and H 6.6 cm (2⅝ in). Handled coffee cup, overglaze enamels in medallion of a deer (Corsica) pursued by a unicorn (England) and lion (Spain), labeled in Spanish with a banner below: HUYE OPROBRIO DEL HUNDO (sic, MUNDO) ("Flee the insults of the world"). Fine Spanish export, perhaps unique. Private collection, Mexico City.

CHAPTER 5

205. Garniture set of five pieces: two beakers, three ovoid vases on a Dutch cupboard (kas), Kangxi, c. 1685–1700, but beakers marked with six-character Chenghua nianhao and ovoid pieces with six-character Jiajing nianhao. Beakers: H 25 cm (9½ in) and H 24.5 cm (9⅜ in). Vases: H 26.5 cm (10¼ in). Underglaze blue, similar beakers separate almost identical ovoid vases, each with two Chinese women "lange lijzen" (Dutch: long Elisa's) and a vase of flowers. Beakers in three sections accentuated by wide waists. Fine domestic/export. Courtesy of the Fries Museum, Leeuwarden (2324, 3179).

206. Flagon, Shunzhi/Kangxi, c. 1645–65. H 23.3 cm, D 12.1 cm (9³⁄₁₆ in, 4¹¹⁄₁₆ in). Spout on rim, long neck, loop handle. Underglaze blue, five sections: 1. neck with stylized tulip and leaf motif, 2. floret-scroll leaf, 3. masque and leaf, 4. lappet-edged band, two landscape vignettes, 5. second masque with floral scrolls. Blend of Western form with Turkish, European, and Chinese decorative motifs. Above-average export. Courtesy of the Ashmolean Museum (1978.792).

207. Chalice, Kangxi, c. 1685–1700. H 14.8 cm, D 9.7 cm (5¾ in, 3¾ in). Modeled on European or English metalwork, over-the-edge cover with double knob finial; small trefoil handles, tapered body, footed base. Underglaze blue tulips similar to Turkish embroidered textile tripartite designs of the middle- to late-seventeenth century and contemporary English earthenware. Fine export. Private collection, the Netherlands.

208. Bowl (covered), Yongzheng/Qianlong, c. 1725–40. Bowl D 40.6 cm, H 31.7 cm (16 in, 12½ in); stand D 55.2 cm (21¾ in). Pointed finial on cover with everted edge; high footed bowl. Overglaze polychrome and gilt, Italianate borders; on cover, each side of bowl and stand: four realistic castles, three from late-seventeenth- and early-eighteenth-century Swedish engravings; bowl 1. Tawastehus Castle, Johann van den Aveelen, engraver, 1710; 2. Nynaes Castle, engraver unknown; stand 3. Laeckoo Castle, Willem Swidde (1669?–1691), engraver. Courtesy of the Metropolitan Museum of Art. Purchase, Joseph Pulitzer Bequest, 1940 (40.133.lab).

209. Stand for bowl in fig. 208. D 55.2 cm, H 7.6 cm (21¹¹⁄₁₆ in, 3 in) (40.133.2).

210. Box with inkwell and sander, Kangxi, c. 1700–1720. H 8.3 cm, D 8.6 cm, W 27.0 cm (3¼ in, 3⅜ in, 10⁹⁄₁₆ in). Footed box, underglaze blue floral-and-leaf motif. Stock Chinese pattern on a Western form. Average export. Courtesy of the Trustees of the British Museum (1949 2-16 2).

211. Figurine, man with monkey, Kangxi, c. 1700–1710. H 30.5 cm (12 in). A molded Westerner seated on a pedestal with a monkey at his knee in overglaze iron-red, green, black, brown with gilt; left hand missing. Possibly similar to the "painted men" listed aboard the Dashwood in 1701 from Amoy. Probably made at Dehua, not far from Amoy. Above-average export. Courtesy of the Victoria and Albert Museum (C.17 1951).

212. Hounds (pair), not identical, Kangxi, c. 1700–1715. OH 16.5 cm, 10.8 cm (6½ in, 4¼ in). Snarling, seated dogs with overglaze brown-spotted coats, red and green floral lappet collars with bells on black ground. Ex. coll. Kitchener. Fine export. Private collection, U.S.A.

213. Fo lion with figures (one of a pair), Kangxi, c. 1700–1710. H 21.3 cm, W 21.0 cm, D 12.7 cm (8⅜ in, 8¼ in, 5 in). In cream-white, mounted couple (the man, Western; the woman, Oriental) on a large lion's back with a small one. Servant with cash (Chinese coin) in hand flanked by two more small lions. Unusual, possibly ironic blend of East and West. In 1774, listed in a Van Cortlandt family inventory. Gift of Miss Charlotte A. Van Cortlandt. Above-average export. Courtesy of Sleepy Hollow Restorations (VC.72.1).

214. Elephant (one of a pair), Kangxi, c. 1700–10. OL 22.2 cm, OH 13.6 cm (8¾ in, 5⅜ in). White elephants are bearers of the Buddha's jewels. Overglaze black lines abstractly simulate wrinkled hide. Above-average export. Private collection, U.S.A.

215. Cup and saucer, Kangxi, c. 1700–20. Cup D 8.9 cm, H 5.1 cm (3½ in, 2 in); saucer D 13.3 cm, H 2.54 cm (5¼ in, 1 in). Molded ("quilted") bamboo, peonies, birds; single honeycomb border. Stock export, now rare. Gift of Mrs. L. P. Dean. Courtesy of the Society for the Preservation of New England Antiquities (1920.137a&b).

216. Chocolate cups (pair, covered), Kangxi, c. 1700–20. H 16.2 cm, OW 12.7 cm (6⅜ in, 5 in). High-domed covers, bracket-shaped double handles with masks highlighted in blue; underglaze blue lappet and leaf border with objects from the scholar's table and artemesia leaves. Example of Western form united with Chinese decoration. Fine blue-and-white. Courtesy of the British Museum (F1578).

217. Bowls (pair), Kangxi/Yongzheng, c. 1720–40. Both D 14.9 cm; left: H 7 cm; right: H 7.3 cm (5⅞ in, 2¾ in, 2⅞ in). Standard design in overglaze gold-red, yellow, green, and blue in peony, daisy and eroded rock with butterfly; brown edges. Typical "sneaker" size. Average polychrome export. Courtesy of Norman Herreshoff.

218. Coffee pot (covered), Japanese, Arita, c. 1680. H 27.5 cm, D (base) 16.5 cm (10¾ in, 6½ in). Tapered body, long loop handle; on opposite side, a low hole to take a metal spout. Metal mount for low-domed cover anticipated by small loop. In underglaze blue, two phoenixes (one perched, one flying) amid peonies and pomegranates; peonies and chrysanthemums on cover. Low-spout models not copied by the Chinese, but Japanese form existed as early as 1680s (compare figs. 155 and 168). Fine export. Courtesy of the

Ashmolean Museum (1978.878).

219. *Porringer* (covered), Kangxi/Yongzheng, c. 1715–25. OW (with handle) 18.3 cm, D 12.8 cm, H 8.7 cm (7³/16 in, 5 in, 3¹/4 in). With a pierced handle, from a Western prototype, probably pewter or silver (except for the Fo lion finial). White with overglaze iron-red, yellow, green, blue, and black, possibly painted in Japan. Courtesy of the Trustees of the British Museum (F944).

220. *Teapots with matching cups*, Kangxi, c. 1710–20. Pots: H 18.7 cm (7²/5 in). Cups with covers H 10.5 cm (4 in). Bamboo-shaped "Fujian" cup handles. "Mirror," underglaze black with worn overglaze gilt. Courtesy of the Trustees of the British Museum (F53, 1923 3-14 193 and 194).

221. *Plate*, Yongzheng/Qianlong, c. 1730–50. D 22.9 cm, H 2.5 cm (9 in, 1 in). Octagonal notched rim; underglaze blue, outer border of lattice, whorls, florets; cavetto border, paired and rayed whorls; peony and floret central design. Average stock design. No. 134 in Elizabeth C. Canby catalogue. An identical plate, owned by Dr. Edward A. Holyoke (1728–1829) of Salem, now at the Essex Institute. Courtesy of Mr. and Mrs. Lewis Rumford II.

222. *Plate*, Yongzheng/Qianlong, c. 1730–40. D 22.8 cm, H 2.8 cm (9 in, 1¹/8 in). Reverse border decoration twice as large as flat edge: underglaze blue peony, willow, and chrysanthemum with stylized chrysanthemum center. First-quality export. No. 305 in Elizabeth C. Canby catalogue. Courtesy of Mr. and Mrs. Lewis Rumford II.

223. *Hot-water dish*, Qianlong, c. 1740–60. D 22. 9 cm, H 4.4 cm (9 in, 1³/4 in). Octagonal notched rim; left handle open for water. Underglaze blue outer border, dotted circles, four polar devices, eight butterflies, whorls, dotted circles; cavetto border, paired and rayed whorls; central islandscape, two-story pagoda with terrace, three figures. Above-average export. Courtesy of Norman Herreshoff.

224. *Cruet set*, Qianlong, c. 1740–50. L 20 cm, H 14.5 cm (7³/4 in, 5¹¹/16 in). Oil and vinegar hexagonal ewers with lids on handled double stand. Underglaze blue scenes of tea production. Stand sides, rare oversize shell and cornucopia border similar but not identical to borders on Rouen faience (compare figs. 202 and 203). First-class export. Courtesy of the Fries Museum, Leeuwarden.

225. *Tureen*, Qianlong, c. 1740–60. H 28.6 cm, OW 25.4 cm (11¹/4 in, 10 in). Metalwork model: high-topped, blossom finial, six paired molded ribs, attached handles; inside near bottom, perforated divider; underglaze blue borders in floral and diaper styles; unusual lappets on cover; on body, ogival-edged lotus-and-scroll border; overglaze gold-red, green, turquoise and white more roughly painted than underglaze blue. From the estate of Emily Verplanck Johnstone (1837–1913) of Staten Island. Above-average export, rare. Courtesy of Mrs. Peter Milliken.

226. *Tureen and stand*, Yongzheng/Qianlong, c. 1730–50. Tureen: H 29.2 cm, OW 35.5 cm (11¹/2 in, 14 in); stand: D 38.1 cm, H 5.1 cm (15 in, 2 in). Metalwork model; high-topped, closely fluted cover (finial replaced) and horizontal narrow bands; bent-leaf handles. Overglaze gold-red, iron-red, orange, blue, brown, green. Fleur-de-lis and paired and rayed whorl borders. Terrace with karst rocks and tree peony; beyond, a cock and hen. Descended in the Otis family of Boston. First-class export. Courtesy of the Society for the Preservation of New England Antiquities (1927.2203a&b).

227. *Dutch junk and plate. Junk*: Yongzheng, c. 1730. H 30.5 cm, L 27.9 cm (12 in, 11 in). Single-masted, three sails, round pagodalike sterncastle, guns in portholes and above Fo lion figurehead, four standing Westerners. Overglaze gold-red, iron-red, blue, green, turquoise, yellow. *Plate*: Qianlong, c. 1756–60. D 22.9 cm (9 in). In cartouche, inscription identifying the Dutch ship *Vryburg*, Capt. Jacob Ryzik, in Canton in 1756. Gilt and gold-red floral and scroll outer border. First-class export. Courtesy of Dr. Wesley Gallup.

228. *Teapot*, Qianlong, c. 1750–75. OW 24.1 cm, H 15.2 cm (9¹/2 in, 6 in). Standard-shaped, large teapot; in black line and enamels, an anonymous ship, flying a British flag. Good export. Courtesy of the Peabody Museum (1975.27.142AB).

229. *Bottle*, Qianlong, c. 1750. H (with top) 24 cm, 9.5 cm sq. (9³/8 in, 3¹¹/16 in sq). Flat with silver top; overglaze gold-red, yellow, and green of birds, peonies, and other flowers; yellow florets on rectangular borders. First-class export. Gift of the estate of Mr. Harry T. Peters, Jr. Courtesy of the Peabody Museum (1982.7.35).

230. *Coffee/chocolate pot*, Qianlong, c. 1750–75. H 24.8 cm, OW 17.8 cm (9³/4 in, 7 in). Dome lid with peach finial, molded spout and handle, pear-shaped. Overglaze iron-red, gold-red, green, black and gilt reserves with Chinese figures indoors and on terrace; dotted circle ground. Fine export. Private collection, U.S.A.

231. *Brownware* (miscellaneous), Yongzheng/Qianlong, c. 1730–50. Left to right: covered bowl H 13 cm, D 11.6 (5¹/16 in, 4¹/2 in); cup H 5.7 cm, D 11.7 cm (2¹/4 in, 4⁵/8 in); teapot H 17 cm, OW 23 cm (6¹¹/16 in, 9 in). Chinese forms with Western quatrefoil, lobed-and-pointed or leaf reserves, also found in overglaze blue, green, and turquoise grounds. Average export. Bowl, gift of T. F. Hunt; pot, gift of Frederick Lamson. Courtesy of the Essex Institute.

232. *Dutch tile and Chinese export borders:*
   a. Dutch tile, late-sixteenth or early-seventeenth century. Underglaze blue except for touches of red on hen's comb and feathers. Corner "ox heads" show stylistic similarities to two plate borders (b) and (c).
   b. Outer border on export porcelain plate, c. 1740. Gilt lacework copied from a Meissen prototype, c. 1725–40. Central decoration of plate shows Dutch ships anchored at Capetown Harbor. After Le Corbeiller, *Patterns*, pl. 33, pp. 84–85.
   c. Cavetto border on export porcelain plate, c. 1735–50, Salem, Mass. Typical inner border on underglaze blue, common in period 1725–75. From a plate at the Peabody Museum. Drawings by Robert Williams.

233. *Shelves of Transitional underglaze blue*, Fries Museum. Courtesy of the Fries Museum, Leeuwarden.

234. *Cup and saucer*, Kangxi, c. 1690–1710. Cup D 5.7 cm, H 3.5 cm (2¹/4 in, 1³/8 in); saucer D 8.9 cm, H 1.9 cm (3¹/2 in, ³/4 in). Fluted; underglaze blue, paneled six-section, three designs of two panels each; early willowware with peony. Average export. In collection of Elizabeth C. Canby (acquired 1849); cup marked No. 132 but not so listed in Canby catalogue. Courtesy of Mr. and Mrs. Lewis Rumford II.

235. *Plate*, Japanese Imari, later Genroku Era, 1688–1703. D 31 cm (12³/16 in). Scalloped rim, fluted border of two reserves and two overglaze enameled panels on a flowered ground. Central flower basket. Common domestic/export. Courtesy of the Museo Nacional del Virreinato, Mexico (54588).

236. *Plate*, Qianlong, c. 1740. D 22.5 cm, H 1.9 cm (8⅞ in, ¾ in). Underglaze blue, outer border of repeat pattern: butterfly, double lozenge, diapered scroll, whorls, feather, floret (four times); cavetto border, paired and rayed whorls; lady with basket on willow trunk; child with fish on right. Brown rim. Fine export. No. 33 in Elizabeth C. Canby catalogue, in Canby family since 1803, possibly earlier. Courtesy of Mr. and Mrs. Lewis Rumford II.

237. *Plate*, Qianlong, c. 1740–50. D 22.8 cm, H 2.54 cm (9 in, 1 in). Overglaze enamels on a pattern usually found in blue-and-white. Brown rim. Listed without a number in the Elizabeth C. Canby catalogue. Courtesy of Mr. and Mrs. Lewis Rumford II.

238. *Cup and saucer*, Kangxi/Yongzheng, c. 1715–30. Cup D 9.3 cm, H 5.3 cm (3⁹/₁₆ in, 2¹/₁₆ in); saucer D 8.9 cm, H 2.2 cm (3½ in, ⅞ in). Swiftly drawn, underglaze blue spotted buck near peony and prunus, karst rock; thin diaper border. Stock pattern, average export, now rare. Gift of Mrs. H. P. Sturgis. Courtesy of the Essex Institute.

239. *Dish*, Kangxi, c. 1700–20. L 19.2 cm (7½ in). Scallop-shaped with ribbing and flat-edge flange. Chinese "Imari" palette. Brought to Canada either by William Woodforde of England, a surgeon's mate, in New Brunswick from 1812, or by his wife's Loyalist family, the Stephen Millers of Massachusetts. Courtesy of the Weldon Collection, University of Kings College, Halifax, (W130).

240. *Charger*, Yongzheng, c. 1720–30. D 39 cm, H 4.6 cm (15²/₅ in, 1²/₅ in). Underglaze blue and overglaze enamels in a plainer variant of the symmetrical Chinese "Imari" style, with two crabs, peonies, and pine; owned by Hugh Cargill of Concord, Mass. (1739–99). Courtesy of the Concord Antiquarian Museum (C-1041).

241. *Charger*, Yongzheng, c. 1720–30. D 41.7 cm, H 4.8 cm (16³/₈ in, 1³/₄ in). Chinese "Imari" palette; two outer borders in alternating quadrant format; cavetto border spaced as outer one; central peonies with karst rock. Descended in the Russell and Gerry families of Marblehead, Mass. Gift from the estate of Mr. and Mrs. Charles Robert Morris by their daughters, Mrs. G. William Helm, Jr., and Mrs. Alan J. Gayer. Courtesy of the Peabody Museum (1438.1).

242. Detail of fig. 241.

243. *Tureen*, Qianlong, c. 1740–60. H 22.8 cm, OW 31.7 cm (9 in, 12½ in). Cover with narrow flattened rim, pointed knob finial, half-circle handles. Underglaze blue, Chinese "Imari"-type, underglaze blue and overglaze iron-red but no gilt; oversize shell border, smaller lattice borders; two fishermen poling rafts with cargo of jars (compare fig. 202). Fine export, rare. Ex. coll. Mr. and Mrs. Bertram Rowland. Courtesy of the Peabody Museum (1977.13.29B).

244. *Charger*, Yongzheng/Qianlong, c. 1730–40. D 34.3 cm, H 3.8 cm (13½ in, 1½ in). Octagonal flattened edge; overglaze blue, green, brown, orange, and touches of gold-red, two water buffalo near banana tree, karst rock, insects, and flowers. Fine export. Bought in England in 1760–63 by Nathaniel Barrell, son-in-law of Jonathan Sayward (1713–97), York, Maine, given to Sayward. Courtesy of the Society for the Preservation of New England Antiquities (1977.403.1).

245. *Plate, tureen, and salt* (same service), Yongzheng/Qianlong, c. 1735–50. Plate D 24.2 cm (8⅝ in); salt H 3.1 cm (1½ in); tureen L 35.5 cm, W 20.3 cm (14 in, 8 in). Metalwork models for notched corners of plate and salt, ribbed tureen. Overglaze enamels. Bequest of Mrs. Sarah J. Schuyler Van Rensselaer. Courtesy of the Newark Museum (25.891-898).

246. *Plates*, Qianlong, c. 1740–60. Left: D 22.9 cm, H 2.2 cm (9 in, ⅞ in); right: D 22.9 cm, H 1.3 cm (9 in, ½ in). Borderless, flattened edges; overglaze gold-red, turquoise, green, orange, and white in landscape with sheep or floral (peonies dominant). Left: brown rim. Owned by Alexander and Elizabeth Schuyler Hamilton (m. 1780), possibly a gift of General Philip Schuyler. Courtesy of the estate of Mrs. John Church Hamilton, on loan to the Museum of the City of New York (L4784.1-4).

247. *Sauceboat and stand*, Qianlong, c. 1750. Boat: OL 19.7 cm, H 5.1 cm (7¾ in, 2 in); stand: OL 18.7 cm, H 1.9 cm (7³/₈ in, ¾ in). European/English metalwork models for scalloped edges, fluted sides, leaf-and-bud base to stand. Evolved Chinese "Imari" palette: underglaze blue, iron-red, gilt plus gold-red, turquoise, green; seated Chinese woman on terrace. Descended in the Van Cortlandt family, the Van Cortlandt Mansion, the Bronx. Courtesy of the National Society of Colonial Dames of the State of New York.

248. *Part of a tea service*, Qianlong, c. 1750. Left to right: milk pot H 12.7 cm, OW 10.2 cm (5 in, 4 in); teacaddy H 14.3 cm, OW 7.6 cm (5⅝ in, 3 in); plate D 20.6 cm, H 4.1 cm (8⅛ in, 1⅝ in); coffee cup D 5.7 cm, H 6.0 cm (2¼ in, 2³/₈ in); tea cup D 7.6 cm, H 6.9 cm (3 in, 2³/₄ in); saucer D 11.7 cm, H 2.5 cm (4⅝ in, 1 in). On plate reverse, a note remains, probably written by its owner, the Providence collector Ann Allen Ives (1810–84), of the Dorr (China trade) family, stating that the set was bought in Surinam in 1757. Fine export. Private collection, U.S.A.

249. *Tureen*, Qianlong, c. 1760–80. H 19.1 cm, OW 26.0 cm (7½ in, 10¼ in). Cover with pomegranate finial, everted lip, boar's-head handles. Overglaze gold-red, iron-red, green, black, and gilt; borders of bamboo and dotted motif; roses, floral sprays in French style. Part of large service associated with Abigail Adams (1744–1818), said to have been purchased in England. Courtesy of Adams National Historic Site.

250. *Plate*, Qianlong, c. 1775, D 22.9 cm, 2.2 cm (9 in, ⅞ in). Overglaze enamels and gilt. An unusually large central rose framed by an inner border of bamboo and roses and modified spearhead outer border. One of eight plates still at the Adams House, also associated with Abigail Adams (see fig. 249). Courtesy of Adams National Historic Site.

251. *Punchbowl*, Qianlong, c. 1760. D 39.3 cm, H 17.8 cm (15½ in, 7 in). Metalwork model, octagonal and ribbed. Overglaze polychrome: four floral and four figural black-outlined panels. Bamboo inner border; individual motif bottom border. Owned by Alexander and Elizabeth Schuyler Hamilton (m. 1780). Gift of Mrs. Anita L. Pearson. Courtesy of the estate of Mrs. John Church Hamilton, on loan to the Museum of the City of New York (39.66).

252. Interior of bowl in fig. 251.

253. Detail of border in fig. 251.

254. Five styles of the so-called "tobacco leaf" pattern, Qianlong, c. 1750–75. Two palettes: left, overglaze gold-red, iron-red, green, brown; right, underglaze blue and other overglaze enamels as shown. Passion flower and undetermined leaf dominate, possibly tobacco. (Design may be a hybrid of East and West by a Western hand; not from a known textile.) Courtesy of Earle D. Vandekar, London.

255. *Soup dish*, Qianlong, c. 1750–75. D 22.9 cm, H 3.8 cm (9 in, 1½ in). Octagonal, notched rim. Underglaze blue, narrow diaper border; four ducks in water scene. Owned by Mary Webb Updegraff (1747–1833) of York, Pennsylvania. Courtesy of Mr. and Mrs. Lewis Rumford II.

256. *Soup dish*, Qianlong, c. 1750–75. D 24.5 cm, H 3 cm (9½ in, 1 in). Slightly foliated rim. Underglaze blue dotted edge; French design of carnation, bell-flower and floral sprays. No mark on base. Courtesy of the Peabody Museum (A8038).

257. *Tureen*, Qianlong, c. 1796. OL 31.7 cm, OW 22.9 cm OH 22.2 cm (12½ in, 9 in, 8¾ in). Double-domed cover with everted lip, strawberry finial, strap handles, flared foot. Overglaze polychrome landscape; wide border with Eight Immortals, cipher DWMC for DeWitt Clinton (1769–1828) and Maria Franklin (1775–1818) (m. 1796). Unique export. Gift of Mrs. James Alexander Miller. Courtesy of the Museum of the City of New York (68.40.lab).

CHAPTER 6

258. *Punch bowl*, Qianlong, c. 1784–85. D 38.7 cm, H 15.9 cm (15¼ in, 6¼ in). Mahogany stand and lid, 46 cm sq, H 17.1 cm (18⅛ in, 6¾ in). Overglaze polychrome border of Greek key in iron-red and gilt, floral swags. Two floral sprays on opposite sides of exterior. Ship appears only on interior (fig. 259), unlike five similar bowls discussed in Mudge, 1981, pp. 130–131, 241. Said to have been brought home by the *Empress of China*, 1785. Gift of Mr. Richard V. Lindabury (69.244a-c). Courtesy of the New Jersey State Museum.

259. Interior of fig. 258. Ship design probably from the British ship *Hall*, shown in the frontispiece engraving in William Hutchinson, *A Treatise on Practical Seamanship* (1777). Banner: JOHN GREEN, EMPRESS OF CHINA, COMMANDER.

260. *Tureen*, Qianlong, c. 1796, H 21.6 cm, L 29.8 cm (8½ in, 11¾ in). Overglaze iron-red strawberry finial and handles; in green, brown, and gilt, figure of Commerce with anchor, left arm extended. Below, scrolled and leaved banner: SPERO ("Hope"). Part of a unique export service (56.550.1). Courtesy of the Henry Francis du Pont Winterthur Museum.

261. Interior, southeast parlor, house of Edward Carrington (1775–1843), built 1810–11, razed 1962. Floor and table jars, bowls, mantle urns, and garniture; porcelains of this quality in Carrington's front hall, other parlors, library, dining room, pantry, and upstairs rooms. Courtesy of the Rhode Island Historical Society.

262. *Urn* (one of a pair on the mantel in fig. 261), Qianlong, c. 1800–10. H 47.6 cm (18¾ in). Overglaze polychrome classical shape with flower handles, sepia vignette, marbelized base. Finial of Chinese woman, restored by an inferior hand. Black borders on shoulder and around vignette, later additions. Original acanthus leaf and gilt-on-blue border at neck. Based on a Western model; two known in "Rose Medallion" (compare figs. 200 and 264). First-class export, rare in its day. Courtesy of the Rhode Island Historical Society (1962-3-349).

263. *Bowl*, Qianlong, c. 1811. D 53.3 cm, H 25.4 cm (21 in, 10 in). Exterior upper border: PRESENTED BY GENERAL JACOB MORTON TO THE CORPORATION OF THE CITY OF NEW YORK, JULY 4, 1812. Foot border: THIS BOWL WAS MADE BY SYNCHONG IN CANTON FUNGMANHI PINXR. Interior border: DRINK DEEP. YOU WILL PRESERVE THE CITY AND ENCOURAGE CANALS. Interior view *"New York from Brooklyn, 1802,"* by William Birch; Samuel Seymour, engraver. Exterior: seals of the U.S. and New York City; unidentified views of ships at anchor, one with an American flag. Unique export. On loan from the City of New York, 1912. Courtesy of the Metropolitan Museum of Art.

264. *Urn* (one of a pair), c. 1803. H 47.6 cm (18¹¹/₁₆ in). On a form identical to the urn in fig. 262, in overglaze enamels, a variant of the English arms of Leslie-Melville, the Earls of Leven and Melville. Arms: Leslie, azure a thistle beneath an imperial crown or quartering Melville, argent on a bend azure (here gules) three buckles or. Crest: a demi-chevalier holding in the hand a dagger (here the arm and dagger only). Two chevaliers hold banners with elements of the American flag. [David, 6th Earl of Leven and Melville, died in 1802. Soon afterward, these urns were probably ordered by his oldest son, Alexander, the 7th Earl. (Alexander's wife, Jane Thornton, was the daughter of John Thornton, a director of the East India Company, and sister of another director.) Alexander's younger brother, William, was killed in the American Revolution in 1777, twenty-five years before the urns were probably made, explaining the use of the American-style banners (compare figs. 200 and 262).] Unique decoration. Private collection, U.S.A. Information courtesy of David S. Howard.

265. Finial of fig. 264, a mourning woman (compare fig. 262, where the woman's nakedness is covered up in the restored or altered finial).

266. Close-up of medallion on fig. 264.

267. *Vase*, Daoguang/Xianfeng, c. 1840–60. H 23.5 cm (9³/₁₆ in). Long neck with three dragons; in relief, scalloped lip and neck base, sloped shoulder, high foot. Overglaze polychrome, four-masted clipper ship, American flag with crew. Floral border on shoulder; on reverse, floral sprays. Possibly unique export. Gift of Frederick S. Colburn. Courtesy of the Art Institute, Chicago (1958.259).

268. *Cup and saucer*, Daoguang, c. 1835. Cup with cover: H 10.2 cm, D 8.9 cm (4 in, 3½ in); saucer: D 12.7 cm, 3.2 cm (5 in, 1¼ in). Underglaze blue and white scene from a drama or narrative: two women, one holding a vase, on narrow raft with large jar; phoenix and moon. Above-average domestic/export. Originally owned by Edward Carrington of Providence. Private collection, U.S.A.

269. *Plates*, left: Tongzhi/Guangxu, c. 1864–1900. D 19 cm, H 2.9 cm (7½ in, 1⅛ in); right: Daoguang, c. 1835. D 19.7 cm, H 2.5 cm (7¾ in, 1 in). Left: cabbage-leaf stock design in overglaze gold-red, green and yellow; on base, four underglaze copper-red bats in polar arrangement. Common domestic/export. Right: overglaze green, white, and blue design in quadrants, stylized lotus and scrolls, butterflies; central chrysanthemum, four *shou* characters in gilt ("long life"); gilt rim. Part of a service owned by Robert Bennett Forbes. Fine domestic/export. Courtesy of the Peabody Museum (1970.278A, 1965.1.491).

270. *Dish*, Daoguang, c. 1820–30. L 26.7 cm, W 22.2 cm, H 3.8 cm (10½ in, 8¾ in, 1½ in). Lozenge-shaped, overglaze scene of Chinese figures in sepia and gilt with no border. From a service owned by Robert Bennett Forbes. Unusual, possibly unique monochrome export. Courtesy of the Peabody Museum.

271. *Soup plate*, Daoguang, c. 1820–30. D 25.4 cm, H 5.1 cm (10 in, 1½ in). Wide outer border in salmon with gilt overscrolls, thin stylized-leaf cavetto border; central medallion: stylized flowers with arrowhead and X border. Owned by Robert Bennett Forbes. Smooth, finely painted; first-class export. Courtesy of the Peabody Museum (A8037).

272. *Dish* (for condiments), Daoguang, c. 1820–40. D 49.0 cm, OH 10.5 cm (19.3 in, 4⅛ in). Five-part, lidded, underglaze blue dish with strawberry finials in "Nanking" design. Variant condiment dishes in blue-and-white or polychrome often have more compartments, may not have lids. Blue-and-white of this quality often more costly than polychrome porcelain. First-class export. Courtesy of the Peabody Museum (A8075).

273. *Vase* (one of a pair), Daoguang, c. 1835. H 43.2 cm, OW 22.2 cm (17 in, 8¾ in). Humped dragon handles, scalloped lip, sloped shoulder and base, high rounded foot; overglaze polychrome lotus and scroll pattern with *shou* and jade gong, one of the Eight Precious Things, on opposite sides in gold-red, green, dark-blue, and white. Decoration slightly off center. Matches right plate in fig. 269. Fine domestic/export. Owned by Robert Bennett Forbes. Courtesy of the Peabody Museum (1965.1.956).

274. *Plate*, Daoguang, c. 1840–50. D 24.5 cm, H 2.4 cm (9⅜ in, ⅞ in). In overglaze green, yellow, blue, gold-orange, brown-pencil, indoor/outdoor view of scholar and his family. In upper right, vase and Chinese characters *Shengxian*, personal name of Chai Shaobing (1616–1670), poet and connoisseur of antiquities. Wide border of four reserves, stylized floral border with gilt rim. First-class domestic/export. Courtesy of the Peabody Museum.

275. *Saucer*, Tongzhi, 1862–74. D 14.5 cm (5¹¹/₁₆ in). Overglaze polychrome, central medallion: in stock pose, Li Taibo (A.D. 701–762), one of two major poets of the Tang dynasty, exponent of freedom in life and verse forms, celebrated friendship and wine (wine jar behind him). Above and below, two Han dynasty figures; top: Zhuge Wuhou, duke of Wuxiang; bottom: Yan Guang, hermit of Mt. Fuchun. "Poetry" on roof and cartouche, uneducated prose. Owned by Augustine Heard, Sr. Above-average domestic/export. Courtesy of the Peabody Museum (A8075).

276. *Cup and cover*, period and mark of Tongzhi, 1862–74; matches saucer in fig. 275.

277. *Tea service* (partial), *bouillon cup*, Xianfeng/Tongzhi, c. 1855–70. White with black-penciled bamboo stands, Chinese characters. Set made for owner, Catherine Van Rensselaer Bonney (1817–90), teacher in China, 1856–71; translator from the Chinese: Teapot cover, Chinese proverbs; top, names of eighteen Chinese provinces; left side, Chinese cities; right side, America, China, England, France. (Teapot lid, deep necked, holds in place while pouring.) Milk pot, plates and saucers, Chinese proverbs. Cup fronts, New Year greetings. Bouillon cup with strawberry finial from another service. In Chinese characters, the imperial dynasties. Above-average export. Courtesy of Historic Cherry Hill, Albany (1681).

278. *Toilet set*, Xianfeng/Tongzhi, c. 1855–70. "Highly painted," "Rose Mandarin" ware: basin, covered bottle, commode, brush box, and soap dish. Probably owned by Catherine Van Rensselaer Bonney. Common export. Courtesy of Historic Cherry Hill, Albany.

279. *Plates*, Daoguang, c. 1835–50. Left: D 21.6 cm, H 3.2 cm (8½ in,

1¼ in); right: D 20.3 cm, H 2.2 cm (8 in, ⅞ in). Left: black ground with polychrome floral pattern, worn gilt rim; on reverse, six-character mark of Qianlong (1736–95) in red-orange, three bats on rim. Right: white ground with flowers, birds and insects, gilt rim. Fine domestic/export. Courtesy of the Peabody Museum (1316.1, 1965.1.477).

280. *Greenware* (not a set), Daoguang/Xianfeng, c. 1845–55. Shaped dish (nappie): left D 26.7 cm, W 24.1 cm, H 5.1 cm (10½ in, 9½ in, 2 in). Can and cups, left to right: D 6.3 cm, 8.3 cm, 9.8 cm, 11.4 cm (2½ in, 3¼ in, 3⅞ in, 4½ in); capacities: ½ C, ⅔ C, ¾ C, 1 C. Nappie: orange and gilt handle, overglaze green ground, exotic birds on lemon tree, insects, flowers; similar decoration on cups. Owned by Robert Bennett Forbes. Above-average export. Courtesy of the Peabody Museum (1965.1.513).

281. *Platter with strainer*, Jiaqing, c. 1810. D 45.0 cm, H 6 cm (17¹¹/₁₆ in, 2⅜ in). Fluted edge with flat, perforated strainer; overglaze floral sprays, iron-red and gilt chain borders. Fine export. Courtesy of the Peabody Museum, Salem (A8076).

282. *Candlesticks* (pair), Daoguang, c. 1820–30. H 17.8 cm, D (base) 8.3 cm (7 in, 3¼ in). Underglaze blue "Canton" ware, fringed and scalloped border. Average-quality export, now rare. Courtesy of Norman Herreshoff.

283. *"Canton" ware* (not a set), Daoguang, c. 1825–35. Left to right: tile 9.5 cm square (3¾ in); dish L 25.4 cm, W 21.3 cm, H 5.1 cm (10 in, 8⅜ in, 2 in); teacup D 8.3 cm, H 6.4 cm (3¼ in, 2½ in); coffee cup D and H 5.7 cm (2¼ in). Underglaze blue, willow pattern. All owned by Robert Bennett Forbes. Common export. Courtesy of the Peabody Museum (1965.1.3121, 1965.1.690, 1965.1.620).

284. *Plate*, Daoguang, c. 1825–50. D 22.8 cm (9 in). Underglaze blue, broad border with three prunus clusters spaced evenly on inner and outer edges. In center, a basket with flowers. Common export. Private collection, Mexico City.

285. *Shards*, the padre's house, Old Plaza Church, downtown Los Angeles, c. 1819–21. "Canton" ware, "Four Seasons" (see fig. 303), and unidentified polychromes recovered from same pit; report in progress. Courtesy of the Northridge Archaeological Research Center, Northridge, California, and El Pueblo de Los Angeles State Historic Park.

286. *Jar*, Jiaqing/Daoguang, c. 1815–30. H 66.0 cm (25⅞ in). Medium dome lid with pointed finial. Underglaze blue Chinese landscape with pagodas and figures. Deep shoulder border of lobed reserves, alternately blue and fishroe backgrounds with flowers and leaves, joined by double-cash motifs with splayed stylized feathers below. Finely wrought brass neck band and lock. Spanish California, with its Mexican tastes, probably had more such jars than New England; export ware was brought to either area by the same shippers. First-class domestic/export. Courtesy of the Essex Institute, Salem (102, 237).

287. *Plate*, Daoguang, c. 1830. D 21.2 cm, H 1.5 cm (8¼ in, ⅗ in). Overglaze polychromes: asymmetrical outer border with karst rock, birds and butterflies on prunus; inner border, lime-green and gilt *ruyi*; in center, floral and fruit bouquet with blue ribbon; gilt rim. Part of service made for Frederick Hall Bradlee and Lucretia Wainwright of Boston (m. 1831). Fine export. Courtesy of the Peabody Museum (E52, 252).

288. *Plate*, Daoguang, c. 1820–30. D 24.1 cm, H 2.5 cm (9½ in, 1 in).

In overglaze salmon, sepia, dark brown, and gilt; broad border in Empire style, four legendary Chinese "Auspicious Figures" with composite emblems of the "Hundred Antiquities" (associated with the Eight Immortals, Buddhism, or Taoism). Also known in polychrome. Monogram in gilt NPH for Nathaniel Perez Hamlen, a Boston ship captain in the mid-nineteenth-century China trade. Fine export. Courtesy of a descendant, Mr. Devlen Hamlen.

289. *Plate*, Daoguang, c. 1825–50. D 25 cm (9⁴/5 in). Overglaze enamels, yellow border with tightly scrolled green and white stems, four reserves of flowers and birds and four peonies. In center, two pheasants and three butterflies in a garden. Fine export. Courtesy of the Peabody Museum (Porter No. 21).

290. *Dish* (covered), Daoguang, c. 1830. Left: D 23.0 cm, W 20.4 cm, H (with cover) 13 cm (9 in, 8 in, 5¹/16 in). Low, sloped lid with bamboo handle; overglaze sepia and gilt birds, butterflies, flowers, and fruits ("bbff"). Courtesy of the Peabody Museum (E52, 521).

291. *Plate and cup*, Daoguang, c. 1830–50. Plate: D 24.1 cm, H 3.2 cm (9¹/2 in, 1¹/4 in); cup: D 6.6 cm, H 5.7 cm (2⁵/8 in, 2¹/4 in). Concave, flattened edge; overglaze purple, yellow, green, iron-red: six scalloped reserves with figures (two sets of each design); central floral medallion. Owned by Robert Bennett Forbes. Above-average export. Courtesy of the Peabody Museum (1967.1.146, 1967.1.47).

292. *Plate* (reconstructed), Daoguang, c. 1825. (P297-307-22), the Cooper-Molera Adobe, Monterey. Underglaze blue, white areas on wide border, loosely drawn basket of one of the Eight Immortals. Rough domestic/export. Courtesy of the California Department of Parks and Recreation (CDPR).

293. *Plate* (reconstructed), Daoguang, c. 1825. (P297-371-9), the same site as fig. 292. On edgeless plate, underglaze blue and copper-red, birds on prunus. Identical design on sale in Jingdezhen antique shop in 1982. Rough domestic/export. Courtesy of CDPR.

294. *Shard* (plate detail), Daoguang, c. 1825. (P297-371-10); same site as figs. 292 and 293. In underglaze blue and copper-red, close-up of phoenix. Rough domestic/export. Courtesy of CDPR.

295. *Cup and plate shards*, Daoguang, c. 1825–35. (P404-6-319, P297-371-6); cup from the Wrightington Adobe Site, Old Town, San Diego, plate from same site as figs. 292 through 294. Underglaze blue abstracted Arabic script and design. Rough domestic/export. Courtesy of CDPR.

296. *Platter shards*, Daoguang, c. 1830–40. (P297-414-81), the same site as figs 292 through 295. Underglaze blue "Canton" ware. Average export. Courtesy of CDPR.

297. *Plate shards*, Daoguang, c. 1825–40. (P297-414-44), the same site as figs 292 through 296. Underglaze blue "Canton" ware. Rough export. Courtesy of CDPR.

298. *Pitchers*, Daoguang, c. 1825–50. Clockwise from top left: H 25 cm, 22 cm, 24 cm, 13.8 cm, 16.2 cm, 13 cm (9³/4 in, 8⁵/8 in, 9³/8 in, 5³/8 in, 6³/8 in, 5 in). Overglaze polychrome: upper left, loop handle, large spout "Mandarin" pattern, shape from an American ceramic designer, Thomas Tucker; rear center, octagonal, gilt-molded spout, below "H M Sowry M Floury" in gilt, angled handle, "Rose Medallion"; remaining three, also octagonal "Mandarin," shape popular in contemporary ironstone. Courtesy of Mrs. Cleveland Alma Porter and the Peabody Museum (E68, 863).

299. *Cup and saucer, dish, teapot. Cup and saucer:* Daoguang/

Xianfeng, c. 1850–70. Cup H 6.9 cm, D 6.4 cm (2³/4 in, 2¹/2 in). Overglaze green and gilt ground to four reserves (compare fig. 280); saucer D 10.8 cm, H 2.5 cm (4¹/4 in, 1 in). *Dish*: Daoguang, c. 1830. D 24.8 cm, H 4.4 cm (9³/4 in, 1³/4 in). "Mandarin" pattern with unusual border. *Pot*: Daoguang/Xianfeng, c. 1850–70. H 12.3 cm, OW 19.05 cm (4⁷/8 in, 7¹/2 in). Earlier form with later flattened finial, dragon above stylized waves (a design also in underglaze blue and polychrome as popular as rose wares). Private collection, U.S.A.; teapot, courtesy of Norman Herreshoff.

300. *Cups and saucer* (from the same service), Daoguang, c. 1825–50. Saucer: D 15.9 cm, H 3.8 cm (6¹/4 in, 1¹/2 in); cups left to right: custard cup D 7.6 cm, H (with lid) 8.9 cm (3 in, 3¹/2 in); breakfast cup D 10.5 cm, H 7.1 cm (4¹/8 in, 2¹³/16 in); teacup D 9.5 cm, H 6 cm (3³/4 in, 2³/8 in); teacup D 8.3 cm, H 6.6 cm (3¹/4 in, 2⁵/8 in). Variety of cup forms within one service. Overglaze polychromes: basket with loose bird/butterfly/fruit/flower ("bbff"); tighter border with same motifs plus emblems. Owned by Edward Carrington of Providence. Stock pattern, above-average export. Private collection, U.S.A.

301. *Plate*, Xianfeng/Tongzhi, c. 1850–75. D 25.4 cm, H 3.0 cm (10 in, 1³/16 in). Swiftly drawn underglaze blue and copper-red carp among abstract waterweeds. Rough, common domestic/export for post-1850 overseas Chinese from Canton area on West Coast and inland. Pattern still popular in China today. Author's collection.

302. *Plate*, Daoguang/Xianfeng, c. 1820–60. D 28.3 cm (11¹/8 in). Underglaze blue and copper-red carp in waterweeds; quality prototype to fig. 301. Above-average domestic/export. Courtesy of the Victoria and Albert Museum (1798–1876).

303. *Overseas Chinese ware*, c. 1850–1920. Imported by Chinese immigrants to the United States. A: "Four Seasons" light green-glazed white porcelain, glaze rather thick and quickly painted with overglaze prunus, peony, lotus, and chrysanthemum (representing the four seasons) and a peach (longevity) in the center. Found in five forms: large serving bowls, small bowls or cups (D 10.6 cm, 4¹/8 in), serving plates/dishes in several sizes, wine cups, and spoons; the larger pieces with red marks stamped on the base, often the mystic knot (one of the eight Buddhist emblems, see Appendix A, fig. 384). B. "Three Circles and Dragonfly" stoneware rice bowls in underglaze dark blue or green-gray; thick clear glaze; outer border of four motifs (counterclockwise): three circles, Chinese character "dragonfly," waterweeds with five large leaves, and a flowering plant with four wide leaves. Drawings by Paul G. Chace, archaeologist, Escondido, Calif.

304. *Overseas Chinese ware*, c. 1850–70. Underglaze blue twin Chinese characters *shuang xi* ("double happiness") appearing on rice bowls found in early Western work camps (railroad and gold mining), but not in urban settlements. Its limited appearance, not yet fully understood, is possibly due to radical changes during the Punti-Hakka Wars, 1856–68. Drawing by Gena R. Van Camp. Courtesy of Paul G. Chace, archaeologist, Escondido, Calif.

305. *Plate*, Qianlong, c. 1750–75. D 21.6 cm, H 2.5 cm (8¹/2 in, 1 in). Octagonal notched rim, four narrow reserves on iron-red and gilt geometric ground; cavetto border, fleur-de-lis; one of several popular patterns: peacock pair on rocks amid tree peony. Also occurs on round dishes; other samples (some platters) now in Ottawa, Boston, Williamsburg, and Charleston, S.C.; this one originally

from Wilmington, Delaware; No. 281 in Elizabeth C. Canby catalogue. Fine export. Courtesy of Mr. and Mrs. Lewis Rumford II.

306. *Plate*, Guangxu, c. 1875–1900. D 25 cm, H 2.5 (9¾ in, 1 in). Underglaze mark on base: *yu* ("jade"). Close-scalloped edge, underglaze blue, four pairs of reserves on diaper border; in center, quadrant design of vases on stands with figures on sides; between them, four birds in fruit trees; medallion with finger citron, two other fruits. Owned by Edward Black Greenshields (b. 1850) of Montreal. Unusual, fine export. Courtesy of Elizabeth Collard.

307. *Tureen and stand*, Jiaqing, c. 1790–1810. Tureen, OL 19.7 cm, H 17.1 cm (7¾ in, 6¾ in); tray L 21.6 cm, W 15.2 cm, H 9 cm (8½ in, 6 in, ⅞ in). Arms vary from the arms of Mackenzie of Seaforth (the only Mackenzie arms): azure, a stag's head cabossed or; crest, a mountain inflamed proper; supporters, two savages wreathed about the loins and head with laurel, each holding in his exterior hand a baton or club erect and inflamed, all proper; motto: LUCEO NON URO ("I shine, not burn"). Often associated with Sir Alexander Mackenzie (1764–1820), but service probably made for his first cousin, Roderick McKenzie [sic] (1761?–1844), of Terrebonne; both men were prosperous fur traders. Courtesy of the Canadiana Department, Royal Ontario Museum, Toronto (962.193.21a-c).

308. *Plate*, Qianlong/Jiaqing, c. 1790–1800. D 24.8 cm (9¾ in). Underglaze blue "Nanking" border, unidentified coat of arms: may or may not be Canadian, not of the Hudson Bay or the North West Company; not a national emblem; probably an independent trading company. Above-average export. Bequest of Mrs. J. Insley Blair. Courtesy of the New York Historical Society (1952.125).

309. Detail of fig. 308. Unidentified arms. Quarterly field, azure and gules: mink, salmon, crayfish, whale. Crest: ship on world. Figures of Commerce and Indian with bow and beaver. Motto: COMMERCIO LIBERALI CRESCUIUS (garbled, "May free trade increase").

310. *Vase* (one of a pair), Daoguang, c. 1840–50. H 63.5 cm (25 in). Wide flaring lip, ovoid body, long-billed duck handles; overglaze gold-red and polychrome ten panels of Chinese figures (three on front and back, two on each side); in background symbols of gentleman-scholar, floral sprays. First-class export. Gift of Mrs. Richard S. Russell. Courtesy of the Essex Institute (123,001).

311. *Assorted "Rose" ware*, Xianfeng/Tongzhi, 1856–70. Pair of vases, punch bowl (one of two), two sets of nesting boxes in "Rose Medallion"; two mugs in "Mandarin." Associated with Catherine Van Rensselaer Bonney of Albany, in China 1856–71. Interchangeable with contemporary imports on the west coast of Canada, the United States, and Mexico. Courtesy of Historic Cherry Hill, Albany.

CHAPTER 7

312. *Tea set* (partial), Qianlong/Jiaqing, c. 1790–1810. Coffee/chocolate pot: H 25 cm, OW 21.5 cm (9¾ in, 8⅜ in); teapot H 14.4 cm, OW 24 cm (5⅝ in, 9⅜ in); teacup D 9 cm, H 6.4 cm (3½ in, 2½ in), saucer D 14.3 (5⅝ in), sugarbowl H 13.8 cm, OW 15 cm (5⅜ in, 5⅞ in), milk pot OH 13.6 cm, OL 17.5 cm (5¼ in, 6¾ in). Typical late-eighteenth-, early-19th-century forms. Overglaze sepia, dark brown, and gilt floral swags with large and small chain borders; unidentified sepia landscape vignette. Gift of Miss Miriam Shaw

and Francis Shaw, Jr. Courtesy of the Essex Institute.

313. *Tea set* (partial), Jiaqing, c. 1802. Coffee/chocolate pot: OH 24.8 cm, OW 23.5 cm (9¾ in, 9¼ in); teapot OH 15.2 cm, OW 24.1 cm (6 in, 9½ in); cup D 9.2 cm, H 6 cm (3⅝ in, 2⅜ in); saucer D 14 cm, H 3.5 cm (5½ in, 1⅜ in); plate D 24.1 cm, H 2.2 cm (9½ in, ⅞ in). Overglaze sepia, black and gilt, gift to Elizabeth Roberts and James Canby of Wilmington, Delaware (m. 1803). (Their son, Samuel, married Elizabeth Clifford in 1832, and this ware, with others (see fig. 321), descended in the family). No. 66 in Elizabeth C. Canby catalogue. Courtesy of Mr. and Mrs. Lewis Rumford II.

314. Detail of landscape vignette in fig. 313, possibly a Philadelphia residence on the Schuylkill River.

315. *Milk pot* (part of a tea service), Qianlong, c. 1790. H 14.6 cm, OW 10.8 cm (5¾ in, 4¼ in). Bellied body, crossed strap handles ending in fern leaves, strawberry finial. Clear glaze on white, overglaze gilt. Part of a tea service made for John Adams, bearing his monogram. Fine export. Courtesy of the Adams Historic Site.

316. Detail of eagle with JA in fig. 315.

317. *Monteith*, Qianlong/Jiaqing, c. 1790–1800. OL 30.5 cm, OW 17.1 cm, OH 10.2 cm (12 in, 6¾ in, 4 in). Wave-shaped rim, plain handles. Overglaze black, sepia, and gilt; unidentified pastoral vignette. Fine export, rare. Gift of Mrs. H. P. Sturgis. Courtesy of the Essex Institute (557).

318. *Condiment set and covered dish*, Qianlong/Jiaqing, c. 1790–1800. Left: OL 36.5 cm, H 18.4 cm (14⅜ in, 7¼ in); right: OL 31.7 cm, H 13.9 cm (12½ in, 5½ in). Probably both modeled on metalwork; condiment set: pierced latticed borders in the style of Meissen (1764–73), nine-piece with six scalloped shells; dish: ribbed, scalloped-rim, strap handles. Overglaze blue and gilt, urn with flowers, blue floral swag and entwined gilt chain borders. Fine export. Originally bought by John Brown (1736–1803). Gift of Agnes Herreshoff. Courtesy of the Rhode Island Historical Society (1958.9.23).

319. *Urns* (pair), Jiaqing, c. 1800. H 44.4 cm, base 10.2 cm sq. (17½ in, 4 in sq.). Molded ovoid shapes on square pedestals with high-domed, perforated tops; elongated Greek key handles. Overglaze blue and gilt leaves, swags and jewel-like bands. Associated with the Montgomery family of Philadelphia. First-class export, unique. Gift of Mrs. Angus W. Morrison in memory of her mother. Courtesy of Gunston Hall, the National Society of the Colonial Dames of America (G-174 (1-4)).

320. *Cups* (pair), Jiaqing, c. 1800. H c. 24.1 cm (c. 9½ in). Ovoid bodies on bell-shaped bases, covers with flattened edge, loop handles, Overglaze gold-red flowers, lime-green leaves, gilt. Pseudo-armorial mantle with monogram TSS for descendant of Isaac Sears (1730–86), early Boston merchant in the U.S.-China trade. Fine export. Courtesy of Elizabeth and Matthew Sharpe.

321. *Garniture set*, Qianlong/Jiaqing, c. 1802. H (ovoids) 29.5 cm, H (beakers) 23.5 cm (11⅝ in, 9¼ in). Three ovoid pieces with covers and Fo-lion finials, two beakers. Underglaze blue and overglaze gilt: "best Nanking" ware with same riverscape painted to fit shape of object. In Canby family since 1803 and possibly earlier (compare fig. 313). No. 96 in Elizabeth C. Canby catalogue. Fine export. Courtesy of Mr. and Mrs. Lewis Rumford II.

322. Detail of an ovoid piece in fig. 321.

323. *Vase* (one of a pair), Qianlong/Jiaqing, c. 1790–1810. H 49.5 cm,

OW 19.7 cm (19½ in, 7¾ in). Molded, vertically indented ovoid shape, cover with everted lip, "cane basket" ground in Meissen style with lobed and pointed reserves, Chinese figure handles. Overglaze iron-red, blue, black, sepia, and gilt; sepia landscapes from European prints. First-class export, rare. Owned by Edward Carrington. Private collection, U.S.A.

324. Handle to vase in fig. 323.

325. *Goblets* (pair), Qianlong/Jiaqing, c. 1795–1812. H 13.9 cm, D (top), 7.6 cm, D (base) 6.2 cm (5½ in, 3 in, 2⁷⁄₁₆ in). Band at bowl base dividing stem from cup. Overglaze blue, iron-red, gold-red, green, brown, black, and gilt. Eagle identical to engraved ship on the 1803 ownership certificate of the New York ship *Elizabeth*, standard for many ships. Bequest of Hope Brown Russell. Courtesy of Museum of Art, Rhode Island School of Design (09.222, 09.223).

326. *Bowl*, Jiaqing, c. 1800–15. H 12.4 cm, D 25.4 cm (4⅞ in, 10 in). Fluted sides and base with scalloped rim, tall stem, based on a metalwork model. Overglaze blue, green, and gilt in French or Swiss cornflower design. Fine export, rare. Part of a service owned by the Middleton family of Charleston, S.C. Private collection, U.S.A.

327. Detail of decoration in fig. 326.

328. *Tea and dinner service* (partial); platter, leaf-shaped dish, covered jug, Daoguang, c. 1825–35. Platter L 43.0 cm, W 38.0 cm (16⅞ in, 14⅞ in); leaf-shaped dish OL 18.0 cm, OW 14.0 cm (7 in, 5½ in); jug H 25.0 cm, OW 23.5 cm (9¾ in, 9³⁄₁₆ in); teapot H 16.5 cm, OW 27.5 cm (6½ in, 10¾ in); sugarbowl H (with lid) 12.0 cm, OL 14.6 cm (4¹¹⁄₁₆ in, 5¹¹⁄₁₆ in); slopbowl H 7.7 cm, D 17.5 cm (3 in, 6¾ in); milk pot OH 9 cm, OL 17.5 cm (3½ in, 6¾ in); breakfast cup D 11.2 cm (4⅜ in); teacup D 9.8 cm (3¾ in). Overglaze salmon, black, sepia, and gilt in French Empire-style border. Medallion on tea pieces with cypher DAP for David A. Pingree (1795–1863), gift of Mrs. John F. Fulton; platter and leaf dish, gift of Mr. Stephen Wheatland; jug with HMB in medallion, gift of Hope W. (Mrs. Francis) Brown. First-class export. Courtesy of the Essex Institute (134, 318, 321, 327–330; 135,337).

329. *Dinner service pieces*, Daoguang, c. 1825–35. Tureen OH 36.2 cm, OL. 35.6 cm (14¼ in, 14 in); sauceboat (with stand) H 13.9 cm, OL 18.4 cm (5½ in, 7¼ in); hot water covered dish H 16.5 cm, OW 22.9 cm (6½ in, 9 in); egg cups H 6.7 cm (2⅝ in). Water buffalo tureen, Chinese-inspired; others, Western in shape; overglaze iron-red, gold-red, salmon, brown, green, gilt; sepia birds in reserves. First-class export. Originally owned by the Forbes family of New York but sold at auction there in 1848 without a monogram. Courtesy of the Rhode Island Historical Society (1975.23.1.26).

330. *Coffee and teapots*, Daoguang/Xianfeng/Tongzhi, c. 1835–70. Left to right by rows, H only: (back row) 25 cm, 24.5 cm, 23 cm (9¾ in, 9⁹⁄₁₆ in, 9 in); (front row) 9.5 cm, 12 cm, 8.5 cm (3¹¹⁄₁₆ in, 4¹¹⁄₁₆ in, 3¼ in). Footed coffeepot in middle back row; cover's deep shaft keeps it in place when pouring. "Mandarin" decoration on pieces c. pre-1850; "Medallion" (with reserves) c. post-1850 (two facing coffeepots). Above-average export. Courtesy of Mrs. Alma Cleveland Porter.

331. *Ewers* (pair), Daoguang, c. 1830–1850. OH 26.8 cm (10¾ in). European silver models for molded, ribbed, and banded bodies on high, bell-shaped bases, scalloped rim, strap handles ending in fern leaves. Overglaze gold-red, green, brown, and gilt: grape and leaf all-over design; in front on one a Chinese landscape vignette, on the other a floral spray. Fine export. Owned by the Cadwalader family of Philadelphia.

332. *Lamp base*, Daoguang, c. 1850, H 20.6 cm, OW 12.4 cm (8⅛ in, 4⅞ in). Hexagonal molded body. Underglaze blue borders of *ruyi*, diaper, prunus, and stylized wave on knobbed areas, plantain leaves with dotted arrows on shaft, Chinese narratives or dramas on well and base. Above-average export. Courtesy of the Peabody Museum.

333. *Seat*, Daoguang, 1850. H 46.2 cm, OD 38.1 cm (18 in, 15 in). Barrel-shaped with imitation brass nails. Overglaze gold-red, polychrome and gilt deep borders of birds, butterflies, fruit, and flowers; central scene possibly from a drama; upper center, perforated double cash motif; crest of Manigault arms with Indian transformed to an aborigine with ostrich feathers; initials LM backward. Bought October 1, 1850, in Canton by Louis Manigault. Fine export. Courtesy of the Rev. Emmet Gribbin.

334. Detail of reverse of fig. 333. Panel above cash in Chinese: "*man-yi-gou*," phonetic spelling of Manigault from part of French tricolor flown in Canton on special occasions by Louis Manigault.

335. *Vase* (one of a pair), Xianfeng, c. 1855–60. H 87 cm (34¼ in). Scalloped rim, fluted base; each handle, two pairs of facing Fo lions; raised dragons between neck and body reserves; overglaze gold-red, polychrome and gilt "Mandarin" ware. Probably bought in 1858 by Admiral Samuel Francis du Pont. Above-average export for period. Gift of Mrs. Rodney Layton. Courtesy of the Winterthur Museum (65.96.1G).

336. *Tureen*, Tongzhi, c. 1865. L 33 cm, W 29 cm, H 17 cm (12⅞ in, 11⅜ in, 6¹¹⁄₁₆ in). Duck-shaped, cover overlaps base beneath neck and tail, body incised, metal handles with gilt boss in center, scroll feet. Overglaze gold-red, black, green, yellow, and gilt, stylized waves with lotus. First-class export. Courtesy of Richard R. Forster III.

337. *Dishes* (obverse, reverse), Daoguang, c. 1825–35. D 25.4 cm, H 6.4 cm (10 in, 2½ in). Scalloped, fluted. Underglaze blue with "Canton" border: large network, scalloped inner line, right side willow and pagoda landscape; reverse, three underglaze blue floral sprays. Common export, "pudding dishes" in dinner services. The Van Cortlandt Mansion Museum, the Bronx. Courtesy of the National Society of Colonial Dames of the State of New York.

338. *Plate*, Daoguang, c. 1800. D 24.4 cm, H 2.5 cm (9⅝ in, 1 in). Octagonal, notched. Underglaze blue with gilt, "best Nanking"; border of lattice, spear and dumbbell, cavetto border with three reserves of emblems; right side two-story pagoda with moon gate, figure on bridge with parasol in foreground. (This landscape and cavetto border are invariably paired, indicating a pattern-book source.) Monogram TADP for Thomas and Anna Dummer Perkins, m. 1801, called the "Tadpole china" by family aunts, the Misses Loring. Fine export. Courtesy of Devlen Hamlen.

339. *Tureen*, Qianlong, c. 1780. L 30.3 cm (12 in). Underglaze blue, "Nanking" ware owned by the grandmother of Henry David Thoreau, Jane Burns Thoreau (m. 1781, d. 1796/97), above-average export. Courtesy of the Concord Antiquarian Society, Concord, Mass (C-344).

340. *Stand* to tureen in fig. 339 (C-345).

341. *Pattypan*, Jiaqing/Daoguang, c. 1815–30. D 12.9 cm, H 5 cm (5⅞ in, 2 in). Thick, crimped ("pie-crust") rim, sloped sides. Underglaze blue four-part border with spearhead innermost; quadrant of floral sprays with ribbons. Common export. The Van Corlandt Mansion Museum, the Bronx. Courtesy of the National Society of Colonial Dames of the State of New York.

342. Examples of "FitzHugh" overglaze polychromes except where noted. Jiaqing/Daoguang, c. 1800–50. Clockwise from upper left: blue and gilt plate, c. 1840–50, SHN for Sylvia Hathaway Nye of Acushnet, Mass., gilt of Miss Sylvia H. Knowles; sepia dish, c. 1820–35 from a service for the Henleys of Philadelphia; gilt dish from only known gilt FitzHugh, c. 1800–15, anonymous loan; orange plate, c. 1810–30, Mary Russell Perkins Estate; underglaze blue soup dish, black JWP for James William Paige, senior partner in Boston China trade firm, c. 1833, gift of Mrs. Reginald Foster; green and gilt plate, crest and motto of Rawsons, part of private English firm at Canton, c. 1820, private collection; yellow, iron-red and gilt plate, blank center, c. 1800–20, private collection; black and gilt teapot, ASC may refer to Bristol, Rhode Island, family, anonymous loan; blue and gilt saucer, c. 1820–30, gift of Mr. and Mrs. Roland B. Hammond. Courtesy of the Peabody Museum.

343. *Cup and saucer*. Qianlong/Jiaqing, c. 1790–1800. Cup D 6.9 cm, H 6.5 cm (2¹¹⁄₁₆ in, 2½ in), capacity 1/2 C; saucer D 14.2 cm, H 3.2 cm (5½ in, 1⅛ in). Overglaze enamels: 1782 U.S. seal; floral swags from blue and gilt band on cavetto border; outer border, entwined gilt leaf and V or dot chains on scalloped blue ground. Identical to one made for Moses Brown (1738–1836) of Providence at the National Museum of History. First-class export. Gift of Mr. Harry T. Peters. Courtesy of the Peabody Museum (1975.27.183AB).

344. Detail of the U.S. seal in fig. 343.

345. *Coffee/chocolate pot*, Qianlong, c. 1790. H 22.9 cm, OW 15.9 cm (9 in, 6¼ in). Pear shape, loop handle, strawberry finial, molded spout. Overglaze enamels: the emblem of the Society for the Cincinnati, composed of French and American officers who served together in the Revolution; Major General Henry Knox (1750–1809), founder. In gilt below insignia, HKL for Henry and Lucy Knox. Bought by Samuel Shaw, Knox's former aide, supercargo on the *Empress of China* and first U.S. consul at Guangzhou (1786–99). Originally with a stand from a set of 150 pieces. First-class export. Gift of de Lancey Kountze, B.A., Yale, 1899. Courtesy of the Yale University Art Gallery (1939.69).

346. *Plates*, Jiaqing/Daoguang, c. 1825–35. Right: D 24.8 cm, H 3.2 cm (9¾ in, 1¼ in); left: soup D 24.4 cm, H 3.8 cm (9⅝ in, 1½ in). Right: outer and inner borders in overglaze iron-red, beige, and gilt. Eagle design from an earlier model (1800–10) with slight variations (compare Mudge, 1981, figs. 84b and 85). Presented by the Chinese government to John C. Calhoun (1782–1850), vice president under John Quincy Adams and Andrew Jackson (1825–37). Left: grape, leaf, tendril outer border in gold-red, brown, and gilt. Pseudo-armorial with eagle crest of Thomas Ap Catesby Jones (1790–1858) and Mary Walker Carter (m. 1823); CMJ, their combined initials. Jones was naval commander in the Pacific. Both: first-class export. Courtesy of Dr. Wesley Gallup.

347. Close-up of typical eagle pattern, c. 1810–20. Probably derived from a ship document. Overglaze enamels: a spread-winged eagle

with a banner in its beak perches on a cannon with horizontal pikes, spears, and U.S. flags to right and left. The grape-and-leaf border is only one of several in which this type of eagle appears. Finely painted. Courtesy of Dr. Wesley Gallup.

348. *Dish*, Jiaqing, c. 1820. D 28.3, H 12.7 cm (11⅛ in, 5 in). Heavy, circular, straight-sided. Overglaze enamels: two scenes of Westerners in eighteenth-century dress from an unidentified print. "FitzHugh" inner border in iron-red. Inside bottom, a brown eagle with striped shield clasps a banner reading E PLURIBUS UNUM (a spread-winged variant of the U.S. seal eagle, compare figs. 343 and 349). Surrounding it, four butterflies in iron-red and gold. Special-order American export, possibly unique. Courtesy of the Edison Institute, the Henry Ford Museum, and Greenfield Village (55.33.10).

349. *Platter*, Jiaqing, c. 1810–20. L 43.2 cm, W 33.7 cm (17 in, 13¼ in). "Well and tree" molded server for meat and gravy, tab feet. Overglaze orange "FitzHugh" pattern, spread-winged eagle with striped shield (compare fig. 348). Associated with John Richard Stockton (1764–1828), lawyer, land holder, U.S. senator (1790–99) and representative (1813–15), son of Richard Stockton, signer of the Declaration of Independence. First-class export. Courtesy of the Old Barracks Association, Trenton (57.5).

350. *Tureen*, Daoguang, c. 1820–40. L 31 cm, H 22 cm (12⅛ in, 8⅜ in). High-domed, high-footed form in overglaze enamels and gilt (latter retouched). Ship with two American flags and banner: AMERICA OF SALEM. Possibly commemorates a ship owned and captained by Jacob Crowninshield of Salem. (In 1796, his ship *America* brought a two-year-old female elephant to Salem from Bengal.) Courtesy of the Dietrich Brothers Americana Corporation. On loan to the Diplomatic Reception Rooms, U.S. Department of State.

351. *Bowl*, Jiaqing, c. 1790–1800. D 28.7 cm, H 11.9 cm (11⁵⁄₆ in, 4¹¹⁄₁₆ in). Overglaze polychrome bust of Washington encircled by a linked chain of thirteen states. Interior border, an undulating stylized laurel with obverse medal of the Society of the Cincinnati. Colonel Richard Humpton, Pennsylvania Continental Line, 2d Regiment (d. 1804), probable first owner. Possible design sources are the first U.S. copper cent or an Amos Doolittle print (both 1787). Unique export. Courtesy of the Historical Society of Pennsylvania.

352. *Butter tub and stand*, c. 1800–10. OL 18.1 cm, OH 8.9 cm (7⅜ in, 3½ in). Oval with sloping sides. Overglaze blue and gilt star border with four reserves, two of landscapes and two of birds. Center of stand and on opposite sides of the tub, overglaze green and sepia views of Mount Vernon after 1792, when a colonnade was built between the main house and the closest outbuilding. Fine-quality export, from a unique service. Private collection, U.S.A.

353. *Saucer*, Qianlong, c. 1795. D 16 cm, H 3.6 cm (6⁵⁄₁₆ in, 1⁷⁄₁₆ in). Gently scalloped rim, raised center to hold cup; in overglaze polychrome and gilt: nationalistic emblems of rising sun of the republic, outer chain of fifteen states (Massachusetts without a second "t"), snake biting its tail, symbol of eternity. Motto refers to the Union: DECUS ET TUTATMENT AB ILLO ("Honor and defense come from it"). MS for Martha Washington. Unique export. Gift of Mrs. Elizabeth Renshaw. Courtesy of the Diplomatic Reception Rooms, U.S. Department of State (77.18).

354. Oil on panel, *Still Life with Strawberries*, American, Raphaelle Peale (1774–1825). 40.6 cm × 55.9 cm (16 in × 22 in). On sugarbowl, a vignette of Commerce with anchor and distant ships, not the arms of Rhode Island. Courtesy of Mr. and Mrs. Robert C. Graham, Graham Gallery, New York.

355. *Punch bowl*, Daoguang, c. 1821–25. D 27.9 cm (11 in). In overglaze polychrome and gilt, European garland border; in sepia, black, yellow, and gilt, American eagle with trumpet, shield and banner, IN GOD WE HOPE (seal of Newport, R.I., 1821). Owned by John Jay (1745–1829). First-class export. Gift of Mrs. George P. Morse. Courtesy of the Diplomatic Reception Rooms, U.S. Department of State (64.68).

356. *Punch bowl*, Tongzhi, c. 1870. D 41.3 cm, H 16.8 cm (16¼ in, 6⅝ in). Low-footed, ridged body; overglaze enamels, an almost complete 1868 seal of the state of Illinois, on the fiftieth anniversary of the state's admission to the Union as the twenty-first state. Outer fleur-de-lis, inner floral swags on borders, and floral sprays are copies of eighteenth- and early-nineteenth-century French prototypes. Possibly unique. Courtesy of the Bayou Bend Collection, Museum of Fine Art, Houston (B.54.19).

357. *Plate*, Republic of China, c. 1915 or later. D 29.2 cm (11½ in). Underglaze T-shaped outer border, waterweed inner border; blue eagle with three arrows in left claw, major element of the seal of New Mexico of 1913 (made a state in 1912) with a smaller eagle to right. Chinese inscription *zheng dian* (?). Original seal of N.M.: CRESCIT EUNDO ("We grow as we go"). Indecipherable motto on banner. Possibly from embroidered prototype (compare Howard and Ayers, II, fig. 521). Courtesy of the Ottema–Kingman Foundation, the Princessehof Museum (OKS 1976.143).

358. *Punch bowl*, Qianlong, c. 1780–90. D 40.6 cm, H 15.8 cm (16 in, 6¼ in). Overglaze blue, iron-red, and gilt with three sepia vignettes of the hunt (hound and hare), the race course (two riders competing), and the steeplechase (a horse and rider with dogs before a fence). Inscribed FOR JOHN SEAWELL OF GLOUCESTER COUNTY VIRGINIA twice, once on body, then overpainted on exterior upper border. Inner border: novel version of grape-and-leaf motif. First-class special-order export, similar but not identical to any known bowl (compare Palmer, pl. 9). Courtesy of P. Hairston Seawell of Virginia.

359. Detail of the punch bowl in fig. 358.

360. End of inscription FOR JOHN SEAWELL OF GLOUCESTER COUNTY VIRGINIA in fig. 358.

361. *Cup and saucer*, Jiaqing/Daoguang, 1815–30. Cup D 8.6 cm, H 5.1 cm (3⅜ in, 2 in); saucer D 13.9 cm, H 3.6 cm (5½ in, 1⅜ in). Handleless cup, smooth-surface saucer. Deep gilt saw-tooth border, gilt tasseled and ribboned swags in French Empire style; AA for Abijah Arden (1759–1832) of New York. Fine export, rare. Courtesy of Mrs. Peter Milliken.

362. *Jug*, Qianlong, c. 1780–1800. H 21.9 cm, D 13.0 cm (8⅝ in, 5⅛ in). Barrel-shaped, strap handles ending in fern leaves. Overglaze polychrome rococo arms of Hancock, penciled floral sprays, gilt diaper and spearhead border. Arms differ from Hancock arms on mug at Winterthur (compare Palmer, fig. 68). Descended in Hancock family from Mary, sister of John Hancock. Fine export. Courtesy of the Bostonian Society (65.26).

363. *Plate*, Jiaqing, c. 1804 or 1805. D 24.5 cm, H 5 cm (9⅝ in, 1⅞ in).

Overglaze polychrome and gilt delicate painting: feather-edge gilt border, cavetto gilt wavy line with florets; peonies, asters, pomegranates; top: crest of the Van Schaick family from rococo arms of John Gerse Van Schaick's bookplate. Part of tea set of Gerrit Wessel Van Schaick (1758–1816) of Albany. Courtesy of the Albany Institute of History and Art.

364. Detail of crest in fig. 363.

365. *Jugs* (pair), Jiaqing, c. 1790–1810. H 28 cm (11 in). Covers with flattened edge, Fo-lion finials; strapwork handles ending in gilded fern leaves; deep gilt borders; in overglaze gold-red, blue and penciled, arms of the Bakers' Guild, New York ("The Bakers' Arms"); beneath gilded spout, TB for Tucker Brown, chief flour inspector, port of New York. Fine export. On loan to the Peabody Museum. Courtesy of Lt. Col. Michael M. Sheedy III (1456.1,.2).

366. *Table service* (partial), Daoguang, c. 1820–23. Clockwise from top: platter L 43.1 cm, W 38.1 cm (17 in, 15 in); shaped dish (nappie), covered custard cup (another on left) H 8.3 cm (3¼ in); covered vegetable dish; sauce boat. Brown and black "FitzHugh" with coat of arms of Charles Izard Manigault (1795–1874) after its alteration in Australia in 1820: belled falcons gules two and one on azure field. Crest: Ostrich-plumed aborigine. Motto: PROSPICERE QUAM ULCISCI ("It is better to anticipate than to avenge"). Courtesy of Mrs. Isaac Northrup.

367. *Coffee can*, Daoguang, c. 1820–1823. H and D 6.4 cm (2½ in). Brown and black "FitzHugh" with post-1820 Manigault crest, motto in medallion (as in fig. 366) with GHM for Gabriel Henry Manigault (1788–1834), brother of Charles Manigault. Service probably ordered by Charles for his older brother. Courtesy of the Reeves Collection, Washington and Lee University.

368. *Cup and saucer*, Qianlong, c. 1790. Cup D 8.6 cm, H 4.1 cm (3⅜ in, 1⅝ in); saucer D 13.9 cm, H 3.2 cm (5½ in, 1¼ in). Overglaze blue and gilt; wave and spearhead outer border; cavetto, lozenge chain; central oval with penciled crest of two facing birds, tripartite flame above them (common anonymous armorial motif). Owned by William White (1748–1836), first Protestant Episcopal bishop of the diocese of Pennsylvania. Above-average export; No. 3 in Elizabeth C. Canby catalogue. Courtesy of Mr. and Mrs. Lewis Rumford II.

369. *Plate*, Daoguang, c. 1830–50. D 20.1 cm, H 2.5 cm (7⅞ in, 1 in). "Mandarin" style with bird, butterfly, fruit, and flower ("bbff") border; two Chinese men and four women on a terrace. Top border, unidentified crest. Fine export, rare as armorial. Associated with a family of Newburyport, Maine. Private collection, U.S.A.

370. Detail of crest in fig. 369. Swan above crown within buckled belt. Motto: OPTIMUS EST QUI MINIMIS URGETUR ("Happy is he who is least harried").

371. *Soup dish*, Tongzhi, 1868. D 20.5 cm, H 4 cm (8 in, 1½ in). Overglaze polychrome on gilt ground, "Rose Medallion" pattern: quadrants of melon-shaped reserves, two with Chinese scholar at desk and three women, two with birds, butterflies, and flowers; in medallion, USG for Ulysses S. Grant (1822–85), elected president 1868. That year, this service was bought for Grant (with another for himself) by Capt. Daniel Ammen of the *Piscataqua* through Oliphant and Co., a U.S. firm in Shanghai. First-class export. Gift of Edith Grant Griffiths. Courtesy of the Peabody Museum.

372. *Soup dish*, Daoguang, c. 1830. D 25.3 cm, H 4.2 cm (9¹⁵⁄₁₆ in, 1³⁄₅

in). Overglaze polychrome wide border of four sections: two of key reserve with flowers and insects, two of melon reserve with birds; Chinese *shou* characters. On right: two scholars; left: warrior from historical drama or narrative. Owned by Mary Jane Derby (1807–92), Salem, wife of Ephraim Peabody (m. 1832) and daughter of Elias Hasket Derby. Courtesy of the Peabody Museum (E69, O34).

373. *Punch bowl*, Daoguang, 1832. D 50.8 cm, H 22.9 cm (20 in, 9 in). "Mandarin" style overglaze polychrome and gilt. Exterior: four reserves with figures. Inscribed in shield with star: FROM/ THE COMMANDER AND WARD ROOM OFFICERS/ OF THE/ U.S. SHIP PEACOCK/ TO/ DWIGHT BOYDEN — TREMONT HOUSE BOSTON 1832. Interior: wide continuous cavetto border of figures inside and out. In bottom: view of Guangzhou. Gift of Dwight Boyden, 1924. Fine export, unique. Courtesy of the Bostonian Society (1.95).

374. Interior of fig. 374; view of the hongs at Guangzhou with national flags.

375. *Cups and saucers*, Tongzhi, c. 1862–74. Left to right: cup (with cover) H 8.3 cm, D 8.9 cm (3¼ in, 3½ in); saucer L 16.5 cm, W 10.8 cm, H 2.2 cm (6½ in, 4¼ in, 7/8 in); cup (with cover) D 13.9 cm, H 3.2 cm (5¾ in, 1¼ in); cup H 9.5 cm, D 8.9 cm (3¾ in, 3½ in). Overglaze polychrome Chinese figures and characters. Left saucer: Li Taibo in center; above, Zhuge Wuhou; on left, An Min; on right, Su Ruolan (a woman); bottom, Dong Fang Shuo (a magician). Right saucer: Li Taibo in center; top, Dong Fang Shuo; bottom, Zhang Qian. From the Edward Carrington House, Providence (may have been owned either by him or by his sons). Private collection, U.S.A.

376. *Cup, saucer, plate*, Daoguang, c. 1830–50. Cup D 9.8 cm, H. 6.6 cm (37/8 in, 25/8 in); saucer D 15.5 cm, H 2.5 cm (61/8 in, 1 in); plate D 24.7 cm, H 4.4 cm (9¾ in, 1¾ in). Overglaze iron-red, blue, and gilt in bird, butterfly, flowers, and fruit ("bbff") pattern; MES monogram not identified. Courtesy of the Peabody Museum (1026.3, 1972.47ab).

377. *Plate and stand*, left: Tongzhi/Guangxu, c. 1870–90; L 23.8 cm, H 2.5 cm (93/8 in, 1 in), overglaze polychrome "hundred butterflies," stock pattern; right: Jiaqing/Daoguang, c. 1810–25; L 27.9 cm, H 2.5 cm (11 in, 1 in). Pierced border overglaze gold-red and gilt, tight rose outer and cavetto borders; medallion butterfly with right wing raised. Owned by Stephen Van Rensselaer (1764–1839), descendant of the 17th-century Van Rensselaers, called "the Patroon," of which he was the last. First-class export. Examples of two treatments of butterfly motif in early and late nineteenth century. Courtesy of Dr. Wesley Gallup.

378. *Plate*, Tongzhi/Guangxu, 1870–1900. D 24.1 cm, H 2.2 cm (9½ in, 7/8 in). Overglaze polychrome, iron-red and green dominant; wide border with two types of reserves in quadrants, symbols of the scholar and birds with flowers; in center, two dragons chasing flaming pearl. Owned by Brooks Adams (1848–1927), greatgrandson of John Adams. Courtesy of Adams National Historic Site.

379. *Vase*, Tongzhi/Guangxu, c. 1870–80. H 25.7 cm, OW 10.2 cm (101/8 in, 4 in). Concave neck, egg-shaped body, high foot, butterfly and ring molded "handles"; overglaze polychrome and gilt view of signers of the Declaration of Independence under spreadwinged eagle; rose sprays. Possibly made to commemorate the

one hundredth anniversary of the Declaration. Courtesy of Dr. Wesley Gallup.

380. *Platter*, Republic of China, c. 1912–28. L 33.7 cm, W 26.7 cm (13¼ in, 10½ in). Overglaze polychrome wide border similar to "hundred butterfly" pattern; crossed flags of the U.S. and the Republic of China, 1912–28. Stripes of Chinese flag: iron-red, yellow, blue, white, and black. Average export; rare. Gift of Mr. and Mrs. Joseph D. Shein. Courtesy of Diplomatic Reception Rooms, U.S. Department of State (81.57).

381. *Plate*, Xuantong, 1909–11. D 27.1 cm (105/8 in). Period and mark of Xuantong. Tightly scalloped rim; underglaze blue wide border of abstract waves; four fishes; central crab with waterweeds suggested by wavy lines. Gift of Edward M. Raymond, 1909. Courtesy of the Essex Institute (102, 253).

382. Reverse of fig. 381; mark of Xuantong, 1909–11.

APPENDIX A

383. *Eight Precious Objects (ba bao)*.
384. *Eight Happy Omens (ba ji xiang)*.
385. *Ming and Qing Dynasty Marks*.
386. *Shard*, Jiaqing, c. 1550–66. Exterior base of a small bowl (compare figs. 115 and 116). Mexico City subway excavations. Private collection.
387. *Shards*, Jiajing, c. 1550–66. Top: interior of a small bowl, underglaze blue abstract floral and scroll design on convex center; bottom: exterior of similar bowl, overglaze yellow and green; part of underglaze blue mark, *fu qui jia qi* ("honorable vessel"). Mexico City subway excavation. Private collection.
388. *Shard*, Wanli, c. 1590–94. Base of a thin, pure white, small bowl. Mark: *yu tang jia qi* ("beautiful vessel of the Jade Hall"). Associated with the wrecked Spanish galleon *San Agustin* (1595), Drake's Bay. Courtesy of the Archaeological Research Facility Collection, University of California, Berkeley.
389. *Shard*, Wanli, from a well filled in 1600. Base of an unidentified vessel with part of a *fu* mark ("good wishes" or "good luck"). Courtesy of the Florida State Museum.
390. *Shard*, interior base of a small bowl, Jiajing, c. 1550–66. Underglaze blue abstract waterweed design. Mexico City subway excavations. Private collection.
391. *Kangxi Period Symbols*.
392. *Ding-like (incense burner) mark* in two concentric circles, Kangxi, c. 1690–1720. Underglaze blue, on base of an underglaze blue and overglaze brown saucer. Courtesy of the Henry Francis du Pont Winterthur Museum (78.71.B).
393. *Saucer base*, Kangxi, c. 1690–1700. D 16.5 cm. Underglaze blue fish in two concentric circles (obverse: overglaze iron-red and gilt in an early willow pattern, see fig. 118). Private collection, Mexico City.
394. *Bowl under-rim*, detail, Kangxi, c. 1685–1700. D 28.9 cm. Underglaze blue, fungus mark with grass (obverse: landscape with Japanese Imari-style wide border, see fig. 106). Private collection, Mexico City.
395. *Dish base*, Kangxi, c. 1680. D 27.3 cm (1011/16 in). Grooved base,

underglaze blue mark and period of Kangxi (1662–1722). Private collection, Mexico City.

396. *Shard*, Kangxi, c. 1690–1710. A thin, white base of a saucer, underglaze blue mark of Chenghua (1465–87); found on the Drummond plantation (see fig. 136). Courtesy of the Virginia Research Center.

397. *Cup base*, Kangxi, c. 1713. H 7.3 cm, D 8.6 cm (2⅞ in, 3⅜ in). Tall sloping body, everted lip, high foot. Underglaze blue six ogival panels with loosely painted peonies; interior, stylized wave border, central floret. Recovered from the 1715 *San José* wreck (see obverse, fig. 109).

398. *Bowl base*, Kangxi, c. 1713. Underglaze blue mark, *yi*? ("appropriate; suitable for progeny"). Private collection.

399. *Cup and saucer*, Kangxi, c. 1700–20. Octagonal shape cup with overglaze light-brown ground, panels of iron-red and green flowers; interior: butterflies and flowers. On base: underglaze blue mark *yi* (different character from above, "happiness"), in two underglaze blue, concentric circles. Courtesy of the Fries Museum, Leeuwarden.

400. *Shard*, Kangxi, c. 1700–20. Exterior: octagonal light brown base. Underglaze blue mark, conch shell in two concentric circles. Mexico City subway excavations. Private collection.

401. *Plates* (identical), Kangxi/Yongzheng, c. 1715–25. D 21.6 cm, H 4.1 cm (8½ in, 1⅝ in). Overglaze polychrome, including gold-red of cock and hen beneath banana tree amid peonies and karst rock; exterior, the same with chicks. Underglaze blue mark in double square, *cai hua tang zhi* ("Made for the Hall of Beautiful Paintings"). First-class imperial ware. Ex. coll. Kitchener. Private collection, U.S.A.

402. *Stand*, Qianlong, c. 1790. L 22.2 cm, W 19.05, H 2.9 cm (8¾ in, 7½ in, 1⅛ in). Pierced border, arms of the English East India Company, part of a service owned by the governor of Bombay. Fine export. Courtesy of Dr. Wesley Gallup.

403. *Vase*, Xianfeng, Tongzhi, c. 1850–75. H 31.8 cm (12½ in). Small-necked, bulbous body; overglaze polychrome figure of Chinese-featured Liberty with raised sword and striped shield, eagle to her right, probably from a ship's paper (no known numismatic source), possibly ironic. Above-average export, rare. (Others of this design at Historic Deerfield.) Bequest of estate of Mr. Harry T. Peters, Jr. Courtesy of the Peabody Museum (1300.97).

404. Detail of fig. 403.

405. *Cups and sauceboat*, Tongzhi/Guangxu, c. 1870–90. Left to right: teacup D 8.3 cm, H 8.1 cm (3¼ in, 2³⁄₁₆ in); coffeecup D 6.9 cm, H 5.4 cm (2¾ in, 2⅛ in); boat L 18.4 cm, H 7.9 cm (7¼ in, 3⅛ in). Overglaze iron-red, blue, green, gilt; seven borders in red ground, three superimposed reserves: a rectangle with peacock and peony, fan with two figures, melon with birds and flowers. Fine export. Descended in the Morgan family of Worcester (possibly purchased from Misses Rice and Barnard of Worcester). Courtesy of Prof. and Mrs. Charles M. Morgan.

406. Detail of overglaze-red mark on cup base in fig. 405.

407. *Dish base*, Guangxu, c. 1895–1900. L 37.1 cm, W 27.9 cm, H 6.9 cm (14⅝ in, 11 in, 2¾ in). Lozenge-shape with foliate and scalloped rim; high sloping foot. Overglaze gold-red, iron-red, blue, yellow, green, turquoise. In overglaze red on base, CHINA, and mark of Guangxu (1875–1908). Above-average export. Associated with the J. Gray Bolton family of Philadelphia. Author's collection.

GLOSSARY

408. *Babyes* (two boys), c. 1690–1720, H 12.0 cm (5 in). Underglaze blue aprons, "chow-chow." Above-average export. Courtesy of the Groninger Museum, Groningen, the Netherlands.

409. *Cup* (burnt), c. 1790, D 8.6 cm (3⅖ in). Overglaze gilt, S W PENNOCK for Sarah Wistar Pennock. (Not in Elizabeth C. Canby catalogue.) Above-average export. Courtesy of Mr. and Mrs. Lewis Rumford II.

410. *Bowl*, c. 1750–70, D 10.8 cm (4¼ in). Overglaze enamels, crackled glaze, gift of David Lewis to Catharine Lewis in 1774, unusual export. No. 91 in Elizabeth C. Canby catalogue. Courtesy of Mr. and Mrs. Lewis Rumford II.

411. *Jar*, c. 1730–50, H 34.3 cm (13½ in). Overglaze gold-red in the leaf reserve and on scrolled turquoise ground, yellow-orange lappets on shoulders and base, carved replacement lid probably Mexican. Fine export. Private collection, Mexico City.

412. *Teapot*, c. 1730–40, H 12.7 cm (5⅛ in). Chinese "Imari," descended from Rebecca Wistar. No. 9 in Elizabeth C. Canby catalogue. Average export, now rare. Courtesy of Mr. and Mrs. Lewis Rumford II.

413. *Platter*, c. 1790–1810, L 54.5 cm (21½ in). Underglaze blue "Nanking" pattern, unusually large and finely painted. landscape right with two pagodas, prunus, and willow; on left, a sampan with fisherman and small island with pagoda in background. Courtesy of the Peabody Museum (E49,440).

414. *Bowl*, c. 1750, D 31.2 cm (12⁵⁄₁₆ in). Overglaze enamels in iron-red, gold-red, and gilt of a group of Chinese figures with an ornate and deep inner border. From the Kip family of New York, gift of Robert Swartwout Talmage. Fine export. Courtesy of the Museum of the City of New York (32.144.1).

415. *Bowls in stands*, c. 1875. Left: H 8.9 cm fluted, overglaze enamels; right: H 10.2 cm rice-grain, underglaze blue; both average ware. Courtesy of Mr. and Mrs. Lewis Rumford II.

416. *Tea caddy and tray*, c. 1700, tray 13.3 cm sq. (5⅕ in), caddy H 10.6 cm. Overglaze enamels with arms of Higginson, owned by Nathaniel Higginson, governor of Madras. Courtesy of the Essex Institute, Salem.

417. *Jar*, c. 1583–1620. H 34 cm (13⅖ in). *Wucai* decoration in the "Hundred Bats" (*fu* means both "bat" and "happiness") design. On shoulder, two of the eight trigrams: 1. three solid lines representing the south, heaven, sky, and the male principle, and 2. three broken lines representing the north, earth, and the female principle. Gift of Mr. Harry T. Peters, Jr. Above-average domestic/export. Courtesy of the Peabody Museum (1977.56.42).

18. Ibid., 182.

19. E. D. Hester, "Catalog of the Hester Collection of Ceramic Wares: Jeffersonville Section," MS, Field Museum of Natural History (Chicago, 1957), i.

20. In 1693, Gemelli Careri describes the "Parian" shops, which dealt in many goods, including porcelains; Francisco Giovanni de Gemelli Careri, *Voyage du tour de monde*, translated by M.L.N., vol. 5 (Paris: E. Ganeau, 1727), 20–21.

21. H. Otley Beyer, "Chinese, Siamese, and Other Oriental Ceramic Wares in the Philippine Islands," Philippine Archaeology Manuscript Series 1 (Manila: 1930), 21–23.

22. The phenomenal growth of the Chinese community in Manila is another way to measure the increase of porcelain imports. From 150 Chinese in 1571, this number had multiplied by 1588 to 10,000, to 24,000 in 1596, to 30,000 in 1603, to 40,000 in 1749, to 67,000 in 1886, and to 100,000 in 1896. Zaide, 324, 341. Another gauge is the accelerated number of Chinese junks arriving in Manila: in 1574, six were recorded; in 1580, forty or fifty. This figure fell by the end of the century to thirty or forty as the trade settled into a pattern that held firm—with ups and downs—through the eighteenth century. Schurz, 71.

23. Schurz, 193.

24. Blair, vol. 3, 239.

25. For Philip's inventory of porcelain and other ceramics, compiled in 1611–13, see J. C. Davillier, *Les origins de la porcelaine en Europe* (Paris: J. Rouam, 1882), 125–35. Donald Lach states that Philip's porcelains numbered over three thousand pieces. *Asia in the Making of Europe* (Chicago: University of Chicago Press, 1965), 15. The king's inventoriers may not have intended Chinese porcelain when using either *porcelana* or *loza* alone; only when these terms are further qualified with "*de Chine*" may one be sure that export ware rather than faience is meant. The Portuguese and Spanish both referred to their own faience in the Chinese style as "porcelain."

26. Blair, vol. 3, 247, 249.

27. Schurz, 190, 193, 194.

28. Among other statistics of the trade in the Archivo de Indias, Seville, are records of imports on Chinese goods entering Manila (1587–1787) and the value of items leaving Manila (1586–1700) or entering Acapulco (1591–1780). These figures would be altered by gaps in these records or by smuggling. Also, one set reflects customs duties, which the government changed from period to period, while the other shows cargo prices that also fluctuated but from outside causes. Taken together, however, they give an overview of a huge increase in activity. In 1586–1620, a 98 percent jump occurred in the total pesos charged vessels coming from China, including Macao and Formosa (Taiwan). For the same years, the value of exports leaving Manila increased 89.4 percent. And in the thirty years 1591–1620, Acapulco's imports rose 73 percent. If documents on Acapulco existed for the first four years (1586–90), then the difference between Manila exports and Acapulco imports, 16.4 percent, would probably have been even less, allowing for other ports as destinations for goods traded at Manila. As it is, the 73 percent figure indicates how primary Acapulco grew to be as a terminus for Mexico's share. Pierre Chaunu, *Les Philippines et le Pacifique des Iberiques*, vol. 1 (Paris: Service

d'Edition et de Vente des Publications de l'Education Nationale (SEVPEN), 1960), 86, 96–97, 200–3; see also graph, vol. 2, p. 53.

29. Schurz, 371–76.

30. Schurz, 366–71; Woodrow Borah, "Early Colonial Trade and Navigation Between Mexico and Peru," *Ibero-Americana*, 38 (1954), 116–59; see also John J. TePaske, ed. and trans., *Discourse and Political Reflections on the Kingdoms of Peru* (Norman, Okla: University of Oklahoma Press, 1978).

31. Harry Tschopik, "An Andean Ceramic Tradition in Historical Perspective," *American Antiquity* 15, no. 3 (1950), 203–4.

32. Schurz, 384–86.

33. Gemelli Careri, vol. 6, 2.

34. D. A. Brading, *Miners and Merchants in Bourbon Mexico, 1763–1810* (Cambridge, Eng.: University Press, 1971), 95–96, 98.

35. P. J. Bakewell, *Silver Mining and Society in Colonial Mexico: Zacatecas, 1549–1700* (Cambridge, Eng.: University Press, 1971), 21. For a brief mention of oriental goods arriving in the Parral area (twice as far from Mexico City as Zacatecas), see Robert C. West, "The Mining Community in Northern New Spain: The Parral Mining District," *Ibero-Americana* 30 (1949), 83–84.

36. Bakewell, 219–20.

37. Ibid., 235.

38. J. E. S. Thompson, ed., *Thomas Gage's Travels in the New World* (Norman, Okla.: University of Oklahoma Press, 1958), 68.

39. Ibid., 33–34.

40. Manuel Toussaint, *Colonial Art in Mexico*, translated by Elizabeth W. Weismann (Austin: University of Austin Press, 1967), 393.

41. Gonzales Lopez Cervantes, "Porcelana Oriental en la Nueva Espana," *Anales del Instituto Nacional de Antropologia e Historia (INAH)* (1976–77), 69–70.

42. Toussaint, 12, 161–69, 173–76, 264–66, 314–16, 339–40, 374–78, 379; Manuel Toussaint, *Planos de la Ciudad de Mexico, Siglos XVI y XVII* (Mexico City: XVI Congreso Internacional de Planificacion y de la Habitacion, 1938), 31, 175–77. Also author's conversation with Sr. Manuel Carballo, Mexican scholar. Sept. 1982.

43. Don Juan de Cervantes Casaus, private archives, MS, Inventory, 1645, p. 12, Mexico City.

44. Richard C. Rudolph, "Chinese Armorial Porcelain in Mexico," *Archives of the Chinese Art Society of America*, vol. 15, 1961, 14, quoting Salvador Ugarte, "La Porcelana de China y su Introducción en México en la Epoca Colonial," *Boletin de la Sociedad Méxicana de Geografía y Estadistica* 59 (1944): 515.

45. Touissant, *Colonial Art*, 169.

46. Author's correspondence with Sra. Marita Martinez del Rio de Redo, March 1982.

47. Ugarte, 515.

48. J. I. Israel, *Race, Class, and Politics in Colonial Mexico*, pt. 1 (London: Oxford University Press, 1975), 75–79. The *chinos* were also used as slaves in the silver mines. P. J. Bakewell, 123–24.

49. Gage quoted in Thompson, 68.

50. Brading, 24.

51. James Lockhart, "The Social History of Colonial America," *Latin American Research Review*, 7, no. 1 (Spring 1972), 11.

52. Antonio Francisco Garabana, "The Oriental Trade with the Mexican Provinces," *El Galeon de Manila, Artes de Mexico*, vol. 18,

no. 143, (Mexico City, 1971), 71; see also C. L. Guthrie, "Colonial Economy, Trade, Industry, and Labor in Seventeenth-Century Mexico City," *Revista de Historia de America*, no. 7 (Dec. 1939), 103–4.

53. Letter to author from John Ayers, 12 Aug. 1983.

54. Rodrigo R. Rivero Lake, "Comercio Artistico con el Oriente del Siglo XVI al Siglo XVIII," *8 Festival Internacional Cervantino* (Guanajuato, Mexico, 1980), 6.

55. The lids of the jars d'Entrecolles described do not correspond to the Valdés pair, but his remarks apply to other jars of its size. D'Entrecolles also wrote, "This year they made some ceramic designs which were supposed to be impossible. These were tall urns three feet and taller, plus pyramidal covers which add another foot in height. These urns are made of three pieces, but they are assembled with such skill and with such technique, that they make one piece, so uniform that it is impossible to find the joints. I was told that eighty urns were made, but that only eight of them were successful and all the others were lost. These pieces were ordered by some Cantonese merchants who dealt with Europeans, whereas in China, nobody is interested in such expensive porcelain." Robert Tichane, trans., *Ching-tê-chen, Views of a Porcelain City* (Painted Post, N.Y.: New York State Institute for Glaze Research, 1983), 120.

56. Jean M. Mudge, "Hispanic Blue-and-White Majolica in the Chinese Style," *Chinese Porcelain and Its Impact on the Western World* (Chicago: David and Alfred Smart Gallery, University of Chicago, 1985), 50.

57. The *San José* bottle had an unusual pewter screw-on top (lead caps or cork seals are commoner). Allen R. Saltus, "Rare Oriental Porcelain Recovered from 1733 Shipwreck," *Archives & History News* 3, no.5, Sept.-Oct. 1972), 1; Patricia Ann Logan, "The *San José y Las Animas*" (Master's thesis, Florida State University, 1977), 15, fig. 6.

58. Sullivan, 47, fig. 22. There are no kendis illustrated in Barbara Harrisson, *Swatow* (Leeuwarden, Holland: Princesshof Museum, 1979).

59. Gonzalo Obregón, "El Aspecto Artistico del Comercio con Filipinas," *El Galeon de Manila*, vol. 18, no. 143 *Artes de Mexico* (Mexico City, 1971).

60. Cf. David Howard and John Ayers, *China for the West*, vol. 2, no. 578 (New York: Sotheby Parke Bernet, 1978), 560.

61. Manuel Excriva de Romani y de la Quintana, *Historia de la Cerámica de Alcora* (Madrid: Fortanet, 1919), pl. 49, f.p. 220; Balbina Martinez Caviro, *Catalogo de Cerámica Española* (Madrid: Instituto Valencia de don Juan, 1968), nos. 250–55.

62. Mudge, 52.

63. Howard and Ayers, 591–92; Michel Beurdeley, *Chinese Trade Porcelain* (Rutland: Vt.: Charles E. Tuttle, 1962), pl. 17, p. 85.

64. Author's conversation with Prof. Tsugio Mikami, 7 Nov. 1982, Hangzhou. See also a bowl with red cranes and gilded clouds, Cécile and Michel Beurdeley, *A Connoisseur's Guide to Chinese Ceramics* (New York: Harper & Row, n.d.), pl. 28, p. 119.

65. R. L. Hobson, *Chinese Pottery and Porcelain*, vol. 1 (New York: Dover, 1976), 161–62.

66. Feng Xianmeng et al., eds., *History of Chinese Ceramics* (Peking: Wen Wu, 1982), 385.

67. Adalbert Klein, *Islamische Keramik* (Baden-Baden: Holle Verlag, 1976), 88, 93; fig. 35.

68. Hobson, pl. 74, figs. 1 and 2; Addis, *South-East Asian and Chinese Trade Pottery*, figs. 141 and 142. Fig. 141 is also reproduced in Laurence C. S. Tam, *An Anthology of Chinese Ceramics* (Hong Kong Museum of Art, 1968); see also John Alexander Pope, ed., *Oriental Ceramics*, The Victoria and Albert Museum (Tokyo: Kodansha, 1977), V, pl. 168; Tokyo National Museum, vol. 1 (Tokyo: Kodansha, 1982), pl. 119. None of the bowls show the Jiajing reign mark, but rather, characters representing good wishes, e.g., "long life, riches, and honors!"

69. Walter Denny, "Textiles," in *Tulips, Arabesques, and Turbans: Decorative Arts from the Ottoman Empire*, edited by Yanni Petsopoulos (New York: Abbeville Press, 1982), p. 123, and figs. 119–22, p. 127.

70. Henry Trubner and Tsugio Mikami, *Treasures of Asian Art from the Idemitsu Collection* (Seattle, Wash.: Seattle Museum of Art, 1981), 82.

71. John Ayers, *World Ceramics* (London and New York: Hamlyn, 1968), 56.

72. Sumarah Adhyatman, *Antique Ceramics Found in Indonesia* (Jakarta: Ceramic Society of Indonesia, 1981), 331.

73. Quoted by Obregón, 104.

74. Harrisson, 11.

75. Seizo Hayashi and Henry Trubner, *Chinese Ceramics from Japanese Collections* (New York: Asia Society, 1977), 123; see also T. Volker, *Porcelain and the Dutch East India Company, 1602–1682* (Leiden: E. J. Brill, 1954), 119.

76. Medley, 224.

77. Letter to author, 28 Jan. 1983 from Gonzalo Lopez Cervantes; Cervantes, 1976–77, 74–80, figs. 1–12; Cervantes, "El Templo Mayor: Excavacionese y Estudios," *Anales del INAH* (Mexico, 1982), 257–59; Florence C. Lister and Robert H. Lister, "Non-Indian Ceramics from the Mexico City Subway," *El Palacio*, 81, no. 2 (1974), 43–45; Lister and Lister, "Mexican Subway Excavations," *Historical Archaeology* 8 (1974), 17–52.

78. R. G. Montgomery et al., "Franciscan Awatovi," *Papers of the Peabody Museum of American Archaeology and Ethnology*, (1949), 36, as quoted in John W. Olsen, "A Study of Chinese Ceramics Excavated in Tucson," *The Kiva* 11, no. 1 (Fall, 1978), 8–9; Cornelia T. Snow, "A Brief History of the Palace of the Governors and A Preliminary Report on the 1974 Excavation," *El Palacio* 80, no. 3 (Fall 1974), 17.

79. In the shard collection of LA 326, Bardolier's Puaray, N.M., in the files of the Museum of Indian Arts and Culture, Laboratory of Anthropology, Museum of New Mexico, Santa Fe, N.M., courtesy of Stewart L. Peckham, curator.

80. D. F. Lunsingh Scheurleer, *Medelingenblad Nederlandse Vereninging Van Virenden Van de Ceramiek* (Amsterdam: Prinsengracht, 1981), 8.

81. Jessica Rawson, *Chinese Ornament: The Lotus and the Dragon* (London: British Museum, 1984), 125–32. The possibilities for cross-fertilization of sources in the decorative arts between the Arab world and China had a venerable history. In the ninth century, Persia bordered China on the east, and Arab merchants were established in Guangzhou. In the west, from the eighth to thir-

teenth centuries, the Muslim empire extended into southern Spain with a lasting influence upon the peninsula. At its height in the eleventh century, this Arab world stretched from Persia and Turkey across North Africa to include two-thirds of present-day Spain. J. H. Parry, *The Spanish Seaborne Empire* (London: Hutchinson, 1966), 284; William R. Shepherd, *Historical Atlas* (New York: Barnes and Noble, 1956), 66–67; for faience prototypes, see Klein, fig. 1, p. 18; also, J. Zick-Nissen, "Nachleben klassischer Typen nach Auflösung des Kalifats," *Islamische Keramik* (Düsseldorf: Hetjens-Museum, 1973), fig. 234, p. 169; and Bearbeitet von Kristian Jakobsen, *Islamische Keramik* (Hamburg, 1959), fig. 2, p. 14.

82. John A. Pope, *Chinese Porcelains from the Ardebil Shrine* (Washington, D.C.: Freer Gallery of Art, 1956), see pls. 75–77.

83. Cf. similar ewers in Southeast Asia, Adhyatman, p. 324, fig. 43 and p. 331, fig. 58.

84. Sir Percival David, ed. and trans., *Chinese Connoisseurship: The Ko Ku Yao Lun* (New York: Praeger, 1971), 144.

85. Addis, *South-East Asian and Chinese Trade Pottery*, 35–36.

86. "Fine and Important Late Ming and Transitional Porcelain," *Catalogues* (14 Mar. 1984, 12–13 June 1984, 14 Feb. 1985), Christie's Amsterdam B.V.; Janet Green, "South China Sea Find," *Canadian Collector* (Nov.-Dec. 1984), 38–43; Colin Sheaf, "The Private Collection of Captain M. Hatcher," *Arts of Asia*, vol. 15, no. 4, 112–15.

87. Philip Wen-chee Mao, "The Shu-Fu Wares," in Addis, South-East Asian and Chinese Trade Pottery, 22.

88. Cf. Scheurleer, 44–48.

89. Feng et al., 407; Mao, 22.

90. Feng et al., 400; Volker, 81.

91. Clarence Shangraw and Edward P. Von der Porten, "The Drake and Cermeno Expeditions' Chinese Porcelains at Drakes Bay, California, 1579 and 1595" (Santa Rosa, Calif.: Drake Navigators Guild, 1981), 56–59.

92. Harrisson, 13, and nos. 97–115.

93. For its unusual size and good painting, compare similar pieces in Scheurleer, 51–53; see also C. L. van der Pijl-Ketel, ed., *The Ceramic Load of the 'Witte Leeuw', 1613* (Amersterdam: Rijksmuseum, 1982), 53–117.

94. Davillier, 135.

95. Van der Pijl-Ketel, 133.

96. Cf., Mary Tregear, "Chinese Ceramics," *Eastern Ceramics* (London: Wilson, 1981), 25, no. 17.

97. Jars without lids of similar decoration are in a Singapore collection. S. T. Yeo and Jean Martin, *Chinese Blue and White Ceramic* (Singapore-Art Orientalis, 1978), fig. 10, p. 33 and at the Princessehof Museum, the Netherlands.

98. Beyer, 97.

99. Private Collection, Mexico.

100. Hobson, vol. 2, 95–97.

101. *Oriental Ceramics*, vol. 6, Percival David Foundation, (Tokyo and N.Y.: Kodansha, 1982) monochrome 173; for decorative similarities to early-sixteenth-century wares, see Tregear, p. 23, nos. 10 and 11; see also Adhyatman, 332.

102. Schurz, 268.

103. Gage in Thompson, 158–59.

104. Rawson, 129–31.

105. J. W. Allan, "Islamic Ceramics," *Eastern Ceramics*, exhibit catalogue, Ashmolean Museum (London: Philip Wilson, 1981), 95–128.

106. Soame Jenyns, "The Wares of the Transitional Period Between the Ming and the Ch'ing, 1620–1683," *Archives of the Chinese Art Society of America*, vol. 9 (1955), p. 20; also see Stephen Little, *Chinese Ceramics of the Transitional Period: 1620–1683* (New York: China Institute in America, 1983), 1.

107. Chaunu, *Les Philippines*, 96–98.

108. Gregorio M. Guijo, *Diario 1648–1684*, vol. 1 (Mexico: Editorial Porrua 1952), 184; vol. 2, 40, 61, 147.

109. Blair, vol. 25, 111–44. The Portuguese continued to crisscross the South China Sea from Macao or Canton with porcelains, a clue to what went to Manila and Mexico as well. In 1637, for example, a number of Portuguese ships were inventoried after their capture by the Dutch. A variety of fine and coarse wares—sometimes packed in wicker hampers—were described according to Dutch use, among them were *gorgelets*, another name for kendi. Michael Sullivan, 51, 52. T. Volker, *Porcelain and the Dutch East India Company* (Leiden: E. J. Brill, 1954), 197–200.

110. Beurdeley, 210; Volker, 193; Little, 27.

111. S. W. Bushell, *Oriental Ceramic Art* (New York: Crown, 1980), reprint of 1896 edition, 65–66.

112. Gemelli Careri, vols. 4 and 5.

113. Manuel Toussaint, *Pintura Colonial en Mexico* (Mexico-Imprenta Universitaria, 1965), pl. 43. In this view of the Crucifixion, the Christ, crowned with thorns, is attended only by two haloed figures, the whole encircled by clouds. A likely possibility of woodcut sources for the Chinese painter were those in Jeronius Nadal, *Images from the Gospels* (Bergamo: Edizioni Monumenta Bergamo, 1976, reprint of Antwerp edition, 1593), a work that Ricci had with him in China for many years. A fellow Jesuit, Father Emmanuel Diaz, borrowed it for his mission work in Nanchang, only 135 kilometers (53 miles) from Jingdezhen. In Beijing, Ricci also had twenty-one woodcut prints of the Passion of Christ by Anthony Wierix, engraver of many of Nadal's prints. Jonathan D. Spence, *The Memory Palace of Matteo Ricci* (New York: Viking, 1984), 62–63. Pages of a book with engravings of Christ's life, in China since the seventeenth century, indicate no close parallels, although elements from several prints could have been selected and recombined on the china. Nino Benti, *Immagini di Storia Evangelica* (Bergamo: Edizioni "Monumenta Bergomensia," 1976), reprint of 1595 edition.

Still another explanation of Christian ware in general is given by d'Entrecolles in his letter of 1712. At the time, he reported, porcelain illustrating the Crucifixion had not been made for sixteen or seventeen years since the time of his writing, its original purpose having been found out: to keep alive the memories of the crucifixion of missionaries and converts earlier in the century when the Japanese feared a political invasion from Spain following a national conversion to Catholicism. Christianity, officially banned, went underground. The porcelains with images of Christ's Crucifixion became reminders for a faithful remnant; they circulated almost unnoticed. Once discovered, however, their usefulness was over. D'Entrecolles in Stephen W. Bushell, *Description of Chinese Pottery and Porcelain* (Oxford: Clarendon

Press, 1910), 207.

114. Robert F. Burgess, *Man: 12,000 Years Under the Sea* (New York: Dodd, Mead, 1980), f.p. 123.

115. See p. 306, n. 81. Also, R. J. Charleston, ed., *World Ceramics* (New York: Hamlyn, 1968), p. 91, figs. 262, 263.

116. Yanni Petsopoulos, ed., *Tulips, Arabesques, and Turbans: Decorative Arts from the Ottoman Empire* (New York: Abbeville Press, 1982), 122, 127.

117. Bernard Rackham, *Islamic Pottery and Italian Maiolica* (London: Faber and Faber, 1959), pl. 58B. no. 76; and pl. 47, no. 103. The whorls are distinct from debased Arabic script. That script first appears on Chinese porcelain in the fifteenth century, but only became popular in the first decades of the sixteenth century. Feng et al., 406. The debased versions in North America are from the nineteenth century.

118. Stig Roth, *Chinese Porcelain Imported by the Swedish East India Company*, translated by Mary G. Clarke (Göteborg: Gothenburg Historical Society, 1965), 12.

119. Toussaint, *Colonial Art*, 339–40.

120. "Among all the silk stuffs brought by the Chinese," wrote one Spaniard, "none is more esteemed than the white,—the snow is not whiter,—and there is no silk stuff in Europe that can approach it." Schurz, 72.

121. The diety mounted on an elephant is actually Samantabhadra; on a lion, Manjuvri. Information courtesy of Amy McNair, graduate student, University of Chicago.

122. Author's conversation with the Reverend Dr. Joseph M. Kitagawa, University of Chicago Divinity School, 26 Feb. 1983.

123. P. J. Donnelly, *Blanc de Chine* (London: Faber and Faber, 1969), 154.

124. C. R. Boxer, ed., *South China in the Sixteenth Century* (London: Hakluyt Society, 1953), 213. On the other hand, Nestorian Christians had been in Xian in the sixth century, although their relationship to symbols on the Guanyin is unknown. More directly, the Chinese Christians in Jingdezhen, some of whom were potters and others who carried on a large exchange in porcelain, may have been responsible for a slight shift of elements in the Guanyin to make her appear like the Christian Madonna. D'Entrecolles, 181.

According to d'Entrecolles, the figurine was being produced in quantity at Jingdezhen as well as Dehua; he also noted that they held children. Further he likened them to the figures of Venus and Diana in the West, except that their long flowing robes made them "très-modestes." D'Entrecolles in Bushell, *Chinese Pottery and Porcelain*, 203. Another magnificent and unusual Guanyin from Jingdezhen, this one in polychrome and without a child, has been dated by its mark to 1717. S. W. Bushell, "Chinese Figure of Kuan Yin Painted with Coloured Enamels of the K'ang Hsi Period," *The Burlington Magazine* 12 (Liechtenstein: Kraus Reprint, 1968), 96–101.

125. Geoffrey A. Godden, *Oriental Export Market Porcelain* (New York: Granada, 1979), 260.

126. Ibid., 259.

127. Jorge René Gonzáles, "La Porcelain China," *El Galeon de Acapulco, Artes de Mexico* 23 (1976), 54, 57.

128. In comparing these Ming shards with late-seventeenth century (Kangxi) ones, Beyer made an important technical point: long exposure to salt water made the earlier enamels extremely fragile and easily lost; only if allowed to dry before touching could their overglaze painting be preserved. In contrast, the Kangxi enamels, also overglaze and in seawater, were much more permanent. Beyer, 21–23.

129. William Willetts and Lim Suan Poh, *Nonya Ware and Kitchen Ch'ing* (Selangor, Malaysia: Oxford University Press, 1981), 95–128.

130. Obregón, 86, 88, 89, 90.

131. Clare Le Corbeiller, *China Trade Porcelain: Patterns of Exchange* (New York: Metropolitan Museum of Art, 1974), 7.

132. Rudolph, 15–16; Marcus B. Burke "The Academy of San Carlos," in *Spain and New Spain: Mexican Colonial Arts in their European Context*, edited by Linda Bantel and Marcus B. Burke (Corpus Christi, Tex.: Art Museum of South Texas, 1979), 46.

133. Schurz, 60 and appendix 1, pp. 409–18.

134. Obregón, 108; Carlos Henze, "La Singular Fuente de la 'Casa del Risco,'" *Excelsior, Magazine Dominical* (Mexico City, 24 Oct. 1982), n.p.; for a similar wall in a tomb in Cirebon, Indonesia, with Chinese and Dutch delftware symmetrically displayed, see Adhyatman, 208–9.

CHAPTER 3

1. Lawrence A. Harper, *The English Navigation Laws*, (New York: Columbia University Press, 1939), 240.

2. Phillip A. Bruce, *Economic History of Virginia in the Seventeenth Century*, vol. 2 (New York: Macmillan, 1896), 299.

3. Donald F. Lach, *Asia in the Making of Europe: The Century of Discovery*, vol. 1 (Chicago: University of Chicago Press, 1965), 121, 122.

4. T. Volker, *Porcelain and the Dutch East India Company* (Leiden: E. J. Brill, 1954), chap. 9, p. 22.

5. Volker, 65–112.

6. Bruce, vol. 1, 57.

7. Hosea B. Morse, *The Chronicles of the East India Company Trading to China*, 1635–1834, vol. 1 (Oxford: Clarendon Press, 1926), 8, 26, 97.

8. Volker, 9.

9. Morse, 1–13.

10. Of several Dutch maps of the early part of the century, two good examples of the East Coast (1621 and 1636) show an increasingly detailed knowledge of the river area: *America Septentrionalis*, 1621, in John Brodhead and Edmund B. O'Callaghan, eds., *Documents Relative to the Colonial History of the State of New York*, vol. 1 (Albany: Weed, Parsons, 1856), f. title p.; Map of Nieuw Nederland, 1636; at exhibition in Amsterdam, "The Birth of New York: New Amsterdam 1624–1664," Amersterdams Historisch Museum, Mar.–Apr. 1983.

11. Bruce, vol. 2, 292.

12. Ibid., 308–9.

13. Volker, 50–59.

14. Ibid., 65–66, 108–10.

15. Ibid., 125, 128.

16. Bruce, vol. 2, 310.

17. Ibid., 309.

18. Harper, 391.
19. Edward Waterhouse, "To Allay the Panic in England, Caused by the News of the Massacre . . . ," in Edward D. Neill, *History of the Virginia Company of London* (Albany: Joel Munsell, 1869), 337.
20. John E. Pomfret, *Founding the American Colonies, 1583–1660* (New York: Harper & Row, 1970), 35.
21. Alain C. Outlaw, "Excavations at Governor's Land," *Notes on Virginia*, no. 19 (Richmond: Virginia Historical Landmarks commission, Summer 1979), 24; Letter to author from Merry A. Outlaw, curator, Research Center for Archaeology, Yorktown, Va., 11 Aug. 1983.
22. C. L. van der Pijl-Ketel, ed., *The Ceramic Load of the "Witte Leeuw"* (Amsterdam: Rijksmuseum, 1982), 143–45.
23. The shard finds from Virginia for this early period are being sifted and counted for future detailed treatment by a number of institutions and individuals: the Virginia Research Center for Archaeology and the National Park Service, both at Yorktown; Colonial Williamsburg; and the University of California at the "Flowerdew Hundred Plantation," to name a few.
24. MS, Nick Luccketti, "North Quarter Salvage Excavation: Interim Report," Kingsmill Plantation, Virginia Research Center for Archaeology, Williamsburg, Va., Jan. 1979.
25. Letter to author from Merry A. Outlaw; William M. Kelso, "Historical Archaeology at Kingsmill: The 1974 Season," (paper prepared for Virginia Research Center for Archaeology, Williamsburg, Va., Mar. 1976).
26. Author's telephone conversations with James Deetz, director of excavations at "Flowerdew," 28 July 1983 and 11 Oct. 1983.
27. Letter from James N. Haskett, chief park historian at Yorktown, 3 July 1978.
28. Ibid.
29. Alain Outlaw, 24.
30. Ivor Noël Hume, "Pottery and Porcelain in Colonial Williamsburg's Archaeological Collections," *Colonial Williamsburg Archaeological Series no. 2* (Williamsburg, Va.: Colonial Williamsburg Foundation; Williamsburg 1976), 43.
31. William M. Kelso, "Historical Archaeology at Kingsmill: The 1972 Season" (Office of Archaeology, Richmond, Va., Apr. 1973), n.p.
32. Inventory of the Estate of Mr. Thomas Pettus, 1692, *Henrico County Miscellaneous Court Records* (1650–1717), vol. 1, 74.
33. Kelso.
34. Pomfret, 50.
35. Ibid., 52–53.
36. Ibid., 65–66, 73.
37. TS, Inventory, Jonathan Newall, storekeeper, 29 Aug. 1671/72, notebook 6, p. 146, York County Inventories, Colonial Williamsburg, Va.
38. Susie M. Ames, *Studies of the Virginia Eastern Shore in the Seventeenth Century* (Richmond, Va.: Dietz Press, 1940); Susie M. Ames, ed., *County Court Records of Accomack-Northampton, Virginia, 1640–1645* (Charlottesville, Va.: University Press of Virginia, 1973); Mary C. Beaudry et al., "A Vessel Typology for Early Chesapeake Ceramics: The Potomac Typological System," *Historical Archaeology*, 17, no. 1 (1983), 18–39; Warren M. Billings, ed., *The Old Dominion in the Seventeenth Century* (Chapel Hill, N.C.: University of North Carolina Press, 1975); and TS, Inventories, 1636–
1720, York County, Inventories, Colonial Williamsburg, Va.
39. TS, Inventory of Gabriell Jones, 24 Feb. 1670/71, notebook 4, p. 348, York County Inventories, Colonial Williamsburg, Va.
40. Called "Virginia" at first; E. B. O'Callaghan, ed., *The Documentary History of the State of New York*, vol. 3 (Albany: Weed Parsons, 1849–51), 33.
41. Peter Nelson, "Government and Land System, 1624–1664," in *History of the State of New York*, Alexander C. Flick, ed., vol. 1 (New York: Columbia, 1933), 264–65.
42. A. Everett Peterson, "Population and Industry," in Ibid., 325–26. Also, O'Callaghan, vol. 1, 689; and vol. 3, 47.
43. Thomas J. Condon, *New York Beginnings* (New York: New York University Press, 1968), 116, 177.
44. O'Callaghan, vol. 1, 44.
45. Ibid.
46. Diane de Zerega Rockman and Nan A. Rothschild, "Excavating New York: The Big Apple," *Archaeology* 33, no. 6 (1980), 58.
47. Author's correspondence with Meta Fayden Janowitz, 20 Sept. and 8 Oct. 1983; interview with Janowitz, 3 Nov. 1983.
48. Eric Nooter, "The Archaeology of Dutch New York," Boudewijn Bakker, ed., *The Birth of New York* (New York: New York Historical Society, 1982) 23; also, Janowitz, correspondence and interview, 3 November 1983.
49. J. H. Innes, *New Amsterdam and Its People* (New York: Scribner's, 1902), 108, 164, and 193.
50. Cf. Brodhead and O'Callaghan, vol. 14, 42–44; Kenneth Scott and Ken Stryker-Redda, eds., *New York Historical Manuscripts: Dutch*, vol. 2 (1642–47), translated by A. J. F. van Laer (Baltimore: Genealogical Publishing Company, 1974), 121–25.
51. Author's telephone conversation with Lloyd Ultan, professor of history, Fairleigh Dickinson University, 13 Aug. 1983.
52. Mark Lerner, *Blue & White: Early Japanese Export Ware* (New York: Metropolitan Museum of Art; 1978), fig. nos. 27–31.
53. Van Doesburgh was also an ancestor of the Dusenbury family of Long Island. Letter from Paul R. Huey, senior scientist of Archaeology, Historic Site Bureau, Peebles Island, Waterford, N.Y., 5 Mar. 1980.
54. Carl Bridenbaugh, *Cities in the Wilderness* (New York: Ronald Press, 1938), 34.
55. Sale of Goods of Pieter Claerbout, 16 July 1659 in Jonathan Pearson, trans., and Arnold J. F. van Laer, ed., *Early Records of the City and County of Albany and the Colony of Rensselaerswyck*, vol. 1 (Albany: University of the State of New York, 1869–1919), 249.
56. Volker, 56.
57. See Inventory of Jan Jansen Damen, July 1651, *New York MSS*, vol. 3, 267–76; Public Sale of Personal Property, Bastian de Winter, 23 Sept. 1658, in Pearson and van Laer, vol. 4, 78; Sale of Estate of Rutger Jacobsen, 9 Dec. 1665, in Pearson and van Laer, vol. 1, 83; Sale of Household Goods of Dirck Janse Kroon (one of the wealthiest men in the colony), 14 May 1664, Pearson and van Laer, vol. 1, 350.
58. Arnold J. F. van Laer, *Correspondence of Jeremias van Rensselaer* (Albany: University of the State of New York, 1932), 291.
59. This reference and most of the other Albany inventories, courtesy of Charlotte Wilcoxen of the Albany Institute of History and Art.

60. Esther Singleton, *Dutch New York* (New York: Dodd, Mead, 1909), 115.

61. Brodhead and O'Callaghan, vol. 1, 577.

62. Shards from Madagascar are in Pierre Verin, "Les Échelles Anciennes du Commerce sur les Côtes Nord de Madagascar," vol. 1 (Service de Reproduction des Théses; Université de Lille III, 1975), 780–97. Reference courtesy of Henry T. Wright, curator, Museum of Anthropology, University of Michigan, Ann Arbor.

63. Brodhead and O'Callaghan, vol. 4, 306, 307; Singleton, 336.

64. Willard H. Bonner, *The World Book*, vol. 11 (Chicago: Field Enterprises, 1966), 242–43.

65. Condon, 121, 123.

66. Brodhead and O'Callaghan, vol. 4, 385–86.

67. Ibid.

68. Ibid.

69. Mrs. Schuyler van Rensselaer, *History of the City of New York in the Seventeenth Century*, vol. 1 (New York: Macmillan, 1909), 155.

70. Bruce, vol. 2, 314–15.

71. Condon, esp. chaps. 5 and 6; Robert C. Ritchie, "London Merchants, the New York Market, and the Recall of Sir Edmund Andros," *New York History* 57 (Jan. 1976), 6.

72. Ritchie, 7–19, 23, 29.

73. J. H. Parry, *The Age of Reconnaissance* (New York: World, 1963), 186–89.

74. Singleton, 85. In 1684, Catrina Darvall of New York City, sister of Maria van Rensselaer, wife of patroon Jeremias Van Rensselaer, supplied her Albany relatives with "two large porcelain jars" costing the sum of fl. 5:10. . . . " Arnold J. F. van Laer, trans., and ed., *Correspondence of Maria van Rensselaer, 1669–1689* (Albany: University of the State of New York, 1935); reference, courtesy of Charlotte Wilcoxen.

75. Singleton, 85.

76. Ibid., 114.

77. John Miller, "A Description of the Province and City of New York in 1695," in Cornell Jaray, *Historic Chronicles of New Amsterdam, Colonial New York, and Early Long Island* (Port Washington, N.Y.: Ira J. Friedman, 1968), 37.

78. MS Inventory of Margrita Van Varick, 29 May 1695/96, Historical Archives, Queens College Library, New York.

79. Volker, 48–49.

80. MS Inventory of the Goods and Estate of the Reverend Mr. Patrick Gordon, New York, 16 Dec. 1702, Archives, Queens College Library.

81. Singleton, 132.

82. Rodris Roth, "Tea Drinking in Eighteenth-Century America: Its Etiquette and Equipage," *United States National Museum Bulletin* 225, Washington, D.C., 1963, f.p. 63.

83. Singleton, pp. 93–94. In the years before 1710, Margareta Schuyler of Albany had similarly enjoyed 8 porcelain dishes upon her "Large Chamber" mantel, or "acht Portulyne Schotells boven d Mantell [sic]." Inventory of Margareta Schuyler, 27 Jan. 1710/11, Albany, by her children, Colonel Peter Schuyler, Captain Philip Schuyler, Lt. Colonel Johannes Schuyler, Alita Livingston, and Margaret Collins, Schuyler Family Papers, CX555, Box 1, Folder 3, No. 6., Albany Institute of History and Art.

84. Singleton, 109.

85. MS Inventory of Capt. Nicholas Dumaresq, New York, 12 June 1701, Historical Archives, Queens College Library.

86. Cf. with later coffee-chocolate pots, fig. 312.

87. Pomfret, 201.

88. James Deetz, *In Small Things Forgotten* (New York: Anchor, 1977), 50.

89. Bernard Bailyn, *The New England Merchants in the Seventeenth Century* (New York: Harper & Row, 1955), 17–18, 28.

90. Pomfret, 201–2.

91. Bridenbaugh, 30–31. William A. Baker, *A History of the Boston Marine Society, 1742–1967* (Boston: Boston Marine Society, 1968), 34–35.

92. Baker, 33–34.

93. Bridenbaugh, footnotes on n. pp. 6, 143.

94. Ames, *Virginia Eastern Shore*, 47.

95. Ibid., 64.

96. Alice Morse Earle, *Customs and Fashions in Old New England* (Detroit: Singing Tree Press, 1968), 182, 180.

97. Alice Morse Earle, *China Collecting in America* (New York: Scribner's, 1892), 56.

98. MS, Inventory of John Winthrop, 17 Feb. 1649, docket 79, Suffolk County Records, Boston, Mass.

99. Davenport was neither the president of Harvard nor John Davenport, the prominent minister, who came to Boston from New Haven only the year before he died in 1669/70, unless Earle misstates his death date. Earle, China Collecting, 56.

100. Ibid.; also, Norman M. Isham and Albert F. Brown, *Early Connecticut Houses* (New York: Dover Reprint, 1965), 290.

101. *Records and Files of the Quarterly Courts of Essex County, Massachusetts*, vol. 1 (Salem, Mass.: Essex Institute, 1911), 120; vol. 2, 370, 418; vol. 3, 361; vol. 4, 16, 379; vol. 5, 95.

102. *Middlesex Court Probate Records*, 1669, 291–94, and 1675, 475–76, quoted by Ann Yentsch, "Expressions of Cultural Diversity and Social Reality in Seventeenth-Century New England" (Ph.D. diss., Anthropology Department, Brown University, 1980).

103. *Suffolk County, Massachusetts, Probate Records*, 1650–1850, vol. 7 (Film: Graphic Microfilm of New England, n.d.), 174–75; vol. 9, 181, as quoted by Garry W. Stone, "Ceramics in Suffolk County Massachusetts Inventories 1680–1775," in *The Conference on Historic Site Archaeology Papers* edited by Stanley South, vol. 3, pt. 2 (Columbia, S.C.: Institute of Archaeology and Anthropology, University of S.C., 1970), 79.

104. Elizabeth Pratt Fox, "Ceramics and Glass" in *The Great River: Art and Society in the Connecticut Valley, 1635–1820* (Hartford, Conn.: Wadsworth Atheneum, 1985), 415.

105. Susan Montgomery, ed., *Unearthing New England's Past* (Lexington, Mass.: Scottish Rite Museum and Library, 1984), 74, 78, 91.

106. The squirearchy included ministers; below them were the "goodmen"—yeomen or tradesmen—tenants, indentured servants, and an occasional foreigner and black. Pomfret, 202.

107. Bailyn, 135–38.

108. But the first shopkeeper of Boston, John Cogan (brother of another merchant, Humphrey, of Exeter, England), had an estate of £1,081.17.02, comparable to Andrews's, with about the same

type, if a few more porcelains: "6 small Chiny Dishes: 20s" and "5 pieces of Cheyney," also worth 20s. With the six plates, thus also perhaps porcelain, two boxes and bottles valued at 5s were listed for a total of £1.5s. But some who might, had no china at all. Two of the most prosperous merchants in Boston, Robert Keayne (d. 1656) and Henry Shrimpton (d. 1666), apparently owned none. Again, their listings may not tell the full story. Bailyn, 35; MSS, Inventories of John Cogan, 20 May 1658, and his wife, Mary Cogan, 31 Oct. 1660, docket 185, Suffolk County Records, Boston, Mass.; MSS, Inventory of Mrs. Anna Keayne, widow of Robert Keayne, 19 Sept. 1657, docket 171; Inventory of Henry Shrimpton, 1666, docket 409, Suffolk County Records, Boston, Mass.

109. Bailyn, 90–91.
110. Earle, *China*, 56.
111. Bailyn, 134–42.
112. J. W. Fortescue, ed., *Calendar of State Papers, Colonial Series, American and West Indies, 1696–1697* (London: Mackie, 1904), 259–60.
113. Jonathan Goldstein, *Philadelphia and the China Trade, 1682–1846: Commercial, Cultural, and Attitudinal Effects* (University Park, Pa., Pennsylvania State University Press, 1978); and Jean Gordon Lee, *Philadelphians and the China Trade, 1784–1844* (Philadelphia: Philadelphia Museum of Art, 1984).
114. Ruth Matzkin, "Inventories of Estates in Philadelphia City, 1682–1710" (Master's thesis, University of Delaware and the Winterthur Museum, 1979), 73.
115. Ibid., 74.
116. MS "Catalogue of China Collection made by Elizabeth C. Canby and Elizabeth C. Rumford of Wilmington, Delaware, prior to 1890," Lewis Rumford II, Baltimore, Md.

CHAPTER 4

1. In 1704, over forty years after New Amsterdam had become New York, a Dutch privateer, Capt. Adrian Claver, brought in two Spanish prizes taken off the coast of Mexico, possibly including porcelains. *The Boston Newsletter*, 24–31 July, 1704, 2.
2. K. N. Chandhuri, *The Trading World of Asia and the English East India Company, 1660–1760* (London: Cambridge University Press, 1978), 409.
3. Geoffrey A. Godden, *Oriental Export Market Porcelain* (London: Granada, 1979), 42, 53.
4. Ibid., 61.
5. William W. Appleton, *A Cycle of Cathay: The Chinese Vogue in England During the Seventeenth and Eighteenth Centuries* (New York: Columbia University Press, 1951), 91.
6. Godden, 80.
7. Chandhuri, 43.
8. Ibid., 519.
9. Ibid., 407.
10. Julius Bloch, et al., *An Account of Her Majesty's Revenue for the Province of New York, 1710–1709* (Ridgewood, N.J.: Gregg Press, 1967).
11. Esther Singleton, *Social New York Under the Georges, 1714–1776* (New York: Appleton, 1902), 120–21; also Alice Morse Earle, *China Collecting in America* (New York: Scribner's, 1892), 60.

12. Earle, 56.
13. "Annapolis and Anne Arundel County, Maryland: A Study of Urban Development of a Tobacco Economy, 1649–1776," Data File, Historic Annapolis Incorporated, Annapolis, Md.
14. Ibid.
15. Gary W. Stone, "Ceramics from the John Hicks Site, 1723–1743: The Material Culture," in *Ceramics in America*, edited by Ian M. Quimby (Charlottesville, Va.: University of Virginia Press, 1972), 119; recent archaeology reveals that in an earlier house from which he moved in 1740, Deacon owned a tea service. Letter to author from Gary W. Stone, 8 Feb. 1984.
16. TS, Oct. 1701, notebook 11, pp. 506–12, York County Inventories, Colonial Williamsburg (hereafter, YCI, CW).
17. TS, 17 Aug. 1702, notebook 12, pp. 27–29, YCI, CW.
18. Dec. and 2 Jan. 1717/18, notebook 15, p. 242–46, YCI, CW.
19. TS, 4 July 1719, notebook 15, pp. 464–66, YCI, CW.
20. TS, 10 June 1720, notebook 15, pp. 628–38, YCI, CW.
21. "An Inventory of the Personal Estate of His Excellency Lord Botetourt began to be taken the 24th of October 1770," copy at Colonial Williamsburg; original document in Botetourt MSS, Virginia State Library, Richmond, Va.
22. Home Miscellaneous Series 14, E/3/97 pp. 56, 92, 113, India Office Library and Records (hereafter IOLR), London.
23. Two weeks later, the *Johanna*, 70 tons, built in New England in 1716, owned by Stephen Perry, followed with European and India goods, this time from Bristol. A month later, on June 23, the *Pink Lark*, also owned by Robert Hackshaw of London, came in with "Eurp & India goods on 56 cocqt" ("cocquet," or customhouse certificate). Colonial [Office] Papers, General Series (hereafter C.O.), 5/1223, pp. 2–4, Public Record Office, Kew, England.
24. C.O. 5/1225, p. 159.
25. New Hampshire (1723–69), Massachusetts (1686–1762), New York (1713–99), Maryland (1689–1765), Virginia (1699–1770), South Carolina (1716–63), Georgia (1765–69), and East Florida (1765–69).
26. Earle, 56–57.
27. *The Boston Weekly News-letter*, 2–9 May, 1728, 2.
28. Earle, 57.
29. Ibid., 59–60.
30. David Howard, *Chinese Armorial Porcelain* (London: Faber and Faber, 1974), 218.
31. Earle, 57.
32. Ibid., 60–62.
33. "Naval Office List of Ships Enter'd Inwards," 29 Dec. 1716–17 June 1717, C.O. 5/508, Public Record Office, Kew, England.
34. Carl Bridenbaugh, *Cities in the Wilderness: The First Century of Urban Life in America, 1625–1742* (New York: Oxford University Press, 1938), 303n.
35. *The South Carolina Gazette,* 7–14 Oct. 1732, 4.
36. Ibid., 1–8 Nov. 1735, 1.
37. Ibid., 13–20 Nov. 1740, 2–3.
38. Ibid., 11–18 Dec. 1740, 2.
39. Ibid., 25 Feb.–1 Mar. 1749, 3.
40. Ibid., 25 Sept.–2 Oct. 1749, 3.
41. Abbott Lowell Cummings, *Rural Household Inventories Establishing the Names, Uses, and Furnishings of Rooms in the Colonial New England Home, 1675–1775* (Boston: Society for the Preserva-

tion of New England Antiquities, 1974); Alice Hanson Jones, *American Colonial Wealth: Documents and Methods* (New York: Arno Press, 1977).

42. *The Boston Weekly News-letter*, 14 Aug. 1755, 1.

43. Robert G. Albion, et al., *New England and the Sea* (Middletown, Conn.: Wesleyan University Press, 1972), 23.

44. Godden, 42, 48, 50.

45. W. T. Baxter, *The House of Hancock, Business in Boston, 1724–1775* (New York: Russell and Russell, 1965), 124; *The Boston Weekly News-letter*, 20 June, 1954, 1.

46. *The Massachusetts Gazette and Boston News-letter*, 14 May 1772 (hereafter *MGBW*).

47. Ibid., Selected issues in the years 1769–74. A collection of Loyalist export ware in Canada was made in the late-nineteenth century by Mrs. John W. Weldon and presented to the University of King's College, Halifax, Nova Scotia. Marie Elwood, "The Weldon Collection," *Canadian Collector* 18, no. 4 (July-Aug. 1983), 26–29.

48. Between Christmas 1769 and mid-May 1770, it was said that £150,000 worth of British merchandise was returned and the names of the importers published in the paper. *MGBW*, 17 May 1770, 5.

49. Ibid., 16 Apr. 1772, 3.

50. Ibid., 17 Feb. 1774, 3.

51. C. J. A. Jörg, *Porcelain and the Dutch China Trade* (The Hague: Martinus Nijhoff, 1982), 92.

52. Ibid., 93.

53. H. H. Kagan, ed., *The American Heritage Pictorial Atlas of United States History* (New York: American Heritage, 1966), 52.

54. *The Boston Weekly News-letter*, 24 Aug. 1755, 1.

55. Louis Dermigny, *La Chine et L'Occident, Le Commerce a Canton au XVIII Siecle, 1719–1833* (Paris: SEVPEN, 1964), 390.

56. Michel Beurdeley, *China Trade Porcelain* (Rutland, Vt. and Tokyo: Charles E. Tuttle, 1962), 101–3.

57. Robert Picard et al., *Les Compagnies des Indes* (Paris: Arthaud, 1966), 32–34.

58. Doing so, some fell into the hands of enemies. In 1757, two French East India ships were taken by the English, their combined cargoes worth £300,000. Two years later, no French ships reached Guangzhou by "missing their passage," i.e., arriving too late for the usual winds to take them up the coast. *The Massachusetts Gazette and The Boston News-letter* 17 Mar. 1757, 1, and 7 June 1759, 2.

59. Letters to author of 12 Oct. 1979 and 9 Apr. 1981 from R. E. Whate, head of Material Culture Research, Archaeological Research Division, National Historic Parks and Sites Branch, Parks Canada, Ottawa.

60. John Lunn, "Colonial Louisbourg and Its Developing Ceramics Collection," in *Ceramics in America,* edited by Ian M. G. Quimby (Charlottesville, Va.: University of Virginia, 1972), 175–76.

61. Letter to author, 28 Jan. 1982, from Andrée Crépeau, Fortress of Louisbourg, National Historic Park, Louisbourg, Nova Scotia.

62. Beurdeley, 104.

63. Lunn, 180, 183.

64. Jacob L. Grimm, "Archaeological Investigation of Fort Ligonier, 1960–1965," *Annals of the Carnegie Museum* 42 (1970), as quoted in John W. Olsen, "A Study of Chinese Ceramics Excavated in Tucson," *The Kiva* 44, no. 1 (Fall 1978), 6.

65. R. E. Whate, "A Cargo of Porcelains for Montreal, 1760," *Canadian Collector* 16, no. 1 (Jan.-Feb. 1981), 24–28.

66. Eugene T. Peterson, "China at Mackinac," *Early Man* 4, no. 4 (Winter 1982), 33–35.

67. Michel Beurdeley, fig. 75, p. 106.

68. Handwritten translation and copy of a letter: 2 Oct. 1937 from Pierre-Georges Roy, archivist, Department du Secretaire de la Province de Quebec to Douglas King Hazen, Chief Justice in St. John, New Brunswick. Letter of Mme. Hazen's descendant, Gertrude Lansing, 18 July 1938. Reference, courtesy of Charlotte Wilcoxen.

69. Hubert H. Bancroft, *The History of California*, vol. 1 (1542–1800), (San Francisco: History Co, 1884), 442.

70. Michael E. Thurman, *The Naval Department of San Blas* (Glendale, Calif.: Arthur H. Clark, 1967), 14.

71. Jean Krase, "The Old World Ceramic Shards from San Diego's Presidio: A Qualitative, Quantitative, and Historical Analysis" (Master's thesis, San Diego State University, 1979), 73.

72. Ibid.

73. Report of Goods Sent to California in 1782, Archivo General y Publico de la Nacion: Californias (hereafter, AGNC), Bancroft Library, University of California, Berkeley. Invoice of Goods for San Diego, 1791, AGNC, vol. 46, no. 4.

74. Krase, p. 76.

75. Ibid., 38.

76. Bancroft, 624.

77. Krase, pl. IV, p. 131. See also David Howard and John Ayers, *China for the West*, vol. 2 (New York: Sotheby, Parke Bernet, 1978), pl. 385, 389.

78. Author's examination, Sept. 1980; letter to author from Jean Krase, anthropologist, 1982, Old Town San Diego Plaza and Street Restoration, Resources Agency of California, Department of Parks and Recreation, Sept. 1977.

79. Russell Ewing, "Mission La Purisima Concepción, California," in *An Archaeological and Restoration Study of Mission La Purisima Concepción*, edited by Richard Whitehead (Santa Barbara Trust for Historic Preservation, Santa Barbara, 1980), 247–48.

80. Nicholas M. Magalousis and Paul A. Martin, "Mission San Juan Capistrano: Preservation and Excavation of a Spanish Colonial Landmark," *Archaeology*, vol. 34 (May-June 1981), 61.

81. 1834 Soledad Mission Inventory; 1834–35 Santa Cruz Mission List, Santa Barbara Mission Archival Library.

82. 1843 Santa Clara Mission Inventory, Santa Barbara Mission Archival Library.

83. *The Massachusetts Gazette*, 8 June 1787, 3.

CHAPTER 5

1. Michel Beurdeley, *Chinese Trade Porcelain* (Rutland, Vt.: Charles E. Tuttle, 1969), 104.

2. C. J. A. Jörg, *Porcelain and the Dutch China Trade* (The Hague: Martinus Nijhoff, 1982), 106, 109, 110, 112, 115, 167.

3. T. Volker, *Porcelain and the Dutch East India Company* (Leiden: E. J. Brill, 1954), 24.

4. Ibid., 73, 74, 88.

5. Ibid., 29.

6. Ibid., 37–38.

7. Ibid., 30–31, 38–41.

8. Arthur Lane, "Queen Mary II's Porcelain Collection at Hampton Court," in *Transaction of the Oriental Ceramic Society*, vol. 15 (1949–50), 21.

9. Clare Le Corbeiller, *China Trade Porcelain, A Study in Double Reflections* (New York: China Institute in America, 1973), fig. 9, p. 24.

10. John Carswell, "Ceramics," in *Tulips, Arabesques, and Turbans: Decorative Arts from the Ottoman Empire*, edited by Yanni Petsopoulos (New York: Abbeville, 1982), #89; Walter Denny, "Textiles," in Ibid., figs. 152, 153, 155; c.f., "Bouteille Polychrome," in Henry Havard, *Histoire des Faïences de Delft*, vol. 2 (Amsterdam: Compagnie Générale d'Éditions "Vivat," 1909), n.p. Reference, courtesy of Charlotte Wilcoxen.

11. Le Corbellier, fig. 38, p. 53.

12. Information provided by Sophie Cadwalader, daughter of Mrs. George Cadwalader, in 1942. Also, genealogical data from "Middleton of South Carolina: A Middleton Family Genealogy," Middleton Place Foundation Occasional Essay, vol. 1, no. 2, 1979.

13. Since about 1704, the English taste for tea had been firmly set and demand would only increase. In the same year, the company bought at a record value for the whole half-century—£20,815—chinaware in which to take tea. In the fifteen years after 1705, values ranged widely from a low of £1,242 in 1712 to a high of £6,233 in 1717. In 1721 and 1722, though, the figures were £9,395 and £9,527 respectively, and in 1730, they reached a high of £11,796, not to be surpassed until 1743 when porcelains valued at £11,995 were recorded. K. N. Chandhuri, *The Trading World of Asia and the English East India Company, 1660–1760* (London: Cambridge University Press, 1978), 388–89, 519.

14. Geoffrey A. Godden, *Oriental Export Market Porcelain, and Its Influence on European Wares* (New York: Granada, 1979), 66–68.

15. Hosea Ballou Morse, *The Chronicles of the East India Company Trading to China, 1635–1834*, vol. 1 (Oxford: Clarendon Press, 1926), Appendix 3.

16. "List of Pepper, Drugs, Calicoes and other Goods for Sale at the East-India-House," India Office Library and Records (hereafter, IOLR), London, Home Miscellaneous Series 10, E/3/97, 28 Mar. 1704, pp. 23–33.

17. "List of Goods to be Provided at Canton by the SupraCargos of the Loyal Blisse," IOLR, Home Miscellaneous Series 10, 1712, pp. 669–71.

18. From the *Hartford* (1718), the *Carnarvon*, the *Sarum*, and the *Bridgewater* (all 1720.)

19. "List of Goods for Sale at the East India House, 6 Mar. 1721/22," IOLR, Home Miscellaneous Series 14, E/3/97 pp. 171–408.

20. Adolphe Coster, ed., "Une description inedite de la demeure de Don Vincenzio Juan de Lastonosa, 1639," *Revue hispanique* vol. 26, (June 1912), 579. Referred to in Alice Frothingham, *Talavera Pottery* (New York: Hispanic Society of America, 1944), 15.

21. Volker, 25.

22. Ibid., 74.

23. "Directions for the Chinaware, 1727–1729," IOLR, Despatch Book, no. 21, E/3/104, n.p.

24. Abraham Wessell et al., China Diary, 10 Aug. 1734, IOLR, G/12/36, pp. 47–48.

25. Ibid., 48.

26. In the same 1734 shipment, a smaller blue-and-white service of seventeen dishes and sixty plates was contracted for with Young Hunqua, Ibid., 54. Still another set, of five dishes and twenty plates, was discussed as an adequate size. Ibid., 57. Hot-water and salad plates appear as separate items in the 1740s, though the latter had already been incorporated into a dinner service. "A Sortment of China Ware for 400 Chests," for the *York* and *Northampton*, IOLR, 1740, E/3/108, pp. 271, 272. By 1739, sets of dishes and plates, in this instance three dishes and twenty plates per set (of blue-and-white), indicate that such groupings were becoming more popular, even though in this order open-stock pieces still far outnumbered sets. Canton Diary of the *Augusta*, IOLR, 1739, G/12/47, p. 14. Eleven years later, an amplified set appeared consisting of eleven dishes in four sizes, thirty-six plates, eighteen soup plates, two tureens and dishes (stands), and two sauceboats. John Misenor, "List of Chinaware bought of Taxia," IOLR, 24 Sept. 1750, E/3/108, n.p. By 1755, a fuller dinner service was possible. A number of old forms were now included, though the simpler dish-and-plate sets were also available, according to a purchase brought to London aboard the *Prince George*. Each "table set" comprised two tureens with covers and stands, thirteen dishes in various sizes, sixty dinner plates, twenty-four soup plates, eight salad dishes, one salad bowl, two sauceboats, and four salts. Godden, 127–28.

27. *The South Carolina Gazette, Supplement*, 16 June, 1759, no. 1289, p. 2.

28. Mary Gelruth, "The Importation of English Earthenware into Philadelphia," (Master's thesis, Henry Francis du Pont Winterthur Museum and University of Delaware, 1964), 121–22.

29. Her nephew, the father of the present owner of the tureen, Mrs. Peter Milliken, purchased it in 1914 from his aunt's estate. Letter to author from Mrs. Peter Milliken, Feb. 1984.

30. Penny J. Sander, "A Choice Sortment," in *Ceramics from New England Homes* (Boston: Society for Preservation of N.E. Antiquities, 1981), p. 15, fig. 46.

31. Jörg, fig. 74, p. 147.

32. Beurdeley, pl. XII, p. 63.

33. "Dispersal of *Sarah* and *Dorothy*," IOLR, Home Miscellaneous Series 9, 1696, p. 9.

34. Ibid., 9, 64, 66.

35. Ibid., 9.

36. Rodris Roth, "Tea Drinking in Eighteeenth-Century America: Its Etiquette and Equipage," *U.S. National Museum Bulletin* 225 (Washington, D.C. 1963), 66.

37. William Butler, "New Yorkers' Taste: Chinese Export Porcelain 1750–1865," *Antiques* vol. 123 (Feb. 1984), 431.

38. Havard, pl. I; H. P. Fourest, *Delftware Faience Production at Delft* (New York: Rizzoli, 1980), 100. References, courtesy of Charlotte Wilcoxen.

39. Jean M. Mudge, *Chinese Export Porcelain for the American Trade, 1785–1835 2nd ed., Rev.* (Cranbury, N.J.: Associated University Presses, 1981).

40. Chandhuri, 97.

41. Walter E. Minchinton, *The Growth of English Overseas Trade in the Seventeenth and Eighteenth Centuries* (London: Methuen, 1969), 24.

42. Ibid.

43. Roth, 68, 74–75.

44. Martha Gandy Fales, "Two New England Dummy Boards," *An-*

tiques 120, no. 6 (Dec. 1981), 1422–23.

45. *The South Carolina Gazette*, Supplement, 16 June 1759, no. 1289, p. 2.

46. Godden, 53.

47. ''China ware items—Images—Animals,'' Manuscript list excerpted from Boston inventories, 1697/98–1769 by Irving Phillips Lyon in the 1930s, Joseph Downs Memorial Library, Henry Francis du Pont Winterthur Museum.

48. 3220–126, YOH Building, room F, feature 1, Department of Archaeology, Temple University, for the Independence National Historical Park, Philadelphia.

49. ''A Sortment of China Ware for 400 Chests sent per *York* and *Northampton*,'' IOLR, 9 Jan. 1740, E/3/108, n.p.

50. John Raper, ''List of ware bought of Tinqua,'' IOLR, 20 Aug. 1734, G/12/36, p. 55.

51. Bevis Hillier, quoting Eberlein, *Pottery and Porcelain* (New York: Meredith Press, 1968), 349, n. 10.

52. Richard Nylander, ''The Jonathan Sayward House, York, Maine,'' *Antiques* 118, no. 3 (Sept. 1979), 570.

53. cf. Clare Le Corbeiller, *Chinese Export Porcelain: Patterns of Exchange* (New York: Metropolitan Museum of Art, 1974), pl. 20, pp. 46–47; and John Goldsmith Phillips, *China-Trade Porcelain* (Cambridge, Mass.: Harvard University Press, 1956), pl. 1, p. 67.

54. H. Crosby Forbes, *Yang-ts'ai: The Foreign Colors* (Milton, Mass.: China Trade Museum, 1982), 11. •

55. Ann Allen Ives (1810–84), of the China-trade Dorr family of Providence, had a large chinaware collection by inheritance and purchase. The larger plate of this service bears the note, presumably in Mrs. Ives's hand: ''This tea set was bought of Miss Shaw & four other heirs of Miss Rebecca Stafford. It was brought from Surinam in 1757 by Capt Soule. Cost of the whole $20, 50cts.''

56. Forbes, 26.

57. Letter to author from Mattiebelle Gittinger, curator, Textile Museum, Washington, D.C., 27 July 1983.

58. Roderick H. Blackburn, *Cherry Hill* (Albany: Historic Cherry Hill, 1976), 119–20.

59. Sander, fig. 47, p. 13; author's inspection, Cherry Hill, Aug. 1979; Butler, 431, referring to Arlene M. Palmer, *A Winterthur Guide to Chinese Export Porcelain* (New York: Crown, 1976), pl. 3.

C H A P T E R 6

1. Benjamin Franklin, *Writings*, edited by Ann H. Smyth, vol. 6 (New York: MacMillan, 1905–1907), 460; Ibid., vol. 9, 110.

2. The advent of the dining room allowed entertaining to be separated from sleeping quarters. Except for tea services, still used in both parlor and bedroom, and for toilette sets, chinaware in quantity was now transplanted to this more public room.

3. Correspondence/Accounts Book, John R. Latimer, May 1815, order of William S. Evans; Downs MS 1138, Joseph Downs Manuscript Library, Winterthur Museum.

4. Record Book of John R. Latimer, 1828–29, 17 Dec. 1829; Downs MS 1140, Joseph Downs Manuscript Library, Winterthur Museum.

5. Jean M. Mudge, *Chinese Export Porcelain for the American Trade, 1785–1835*, 2d ed., rev. (Cranbury, N.J.: Associated University Presses, 1981), 104–29.

6. Ibid., 38–39, 92.

7. Robert B. Forbes, *Personal Reminiscences*, 3d ed., rev. (Boston: Little, Brown, 1892), 144.

8. John K. Fairbank, *The United States and China*, 4th ed. (Cambridge, Mass.: Harvard University Press, 1979), 165–67; Mudge, 146.

9. Fairbank, 181–88.

10. Robert Tichane, *Ching-tê-chen: Views of a Porcelain City* (Painted Post, N.Y.: New York State Institute for Glaze Research, 1983), 326–27.

11. Octavius T. Howe and Frederick C. Matthews, *American Clipper Ships, 1833–1858* (Salem, Mass.: Marine Research Society, 1926–27), vii.

12. Thomas Cary, ''Clipper Ships and the China Trade,'' in *Sketches of California* (Philadelphia: 1887), 130.

13. Howe and Matthews, vii.

14. Basil Lubbock, *The China Clippers* (Glasgow: James Brown, 1914), 104.

15. Letter of Robert Bennett Forbes to his wife, Rose Smith Forbes, 30 Dec. 1938, Robert B. Forbes's Letterbook, no. 3 (1838–39), Peabody Museum Archives, Salem, Mass.: 2; also Forbes, *Reminiscenses*, 144.

16. Ibid.

17. Ibid.

18. Ibid.; Letter to Rose S. Forbes, 28 Jan. 1839.

19. Ibid.

20. Letters of 5 June and 15 June 1839, Rose S. Forbes to Robert B. Forbes, Forbes Papers, no. 6, F2, Peabody Museum Archives, Salem, Mass.

21. Ibid., 29 Oct. 1839, F5.

22. Letters of Robert B. Forbes to Rose S. Forbes, 24 Oct., 22 and 24 Nov. 1839, Forbes papers, no. 6, Peabody Museum Archives, Salem, Mass.

23. E. K. Haviland, ''Early Steam Navigation in China,'' *The American Neptune* vol. 16 (1956), 12–16; vol. 17 (1957), 60–63.

24. Thomas Hunt and Company MS. 761, 1861–1869; H 943, vol. 26, Baker Library, Harvard Business School, Cambridge, Mass.

25. Kwang-Ching Liu, *Anglo-American Steamship Rivalry in China, 1862–1874* (Cambridge, Mass.: Harvard University Press, 1962), 168, 170.

26. Ibid., 3.

27. Letter of Augustine Heard, Sr., to Augustine Heard, Jr., 29 Nov. 1848, Heard MSS, v. BL-4, Letters 1814–1868, folder 6, BL.

28. Ibid., 30 May 1848.

29. Ibid., 5 Mar. 1850.

30. Ibid., 3 June 1850.

31. Ibid., 31 Oct. 1850.

32. Ibid., 6 Dec. 1852.

33. Ibid., 18 Feb. 1853.

34. Ibid., 10 May, 4 July 1853.

35. Ibid., 1 and 23 May 1854.

36. Letter of Augustine Heard, Sr., to Albert Heard, 5 Oct. 1855, Ibid.

37. Ibid., 18 Aug. 1856.

38. The invoice of a Shun Lee included a white and gilt dinner service, a blue line and gilt dinner service, and miscellaneous pieces in ''Pink Roman,'' ''Unique Alexander,'' and ''Unique Gothic.''

Other ceramics denoted "earthenware" were "white granite" in "French shape" shipped by the "Violet." Invoice, 14 Aug. 1866 and invoice, n.d., 1866, Thomas Hunt & Co., MS. pp. 76, 86–87, Baker Library, Harvard Business School, Cambridge, Mass.

39. Adele Ogden, *The California Sea Otter Trade, 1784–1848* (Berkeley, University of California Press, 1941), 157.

40. Ibid., 157–58.

41. Ibid., 158–59.

42. Ibid., Chap. 3, pp. 32–44, 52.

43. Hubert H. Bancroft, *The History of California* vol. 2 (San Francisco: History Co., 1886), 103.

44. Ogden, MS: "Trading Vessels on the California Coast, 1786–1848," Bancroft Library, University of California.

45. Ogden, *Sea Otter*, 159–62.

46. Ibid., 160–64.

47. Ibid., 43, 52, 67.

48. Jean Krase, "The Old World Ceramic Shards from San Diego's Presidio," Master's thesis (San Diego State University, 1979), 84.

49. Ogden, *Sea Otter*, 67.

50. Krase, 85.

51. Bancroft, 194–95.

52. Ogden, "Trading Vessels."

53. Ogden, *Sea Otter*, 87, 90.

54. List of Goods sold to Mission and Individuals, Blanchard and Door, San Francisco, 9 June 1823, Documentos para la Historia de California, 1770–1875, 4 vols., XVII, pp. 188–89 (transcript, San Diego Historical Society Library; original at Bancroft Library, University of California).

55. Ibid., 87–88.

56. "Invoice of Merchandise shipped by Perkins & Co. on board the American Brig *Nile*, Robert B. Forbes Master, Canton, June 15, 1825," Forbes MSS. E-1, Baker Library, Harvard Business School, Cambridge, Mass.

57. Ogden, *Sea Otter*, 90.

58. Bancroft, 392, 668–69.

59. Instructions for purchase and sale of goods on the Brig *Mary Esther*, 13 Feb. 1827, Archivo Particular de la Sra. Dna. Josefa Carrillo de Fitch, Vuida del Capitan Don Enrique D. Fitch, Fitch papers, vol. 1, 1827–1856, Documentas para la Historia de California (TS, San Diego Historical Society Library, original at the Bancroft Library, University of California).

60. Letter to author from Robert Edberg, archaeologist, Northridge Archaeological Research Center, Northridge, Calif. 19 Mar. 1832.

61. Letter of Alfred Robinson to Bryant and Sturgis, San Francisco, 1834, in Adele Ogden, ed., "Business Letters of Alfred Robinson," *California Historical Quarterly* 23, no. 4 (1924), 314.

62. Ibid., San Diego, 5 May 1836; 320–21.

63. "Invoice of Merchandise, shipped by William S. Hinckley, on board Brig *Crusader*, Thomas Sturgis Master . . . ," dated by Adele Ogden 1832–1833, Bancroft Library CB 106, vol. 4, n.f. [1832–1839].

64. "Account of Sales of Sundry Merchandise Shipped on Board Brig *Crusader* 2nd Voyage by Mr. William S. Hinckley . . . ," Bancroft Library CM 106, vol. 2, n.f. [1832–1837].

65. "Account of Sales of Merchandise recd for Brig *Avon* . . . ," dated by Adele Ogden 1834, Bancroft Library CB 106, vol. 2, [1832–

1837]. In 1835, William Henry Dana witnessed the arrival of the *Avon* at San Pedro, the port serving Los Angeles, with a full cargo of "Canton and American goods." Richard Henry Dana, *Two Years Before the Mast* (New York: Macmillan, 1909), 205.

66. "Invoice of Merchandize [sic] Shipped on Board E. & O.E. Schooner *Iolani*, Joseph Rogers Masters . . . , Honolulu, Hawaii, 25 Jan. 1835, William S. Hinckley, Bancroft Library CB 106, vol. 3, n.f.

67. "Account of Sales of Merchandise Rcd c/o *Clementine*—2d Voyage . . . ," dated by Adele Ogden, 1836–1837, Bancroft Library CB 106, vol. 2, n.f. [1832–1837]; William Hinckley to Nathan Spear, Honolulu, 24 Apr. 1836, Nathan Spear Correspondence, Bancroft Library, Univ. of Calif.

68. "Invoice of Merchandise Shipped by William S. Hinckley aboard the Brig *Clementine*, William I. Handley Master, Feb. 15, 1836 . . . ," Bancroft Library CB 106, vol. 3, [1834–1837].

69. David L. Felton and Lee Motz, MS Preliminary Draft, "A Summary of Archaeological Features Encountered During the Restoration of the Cooper-Molera Adobe Complex, Monterey, California," Cultural Resource Management Unit, California Department of Parks and Recreation, Sacramento, Calif., June 1982, 25.

70. Mudge, 144.

71. Bancroft, 670; Ogden, *Sea Otter*, 152.

72. Ogden, *Sea Otter*, 170–71.

73. Letter to author from David L. Felton, Sacramento, 8 Nov. 1982; also, H. H. Bancroft on Spear, *California Pioneer Register and Index* (Baltimore: Regional, 1964), 338.

74. William Willetts, *Nonya Ware and Kitchen Ch'ing* (Selangor, Malaysia: Oxford University Press, 1981), 63.

75. Willetts, 3–5; letter to author from Andrée Crépeau, archaeologist, Louisbourg, Nova Scotia, 1982.

76. Ogden, *Sea Otter*, 175 ff.; Ogden, "Trading Vessels."

77. "Invoice of Merchandise of ship *Alert*, 1840," Bill of Lading, Bryant and Sturgis Co., xerox copy, Tom Han Collection, Serra Museum, Calif., original at Harvard University.

78. "Invoice of D. H. Bartlett, August 30, 1841," Documentos para la Historia de California, Archivo Particular de la Sra. Doña Josefa Carrillo de Fitch, Vuida del Capitan Don Enrique D. Fitch, vol. 2, 1874, Collection no. 179, p. 296 (transcript, San Diego Historical Library, original at Bancroft Library).

79. Robert L. Schuyler, "Indian-Euro-American Interaction: Archaeological Evidence from Non-Indian Sites," in R. F. Heizer, ed., *Handbook of North American Indians*, vol. 8 (Smithsonian Institution, 1978), 69–79.

80. Oscar Lewis, *San Francisco: Mission to Metropolis* (Berkeley, Calif.: Howell-North Books, 1966), 135–36.

81. L. Eve Armentrout-Ma, "Big and Medium Businesses of Chinese Immigrants to the United States, 1850–1890: An Outline," *Bulletin of the Chinese Historical Society of America* 13, no. 7 (Sept. 1978), 1.

82. Amelia Ransome Neville, *The Fantastic City*, edited by Virginia Brastow (Boston: Houghton, Mifflin, 1932), 193, 194.

83. *Daily Alta California*, 4 Aug. 1949; reference, courtesy of Thomas Layton, Department of Anthropology, San Jose State University.

84. *Bogardus' Business Directory for San Francisco, Sacramento*

City (May 1850), California Historical Society, San Francisco.

85. *Register of First-Class Business Houses in San Francisco* (F. A. Bonnard, 1852), California Historical Society, San Francisco.

86. "Invoice of Merchandise shipped by Russell & Co. on board the Brig *Eagle* . . . consigned to Mess. S. H. Williams & Co., 8 February 1850," Forbes Collection, L-2, Baker Library, Harvard University.

87. John Quentin Feller, *The Canton Famille Rose Porcelains* (Salem, Mass.: Peabody Museum, 1982), p. 31, figs. 42 and 43.

88. H. A. Van Oort, *Chinese Porcelain of the 19th and 20th Centuries* (Lochem, the Netherlands: Uitgeversmaatschauppij de Tijdstroom B.V., 1977), 18–39.

89. *Tariff Acts Passed by the Congress of the United States, 1789 to 1909*, House of Representatives, Document 671; 61st Cong., 2d sess., 1909. Reference, courtesy of George L. Miller, Colonial Williamsburg.

90. Van Oort, 39–41.

91. Ibid., 48.

92. Vickery, Atkins and Torrey MSS, California Historical Society, San Francisco.

93. Eugen Neuhaus, MS: "Frederick Cheever Torrey, 1864–1935," California Historical Society, San Francisco.

94. Carol G. Wilson, *Gump's Treasure Trade* (New York: Thomas Y. Crowell, 1949), 56.

95. Elizabeth Collard, *Nineteenth-Century Pottery and Porcelain in Canada* (Montreal: McGill University Press, 1967), 163, 164.

96. Ibid., 165–66, 170.

97. Marie Elwood, "The Weldon Collection: Specimens of China Brought to the Colonies by the Early Settlers, I & IV," *Canadian Collector* (July-Aug. 1983), 26–29; *Canadian Collector* (Jan. 1984), 37–42; letter to author from Marie Elwood, Curator of History, Nova Scotia Museum, 21 Apr. 1980.

98. Letter to author from Elizabeth Collard, Canadian ceramic scholar [see note 95], 1984.

99. On a covered cup and saucer at the National Museum of Man, Ottawa, now damaged. Letter to author from Elizabeth Collard, 3 Oct. 1979. The Durell armorial is not, strictly speaking, Canadian, but rather, English colonial. Philip Durell (1707–1766) was present at Louisbourg in 1745 and 1758 for both English attacks on the then French fort. Shortly after Durell was named commander-in-chief of North America in 1766, he was taken ill and died before assuming office. Ronald Whate, "The Durell Service," *Canadian Collector*, vol. 20, no. 2 (March/April 1985), 48–50.

100. Collard, *Nineteenth-Century Pottery and Porcelain*, 165.

101. The following institutions were unable to identify these arms: the Archives Publique, Ottawa; the Flag Research Center, Winchester, Mass.; the College of Arms, London; and the Royal Ontario Museum, Toronto.

102. Lester A. Ross, MS: "Fort Vancouver, 1829–1860," Fort Vancouver National Historic Site, U.S. Department of the Interior, June 1976, p. 237.

103. Ibid., 238–41.

104. Letter to author from Lester A. Ross, 9 Nov. 1981.

105. Collard, *Nineteenth Century Pottery and Porcelain*, 51.

106. Ibid., 52, 59.

107. Ibid., 197.

108. Ibid.

CHAPTER 7

1. Clare Le Corbeiller, *China Trade Porcelains: Patterns of Exchange* (New York: Metropolitan Museum of Art, 1974), 36–67.

2. Jean M. Mudge, *Chinese Export Porcelain for the American Trade, 1785–1835,* 2d ed., rev. (Cranburg, N.J., 1981), fig. 57, p. 142.

3. Author's conversation with Elizabeth Sharpe, antique dealer, Conshocken, Pa., 1982.

4. Invoice, 16 Feb. 1774, Hodgson and Donaldson, London, Daybook, 1772–1774, Frederick Rhinelander, Rhinelander Manuscripts, New York Historical Society.

5. Mudge, 190.

6. A plate of this service is at the Peabody Museum, Salem, Mass.

7. In an 1848 New York auction, Crawford Allen bought the service; his daughter, Anne Crawford Allen Brown (Mrs. John Carter Brown), inherited the set. Letter, 27 Nov. 1974, Mrs. H. D. Sharpe to Duncan H. Mauran, Rhode Island Historical Society.

8. Letter to author from Jane Gaston Mahler, Manigault descendant and scholar, 19 Jan. 1982.

9. Jane Gaston Mahler, "Huguenots Adventuring in the Orient: Two Manigaults in China," *Transactions of the Huguenot Society of South Carolina,* no. 76, (1971), 16.

10. Illustrated, Mudge, 73; Patricia C. Fleming, "A Porcelain Story: Admiral S. F. du Pont's Voyage to the Orient. 1857–58," *The Delaware Antiques Show* (Wilmington, Del.: Delaware Museum of Art, 1965), 87.

11. Ibid., 83, 85.

12. "Catalogue of the Chinese Section," *Catalogue of the Philadelphia Exhibition* (Philadelphia: 1876), 5–14.

13. Arlene Palmer, *A Winterthur Guide to Chinese Export Porcelain* (New York: Crown, 1976), 56, fig. 24d.

14. Mudge, figs. 75–78, pp. 161–63.

15. In 1876, the author of the Chinese section of the catalogue to the Philadelphia Exhibition noted, "A small quantity of chinaware of the coarser kind is made in the vicinity of Canton for export to India and Europe." *Catalogue of the Philadelphia Exhibition*, 6.

16. Mary Gelruth, "The Importation of English Earthenware into Philadelphia," Master's thesis, University of Delaware and the Henry Francis du Pont Winterthur Museum, 1964, 121.

17. H. Crosby Forbes, *Hills and Streams: Landscape Decoration on Chinese Export Blue-and-White Porcelain* (Baltimore, Md.: International Exhibitions Foundation, 1982), 4.

18. Ibid., 4–12.

19. Mudge, 163–65.

20. Herbert, Peter, and Nancy Schiffer, *China for America* (Exton, Pa.: Schiffer, 1980), 109–10.

21. David Howard and John Ayers, *China for the West*, vol. 2 (New York: Sotheby Parke Bernet, 1978), 499.

22. David Howard, *New York and the China Trade* (New York: New York Historical Society, 1984), 78.

23. Susan G. Detweiler, *George Washington's Chinaware* (New York: Harry N. Abrams, 1982).

24. Jean Gordon Lee, *Philadelphians and the China Trade, 1784–1844* (Philadelphia: Philadelphia Museum of Art, 1984), 88.

25. Mudge, 177.

26. Ibid.

27. Worthington Chauncey Ford, ed., *Inventory of the Contents of Mount Vernon* (Cambridge, Mass.: University Press, 1909), xii.

28. Ibid., xvi.

29. Mudge, frontispiece.

30. Ibid.

31. Most of the china is "Rose Medallion" or "Rose Mandarin" with a few pieces of blue-and-white and green (celadon). Visit of author to Hyde Park, Aug. 1981; letter to author from Susan J. Brown, curator, Hyde Park, N.Y., 6 Oct. 1983; the vases are illustrated in Howard, 134–35.

32. Mudge, 172–73.

33. Howard, 87–94; also see William Butler, "New Yorker's Taste: Chinese Export Porcelain, 1750–1865," *Antiques* 125, no. 2 (Feb. 1984), 434.

34. Howard M. Chapin, *Illustrations of the Seals, Arms, and Flags of Rhode Island* (Providence, R.I.: Rhode Island Historical Society, 1930, 19. Reference, courtesy of Elizabeth Sharpe.

35. Betty I. Madden, *Art, Crafts, and Architecture in Early Illinois* (Chicago: University of Illinois Press, 1974), 81; Joyce R. Ahearn, "A Provisional Docent Research Paper on the Armorial Punch Bowl in the Bayou Bend Collection," MS prepared for Museum of Fine Arts, Houston, Tex., 1982.

36. Author's correspondence and conversation with Mrs. Peter Milliken, descendant and owner of the Arden china, 1981–83.

37. "Catalogue of China," the collection of Elizabeth C. Canby and her daughter, Elizabeth Canby Rumford, before 1890, MS, Lewis Rumford, Baltimore, Md.

38. Mudge, 177–80.

39. Harriet Ropes Cabot, *Handbook of the Bostonian Society* (Boston: Bostonian Society, 1979), 31; cf. Palmer, fig. 68, p. 104.

40. Letter from George Hayley to John Hancock, Miscellaneous Hancock Family Papers (1728–1815), Massachusetts Historical Society, Boston, Mass.

41. Suffolk County, MS. 25 July 1755, "Persons licens'd to Sell Tea, Coffee and China Ware the Ensuing Year," Massachusetts Historical Society, Boston, Mass.

42. Letter of John Jacob Astor to G. W. Van Schaick, 21 Apr. 1804, Van Schaick Papers, Box 1, Manuscript Division, New York Public Library.

43. The complete order read as follows: four sauceboats and cups (stands), one coffeepot, two sugar cups (bowls), four fruit baskets, forty-eight flat plates, four pudding dishes, one punch bowl, two smaller punch bowls, one dozen cups and saucers, six pickle dishes, four cake dishes, totalling $81.00 with extra charges. Invoice of John Jacob Astor for a box of chinaware for Dr. G. W. Van Schaick, New York, 21 Mar. 1805, Van Schaick Papers, Manuscript Division, New York Public Library.

44. Louis Manigault, MS, description of the Manigualt arms, written for his cousin, Henry Middleton Manigault, xerox copy courtesy of Jane Gaston Mahler, Charleston, S.C.

45. A. S. Salley, "The Book Plate in Colonial Times: Mark of a Scholar," *The State Magazine* (4 Nov. 1951), 14–15; Jane Gaston Mahler, "Huguenots," letters to the author from Jane Gaston Mahler, 1981–82.

46. John Q. Feller, *The Canton Famille Rose Porcelains* (Salem, Mass.: Peabody Museum, 1982), 23–27.

47. Mudge, 215–16.

48. Accession card no. 102, 253, Essex Institute, Salem, Mass.

APPENDIX A

1. Carolina Sassoon, *Chinese Porcelain Marks from Kenya* (Oxford, England: British Archaeological Reports International Series, 1978), (Supplementary) 43.

2. Michel Beurdeley, *A Connoisseur's Guide to Chinese Ceramics* (New York: Harper & Row, n.d.), 301. According to Hobson, marked wares are known as early as the Han, but he states that examples known to him have been incised after firing, thus the date, he admits, is questionable. R. L. Hobson, *Chinese Pottery and Porcelain*, 1, reprint of 1915 ed. (New York: Dover, 1976), 107.

3. Feng Xianmeng, et al., *History of Chinese Ceramics* (Beijing: Chinese Silicate Society, 1982), 224, 225.

4. H. A. Van Oort, *Chinese Porcelain of the 19th and 20th Centuries* (Lochem, The Netherlands: Uitgeversmaatschappij de Tijdstroom B. V., 1977), 181.

5. John A. Pope, *Chinese Porcelains from the Ardebil Shrine* (Washington, D.C.: Freer Gallery of Art, Smithsonian Institution, 1956), 34–35, pls. 76, 77, 79, 80, 84–87, 89–91, 96, 115–17, 118, 138; "Topkapu," 20–23.

6. Ibid., 130.

7. Hobson, i, 208.

8. Doreen Stoneham, Research Laboratory for Archaeology and the History of Art, Oxford, "Thermoluminescent Dating of Chinese Porcelain and the Detection of Imitations"; Wei Qingyun, Institute of Geophysics, Academia Sinica, Beijing, and M. J. Aitken, Research Laboratory for Archaeology and the History of Art, Oxford, "The Magnetic Record Carried in Ancient Chinese Pottery," unpublished papers, The International Conference on Ancient Chinese Pottery and Porcelain, Shanghai, November 1982.

9. T. Volker, *Porcelain and the Dutch East India Company*, 1602–1682 (Leiden, Holland: E. J. Brill, 1954), 66.

10. Ibid., 67.

11. Ibid., 88–89.

12. Ibid., 130.

13. Ibid.

14. Clarence Shangraw and Edward P. Von der Porten, MS, "The Drake and Cermeno Expeditions' Chinese Porcelains at Drakes Bay, California" (Santa Rosa, Calif.: Santa Rose Junior College and Drake Navigators Guild, 1981), 61.

15. Hobson, vol. 1, 208.

16. Ibid., 209.

17. Illustrated lists of pre-1956 shards (with no context) and post-1956 (in context, in part) provided by Audrey Noël Hume, 1983–84.

18. Jean M. Mudge, *Chinese Export Porcelain for the American Trade, 1785–1835*, 2nd ed., rev. (Cranbury, N.J.: Associated University Presses, 1981), 217.

APPENDIX B

1. R. L. Hobson, *Chinese Pottery and Porcelain*, vol. 2 (New York: Dover, 1976), 102.

2. Ibid., 75.

3. Herbert H. Sanders, *The World of Japanese Ceramics* (Palo Alto, Calif.: Kodansha, 1967), 225.

4. Feng Xianmeng et al., *History of Chinese Ceramics* (Beijing: Chinese Silicate Society, 1982), 385.

5. Letter of Père d'Entrecolles, 1 Sept. 1712, in S. W. Bushell, *Description of Chinese Pottery and Porcelain* (Oxford, Eng.: Clarendon Press, 1910), 182, 193.

6. Ibid., 196.

7. Ibid.

Selected Bibliography

For complete references see Notes, pages 274–289.

I Archives

Archivo General de Indias, Seville, Spain
Registros de Navíos, Manila Galleon trade documents. Selected copies of these manuscripts and others at the Bancroft Library, University of California, Berkeley, and the University of Texas Library, Austin.
Archivo General de la Nación, Mexico City
El Ramo de la Inquisición, household inventories
Baker Library, Harvard Business School
Forbes Collection, E-1, L-2
Heard Collection, v. BL-4, Letters 1814–68, Folder 6
Hunt and Company Manuscripts: 761, 1861–69; H943, vol. 26
Bancroft Library, University of California, Berkeley
Documentos para la Historia de California, 1770–1875: Fitch Papers. 4 vols. (transcripts at San Diego Historical Society Library)
Nathan Spear Manuscripts:
Account Books: [1830–35, 1832–37, 1834–37]
Correspondence; miscellaneous business papers
British Public Record Office, Kew, England
Colonial Papers, General Series 5/505, 508–12, 573, 709, 710, 749, 750, 848–51, 967–69, 1035, 1036, 1222–29, 1441–50.
California Historical Society, San Francisco
Business Directories, California 1850s
Vickery, Atkins, and Torrey Manuscripts
Colonial Williamsburg, Williamsburg, Va.
Archaeology and Ceramics Departments, Records
History Department, York County Virginia Inventories, June 1637–Mar. 1715/16; notebooks (TSS) 11, 12, 15
Field Museum of Natural History
Anthropology Department, Records
Historic Annapolis, Inc., Annapolis, Md.
Data File of Ceramics in Annapolis and Anne Arundel County, Md: "Annapolis and Anne Arundel County, Md: A Study of Urban Development of a Tobacco Economy, 1649–1776."
India Office Library and Records, London
Court of Directors
Court Books
General Correspondence
Despatch Books
Factory Records
Diary and Consultations
Copies of Letters Dispatched and Received
China
Marine Records
Ships Logs
Proceedings
China General Ledgers and Journals
Home Miscellaneous Series
Vol. 10 and 14
New England Genealogical Society, Boston
Peter Faneuil Papers
Thomas and John Hancock Papers
Daniel Henchman Papers
New York Historical Society, New York
Frederick Rhinelander Papers, Daybook 1772–74.
Robert Sanders Papers, Letterbook, 1752–58.
New York Public Library
Van Schaick Papers, Correspondence, 1804
Peabody Museum, Salem, Mass.
Robert B. Forbes Papers: Letterbook no. 3; no. 6, F 2 and 5.
Augustin F. Heard, Jr., Letters from Canton, 1854–58.
Queens College Library Archives, Flushing, New York
MSS Inventories:
Capt. Nicholas Dumaresq, 12 June 1702
Rev. Patrick Gordon, 16 Dec. 1702
Margrita van Varick, 29 May 1695/96
Rhode Island Historical Society
Edward Carrington Business Papers, 1799–1808
Santa Barbara Mission Archival Library, Santa Barbara, Calif.
1834 Soledad Mission Inventory
1843 Santa Clara Mission Inventory
Suffolk County Records, Boston
MSS Inventories, Docket nos.:
185, John Cogan, 20 May 1658; Mary Cogan, 31 Oct. 1660
171, Anna Keayne, 19 Sept. 1657
409, Henry Shrimpton, 1666
unnumbered, John Winthrop, 17 Feb. 1649

Widener Library, Harvard University, Cambridge, Mass.
  Bryant and Sturgis Collection (copies in Tom Han Collection, Serra Museum, San Diego, Calif.)
Winterthur Museum, Joseph Downs Manuscript Library
  "China Ware items—*Images—Animals*," unnumbered Index of Irving Whitall Lyon, n.d.
  John R. Latimer Papers, MS. 1138, Correspondence/Accounts Book, 1815; MS. 1140, Record Book, 1828–29

II Newspapers

The Boston News-letter, Boston, 1704–26
The Weekly News-letter, Boston, 1727–30
The Boston Weekly News-letter, Boston, 1730–57
The Massachusetts Gazette and the Boston News-letter, Boston, 1757–59, 1765–75
The Massachusetts Gazette, Boston, 1787–88
Daily Alta California, San Francisco, 4 Aug. 1849
The Maryland Gazette, Annapolis, 1728–34, 1775–1813
The Pennsylvania Packet, Philadelphia 1771–90
The South Carolina Gazette, Charleston, 1732–78
Supplement to *The South Carolina Gazette*, 16 June 1759, no. 1289, p. 2.
The Virginia Gazette, 1736–40, 1745–46, 1751–71

III Books

Adhyatman, Sumarah. *Antique Ceramics Found in Indonesia, Various Uses and Origins*. Jakarta: The Ceramic Society of Jakarta, 1981.
Ayers, John. *The Baur Collection*. 4 vols. Geneva: Collections Baur, c. 1968–74.
_____. *Far Eastern Ceramics in the Victoria and Albert Museum*. London: Sotheby, Parke Bernet, 1980.
Bailyn, Bernard. *The New England Merchants in the Seventeenth Century*. New York: Harper & Row, 1964.
Bakewell, P. J. *Silver Mining and Society in Colonial Mexico: Zacatecas, 1546–1700*. Cambridge, Eng.: Cambridge University Press, 1971.
Bancroft, Hubert Howe. *The History of California*. Vols. 1–5. San Francisco: History Company, 1886.
Barber, Edwin A. *The Ceramic Collector's Glossary*. Reprint of 1914 ed. New York: Da Capo Press, 1967.
Beurdeley, Cécile and Michel. *A Connoisseur's Guide to Chinese Ceramics*. Translated by Katherine Watson. New York: Harper & Row, 1975.
Beurdeley, Cécile and Michel. *Castiglione, Peintre Jésuite à la Cour de Chine*. Paris: Bibliothèque des Arts, 1971.
Beurdeley, Michel. *Chinese Trade Porcelain*. Rutland, Vt.: Charles E. Tuttle, 1962.
Billings, Warren M., ed. *The Old Dominion in the Seventeenth Century*. Chapel Hill, N.C.: University of North Carolina Press, 1975.
Blair, E. H., and J. A. Robinson, eds. *History of the Philippine Islands*. Vols. 2, 3, 5, 45. Cleveland: Arthur H. Clark, 1907.
Boger, Louise Ade. *The Dictionary of World Pottery and Porcelain*. New York: Scribner's, 1971.
Brading, D. A. *Miners and Merchants in Bourbon Mexico, 1763–1810*. Cambridge, Eng.: University Press, 1971.

Brodhead, John, and Edmund B. O'Callaghan, eds. *Documents Relative to the Colonial History of the State of New York*. Albany: 1856.
Bruce, Philip A. *Economic History of Virginia in the Seventeenth Century*. 2 vols. New York: Macmillan, 1896.
Bushell, S. W. *Description of Chinese Pottery and Porcelain*. Oxford: Clarendon Press, 1910.
Castillo, Carlos and Otto F. Bond, compilers. *The University of Chicago Spanish-English, English-Spanish Dictionary*. New York: Washington Square Press, 1966.
Chambers, Ephraim. *Cyclopedia, or, an Universal Dictionary of Arts and Sciences*. 7th ed. London: W. Innys, 1751–52.
Chandhuri, K. N. *The Trading World of Asia and the English East India Company, 1660–1760*. London: Cambridge University Press, 1978.
Chaunu, Pierre. *Seville et l'Atlantique, (1504–1650)*. 8 vols. Paris: A. Colin, 1955–56.
_____. *Les Philippines et le Pacifique des Iberiques*. 2 vols. Paris: Service d'Edition et de Vente des Publications de l'Education Nationale (SEVPEN), 1960–66.
Collard, Elizabeth. *Nineteenth-Century Pottery and Porcelain in Canada*. Montreal: McGill University Press, 1967.
Condon, Thomas J. *New York Beginnings*. New York: New York University Press, 1968.
Dermigny, Louis. *La Chine et L'Occident: Le Commerce de Canton au XVIIIe Siècle, 1719–1833*. 3 vols. Paris: SEVPEN, 1964.
Donnelly, P. J. *Blanc de Chine*. London: Faber and Faber, 1969.
Earle, Alice Morse. *China Collecting in America*. New York: Scribner's, 1892.
_____. *Customs and Fashions in Old New England*. Reprint of 1893 ed. Detroit: Singing Tree Press, 1968.
Feng, Xianmeng, et al. *History of Chinese Ceramics*. Beijing: Chinese Silicate Society, 1982.
Forbes, Robert B. *Personal Reminiscences*. 3d ed., rev. Boston: Little, Brown, 1892.
de Gemelli Careri, Giovanni Francisco. *Voyage du Tour du Monde, 1693*. Translated by M.L.N. [full name not given] from Italian original, 1699–1700. Paris: E. Ganeau, 1727.
Gibson, Charles. *The Aztecs Under Spanish Rule*. Stanford, Calif. Stanford University Press, 1964.
_____. *Spain in America*. New York: Harper & Row, 1966.
Godden, Geoffrey A. *Oriental Export Market Porcelain, and Its Influence on European Wares*. New York: Granada, 1979.
Guijo, Gregorio M. *Diario 1648–1684*. 2 vols. Mexico: Editorial Porrua, 1952.
Haring, Clarence R. *The Spanish Empire in America*. New York: Oxford University Press, 1947.
Harrington, Virginia D. *The New England Merchant on the Eve of the Revolution*. New York: Columbia University Press, 1935.
Harrisson, Barbara. *Swatow in Het Princessehof*. Leeuwarden, Holland: Gemeentelijk Museum Het Princessehof, 1979.
Hobson, R. L. *Chinese Pottery and Porcelain*. 2 vols. in 1; reprint of 1915 ed. New York: Dover, 1976.
_____. *The Wares of the Ming Dynasty*. Reprint of 1923 ed. Rutland, Vt.: Charles E. Tuttle, 1975.
Honey, W. B. *Guide to the Later Chinese Porcelain Periods of K'ang Hsi, Yung Cheng, and Chienlung*. London: Board of Education, the Victoria and Albert Department of Ceramics, 1927.

_____. *The Ceramic Art of China and Other Countries of the Far East*. London: Faber and Faber, 1944.

Howard, David Sanctuary. *Chinese Armorial Porcelain*. London: Faber and Faber, 1974.

Howard, David, and John Ayers. *China for the West*. 2 vols. London: Sotheby Parke Bernet, 1978.

Hume, Ivor Noël. *Archaeology and Wetherburn's Tavern*. Colonial Williamsburg Archaeology Series, no. 3. Williamsburg: Colonial Williamsburg Foundation, 1969a.

_____. *Pottery and Porcelain in Colonial Williamsburg's Archaeological Collections*. Colonial Williamsburg Archaeological Series, no. 2. Williamsburg: Colonial Williamsburg Foundation, 1969b.

Hyde, J. A. Lloyd. *Chinese Export Porcelain*. Newport, Eng.: Ceramic Book, 1954.

Israel, J. I. *Race, Class, and Politics in Colonial Mexico, 1610–1670*. London: Oxford University Press, 1975.

Jakobsen, B. von Kristian. *Islamische Keramik*. Hamburg: Bilderhefte des Museums für Kunst und Gewerbe, 1959.

Jenyns, Soame. *Japanese Porcelain*. London: Faber and Faber, 1965a.

_____. *Later Chinese Porcelains*. London: Faber and Faber, 1965b.

Jones, Alice Hanson. *American Colonial Wealth: Documents and Methods*. New York: Arno Press, 1977.

Jörg, C. J. A. *Porcelain and the Dutch China Trade*. The Hague: Martinus Nijhoff, 1982.

Kerr, Robert, ed. *A General History and Collection of Voyages and Travels*. Vol. 10. Edinburgh: Blackwood, 1924.

Klein, Adalbert, ed. *Islamische Keramik*. Düsseldorf: Hetjens-Museum, 1969.

Klein, Adalbert. *Islamische Keramik*. Baden-Baden: Holle Verlag, 1976.

Krell, Dorothy, ed. *The California Missions*. Menlo Park, Calif.: Lane, 1979.

Kurita, Hideo. *Kurita Museum*. Tokyo: Kurita Museum, 1981.

Lach, Donald F. *Asia in the Making of Europe: The Century of Discovery*. Vol. 1. Chicago: University of Chicago Press, 1965.

_____. *Asia in the Making of Europe: A Century of Wonder*. Vol. 2. Chicago: University of Chicago Press, 1970.

Le Corbeiller, Clare. *China Trade Porcelain: Patterns of Exchange*. New York: Metropolitan Museum of Art, 1974.

Liggett, Barbara. *Archaeology at Franklin's Court*. Harrisburg, Pa.: Eastern National Park and Monument Association, 1973.

_____. *Archaeology at New Market*. Philadelphia: Athenaeum, 1978.

Lockwood, Stephen C. *Augustine Heard and Co., 1858–1862: American Merchants in China*. Cambridge, Mass.: Harvard University Press, 1971.

Locsin, Leandro and Cecilia. *Oriental Ceramics Discovered in the Philippines*. Rutland, Vt.: Charles E. Tuttle, 1967.

Marx, Robert F. *Pirate Port: the Story of the Sunken City of Port Royal*. New York: World, 1967.

_____. *The Treasure Fleets of the Spanish Main*. Cleveland: World, 1968.

_____. *Shipwrecks of the Western Hemisphere, 1492–1825*. New York: World, 1971.

_____. *Port Royal Rediscovered*. New York: Doubleday, 1973.

Medley, Margaret. *The Chinese Potter: A Practical History of Chinese Ceramics*. New York: Scribner's, 1976.

Meng, Ho Wing. *Straits Chinese Porcelain*. Singapore: Times Books International, 1983.

Mikami, Tsugio. *The Art of Japanese Ceramics*. New York: Weatherhill, 1972.

Minchinton, Walter E. *The Growth of English Overseas Trade in the Seventeenth and Eighteenth Centuries*. London: Methuen, 1969.

Morse, Hosea Ballou. *The Chronicles of the East India Company Trading to China, 1635–1834*. 5 vols. Oxford: Clarendon Press, 1926.

Moule, A. C., and Paul Pelliot. *Marco Polo: The Description of the World*. London: Routledge, 1938.

Muckelroy, Keith, ed. *Archaeology Under Water*. New York: McGraw-Hill, 1980.

Mudge, Jean McClure. *Chinese Export Porcelain for the American Trade, 1785–1835*. 2d ed., rev. Cranbury, N.J.: Associated University Presses, 1981.

O'Callaghan, Edmund B., ed. *The Documentary History of the State of New York*. Vols. 1, 3. Reprint of 1849–51 ed. New York: Columbia University Press, 1933.

Ogden, Adele. *The California Sea Otter Trade, 1784–1848*. Berkeley, Calif.: University of California Press, 1941.

Parry, J. H. *The Spanish Seaborne Empire*. London: Hutchinson, 1966.

_____. *Trade and Dominion: The European Overseas Empires in the Eighteenth Century*. New York: Praeger, 1971.

Pearson, Jonathan, trans., and Arnold J. F. van Laer, ed. *Early Records of the City and County of Albany and the Colony of Rensselaerwyck*. Vols. 1, 4. Albany, N.Y.: University of the State of New York, 1869–1919.

Picard, Robert, et al. *Les Compagnies des Indes*. Grenoble, France: Artaud, 1966.

Pomfret, John E. *Founding the American Colonies, 1583–1660*. New York: Harper & Row, 1970.

Pope, John Alexander. *Chinese Porcelains from the Ardebil Shrine*. Washington, D.C.: Freer Gallery of Art, Smithsonian Institution, 1956.

_____, ed. *Oriental Ceramics: The World's Great Collections*. 12 vols. Tokyo: Kodansha, 1976–1978.

Quimby, Ian M. G., ed. *Ceramics in America*. Charlottesville, Va.: University of Virginia Press, 1973.

Rawson, Jessica. *Chinese Ornament: The Lotus and the Dragon*. London: British Museum, 1984.

Records and Files of the Quarterly Courts of Essex County, Massachusetts, 1636–1683. Vols. 1–8. Salem: Essex Institute, 1911.

Roth, Stig. *Chinese Porcelain Imported by the Swedish East India Company*. Translated by Mary G. Clarke. Göteborg, Sweden: Gotenburg Historical Society, 1965.

Sanders, Herbert H. *The World of Japanese Ceramics*. Palo Alto, Calif.: Kodansha, 1967.

Scheurleer, D. F. Lunsingh. *L'Armoire Hollandaise aux Porcelaines de Chine*. Paris: Les Presses Artistique, 1971.

_____. *Chinese Export Porcelain*. New York: Faber and Faber, 1974.

Schurz, William L. *The Manila Galleon*. Reprint of 1939 ed. New York: Dutton, 1959

Scott, Kenneth, and Ken Stryker-Rodda, eds. *New York Historical Manuscripts: Dutch*, vols. 1–4. Translated and annotated by Arnold J. F. van Laer. Baltimore: Genealogical Publishing Company, 1974.

Singleton, Esther. *Social New York Under the Georges, 1714–1776*. New York: Appleton, 1902.

_____. *Dutch New York*. New York: Dodd, Mead 1909.

South, Stanley, ed. *The Conference on Historic Archaeology Papers, 1968*. Vol. 3, pt. 2: "Historical Archeology Forum." Columbia, S.C.: 1970.

_____. *Research Strategies in Historical Archaeology*. New York: Academic Press, 1977.

Sullivan, Michael. *The Meeting of Eastern and Western Art: From the Sixteenth Century to the Present Day*. Greenwich, Conn.: New York Graphic Society, 1973.

Tariff Acts Passed by the Congress of the United States, 1789–1909. House of Representatives, Document 671, 61st Cong., 2d sess., 1909.

Taylor, Joan du Plat, ed. *The International Journal of Nautical Archaeology and Underwater Exploration*. Vols. 1, 4–9. London, New York, and San Francisco: Academic Press, 1972–1981.

Tichane, Robert. *Ching-tê-chen: Views of a Porcelain City*. Painted Post, N.Y.: New York State Institute for Glaze Research, 1983.

Toussaint, Manuel. *Pintura Colonial en México*. Mexico City: Universidad Nacional Autónoma de México: Instituto de Investigaciones Estéticas, 1965.

_____. *Colonial Art in America*. Translated by Elizabeth W. Weismann. Austin, Tex.: University of Austin Press, 1967.

Van der Pijl-Ketel, C. L., ed. *The Ceramic Load of the "Witte Leeuw," (1613)*. Amsterdam: Rijksmuseum, 1982.

van Laer, A. J. F., ed. and trans. *Correspondence of Jeremias van Rensselaer, 1651–1674*. Albany, N.Y.: University of the State of New York, 1932.

_____. *Correspondence of Maria van Rensselaer, 1669–1689*. Albany, N.Y.: University of the State of New York, 1935.

Van Oort, H. A. *The Porcelain of Hung-Hsien*. Lochem, The Netherlands: Uitgeversmaatschappij De Tijdstroom B. V., 1970.

_____. *Chinese Porcelain of the 19th and 20th [sic] Centuries*. Lochem, The Netherlands: Uitgeversmaatschappij De Tijdstroom B. V., 1977.

Van Rensselaer, Mrs. Schuyler. *History of the City of New York in the Seventeenth Century*. 2 vols. New York: Macmillan, 1909.

Volker, T. *Porcelain and the Dutch East India Company, 1602–1682*. Leiden, The Netherlands, E. J. Brill, 1954.

_____. *The Japanese Porcelain Trade of the Dutch East India Company After 1683*. Leiden: E. J. Brill, 1959.

Willetts, William, and Lim Suan Poh. *Nonya Ware and Kitchen Ch'ing*. Selanyor, Malaysia: Oxford University Press, 1981.

Woodward, Caroline S. *Oriental Ceramics at the Cape of Good Hope, 1652–1795*. Cape Town, South Africa: A. A. Balkema, 1974.

Yeo, S. T., and Jean Martin. *Chinese Blue and White Ceramics*. Singapore: Arts Orientalis, 1978.

Yule, Sir Henry. *Hobson-Jobson, Being a Glossary of Anglo-Indian Colloquial Words and Phrases*. London: J. Murray, 1886.

Zaide, Gregorio F. *The Philippines Since Pre-Spanish Times*. Manila: R. P. Garcia, 1949.

IV Archaeological Articles and Reports

Addis, Sir John M. "Chinese Porcelain Found in the Philippines." *Transactions of the Oriental Ceramic Society*, 37 (1967–69) (1968a): 17–36.

_____, ed. *Manila Trade Pottery Seminar*. 9 pamphlets. Manila (1968b).

Aga-Oglu, Kamer. "Late Ming and Early Ch'ing Porcelain Fragments from Archaeological Sites in Florida." *Florida Anthropologist* 8, no. 4 (Dec. 1955): 111–16.

Ayers, John. "Chinese Porcelain of the Sultans in Istanbul." *Transactions of the Oriental Ceramic Society* 47 (1982–83), (1983): 77–102.

Beaudry, Mary C., et al. "A Vessel Typology for Early Chesapeake Ceramics." *Historical Archaeology* 17, no. 1 (1983): 18–39.

Benchley, Peter. "Bermuda: Balmy, British, and Beautiful." *National Geographic* 140 (July 1971): 93–121.

Butler, Joseph T. "Chinese Porcelain Figures of Westerners." *Antiques* 79, no. 2 (Feb. 1961): 170–73.

Cervantes, Gonzalo Lopez "Porcelana Oriental en la Nueva Espana." *Anales del Instituto Nacional de Antropologia e Historia* [INAH] (1976–77): 65–82.

_____. "El Templo Mayor: Excavacionese y estudios." INAH (1982): 255–82.

Cole, Fay-Cooper. "Chinese Pottery in the Philippines." *Fieldiana*. Publication 162, Anthropological Series 12, no. 1 (New York: Kraus Reprint, 1968): 3–16.

Crossman, Carl L. "The Rose Medallion and Mandarin Patterns in China Trade Porcelain." *Antiques* 92, no. 4 (Oct. 1967): 530–35.

De Mello, Ulysses P. "The Ship Wreck of the Galleon *Sacramento*— 1668 off Brazil." *International Journal of Nautical Archaeology and Underwater Exploration* [IJNA] 8 (1979), 211–23.

Elwood, Marie. "The Weldon Collection: Specimens of China Brought to the Colonies by the Early Settlers, Particularly the Loyalists." *Canadian Collector* 18, no. 4 (July–Aug. 1983): 26–29.

_____. "The Weldon Collection: Specimens of China Brought to the Colonies by the Early Settlers, Particularly the Loyalists, Part IV." *Canadian Collector* 19, no. 1 (Jan. 1984): 37–42.

Evans, William S., Jr. "Food and Fantasy: Material Culture of the Chinese in California and the West, c. 1850–1900." In *Archaeological Perspectives on Ethnicity in America*, edited by Robert L. Schuyler. Farmingdale, N.Y.: Baywood, 1980, 89–90.

Feister, Lois. "Analysis of the Ceramics Found at the Vereberg Tavern Site, Albany Co., N.Y." *Man in the Northeast* 10 (1975): 2–16.

Feller, John Quentin. "Canton *Famille Rose* Porcelain; Part I: Rose Medallion." *Antiques* 124, no. 4 (Oct. 1983): 748–57.

_____. "Canton *Famille Rose* Porcelain; Part II: Mandarin." *Antiques* 125, no. 2 (Feb. 1984): 444–53.

Fontana, Bernard L., and J. C. Greenleaf. "Johnny Ward's Ranch: A Study in Historic Archaeology." *The Kiva* 28 (1962): 92–93.

Fox, Elizabeth Pratt. "Ceramics and Glass." In *The Great River: Art and Society in the Connecticut Valley, 1635–1820*. Hartford, Conn.: Wadsworth Atheneum, 1985.

Goggin, John M. "Stratigraphic Tests in the Everglades National Park." *American Antiquity* 15, no. 3 (1950): 228–46.

Gourley, Hugh, III. "History in Houses: Carrington House, Providence, R.I." *Antiques* 79, no. 2 (Feb. 1961): 183–86.

Greenwood, Roberta S., ed. *3500 Years on One City Block: San Buenaventura Mission Plaza Project Archaeological Report, 1974*. Ventura, Calif.: Redevelopment Agency, 1975.

_____. *The Changing Faces of Main Street: Ventura Mission Plaza Archaeological Project*. Ventura, Calif.: Redevelopment Agency, 1976.

_____. *The Ontiveros Adobe: Early Rancho Life in Alta California*. Santa Fe Springs, Calif.: Redevelopment Agency, 1982.

____. *The Bandini-Cota Adobe, Prado Dam, Riverside City, California*. Los Angeles: U.S. Army Corps of Engineers, 1983a.

_____. *New Melones Archaeological Project, Calif.: Review and Synthesis of Research at Historical Sites*. Final Report of the New Melones Archaeological Project 7, 1983b, 175–200.

Guthrie, C. L. "Colonial Economy: Trade, Industry, and Labor in Seventeenth-Century Mexico City." *Revista De Historia de América* 7 (Dec. 1939): 103–34.

Hanson, Lee, and Dick Ping Hsu. "Casemates and Cannonballs: Archaeological Investigations at Fort Stanwix, Rome, N.Y." *National Park Service Publications in Archaeology* 14 (1975).

Haskell, Helen W. *The Middleton Place Privy House: An Archaeological View of Nineteenth-Century Plantation Life*. Columbus, S.C.: Institute of Archeology and Anthropology, University of South Carolina, 1981.

Henderson, Graeme. "Indiamen Traders of the East." *Archaeology* 33, no. 6 (Nov.–Dec. 1980): 18–25.

Herman, Lynne L., et al. "Ceramics in St. Mary's City, Maryland, During the 1840s: A Socioeconomic Study." *The Conference on Historic Site Archaeology Papers*, vol. 8, pt. 1 (1973): 52–93.

Hume, Audrey Noël. "The Wetherburn Site Block 9, Area N, Col. Lots 20 and 21." *Report on the Archaeological Excavations of 1965–66*, vol. 2, pt. 3 (Aug. 1970).

Hume, Ivor Noël. "Excavations at Rosewell in Gloucester County, Virginia, 1957–1959." *U.S. National Museum Bulletin* 225 (1962), 155–228.

_____. "Excavations at Tutter's Neck in James County, Virginia, 1960–1961." *U.S. National Museum Bulletin* 249 (1968), 29–72.

Johnson, Paul F., et al. "The Cornwallis Cave Shipwreck, Yorktown, Virginia." *IJNA* 6 (1978): 205–26.

Keith, Donald H. "A 14th-century Cargo Makes Port At Last." *National Geographic* 156, no. 2 (Aug. 1979): 231–42.

Kirkman, J. S. "A Portuguese Wreck Off Mombasa, Kenya." *IJNA* 1 (1972): 153–57.

Lake, Rodrigo R. Rivero. "Comercio Artistico con el Oriente del Siglo XVI al Siglo XVIII." *Catalogo 8 Festival Internacional Cervantino*. Guanajuato, Mexico, (1980): 3–6.

Laufer, Berthold. "The Relations of the Chinese to the Philippine Islands." *Smithsonian Miscellaneous Collections* 50 (1907): 248–84.

_____. "Chinese Pottery in the Philippines, a Postscript." *Fieldiana*. Publication 162, Anthropological series 12, no. 1 (New York: Kraus Reprint, 1968): 17–31.

Le Corbeiller, Clare. "China Trade Armorial Porcelain in America." *Antiques* 112 (Dec. 1977): 1124–29.

Lightley, Robert A. "An Eighteenth-Century Dutch East Indiaman Found at Capetown, 1971." *IJNA* 5 (1976): 305–16.

Link, Marion Clayton. "Exploring the Drowned City of Port Royal." *National Geographic* 117 (Feb. 1960): 151–83.

Lister, Florence C. and Robert H. "Mexican Subway Excavations." *Historical Archaeology* 8 (1974a): 17–52.

_____. "Non-Indian Ceramics from the Mexico City Subway." *El Palacio* 81, no. 2 (1974b): 25–97.

Mahler, Jane Gaston. "Huguenots Adventuring in the Orient: Two Manigaults in China." *Transactions of the Huguenot Society of South Carolina*, no. 76 (1971): 1–42.

Martin, Colin M. "Spanish Armada Pottery." *IJNA* 8 (1979): 179–302.

Magalousis, Nicholas M., and Paul A. Martin. "Mission San Juan Capistrano: Preservation and Excavation of a Spanish Colonial Landmark." *Archaeology* (May/June 1981), pp. 60–63.

Miller, Jefferon J., II. "Ceramics from an Eighteenth-Century Wilderness Fort." *Antiques* 117, no. 2 (June 1970): 888–92.

Montgomery, R. G., et al. "Franciscan Awatovi." *Papers of the Peabody Museum of American Archaeology and Ethnology* 36 (1949): 94–95.

Moran, Geoffrey P., et al. "Archeological Investigations at the Narbonne House." Salem Maritime National Historic Site, Cultural Resources Management Study no. 6. U.S. Dept. of the Interior, Boston, Mass. 1982.

Mudge, Jean McClure. "Chinese Export Porcelain in Salem." In *Ceramics and Glass at the Essex Institute*. Salem, Mass.: Essex Institute, 1985, 6–23.

Nicks, Gertrude. "Toward a Trait List for the North Saskatchewan River in the Late-Eighteenth and Early-Nineteenth Centuries." *The Western Canadian Journal of Anthropology* 1, no. 2 (1969): n.p.

Norman-Wilcox, Gregor. "American Ships in the China Trade." *Bulletin of the Los Angeles Country Museum* 7 (Winter 1955):

Nylander, Richard C. "The Jonathan Sayward House, York, Maine." *Antiques* 116, no. 3 (Sept. 1979): 567–75.

Ogden, Adele, ed. "Business Letters of Alfred Robinson." *California Historical Quarterly* 23, no. 4 (1944): 301–34.

Olsen, John W. "A Study of Chinese Ceramics Excavated in Tucson." *The Kiva* 44, no. 1 (Fall 1978): 1–50.

Otto, John S. "Artifacts and Status Differences: a Comparison of Ceramics from Planter, Overseer, and Slave Sites on an Antebellum Plantation." In *Research Strategies in Historical Archaeology*, edited by Stanley South. New York: Academic Press, 1977, 91–118.

Outlaw, Alain. "Excavations at Governor's Land, 'A Suburb of James Citty.'" *Notes on Virginia*, no. 19 (Summer 1979): 24–27.

Peterson, Eugene T. "China at Mackinac." *Early Man* 4, no. 4 (Winter 1982): 33–35.

Peterson, Mendel. "Reach for the New World." *National Geographic* 152, no. 6 (Dec. 1977): 724–67.

_____. "Graveyard of the Quicksilver Galleons." *National Geographic* 156, no. 6 (Dec. 1979): 850–76.

Piercy, R. C. M. "Portuguese Ship Sunk Off Ft. Jesus, 1697." *IJNA* 7 (1978): 303–5.

Pope, John Alexander. "Fourteenth-Century Blue-and-White, a Group of Chinese Porcelains in the Topkapu Sarayi Muzesi, Istanbul." *Freer Gallery of Art Occasional Papers* 2, no. 1, Smithsonian Institution (1952): 1–85.

Quellmalz, C. R. "Chinese Porcelain Excavated from North American Pacific Coast Sites." *Oriental Art*, New Series, vol. 18, no. 2 (Summer 1972): 148–54.

_____. "Late Chinese Provincial Export Wares." *Oriental Art* 22, no. 3 (Autumn 1976): 289–98.

Ritchie, Robert C. "London Merchants, the New York Market and the Recall of Sir Edmund Andros." *New York History* 57 (Jan. 1976): 5–29.

Ross, Lester A. "Fort Vancouver, 1829–1860." U.S. Dept. of the Interior National Park Service, Ft. Vancouver National Historic Site, 1976.

Rudolph, Richard C. "Chinese Armorial Porcelain in Mexico." *Archives of the Chinese Art Society of America* 15 (1961): 13–20.

Saltus, Allen R. "Rare Oriental Porcelain Recovered from 1733 Shipwreck." *Archives and History News* 3, no. 5 (Sept.–Oct. 1972): 1.

Sassoon, Caroline. "Chinese Porcelain Marks from Kenya." British Archaeological Reports International Series (supplementary) 43 (1978).

Sassoon, Hamo. "Ceramics from the Wreck of a Portuguese Ship at Mombasa." *Azania*, Journal of the British Institute in Eastern Africa, vol. 16 (1981): 97–130.

Schulz, Peter D. "Archaeological Investigations in Old Town San Diego: Architectural Features." Cultural Resource Management Unit, California Department of Parks and Recreation, Sacramento, 12 July 1982.

Sheaf, Colin. "The Private Collection of Captain M. Hatcher." In *Arts of Asia* 15, no. 4, 112–115.

Shenk, Lynette, and George A. Teague. "Excavations at the Tubac Presidio." Arizona State Museum: Archaeological Series, no. 85 (1975): 92–94.

Smith, Hale G. "Archaeological Significance of Oriental Porcelains in Florida Sites." *Florida Anthropologist* 8, no. 4 (Dec. 1955): 111–16.

Snow, Cordelia T. "A Brief History of the Palace of the Governors and a Preliminary Report of the 1974 Excavation." *El Palacio* 80, no. 3 (Fall 1974): 1–21.

South, Stanley, and Michael Hartley. "Deep Water and High Ground, a Seventeenth-Century Low Country Settlement." Research Manuscript Series 166. Institute of Archeology and Anthropology, University of South Carolina, 1980.

Sténuit, Robert. "The Sunken Treasure of St. Helena." *National Geographic* 154 (Oct. 1978): 562–76.

_____. "The Treasure of Porto Santo." *National Geographic* 148 (Aug. 1975): 260–75.

Stone, Garry W. "Ceramics in Suffolk County Massachusetts Inventories, 1680–1775." In *The Conference on Historic Site Archaeology Papers*, edited by Stanley South, pt. 2. Columbia, S.C.: University of South Carolina, 1970, 73–90.

Sullivan, Michael. "Kendi." *Archives of the Chinese Art Society of America* 11 (1957): 40–58.

_____. "Notes on Chinese Export Wares in Southeast Asia." *Transactions of the Oriental Ceramic Society* 33 (1960–62): 61–77.

Teague, George A. "Reward Mine and Associated Sites: Historical Archaeology on the Papago Reservation." *Western Archaeological Center Publications*, no. 11 (1980): 70–77.

Teller, Barbara Gorley. "Ceramics in Providence, 1750–1800." *Antiques* 106, no. 4 (Oct. 1968), 570–77.

Theoret, Marc A. "Canada: Quebec Province: Ft. St. Jean Project." *IJNA* 5 (1976): 348–53.

Tschopik, Harry. "An Andean Ceramic Tradition in Historical Perspective." *American Antiquity* 15, no. 3 (1950): 196–218.

Von der Porten, Edward P. "The Drake Puzzle Solved." *Pacific Discovery* 37, no. 3 (July–Sept. 1984): 22–26.

Wagner, Kip. "Drowned Galleons Yield Spanish Gold." *National Geographic* 127 (Jan. 1965): 1–37.

Wenwu (Cultural Relics), 1980: nos. 4, 11; 1981, no. 1.

West, Robert C. "The Mining Community in Northern New Spain: The Parral Mining District." *Ibero-Americana* 30 (1949).

Whate, Ron E. "The Ceramic Artifacts from Ft. St. Joseph." *Research Bulletin*. National Historic Parks and Sites Branch, Ottawa, 1977.

_____. "A Cargo of Porcelains for Montreal, 1960." *Canadian Collector* 16, no. 1 (Jan.–Feb. 1980): 24–28.

V Exhibition Catalogues

Addis, Sir John M. *South-East Asian and Chinese Trade Pottery*. Hong Kong: Oriental Ceramic Society of Hong Kong, 1979.

Carswell, John, ed. *Blue and White Chinese Porcelain and Its Impact on the Western World*. Chicago: David and Alfred Smart Gallery, University of Chicago, 1985.

Catalogue of the Philadelphia Exhibition, Philadelphia: 1876.

Curtis, Phillip H. *Chinese Export Porcelain: A Loan Exhibition from New Jersey Collections*. Newark, N.J.: Newark Museum, 1979.

Eastern Ceramics and Other Works of Art from the Collection of Gerald Reitlinger. London: Ashmolean Museum, 1981.

Exhibition of the Archaeological Finds of the People's Republic of China. London: 1975.

Feng Xianming. "Archaeological Research on Chinese Ceramics." In *Exhibition of Ceramic Finds from Ancient Kilns in China*. Hong Kong: Fung Ping Shan Museum, University of Hong Kong, 1981, 15–18.

Forbes, H. Crosby. *Hills and Streams: Landscape Decoration on Chinese Export Blue-and-White Porcelain*. Baltimore: International Exhibitions Foundation, 1982a.

_____. *Yang-ts'ai: The Foreign Colors*. Milton, Mass.: China Trade Museum, 1982b.

Howard, David Sanctuary. *New York and the China Trade*. New York: New York Historical Society, 1984.

Kilburn, Richard S. *Transitional Wares and Their Forerunners*. Hong Kong: Hong Kong Oriental Ceramic Society, 1981.

Lang, Gordon, and Eric Till. Untitled catalogue, the Japanese and Chinese Porcelains of the Seventeenth and Eighteenth Centuries at Burghley House, Stamford, Lincolnshire, England, n.d. [c. 1981].

Le Corbeiller, Clare. *China Trade Porcelain: A Study in Double Reflections*. New York: China Institute of America, 1973.

Lee, Jean Gordon. *Philadelphians and the China Trade, 1784–1844*. Philadelphia: Philadelphia Museum of Art, 1984.

Lerner, Martin. *Blue and White: Early Japanese Export Ware*. New York: Metropolitan Museum of Art, 1978

Little, Stephen. *Chinese Ceramics of the Transitional Period: 1620–1683*. New York: China Institute in America, 1983.

Montgomery, Susan, ed. *Unearthing New England's Past: the Ceramic Evidence*. Lexington, Mass.: Museum of Our National Heritage, 1984.

Sander, Penny J. *"A Choice Sortment:" Ceramics from New England Homes*. Boston: Society for the Preservation of New England Antiquities, 1981.

Scheurleer, D. F. Lungsingh. *Mededelingenblad Nederlandse vereniging van vrienden van de ceramick*. Amsterdam: Frits Lugt Collection, 1981.

Tam, Laurence C. S., ed. *Chingtechen Porcelains of the Ming and Ch'ing Dynasties from the Collection of the T. Y. Chao Family Foundation*. Hong Kong: Hong Kong Museum of Art, 1978.

_____. *An Anthology of Chinese Ceramics*. Hong Kong: Hong Kong Museum of Art, 1980.

Trubner, Henry, and Tsugio Mikami. *Treasures of Asian Art from the Idemitsu Collection*. Seattle: Seattle Museum of Art, 1981.

Trubner, Henry, and William Jay Rathbun. *China's Influence on American Culture in the 18th and 19th Centuries*. New York: China Institute in America, 1976.

Index

Numbers in italics refer to pages with illustrations.

PHOTO CREDITS

All photos not attributed to the following photographers were taken by the author.

Albany Institute of History and Art: Figs. 200, 363.
Armen Photographers: Figs. 164, 245.
David L. Arnold: Fig. 112.
The Ashmolean Museum: Figs. 8, 141, 142, 143, 145, 147, 160, 206, 218.
J. David Bohl: Figs. 14, 192, 215, 226, 244, 288, 326, 338.
British Museum: Figs. 26, 134, 148, 151, 153, 210, 216, 219, 220.
Will Brown: Fig. 350.
Rudolph Burckhardt: Fig. 354.
R. Chan: Figs. 197, 198, 199.
The Charleston Museum: Figs. 187, 188.
Richard Cheek: Figs. 362, 373.
Cincinnati Art Museum: Fig. 103.
Colonial Williamsburg: Figs. 135, 137, 178, 179.
Edward S. Cooke: Figs. 240, 339.
Joseph Crilley, Fig. 258.
The David Foundation: Fig. 80.
Kathleen Deagan: Fig. 389.
Dr. Charles H. Fairbanks: Figs. 397, 398.
Clifton L. Fasch: Fig. 342.
David L. Felton: Figs. 292, 293, 294, 295, 296, 297.
P. A. Ferrazini: Fig. 31.
Field Museum: Fig. 43.
Fondation Custodia: Fig. 154.
Henry Ford Museum: Fig. 348.
Fries Museum: Figs. 149, 224.
David Gilliland: Fig. 48.
The Groningen Museum: Figs. 167, 207.
John Harkey: Figs. 13, 22, 28, 29, 176, 177, 180, 182, 184, 185, 202, 203, 217, 223, 228, 243, 248, 249, 250, 262, 268, 269, 273, 279, 280, 282, 283, 291, 299, 300, 315, 318, 323, 329, 332, 343, 375, 376, 377, 378, 403, 417.
Courtesy of Mrs. Bertram C. Harrison and Miss Janet Fauntleroy Taylor: Fig. 21.
Historic Cherry Hill: Figs. 277, 278.
Idemitsu Museum: Fig. 81.
Al Kilbertus: Fig. 306.

Jerry Kobylecky: Figs. 24, 30, 42, 122, 128, 165, 195, 227, 346, 379.
Courtesy of Lic. Rodrigo R. Rivero Lake: Figs. 7, 17, 49, 51.
Bates Littlehales: Fig. 97.
Frank Lusk: Figs. 32, 127, 130, 166, 169, 212, 214, 225, 230, 246, 247, 251, 252, 253, 257, 264, 337, 341, 352, 361, 401, 414.
Courtesy of Dr. Jane Gaston Mahler: Figs. 333, 366.
Metropolitan Museum of Art: Figs. 208, 209.
George D. Miller: Figs. 11, 61, 67, 76, 78, 88, 284, 412.
William Mudge: Figs. 1, 2, 3, 108, 193, 347, 402, 405, 407.
Museo Nacional del Virreinato: Figs. 59, 235.
Museum of Fine Art, Houston: Fig. 356.
Newark Museum: Fig. 168.
New Jersey State Museum: Fig. 258.
New York State Parks and Recreation: Fig. 196.
Princessehof Museum: Figs. 116, 146, 173, 357.
Rhode Island Historical Society: Fig. 261.
Rhode Island School of Design: Fig. 325.
Rijksmuseum: Fig. 84.
William Sargent: Figs. 33, 34, 35, 36, 37, 229, 241, 242, 356.
Mark Sexton: Figs. 183, 189, 190, 191, 201, 231, 238, 256, 270, 271, 272, 274, 275, 281, 286, 287, 289, 290, 298, 310, 312, 317, 328, 330, 336, 371, 372, 381, 413, 416.
Courtesy of Matthew and Elizabeth Sharpe: Figs. 319, 320, 331.
Sleepy Hollow Restorations: Fig. 213.
Robert Sténuit: Figs. 101, 158.
Duane Suter: Figs. 150, 171, 172, 175, 181, 186, 221, 222, 234, 236, 237, 255, 305, 313, 368, 369, 409, 410, 411, 415.
Earle D. Vandekar: Fig. 68.
The Victoria and Albert Museum: Figs. 15, 58, 60, 113, 155, 211, 302.
The Virginia Research Center: Figs. 136, 139, 140, 396.
Edward P. Von der Porten: Fig. 388.
Michael J. Wade: Fig. 358.
The Weldon Collection: Fig. 10.
Winterthur Museum: Figs. 38, 260, 335.